Upper Intermediate Teacher's Book

ASPIRE

Discover
Learn
Engage

Mike Sayer with Paul Dummett, Rebecca Robb Benne and David A. Hill

NATIONAL GEOGRAPHIC LEARNING | HEINLE CENGAGE Learning

Australia • Brazil • Japan • Korea • Mexico • Singapore • Spain • United Kingdom • United States

**Aspire Upper Intermediate
Teacher's Book**
Mike Sayer with Paul Dummett, Rebecca
Robb Benne and David A. Hill

Publisher: Jason Mann

Development Editors: Madeleine Burgess
    and Kathryn Eyers

Editorial Project Manager: Karen White

Project Editor: Amy Smith

Production Controller: Tom Relf

Senior Marketing Manager:
    Ruth McAleavey

National Geographic Liaison: Leila Hishmeh

Art Director: Natasa Arsenidou

Cover Designer: Ioanna Ioannidou

Text Designer: Natasa Arsenidou

Compositor: PreMediaGlobal

Audio: The Soundhouse Ltd.

© 2013 National Geographic Learning, a part of Cengage Learning

ALL RIGHTS RESERVED. No part of this work covered by the copyright herein may be reproduced, transmitted, stored or used in any form or by any means graphic, electronic, or mechanical, including but not limited to photocopying, recording, scanning, digitizing, taping, Web distribution, information networks, or information storage and retrieval systems, except as permitted under Section 107 or 108 of the 1976 United States Copyright Act, without the prior written permission of the publisher.

For permission to use material from this text or product, submit all requests online at **www.cengage.com/permissions** Further permissions questions can be emailed to **permissionrequest@cengage.com**

ISBN-13: 978-1-133-56453-9

National Geographic Learning
Cheriton House, North Way, Andover, Hampshire, SP10 5BW
United Kingdom

Cengage learning is a leading provider of customised learning solutions with office locations around the globe, including Singapore, the United Kingdom, Australia, Mexico, Brazil and Japan. Locate our local office at: **international.cengage.com/region**

Cengage Learning products are represented in Canada by Nelson Education, Ltd.

Visit National Geographic Learning online at **http://elt.heinle.com**
Visit our corporate website at **cengage.com**

Photo credits

The publisher would like to thank the following sources for permission to reproduce their copyright protected images:

Cover: © 2006 CERN

Inside: 5 (Jim Richardson/National Geographic Image Collection), 6a (Melissa Farlow/National Geographic Image Collection), 6b (David Burton/Alamy), 6c (Ace Stock Limited/Alamy), 7 (Shutterstock), 8a (Tetra Images/Alamy), 8b (Scott Enlow/Studio E), 9a (Shutterstock), 9b (Shutterstock), 9c (Travelpix/Alamy), 10a (Ian Bird/Rex Features), 10b (Shutterstock), 10c (Tao Images/Alamy), 11a (Hemis/Alamy), 11b (b/g) (Shutterstock), 11c (landio), 11d (travelibsulawesi/Alamy).

Printed in China by RR Donnelley
1 2 3 4 5 6 7 8 9 10 – 16 15 14 13 12

Contents

Dear Teacher

Thank you for choosing to use **Aspire Upper Intermediate** with your students. As you are probably aware, this course series is different in a number of ways from other courses. Most noticeably, a great deal of the content (photography, text, and video) is drawn from the vast resources of National Geographic.

For this reason, you will find that many of the topics are more varied than normal. Students will find they are learning about diverse topics such as new technology, ancient traditions and exotic places but at the same time relating the issues to the world they already know. For example, a unit such as *Get to work* (Unit 8) clearly provides a forum for students to express their own ideas about work and jobs but the influence of National Geographic content means that they are exposed to jobs and work culture in other parts of the world. In this way their critical-thinking skills are made to work in tandem with effective language learning.

As a language teacher, you will also find a great deal that is reassuringly familiar in this book. For example, there is a carefully graded grammar syllabus with key vocabulary needed at Upper Intermediate level. Students will have plenty of opportunities to practise useful functional and communicative English.

National Geographic magazine was first published in 1888 and its extensive website (www.nationalgeographic.com) of resources sets out a clear mission statement: 'Inspiring people to care about the planet'. In many ways this goal was always uppermost in our minds when writing this book. To produce a course that would *inspire students to care about the planet and inspire them to learn English*. We hope it achieves this for your students.

Good luck!

Paul Dummett and Rebecca Robb Benne

Unit opener

The first activity, **Let's get started**, has three questions: the first question refers to the Opener photo, the second question focuses on the students' opinions on a topic connected with the photo and the third question asks about the students' personal experience related to the topic.

7

Important events

Locals celebrate the annual blessing of the fishing fleet in the small community of Camarinas in Galicia, Spain

Let's get started

1 Look at the picture and caption. Why is this occasion important for the people of this town? What specific events are celebrated in your town or country each year?

2 Read the quotations. Which do you agree with more? Why?

'What ought to be done to the man who invented the celebrating of anniversaries? Mere killing would be too light.'
Mark Twain, American author (1835–1910)

'Make every day a holiday and celebrate just living!'
Amanda Bradley, American contemporary poet

Vocabulary and speaking

3 Work with a partner. Complete the table with the words in the box. Use a dictionary if necessary.

> acrobats   banner   clapping   fireworks   garland
> hat   making a speech   mask
> parade   sash   singing   streamers

Decorations	Clothing	Actions	Entertainment
balloons	costume	dancing	music

4 What is celebrated at each of these types of party? What happens at them? Use words from Exercise 3 to help you describe them.

- a street party
- a housewarming party
- a fancy dress party
- a farewell party

In this unit you will learn

- **Communication:** describing festivals and traditions, presenting a proposal, choosing a present
- **Vocabulary:** festivals, stages of life, weddings
- **Reading and Listening:** coming of age, birthdays and families, festivals
- **Writing:** a description of an event
- **Grammar:** passive gerund and infinitive, passive reporting verbs

83

The **Unit Opener** gives the language aims for the unit. These aims are reviewed in the Review pages and in all the tests. Your students can use them as a checklist for revision at the end of each unit as well as for end-of-term and end-of-year revision. The photographs and discussion tasks are intended to activate students' previous knowledge of both topic and key language.

Main lesson types – A

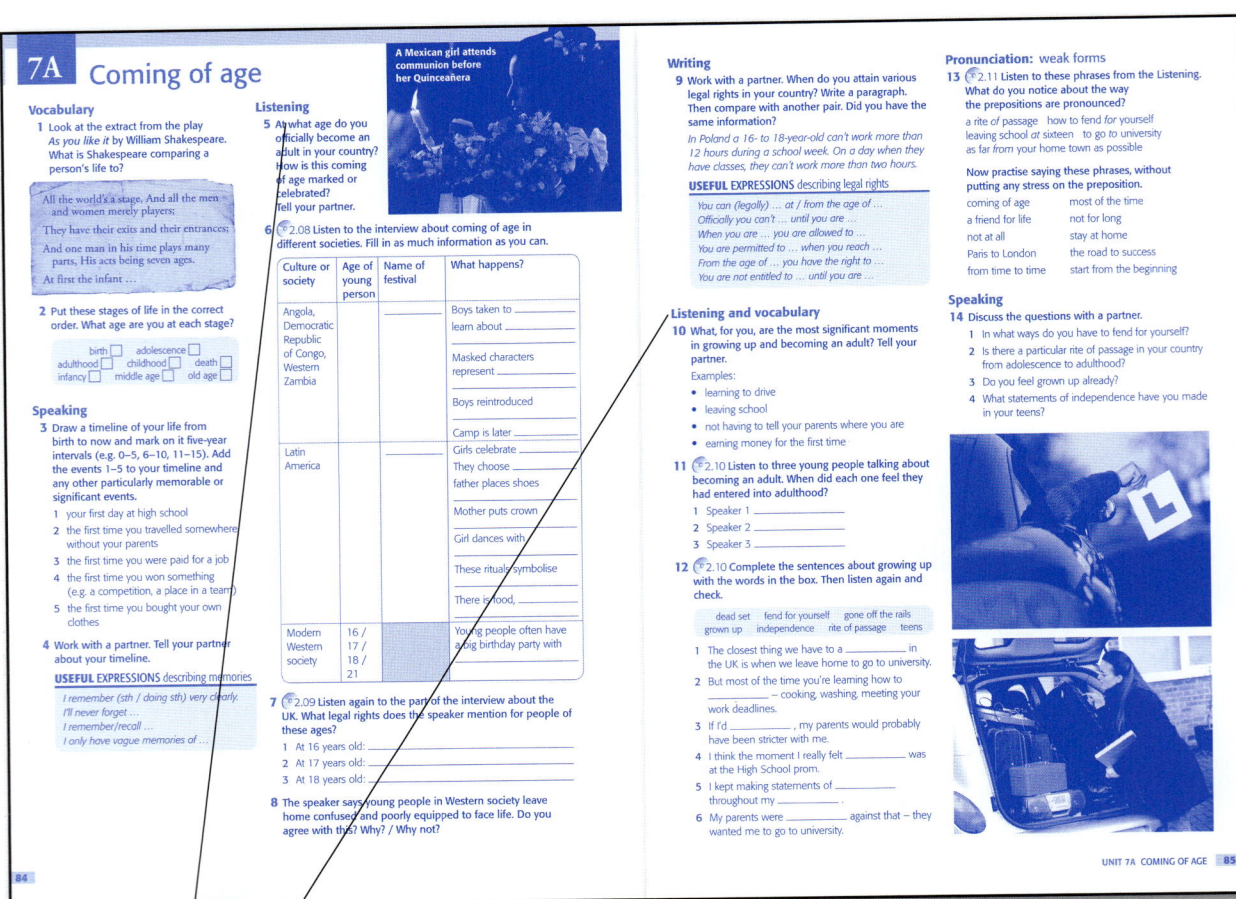

Coming of age

A Mexican girl attends communion before her Quinceañera

Vocabulary

1 Look at the extract from the play *As you like it* by William Shakespeare. What is Shakespeare comparing a person's life to?

All the world's a stage, And all the men and women merely players;

They have their exits and their entrances;

And one man in his time plays many parts, His acts being seven ages.

At first the infant …

2 Put these stages of life in the correct order. What age are you at each stage?

birth ☐ adolescence ☐
adulthood ☐ childhood ☐ death ☐
infancy ☐ middle age ☐ old age ☐

Speaking

3 Draw a timeline of your life from birth to now and mark on it five-year intervals (e.g. 0–5, 6–10, 11–15). Add the events 1–5 to your timeline and any other particularly memorable or significant events.
1 your first day at high school
2 the first time you travelled somewhere without your parents
3 the first time you were paid for a job
4 the first time you won something (e.g. a competition, a place in a team)
5 the first time you bought your own clothes

4 Work with a partner. Tell your partner about your timeline.

USEFUL EXPRESSIONS describing memories

I remember (sth / doing sth) very clearly.
I'll never forget …
I remember/recall …
I only have vague memories of …

Listening

5 At what age do you officially become an adult in your country? How is this coming of age marked or celebrated? Tell your partner.

6 ⓟ2.08 Listen to the interview about coming of age in different societies. Fill in as much information as you can.

Culture or society	Age of young person	Name of festival	What happens?
Angola, Democratic Republic of Congo, Western Zambia			Boys taken to learn about _____ Masked characters represent _____ Boys reintroduced _____ Camp is later _____
Latin America			Girls celebrate _____ They choose _____ father places shoes Mother puts crown Girl dances with _____ These rituals symbolise _____ There is food, _____
Modern Western society	16 / 17 / 18 / 21		Young people often have a big birthday party with

7 ⓟ2.09 Listen again to the part of the interview about the UK. What legal rights does the speaker mention for people of these ages?
1 At 16 years old: _____
2 At 17 years old: _____
3 At 18 years old: _____

8 The speaker says young people in Western society leave home confused and poorly equipped to face life. Do you agree with this? Why? / Why not?

Writing

9 Work with a partner. When do you attain various legal rights in your country? Write a paragraph. Then compare with another pair. Did you have the same information?

In Poland a 16- to 18-year-old can't work more than 12 hours during a school week. On a day when they have classes, they can't work more than two hours.

USEFUL EXPRESSIONS describing legal rights

You can (legally) … at / from the age of …
Officially you can't … until you are …
When you are … you are allowed to …
You are permitted to … when you reach …
From the age of … you have the right to …
You are not entitled to … until you are …

Listening and vocabulary

10 What, for you, are the most significant moments in growing up and becoming an adult? Tell your partner.
Examples:
• learning to drive
• leaving school
• not having to tell your parents where you are
• earning money for the first time

11 ⓟ2.10 Listen to three young people talking about becoming an adult. When did each one feel they had entered into adulthood?
1 Speaker 1 _____
2 Speaker 2 _____
3 Speaker 3 _____

12 ⓟ2.10 Complete the sentences about growing up with the words in the box. Then listen again and check.

dead set   fend for yourself   gone off the rails
grown up   independence   rite of passage   teens

1 The closest thing we have to a _____ in the UK is when we leave home to go to university.
2 But most of the time you're learning how to _____ – cooking, washing, meeting your work deadlines.
3 If I'd _____ , my parents would probably have been stricter with me.
4 I think the moment I really felt _____ was at the High School prom.
5 I kept making statements of _____ throughout my _____ .
6 My parents were _____ against that – they wanted me to go to university.

Pronunciation: weak forms

13 ⓟ2.11 Listen to these phrases from the Listening. What do you notice about the way the prepositions are pronounced?

a rite *of* passage   how to fend *for* yourself
leaving school *at* sixteen   to go *to* university
as far *from* your home town as possible

Now practise saying these phrases, without putting any stress on the preposition.

coming of age   most of the time
a friend for life   not for long
not at all   stay at home
Paris to London   the road to success
from time to time   start from the beginning

Speaking

14 Discuss the questions with a partner.
1 In what ways do you have to fend for yourself?
2 Is there a particular rite of passage in your country from adolescence to adulthood?
3 Do you feel grown up already?
4 What statements of independence have you made in your teens?

The **listening activities** include **a wide range of listening types** (interviews, radio programmes, news reports, etc.) and many of them are drawn from **National Geographic** content.

Main lesson types – B

Grammar is usually presented alongside a reading or listening text so that students can see how grammatical structures are used in a variety of authentic contexts. Students learn both by reading formal grammar presentations and also with learn-through-discovery tasks. Discovery tasks are used for structures the students will have seen before. Each presentation is accompanied by controlled practice exercises as well as free practice and speaking tasks so that the new grammar can be used in meaningful situations.

7B Wedding traditions

Speaking and vocabulary

1 Guess the answers to the quiz about weddings. Then look at the answers on page 144 and discuss them with your partner.

> 1 How many years did the longest marriage between two people last?
> 2 How heavy was the world's largest wedding cake?
> 3 What is the record for the most guests at a wedding reception?
> 4 In which country …
>   do they throw peas instead of rice or confetti?
>   do the guests often bring the flowers for their own table?
>   does the bride step on the groom's foot during the wedding vows?
> 5 How many couples get married …
>   per year in China?
>   per day in Las Vegas?
> 6 Why might someone object to being asked to be a bridesmaid for the third time?
> 7 Why is the person who helps the groom at a wedding called the 'Best Man'?
> 8 Why are ducks associated with weddings in South Korea?
> 9 Why is it customary for a plate to be broken at the feet of the bride and groom during a Czech wedding?
> 10 In the USA …
>   what is the average age for first-time brides? for grooms?
>   how much is spent on a wedding on average?
>   what is the average number of wedding guests?

Grammar: passive gerund and infinitive

2 Study how these two sentences from Exercise 1 are expressed as passive forms and active verbs. Then transform sentences 1–4 using either the passive gerund or the passive infinitive form.

Passive gerund

Why might somone object to be **being asked** to be a bridesmaid for the third time?

Active: Why might someone object to a couple asking her to be a bridesmaid for the third time?

Passive infinitive

Why is it customary for a plate **to be broken** at the feet of the bride and groom during a Czech wedding?

Active: Why is it customary for someone to break a plate at the feet of the bride and groom during a Czech wedding?

1 He insisted on including everyone in the group photograph.
  He insisted on everyone _____

2 The law doesn't allow anyone under 16 to marry.
  No one under 16 is allowed _____
  _____

3 I don't mind you keeping me waiting.
  I don't mind _____

4 They arranged for a Rolls-Royce to take them to the ceremony.
  They arranged _____

Reading

3 Work in pairs. Each choose one of the passages on page 87 to read. Then tell your partner about it. Don't worry if you don't understand all the words – try to convey the main points.

See Grammar Reference, page 154

Different approaches to marriage

A

A traditional wedding in the UK used to be paid for by the bride's parents and it took place in the bride's local church. **These days, it is believed that the costs are often shared between the two families.** In addition, an increasing number of couples pay for their own weddings. And there has been an increase in the number of civil ceremonies that are being carried out – currently about 67% of weddings in the UK are non-religious. In the past, the number of people getting married rose every year, but since 1972, the annual number of marriages has been in decline. **Many young couples today are understood to be waiting until they are older before getting married.** The average age for getting married is now around 36 for both men and women. This contrasts with figures we have from 50 years ago, when 50% of men and 75% of women were married by the age of 25.

B

As in many rural settings the world over, weddings in the area now on the borders with Albania, Bulgaria and northern Greece used to be grand affairs. Traditions differ through the years and between the tribes, but any of the following may have been included. There could be several formal visits when the man asks the father of the woman for her hand in marriage. After the announcement of the engagement, rings would be exchanged and preparations would begin. The dowry system, when it was observed, meant that the bride would have to contribute materially to the marriage. This might mean money or animals, or furnishings for their home. **It is said that the bride often arrived at the ceremony on horseback.** The wedding dress was usually decorated with gold and had coins on the belt. The man might have worn national costume with a white shirt and an open, elaborately-embroidered waistcoat. **The feasting and dancing are said to have lasted three days.**

Grammar: passive reporting verbs

4 Working with the same partner as before, discuss what you have read and what the highlighted words might mean.

5 When we report what people generally say, think or believe, we use passive reporting verbs. Look at the examples in bold in the texts. Then complete the examples below.

Passive reporting verbs

Passive reporting verbs take two forms:

A: *It is believed/thought/said that* + a clause
It is believed that many people are happier living alone.

B: *subject* + *is/are believed/thought/said* + *to-infinitive*
Many people are _____ happier living alone.

If you are reporting something that happened in the past, you will need to change the tense of the verb or the form of the infinitive.
It is understood that last year's wedding _____ paid for by the bride and groom.

See Grammar Reference, page 154

6 Rewrite the sentences using passive reporting verbs.

1 Many people **say** that English people are quite reserved.
  English people are said to be quite reserved.

2 In Sweden, in a restaurant, men **expect** women to pay half the bill.
  In Sweden, women in a restaurant _____

3 In the past people **supposed** that the man would always propose to the woman.
  In the past the man _____

4 People **report** that there has been an increase in the number of civil ceremonies every year.
  The number of civil ceremonies _____

Speaking

7 Work with a partner. Discuss your views on marriage and the information presented on these two pages. Remember to use passive forms. You might like to consider the following questions.

- What was a traditional wedding like in your country?
- What are weddings today like? What happens?
- Do people usually have a long engagement before getting married?
- Are more or fewer people getting married? Why do you think this is?

86 See Grammar Reference, page 154

Main lesson types – C

Vocabulary presentations appear throughout the units but are especially prominent on the **Reading** and **Culture** pages. The vocabulary is either pre-taught to help students with extended reading, or students are encouraged to guess the meaning of new words from context. At Upper Intermediate level **word formation tasks** and **transformation tasks** have been added, as well as tasks in which students are asked to define the difference between semantically close words.

Reading texts are often taken from the **National Geographic** magazine and other National Geographic resources. These texts tend to be information-rich and challenging both in terms of content and language. The accompanying tasks are designed to enhance students' critical thinking. Here you can see an example of a text taken from the National Geographic *Footprint Reading Library*.

7C Birth and birthdays

Speaking and listening

1 Work with a partner.
   Student A: Look at page 142.
   Student B: Look at page 144.

   Each read your two birthday facts. Then tell your partner about them. Which fact most surprised you? Why? Can you find anyone in your class for whom Student A's facts are true?

2 What are the most important (or most celebrated) birthdays in a person's life? What do people usually do to celebrate these birthdays?

3 2.12 Listen to someone describing important birthdays in the UK. Which birthdays does she mention? How do people celebrate them?

4 2.12 Listen again and complete the sentences with phrasal verbs. Then discuss with your partner what each one means.
   1 They might _____ in 1980's fashion or go as characters from films.
   2 It's not just the younger generation that _____ big celebrations.
   3 Not so much 30 – that's one people try to _____ more.
   4 Old friends and family that you don't see very often all _____ for a big celebration.

Reading

5 How many children are there in your family? Is that typical of a family in your country? What are the benefits of being in a small family? What about in a large family?

6 Work with a partner. Do the tasks 1–4.
   1 Look at the title of the article on page 89. Make a list of the difficulties of having a family of this size.
   2 Use the list to make questions that you would like to be answered by the article.
   3 Read the article. Were your questions answered?
   4 What do you imagine the answers to your other questions would be? Tell the class.

7 Read the article again and choose the correct option to complete the sentences. Circle A, B, C or D.
   1 The fertility rate at which the population remains the same is …
      A 2.5.   B 1.3.   C 2.   D 2.1.
   2 Officials in some countries are worried about …
      A their population slowly disappearing.
      B their population quickly disappearing.
      C their population growing older.
      D their population being replaced.
   3 The Duggars believe that …
      A it is their duty to have a lot of children.
      B two or three children is enough for most people.
      C having children is like a tree bearing fruit.
      D we should be grateful for each child we are given.
   4 For Jim Bob, each new birth …
      A is as exciting as the last.
      B makes him feel younger.
      C makes him feel a little older.
      D is a surprise.
   5 Their policy for keeping a peaceful home is …
      A to congratulate the children on the positive things they do.
      B to make sure the children don't misbehave.
      C to be strict about what the priorities are.
      D a mixture of reward and punishment for the children.
   6 They have been able to afford to raise a family of 18 because …
      A in the past they borrowed a lot of money.
      B early on they went out and got a TV deal.
      C they manage not to spend much on food.
      D they don't live very extravagantly.

8 Discuss the questions.
   1 What did you think of the Duggars' family life? Does it appeal to you?
   2 Do you know any large families? What is life like for the children in them?

Nineteen children and counting

The world average fertility rate is 2.5 children per woman. In most European countries (Germany, Poland, Italy, etc.), the rate is around 1.3 children, well below the so-called population replacement level of 2.1. If this were to continue, the logical conclusion would be the disappearance of certain races. No one actually expects this to happen, but the ageing population is nevertheless a real concern for officials in these countries. Imagine what they would give for citizens like Michelle and Jim Bob Duggar, of Arkansas, USA, who announced recently that they are expecting their twentieth child.

Originally their intention was to have only two or three children, but after Michelle suffered a miscarriage* early on, nature took its own way and she has given birth to a new baby, or to twins, every 18 months.

Nineteen children later, all with names beginning with 'J' – from Josh who is 20 to baby Josie – it seems the sky is the limit for the Duggar clan. But surely a new birth can't hold the same excitement as the first or even the fifth? Not according to Jim Bob. 'This never gets old. We are so grateful for each child.' And what about Michelle, who has spent over 150 months of her life pregnant? 'We are so thrilled,' she said.

Given that it can be a full-time job looking after just two or three children, the Duggars have had to organise their life very carefully. The children are all home-schooled; each child learns to play the piano or violin and shares the domestic chores*. They also employ a kind of 'buddy system', in other words each older child looks out for one of the younger ones and helps to mentor them. You might think this would put them off having children themselves, yet Josh,

the eldest, is now expecting his own little girl with his wife Anna next year.

Keeping peace in a home of 20 people is a priority and it has been achieved by adhering to strict principles of praising each child for the good qualities they show rather than by getting angry with them for wrong behaviour. While all this seems positive enough, the Duggars do have their critics, who think that this micro-management of family life is not very natural.

> 'Originally their intention was to have only two or three children.'

Many people will wonder how the Duggars manage to make ends meet. Quite early in their married life Jim Bob and Michelle went to a seminar on financial freedom that they say changed their approach to money. The basic message was 'get out of debt and stay out of debt'. By shopping carefully and making sacrifices on luxuries, this is what they did. They use garage sales and thrift stores and always buy second-hand cars. They spend $3,000 a month on food and other essentials, which is a lot for a family, but that does include nappies*! But things seem to be getting easier rather than harder. The Duggars have their own TV show and Jim Bob himself has had a successful career in commercial real estate.

miscarriage losing a baby before birth
chores boring household jobs
nappies protective pants for babies

DVD – half of the units in the course are supported by films from National Geographic. **Video worksheets** can be found at the end of the Student's Book and the film is available on both the Teacher's DVD and the Student's Multi-ROM. The video worksheets are designed to maximise students' learning while they watch the videos. The activities help students prepare for watching and listening by activating their existing knowledge and pre-teaching the most important new vocabulary. Comprehension activities then ensure that students have a good understanding of what they have seen and heard. The last activity always takes the film topic further, involving students in discussion, group work or role play.

Main lesson types – D

Writing sections always appear on this spread. At Upper Intermediate level students revise basic text types (notices, adverts, emails, letters) and learn how to write all extended text types (description, review, 'for and against' essay, short story). Apart from that, there appear some very useful hints on how to write a CV or job application. Exercises often draw attention to the structure of a text before analysing the language features used. Every writing section concludes with a task in which students produce their own text. Note that the Workbook also offers further writing practice.

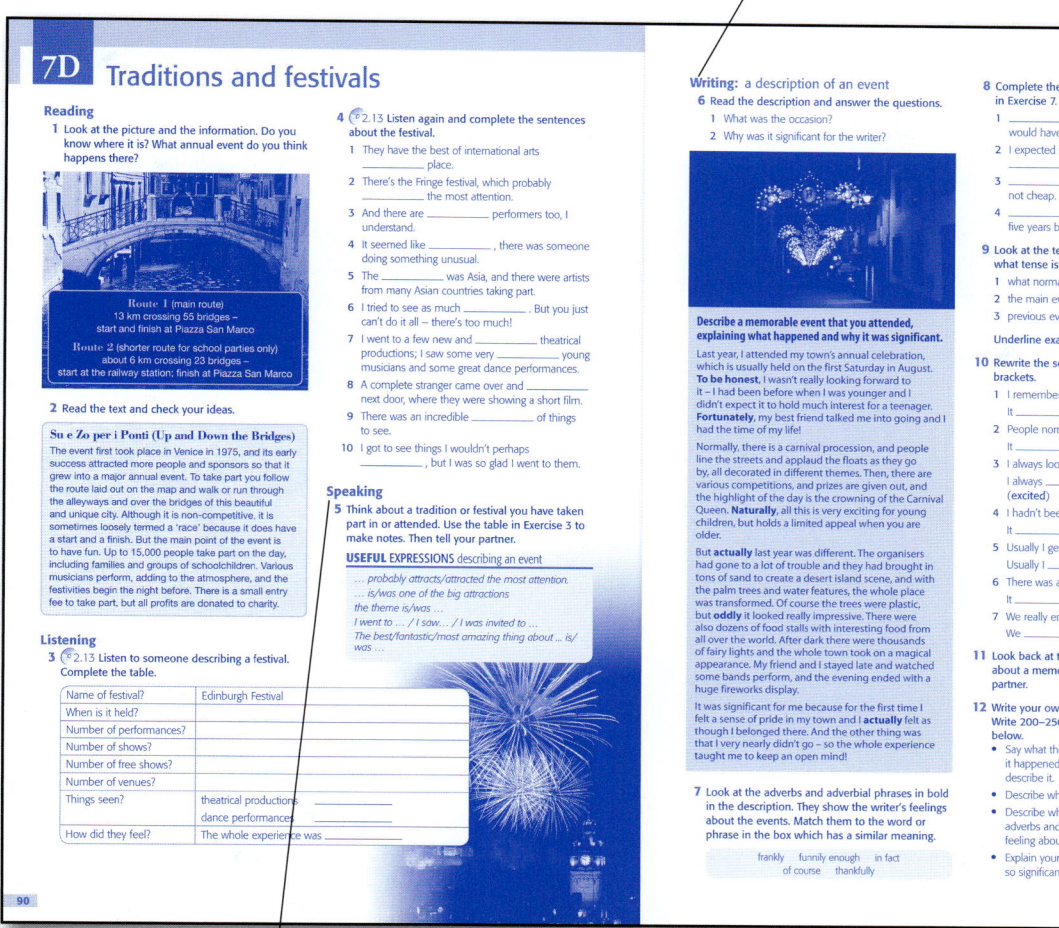

This spread focuses on developing **speaking skills** by giving students useful tips on speaking techniques. On this particular spread students learn how to start a conversation about a problem, how to ask for clarification, how to express the same idea in a different way – in other words how to communicate successfully. Typically students listen to a model conversation and look at the kind of phrases used. Then they work in pairs or groups to practise fluency and functional language.

Main lesson types – E

Culture sections expose students to authentic texts from National Geographic. The extended readings provide interesting insights into cultural life in other countries and ask students to compare their own experiences. The readings also offer a springboard into language practice and exam preparation.

7E How people celebrate

Speaking

1 Which of these would be your idea of a fun way to spend a day off? Tell your partner and explain the reasons for your choice.
- go shopping and out for lunch
- meet up with friends for a picnic or barbecue
- do something active like cycling or playing football
- go to see a sporting event
- go to see a film or a show
- enjoy a big meal with your family

2 What kind of celebrations do you associate with the following days?

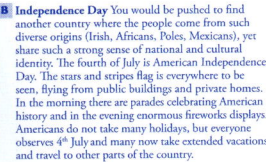
Thanksgiving   New Year's Day   birthdays
Mother's Day

Example:
On New Year's Day everybody dresses up in their best clothes and then we sit down to a big family meal.

National Days

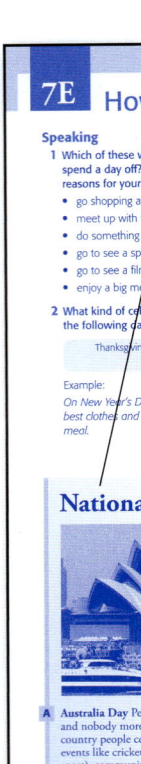

A **Australia Day** People love a reason to have a party and nobody more than the Australians. All over the country people celebrate their culture with sporting events like cricket matches (Australians are crazy about sport), community barbecues, music festivals and parties on the beach (Australians love the beach too!). Celebrations are held on 26 January, the height of summer and the day when the first British colonists landed in Australia, a fact marked by ferry and ship races across Sydney Harbour. But the day is also controversial, since many native Aborigines feel it marks the end of independence, not the beginning.

Reading

3 Read the extract from an article describing National Days in English-speaking countries around the world. Which celebration(s) A–C …
1 seems to be the most patriotic?
2 is a source of disagreement?
3 include competitive games?
4 involve people just getting together to enjoy each other's company?
5 takes place all over the world?
6 is a welcome day off for a hard-working nation?

4 Find a word or expression in the article that means …
1 like something passionately (paragraph A)
2 causing debate and arguments (paragraph A)
3 have difficulty doing (paragraph B)
4 different (paragraph B)
5 longer in time (paragraph B)
6 to change the colour of something (paragraph C)
7 sociable (paragraph C)

5 Is your country's National Day very important to people? What traditional activities take place?

B **Independence Day** You would be pushed to find another country where the people come from such diverse origins (Irish, Africans, Poles, Mexicans), yet share such a strong sense of national and cultural identity. The fourth of July is American Independence Day. The stars and stripes flag is everywhere to be seen, flying from public buildings and private homes. In the morning there are parades celebrating American history and in the evening enormous fireworks displays. Americans do not take many holidays, but everyone observes 4th July and many now take extended vacations and travel to other parts of the country.

C **St Patrick's Day** It is said that over 80 million 'Irish' people live in the world – pretty amazing for a country whose population totals just over 6 million. These are the descendants of emigrants who have been leaving Ireland since the mid-nineteenth century. Thus it is that on 17th March, whatever country you are in, you will probably find St Patrick's Day festivities going on somewhere. People wear something green to commemorate the day and in Chicago and Indianapolis they dye their river and canal green. It is, above all, a time to be happy and convivial and so most people go to bars and restaurants to celebrate – eating, drinking, joking and singing.

Reading and listening

6 How many public holidays are there in your country? Which are the most important ones? Tell your partner.

7 Read the text about the Dragon Boat festival and answer the questions.
1 What, according to the legend, is the reason people race boats during the festival?
2 What special food do people eat and why?

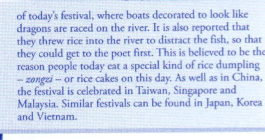

In its modern form, the *Duanwu* Festival, or Dragon Boat festival has been recognised as a public holiday in the People's Republic of China on the fifth day of the fifth lunar month since 2008. However, the tradition is far older and it is said that its origins go back over 2,000 years when, according to one of the many legends surrounding the festival, the poet Qu Yuan died in the river. In their attempt to find his body the local people took their boats out. This is said to be the origin of today's festival, where boats decorated to look like dragons are raced on the river. It is also reported that they threw rice into the river to distract the fish, so that they could get to the poet first. This is believed to be the reason people today eat a special kind of rice dumpling – *zongzi* – or rice cakes on this day. As well as in China, the festival is celebrated in Taiwan, Singapore and Malaysia. Similar festivals can be found in Japan, Korea and Vietnam.

Speaking

10 Work in a small group. Look at the list of holidays that celebrate particular people or groups in society. Discuss what benefits the holidays have for society and what commercial opportunities they bring.

Mother's Day   Father's Day
International Children's Day   Labour Day
International Women's Day

11 Still in your group, invent your own public holiday. Complete the table with notes.

Name of holiday
Proposed date
Significance for people
Possible celebrations
Benefits for society
Possible commercial benefits

8 **2.14** Listen to two people talking about the Dragon Boat festival and tick which speaker mentions the things below. Three of the things are mentioned by both speakers.

	Wendy	Harry
a drummer		
important family gathering		
firing a gun		
jumping in the sea		
a flag		
a competition		
hanging something up		
different fillings		
rowers/oarsmen		
bamboo leaves		
a good-luck ritual		
family walks		

12 Present your idea for a public holiday to the class. Follow this structure for each point in your presentation.
- We'd like to propose a holiday to commemorate / to celebrate …
- The holiday would take place on …
- The reasons for this are … / The idea behind this is …
- One way to mark the occasion would be …
- It would serve / help to …
- There would be several commercial benefits of such a holiday. First, …

Watch a video about a kite festival. Turn to page 138.

9 **2.14** Listen again. This time, note down only the *adjectives* that the two people use. Compare your lists with a partner and try to remember what nouns the adjectives described. Then discuss what details you can remember about the festival.

The **Everyday English** page offers students the chance to hear and use English in real situations. The situations chosen reflect the situations that students may find themselves in if they ever visit a country where English is the first language.

Students may use **Useful expressions** to role play a similar dialogue, or – as it is on this page – use these expressions to describe the photos.

The **Case Study** pages focus on real-world events, people and issues. The material includes comprehension tasks to ensure understanding and also offers questions for stimulating class discussions. Teacher's notes include suggestions for the project-based development of the themes as well as directions to the National Geographic website for further exploration.

Everyday English

Choosing a present

Listening and speaking

1 'It is better to give than to receive.' What does this mean? Do you agree with this saying?

2 Which of these comments about present giving do you agree with?

'You should only buy presents for people when you see something that they will really like.'

'It's never a good idea to buy clothes for someone else.'

'People always prefer to get something that the giver has made themselves.'

'You shouldn't base your choice of present on what you would like to receive yourself.'

'You should spend no more on a present than the receiver would spend themselves.'

'Don't give couples combined presents – always give separate presents.'

3 Choose the correct word to complete each of these statements.

1 That's such a *thoughtful / considered* present. How did you know I liked modern art?

2 Oops. I think I've left the price *marker / tag* on.

3 Oh, you *favour / spoil* me. That must have cost you a *fortune / bargain*.

4 Oh, what lovely flowers! You really *mustn't / shouldn't* have.

5 Sorry, I didn't have time to *pack / wrap* it up.

4 2.15 Listen to the conversation between a shop assistant and someone looking for a present. Answer the questions.

1 Who is the present for?

2 What does he decide to buy?

3 What are the reasons for his choice?

5 2.15 Listen again and complete the phrases that the shopper uses.

1 I'm looking _____ something for my little sister and I'm _____ stuck.

2 Yes, something _____ a clutch bag, _____ that is.

3 Can I have a _____ what you've got?

4 That's _____ nice. What's it made _____?

5 That's a _____ . Have you got anything _____?

6 What happens if she doesn't like it? Can I _____ ?

7 And how _____ is the blue _____?

8 OK. Let's _____ that then. Can you _____ it?

6 Work with a partner. Role play the conversation.

Student A: You are a shopper in a big department store. Look at page 142.

Student B: You are a shop assistant. Help the shopper find a suitable present.

Start like this:

B Hello can I help you?

A Yes, I'm looking for a present for my …

7 Work with the same partner and swap roles.

Student A: You are now the shop assistant.

Student B: You are now the shopper. Look at page 144.

94

Each page includes **a dialogue** with listening and comprehension tasks.

🔍 ## Case Study 4 〉 Celebrations and customs

NAVAJO HOUSE BLESSING

For the Navajo people, the home is treated in many ways as if it were a living person. The ritual of house blessing shows respect for the building and creates an environment where the house will look after its inhabitants. A special song is chanted, happiness is invited into the building, and the walls are marked to show that this has been done. Large, public buildings like schools and museums can also be blessed in ceremonies with costumes, singing and dancing, which may last several days.

THE SEFROU CHERRY FESTIVAL IN MOROCCO

In mid-June (the exact date depends on the harvest being ready), local people celebrate the cherry harvest with singing, dancing and sometimes sporting competitions or a torch-lit procession. A highlight of the festival is the crowning of Miss Cherry, who is then paraded through the streets. The festival also usually hosts a fairground and a market.

THE LANTERN FESTIVAL IN CHINA

During this festival, which is held at full moon, multi-coloured lanterns are displayed in the streets and lit up at night. Puzzles or riddles are written on the lanterns and people try to solve them. It is a time of family reunion, often marked by the eating of a special kind of rice ball. The festival is associated with many stories and legends, and some say that it originated as a way for families to meet each other.

WEDDING CELEBRATIONS IN INDONESIA

Guests are rarely invited to the ceremony itself, as it is considered to be for very close family. The reception typically begins with a procession into the room, after which gifts are given, often in the form of money which is placed in an envelope. Not until speeches have been made and guests have been invited to shake hands with the couple is the food served.

1 Discuss these questions with reference to your own country.

1 Are there any customs related to moving into a new home or opening a public building?

2 How do you celebrate the New Year?

3 Does your country or town have a carnival or festival? What happens?

4 On what occasions do people normally give flowers?

2 Read the text and complete these sentences.

1 The walls of a Navajo home are marked to show that _____ and the house has been blessed with a special song.

2 After _____, Miss Cherry is paraded

3 Complete the following sentences using the information on this page.

1 The Navajo perform a house blessing, which _____

2 Instead of wedding presents, Indonesian couples appreciate being _____

3 People are expected to solve riddles _____

4 Only when the cherry harvest is ready _____

4 In pairs or small groups, discuss how these celebrations and customs are similar to or different from the ones you know.

Review 〉 Unit 7

Vocabulary

1 What would you see at these parties? Complete the phrases with the words in the box.

acrobats balloons clapping costumes masks
making a speech parade streamers

1 a fancy dress party: people wearing _____ and _____

2 a children's birthday party: a room decorated with _____ and _____

3 a farewell party: someone _____ and people _____

4 a carnival or street party: a _____ and _____

Grammar

2 Rewrite the sentences about May Day traditions using passive reporting verbs.

1 People think it started as a celebration of the beginning of summer.

It is _____

2 They say that in the past people decorated their houses with flowers for good luck.

In the past people are _____

3 We know that the crowning of the May Queen is a popular tradition still.

The crowning of the May Queen _____

4 Commentators report that it is the busiest time of the year for English morris dancers.

It is _____

3 Choose the correct forms to complete the text.

Musical chairs is a traditional children's party game which is said to have first (1) *played / been played* in the 19th century. It involves a group of children (2) *dancing / being danced* around a circle of chairs while music is played. There is always one fewer chair than there are children. When the music stops, the children have (3) *to find / to be found* a chair to sit on. Each chair is allowed (4) *to occupy / to be occupied* by only one child. The child who is left without a chair is told (5) *to leave / to be left* the game. A chair is also taken out of the game and they start again. Chairs and children continue (6) *taking out / being taken out* until there are only two children and one chair left. The one who sits on it first is declared the winner.

Everyday English

4 Complete the conversation.

SA = Shop assistant, C = Customer

SA Can I help you?

C I hope so. I'm looking (1) _____ a luxury pen for my dad's birthday.

SA We have some lovely Mont Blanc pens. They're around £200.

C That's a lot. Have you got anything (2) _____?

SA What (3) _____ these Schaeffer pens? They're around £50.

C I like that one. Can I (4) _____ it back if he doesn't like it?

SA Of course, as long as you keep the (5) _____.

C Great, can you (6) _____ it for me?

SA Sure, blue paper or green paper?

Now I can …

☐ talk about traditions and celebrations.
☐ talk about important events in people's lives.
☐ use passive reporting verbs.
☐ use the passive gerund and infinitive.
☐ shop for a present.

The **Review** page revises the key language presented in the unit. Students review the target language (**grammar, vocabulary** and **functional language**) by completing discrete item tasks individually. Then they complete a short self-assessment task. The Review page can be done in class or set for homework.

Contents

1 Artists

UNIT OVERVIEW

Topic	art, music and theatre
Reading	putting on a play, Yann Arthus-Bertrand's photography, a youth orchestra, Banksy the people's artist
Listening	radio programme about music piracy, talking about going to a concert
Grammar	present perfect simple and present perfect continuous, present simple, present continuous and *will*, articles
Function	talking about tastes, phoning the box office (making a booking)
Vocabulary	art, theatre
Pronunciation	linking sounds
Writing	a review of a concert
Speaking	conversation between a musician and a music fan about music piracy, talking about tastes in music, survey on the arts
Culture	the graffiti artist Banksy, the arts in Britain

Let's get started

Books closed lead-in activity

Write *Artists* and *Musicians* on the board.

Ask students, *Who is your favourite artist or musician? What do you know about them and why do you like them?*

Exercise 1

- Ask students, *What is the musician doing? How does he feel?*
- Check students understand the useful expressions (see box below). For lower-level classes, you could spend some time going over the *Useful expressions* box. Say the expressions aloud and ask students to repeat. Then ask them to work in pairs to discuss the quotations. Elicit several responses.

> **Vocabulary note**
> *express yourself* = do creative things in order to show how you think and feel.
>
> *lose yourself in something* = concentrate on producing or experiencing a piece of art so much that you don't notice anything else around you.
>
> We use *do* with an activity (*do a class*) and *make* when we create something (*make films*). Note that *do a play* means to perform it, not write it.

Vocabulary

Alternative activity

Divide the class into groups of four and ask each group to brainstorm one or two of the words in the vocabulary box for one minute. Then ask the groups to share their results with the class.

Exercise 2

- Write *music* on the board and elicit as many words as you can from the students in 30 seconds. Then put students in pairs or groups of three to brainstorm the other words. Tell them to spend no more than 30 seconds on each word.

Exercise 3

- Divide students into groups of four to talk. Ask a few students to tell the class what they found out about others in their group.
- Point out the stress and pronunciation of some of the more difficult words: *amateur dramatics* /ˈæmətə(r) drəˈmætɪks/; *instrument* /ˈɪnstrʊmənt/; *poem* /ˈpəʊɪm/.

Making music

Books closed lead-in activity

Write *African music* on the board. Ask, *What sort of music is Africa famous for? How would you describe African music?*

Alternatively, bring in a recording of African music. Play a brief extract and ask students to describe the type of music, how it makes them feel, and what they like about it.

Reading

Exercise 1

- Ask students to look at the photograph. Ask, *Where do you think he is from? What sort of music does he play?* Elicit several responses.
- Ask students to read the text quickly then discuss the question in pairs. Ask students what other information they can remember about the text.

Answers
He uses his music and reputation to make people aware of social issues such as poverty, economic exploitation and music piracy.

Vocabulary note
immense = huge; *blend* = mix; *profusely* = a lot; *music piracy* = illegally recording or downloading music

Exercise 2

- Divide students into pairs or small groups to discuss the questions.

Example answer
1 If musicians and other artists use their influence to make people aware of important social issues, then I think that's a good thing. However, I don't think artists should misuse their status to influence young people in a negative direction or get involved in issues where they have little experience or knowledge.

Listening

Exercise 3

- Ask students to work in pairs to write a definition. Elicit two or three good examples. In feedback, ask students how they feel about music piracy. Ask, *How widespread is it in your country? Why is it a bad thing?*

Example answer
Music piracy is when people share music illegally. For example, when people copy CDs, upload music to the Internet without the artist's permission or download music from the Internet without paying for it.

Exercise 4 CD1/02

- Give students time to read the statements and check any vocabulary. Play the recording and then ask students to compare their answers in pairs.

Audioscript

Presenter Welcome back. Today we're looking at the question of music downloads, and to discuss this topic, Denise Lewis from the British Association of Music Rights has joined me. Welcome, Denise.

Denise Thank you.

Presenter Let's start with basic definitions because I think most people … when we talk about internet downloads … most people presume we mean illegal copying, music piracy. And that's not true, is it?

Denise No, of course not. Many downloads are in no way illegal. It's been quite common for a few years to purchase downloads for a fee and, in addition, an increasing number of artists have been offering music for free on their websites.

Presenter Yes, that's an interesting area, isn't it? I mean why are artists whose livelihood depends on selling music offering songs for free?

Denise Well, we've been following developments in this direction very closely, as you can imagine, and it seems that offering samples of music leads to fans actually buying music or concert tickets. So it's quite an effective promotion tool and actually boosts … promotes sales rather than hurting them.

Presenter	But what about illegal downloads? I mean, people are also downloading illegally and that does hurt sales.
Denise	Of course. Research among 14–24-year-olds shows that on average 48 per cent of a collection on a digital music player is copied illegally – although illegal downloading isn't just limited to young people, of course. But, I think we mustn't forget that this isn't a new problem. People have been copying music illegally for years. In the past people used to tape their favourite songs off the radio, and pirate CDs are a big issue in many countries … so the music industry has known about the problem for a long time. What is new is that it … it's much easier and quicker to download and share music nowadays – among peers or on social networking sites – so the problem has become more widespread and more visible.
Presenter	But the basic problem remains, doesn't it? Artists are losing out on money from sales of their music.
Denise	Yes, certainly. I think people often forget that songs aren't common property. They belong to musicians and record companies who have invested a lot of time and money to produce them, and therefore they should be paid for their songs. Downloading illegal music is stealing pure and simple, just like stealing a CD or a DVD from a shop.
Presenter	Mmm, but how exactly …

Answer
Statement 3

Vocabulary note
widespread = in many places; *download music* = take it from the Internet; *hurt sales* = make sales go down

---

Exercise 5  CD1/02

- Give students time to read the true or false statements and check any vocabulary. Play the recording and then ask students to compare their answers in pairs.

Answers
1 True 2 False 3 True 4 True 5 True

Exercise 6

- Divide students into pairs or small groups to discuss the questions.

Pronunciation: linking sounds
Exercise 7  CD1/03

- Play the recording. Ask students to listen and mark the linking then check their answers in pairs.
- Ask students to discuss the questions in pairs. Then model the way the sounds link.
- Play the recording again. Students listen and repeat.

Answers
a to a b to my c copy a
1 When a word ends in a consonant and the next word starts with a vowel, the consonant joins the vowel sound to make a single sound. There is no pause between the sounds (download a music file).
2 When an 'r' links to a vowel, the 'r' is pronounced as a definite 'r' sound (share a music file).
3 When a vowel links to another vowel, the words are linked with an extra sound: after 'o' it sounds like 'w' (listen to a song); after 'y' or 'i' it sounds like 'y' (copy a music file).

Extra activity

Write on the board: *Music on the Internet should be free for everyone*. Divide the class into groups of four and ask each group to prepare and present arguments in favour of or against the motion. Then have a class debate.

Speaking

Exercise 8

- For lower-level classes, spend some time going over the *Useful expressions* box. Say the expressions aloud and ask students to repeat. You could brainstorm other reasons for and against being able to download music for free, and write them up on the board before students start the main exercise.
- Give pairs two minutes to decide on their roles and prepare things to say before they do the role play.

> **Vocabulary note**
> *make a living* = earn enough money to live; *lose out on* = miss the opportunity to do or have something; *copyright laws* = legal protection against piracy of books or music

Grammar: present perfect simple and continuous

Exercise 9

- Check the form by asking students to look at sentences 1–4 and label them as present perfect (*have* + past participle) or present perfect continuous (*have* + *been* + present participle). Then ask students to complete the rules. They could work in pairs or do the task individually, then check in pairs.

> **Answers**
> 1 result 2 Is used 3 duration 4 Isn't used

> **Extra activity**
> Write the two sentences in the grammar note on the board and see if students can tell you how they are similar and different in meaning.

> **Grammar note**
> When students have completed Exercise 9, point out that often both forms are possible. For example, we can say *I've lived here for years* or *I've been living here for years*. We choose to say the first to emphasise the result (I'm a long-term resident) and the second to emphasise the duration (this is a long, ongoing activity).

- Refer students to the Grammar Reference on page 145.

Exercises 10 and 11

- Ask students to work individually to complete the sentences and then make them true for themselves. Then divide the students into groups to tell each other what they have been doing.

> **Answers**
> 1 downloaded 2 been 3 been having 4 liked 5 been following 6 never bought
> 7 started 8 been wondering

Books closed lead-in activity

Write *Theatre* on the board. Ask, *Have you ever been to the theatre? What did you see?* If possible, divide the class into groups with at least one student with experience of going to the theatre in each group. Write, *When? Where? What?* on the board and ask students to ask each other about their theatre experiences using the question words.

Extra activity

Ask students what clues helped them find the answers. For example, the word *usually* tells them answer 4 must be present simple passive, and the fact that the missing word is followed by a noun not a clause in 5 tells students it must be *during* not *while*.

Extra activity

Ask students to work in pairs to write their own definition for each of the following people: *the director; the producer; a dresser; the casting director; the scenic artist; the lighting technician.*

Reading and vocabulary

Exercise 1

- Ask students to look at the photograph. Ask, *What do you think it shows? Where do you think it is?* Elicit several responses.
- Ask students to discuss the questions in pairs. In feedback, ask students to tell you what particular plays or musicals are currently popular.

> **Culture note**
> The **West End** in London and **Broadway** in New York are home to some of the most respected and popular theatres in the English-speaking world. Agatha Christie's play *The Mousetrap* has been showing in the West End since 1958. However, in general, musicals tend to run the longest and have the biggest audiences.
>
> **Pantomimes** are musical comedy plays aimed at children and based on traditional stories such as *Cinderella* and *Snow White.* They are really popular in Britain.

Exercise 2

- Ask students to predict what the text is about from the title. Then ask them to read it quickly without worrying about the missing words. Set a gist or focus question: *What things are involved in 'making theatre'?*
- Ask students to complete the text individually and then check in pairs.

> **Answers**
> 1 C 2 B 3 D 4 A 5 B 6 C

Exercise 3

- Ask students to look through the text quickly and find as many words as they can connected with the theatre and acting. Ask them to check their answers in pairs. Then tell them to match the words to the definitions.
- Find out what other words students found in the text.

> **Answers**
> 1 f 2 b 3 d 4 e 5 h 6 c 7 g 8 a

> **Vocabulary note**
> *part* = role in the play; *interpret* = understand and bring to life; *wigs* = hair pieces; *dressers* = people who help actors put clothes on; *scenes* = short parts of a play

Exercise 4

- Divide students into pairs or small groups to discuss the questions.

Grammar: present tenses

Exercise 5

■ Ask students to find and underline the tenses, then check their answers in pairs. Do the first one as an example.

Answers
Present simple for regular actions: the casting director works with the director of a play; the director and designers decide together on the look of the stage; an in-house team makes many of the objects
will **for repeated actions:** casting staff will watch hundreds of plays every year; a director will often invite actors for two auditions; a large team of maintenance staff will wash and look after the costumes
Present continuous with *always:* theatres are always looking for both experienced actors and new talent; actors are always damaging costumes

■ Ask students to work in pairs to complete the rules with the names of tenses. You could write the tense names on the board first to guide them.

Answers
1 the present simple 2 will 3 the present continuous 4 the present continuous

■ Refer students to the Grammar Reference on page 145.

Exercise 6

■ Ask students to complete the exercise individually, then check in pairs.

Answers
1 are always picking up; don't do it 2 will do / do; will make / make; 3 are acting; are living 4 really enjoy 5 always visit 6 won't work / doesn't work; won't happen / doesn't happen

> **Grammar note**
> Notice that in 1 the present continuous is used because it is an irritating habit, but in 5 the present simple is used because it is a regular habit. In 2 and 6, the present simple could be used to describe a regular habit, or *will* could be used to emphasise that these are repeated actions. In 3, *at the moment* reveals that this is happening now, and in 4 the speaker is describing a permanent state (her job).

Exercise 7

■ Ask students to discuss the question in pairs.

Answers
1 costume maintenance staff 2 costume designer 3 actors 4 director 5 casting director 6 (specialised) technician

Exercise 8

■ Give students a few minutes to choose a role and think of what to say. With lower-level classes, you could give them time to write down a few notes or whole sentences. Divide the class into pairs or fours to describe their person's daily routine.

Exercise 9 CD1/04

■ Start by brainstorming what things irritate students in general. Use mime to elicit some of the more difficult vocabulary in the list (chewing gum; slurping drinks; biting nails).
■ Ask students to look at the list in pairs and predict what the speaker will say.
■ Play the recording. Let students check their answers in pairs.
■ Ask students to say what they find irritating in the cinema.

Extra activity

Extend this idea further by asking students to write a list of any ten jobs. Put students in pairs. They must describe the daily routine of each job, and their partner must guess all the jobs. See which pair finishes first.

Audioscript

Woman I really hate it when people come in late. You're sitting ready to watch a play and then you have to get up and down and move your bag or coat so people can get past. It's so rude!

Teenage boy Why do people talk during a film? My friend is always whispering to me or asking questions about the film, it drives me crazy. I just want to watch something in peace.

Man I can't stand people unwrapping sweets. I'm always sitting next to somebody at the theatre who does that.

Woman Leaving early at the end of a film really irritates me. People are always leaving before the film is properly finished. I like to stay right till the end of the music and the credits.

Teenage girl I hate people texting during a film. My brother's always doing it and I find the light on his phone really distracting.

Answers
arriving late; whispering; unwrapping sweets; leaving early; texting

---

Vocabulary note
slurping = making a horrible noise by sucking drink into your mouth

---

Exercise 10

■ For lower-level classes, spend some time going over the *Useful expressions* box. Say the expressions aloud and ask students to repeat.

Pronunciation note
Point out that students should strongly stress certain syllables in order to emphasise their annoyance: *She is <u>always</u> …; I can't <u>stand</u> it when …*

■ To help students get started, ask two or three to share sentences about their brothers or sisters, then put students in pairs or threes to describe their family/ friends.

Photographic art

Vocabulary

Exercise 1

Books closed lead-in activity

- Ask students to complete the definitions then check in pairs. Check understanding by asking students if they can think of a famous portrait (e.g. The Mona Lisa) or if they can say what they would find in a landscape (e.g. fields and hills).

Answers
2 landscape 3 portrait 6 sketch 7 seascape

> **Pronunciation note**
> Point out stress (<u>land</u>scape; <u>por</u>trait) and difficult pronunciation (portrait /ˈpɔː(r)trɪt/; drawing /ˈdrɔːɪŋ/).

Speaking

Exercise 2

- Ask students to read the statement and think about what it means. Ask a student to put the statement in their own words. Ask, *Do you agree with the statement? What else does it take to be a good photographer?*

Reading

Exercise 3

- Ask students to work in pairs to describe the photos. You could introduce a set of useful language on the board to help them before they speak: *It depicts/ shows …; It seems to be …; It looks like …; It makes me feel/think of …*
- Ask students to compare their ideas with the descriptions on page 143.

Exercise 4

- Ask students to read the title of the article and the six sentences A to F. Then ask them to work in pairs to briefly predict what the text is about. Check that students understand that *uplifted* (feeling positive) is the opposite of *disheartened* (feeling negative or depressed).
- Ask students to read and match sentences A–F to gaps 1–4. Let them check in pairs before discussing the answers as a class.

Answers
1 E 2 D 3 C 4 A

Exercise 5

- Ask students to discuss the questions in pairs or small groups.

Grammar: articles

Exercise 6

- Ask students to read the text and think about why *a*, *the* or no article is used in each case. Tell them not to look at the grammar box yet.
- Ask students to work in pairs to discuss why they think the articles are being used, and to match the uses to the rules in the box.

Answers
1 A (first mention) 2 B (plural generalisation) 3 C (unique thing) 4 A (first mention)
5 A (already mentioned) 6 A (first mention) 7 B (plural generalisation) 8 C (unique thing)

Books closed lead-in activity

Write *My favourite photo* on the board. Briefly describe a photo you have. Tell students who is in the photo, where it was taken, why it is special (bring the photo in if you can). Then put students in pairs or threes to describe their own favourite photos.

Extra activity

Ask students in pairs to complete the sentence *A good photographer has to …* Find out who has the best description.

Extra activity

Ask students to find and analyse other examples of the use of articles in the fourth paragraph of the text.

Grammar note
You may wish to point out in feedback that the planet we live on can be referred to as *Earth* (as in its name, like *Mars* or *Jupiter*) or *the Earth* (as in a unique thing, like *the Sun* or *the Moon*). So, the title of the book, *Earth from the Air*, is correct English.

- Refer students to the Grammar Reference on page 146.

Exercise 7   CD1/05

- Lead in by asking students if they have heard of underwater photography. Ask them to read the text briefly and say what David Doubilet does and where he has been. You may also wish to check the difficult words (see below).
- Ask students to work individually or in pairs to complete the text. Then play the recording so that they can check their answers.

Answers and grammar notes
1 the (unique) 2 the (unique) 3 ø (plural generalisation) 4 the (specific)
5 ø (plural generalisation) 6 a (first mention) 7 a (first mention) 8 a (first mention)

Culture and vocabulary note
A **Brownie Hawkeye** is a camera from the 1950s.

groundbreaking = original – the first to do it; *fluorescent* = bright and shiny;
wrecks = ships on the bottom of the sea

Extra activity

Divide students into groups of four. Each student must describe an artist or musician they know well, using complete sentences. The other students in the group must listen. If the student makes a mistake with an article, they shout *challenge* and correct the article. Find out which student can speak the longest without making a mistake.

Taste in music

Play short extracts of three different pieces of music to the class (pop, jazz and classical, for example). Ask students to write adjectives to describe how they feel about the music then discuss their feelings in pairs.

Extra activity

Follow up with a discussion to see what your students think. Ask, *Do you think it is a good idea and why (not)? How could a similar idea help young people in your country? Would you like to see the orchestra and why?*

Reading

Exercise 1

■ Ask students to look at the photographs. Ask, *What can you see?* Elicit several responses. Ask students to think about the connection between the photos in pairs.

Exercise 2

■ Ask students to read the text quickly and check their answers.
■ Ask students to tell you what other information they can remember about the text.

> **Answers**
> The connection between the photos is that one shows a slum (possibly in Venezuela) and the other shows a young girl playing the violin – possibly a musician who came from the slum.

> **Culture and vocabulary note**
> Caracas/kəˈrækəs/ is the capital of Venezuela, a Spanish-speaking country on the north-east coast of South America. It has a mixed population of Hispanic and black African descent, and extremes of wealth and poverty.
>
> *slums* = areas of poverty and bad housing on the edge of developing cities; *conviction* = strength of belief; *limited prospects* = few opportunities in life

Exercise 3

■ Divide students into pairs or small groups to discuss the questions.

> **Answers**
> The two aims of the Venezuelan Youth Orchestra are to give youngsters with limited prospects a new chance in life and to help make classical music more a part of popular culture. It is seen as the most exciting thing happening in the world of classical music and it has inspired many similar projects in countries around the globe.

Listening: expressing likes and dislikes

Exercise 4   CD1/06

■ Ask students to read the statements carefully. To help students prepare for listening ask, *Which two people will you hear in the conversation? What will they talk about? What do you expect them to say?* It is a good idea to get students to predict as much as they can.
■ Play the recording. Ask students to discuss answers in pairs.

Audioscript

Liz	Hey, Sarah, I've got a spare ticket for the Venezuelan Youth Orchestra. They're playing at The South Bank on Saturday night. Do you fancy coming with me?
Sarah	Er … Youth Orchestra? Is that a classical concert?
Liz	Yeah, it is, but I think it'll be really good.
Sarah	Mmm … classical isn't really my thing, I'm afraid.
Liz	Look, I didn't use to be a big fan either, but I'm really keen on it now. My parents took me to a Beethoven concert a couple of years ago and it was absolutely fantastic. It's actually very different hearing classical music live to just listening to a CD or the radio. It can be very powerful.
Sarah	Mmm … well, I do quite like some classical music … when I'm in the right mood, that is. There's a piano piece called 'Pathetique'. Do you know it?
Liz	Yes, of course. It's lovely.

Sarah	It is. My dad loved it … He always used to listen to it when he was working. It's very soothing … and beautiful. It reminds me of sitting quietly in the evening, reading or sometimes just watching him concentrating.
Liz	Well, I don't know if this Youth Orchestra is going to play Beethoven necessarily, but it's kids from poor backgrounds in Venezuela who are the musicians, and I read that when Placido Domingo saw them, he found it so moving that he cried.
Sarah	OK. I'll say yes then. I'd hate to miss it and then regret it.
Liz	That's great. Shall we arrange to meet there about half an hour before the start? It's at the Royal Festival Hall at 8 p.m. …

Answers
1 True 2 False 3 False 4 False

Exercise 5 CD1/06

■ Give students time to read the sentences and complete as much as they can. Then play the recording again. Ask students to compare their answers in pairs.

■ Get students to categorise the ways of expressing likes and dislikes in terms of strength of feeling.

Answers
1 thing 2 fan; keen 3 quite like; mood 4 loved 5 beautiful; reminds 6 moving

> **Vocabulary note**
> Note that *It's not my thing* and *I'm not a big fan (of)* … are gentle ways of saying you don't like something. You are saying that something may well be good but it's not to your taste.
> *soothing* = relaxing; *moving* = makes you feel emotional

Speaking: talking about tastes

Exercise 6

Extra activity —————→

■ Give students a couple of minutes to think of two pieces of music and consider the questions. Tell them to take notes if they wish. Focus them on the expressions used in exercise 5 and tell them to try to use some of them.

■ Ask students to discuss the questions in pairs or small groups. Ask a few students to tell the class what they heard from their partner(s).

Extra activity

Lead in to this activity by playing a piece of music you like. Tell the class why it is special to you. Encourage questions from the students.

Vocabulary

Exercise 7

■ Ask students to look at the words in pairs and decide how many they know or think they know. If they know a lot, ask them to work in groups of four to explain them. If they only know a few, ask them to use a dictionary to research.

■ Use concept-check questions to check meaning. For example, *Is a gig usually in a smaller or larger place than a concert?*

> **Vocabulary note**
> A *gig* is a concert in a small venue. An *arena* is a really large venue such as a football stadium. *Lyrics* are the words of a song. A *support act* is the band that plays first, before the most important act comes on. When somebody famous appears in a show or performance for a brief time, it is a *guest appearance*. An *encore* is when a performer comes back on stage to sing an extra song because the audience are applauding a lot.

Exercise 8

■ Ask students to discuss the questions in pairs. You could brainstorm some positive and negative adjectives to describe concerts first in order to get students started (for example, *exciting, loud, crowded, disappointing*).

Writing: a review of a concert

Exercise 9

- Ask students to look at the picture. Ask, *Who is he? What do you know about him? What sort of music do you think he plays?*
- Ask students to read the text quickly and answer the question.

> **Answer**
> He has mastered Chopin's moods and emotional difficulties.

> **Culture and vocabulary note**
> **Rafał Blechacz** was born in June 1985 in Nakło n. Notecią, in Poland. In 2005, he won the first prize at the 15th International Frederick Chopin Piano Competition in Warsaw, outclassing his rivals. Blechacz completed his secondary education in the National Arthur Rubinstein Music School in Bydgoszcz, and in May 2007 he graduated from the Feliks Nowowiejski Music Academy in Bydgoszcz.
> *compelling* = powerful; *engaging* = appealing; *Op.17* = opus 17 (i.e. a musical work)

Exercise 10

- Ask students to work individually or in pairs to make notes. Give students an opportunity to share their notes with another student or another pair once they have finished.

Exercise 11

- This could be done in class or for homework. If students rewrite the description of the classical concert, remind them to do so from their notes in exercise 10 without looking at the original text.
- If students are to write about a concert they have been to, it is a good idea to do the planning in class. Ask students to write ideas next to each heading first, then compare what they have done with a partner. Encourage students to comment on each other's ideas. Monitor and help. Then ask students to decide which useful expressions to include in their review before starting to write.

Extra activity

Once students have completed their reviews, use them as reading comprehensions for the class. You could attach the reviews to the class walls. Students walk round and read them, and prepare questions to ask a reviewer about one of the concerts. Or students could pass round and read their reviews in groups of four.

Books closed lead-in activity

Ask what examples of public art the students see around their town every day (statues, buildings, etc.). Put students in pairs to build up a list and to say why they think any of the examples are important or interesting.

Reading

Exercise 1

- Ask students to look at the photographs. Ask, *What can you see? How can you describe these photos?* Elicit several responses.
- Check the meaning of *defaced* (made to look ugly). Then ask students to discuss the questions in pairs.

Exercise 2

- Ask students if they can predict the answers to the three questions from the lead-in in exercise 1 and the title of the text. Then ask them to read the article quickly to find answers. Let students check answers in pairs.

> **Answers**
> 1 Banksy is an anonymous graffiti artist. 2 The public like him – they voted him an art hero. 3 Critics give him negative reviews or ignore him.

Exercise 3

- Ask students to work individually to choose the correct word for each gap.
- In feedback, ask students to say which clues helped them reach the correct answer (for example, in 4 it had to be *should* because *ought* is followed by *to*. In 5, it had to be *despite* because *in spite* is followed by *of* and *although* is followed by a clause).

> **Answers**
> 1 B 2 D 3 A 4 C 5 A

Extra activity

Banksy says, 'Galleries are just trophy cabinets for a handful of millionaires,'. Ask students, *What does he mean? Do you agree and why? If you opened a gallery, what type of art would you put in it?*

Exercise 4

- Ask students to work individually to decide if the statements are true or false. Discuss the answers as a class.

> **Answers**
> 1 False (he sprayed pictures on the walls) 2 True 3 True 4 False (a huge hit) 5 False
> 6 True

> **Culture and vocabulary note**
>
> **Banksy** is the pseudonym of a British graffiti artist and political activist who started out producing graffiti in Bristol, England. His identity is unconfirmed. He combines stencil drawings with epigrams which are satirical and darkly humorous. Banksy has also won acclaim for his short faux-documentary *Exit Through the Gift Shop,* which was longlisted for an Oscar.
>
> **Warholesque** refers to Andy Warhol, the twentieth-century American pop artist who famously produced paintings of Campbell's soup cans.
>
> **Tate Modern**, on London's South Bank, opened in the 1990s to display international modern art. It is housed in a huge former power station. **The Cans Festival** took place in May 2008. The name is a joke – it sounds like the English pronunciation of Cannes Festival, the glitzy film festival held in the south of France.
>
> *crumpled* = old, broken; *sneaked* = went into secretly and unnoticed

Listening

Exercise 5

- Read out the statistics in the box. Point out the pronunciation of *per cent* /pə(r)ˈsent/.
- Ask students to work individually to complete the gaps, and then check with a partner.

Exercise 6 CD1/07

- Play the recording. Ask students to listen and check their answers. Discuss the questions in feedback.

> **Answers**
> 1 90% 2 Two 3 26% 4 once 5 quarter 6 twice 7 five 8 ten 9 biggest
> 10 second biggest

Exercise 7

- Ask students to work individually to complete the statistics then check in pairs.

> **Answers**
> 1 in 2 of 3 group 4 quarter 5 Over 6 as

> **Vocabulary note**
> Note that we say *a quarter of, a third of, a percentage of, a number of,* but we don't usually use *of* with *half.*
> *one in three* = 33 per cent or one third; *over* = more than; *under* = less than

Speaking

Exercise 8

- Divide the class into four groups to prepare the questions. You could start them off by eliciting a few (for example, *What kind of music do you like?*).
- When students are ready, ask them to walk round the class and interview the other students, making a note of their answers.
- After five or six minutes of mingling, put groups back together to compare statistics and prepare to present their statistics to the class.
- Correct any errors in their presentations.
- Refer students to the DVD about a Chinese artist in Harlem. Video worksheet on page 136.

Extra activity

Ask students to think of as many alternative ways of expressing the following as they can: 25%; a third; 12 in comparison to 6; 18% in comparison to 30%.

Phoning the box office

Listening and speaking

Books closed lead-in activity

Exercise 1

- Ask students to look at the posters and discuss the questions in pairs.
- Find out which is most popular with the majority of the class. Revise the previous lesson by asking what percentage like which.

Write on the board the name of a show or play that is currently on in your town. Tell students to think of as many questions as they can to ask you about it. Tell them to ask about price, location, actors, times, etc. Answer the questions the students ask you.

Example Answers

1 The photos show two posters. The first is for *The Lion King*, a musical. The second poster is for a pop punk festival.

2 The musical looks like good fun. The second event looks quite cool – the design of the poster is really colourful and abstract. It's probably aimed at young people.

3 I'd prefer to go to the musical because I like events which make me feel good. I don't like pop punk, so the concert doesn't interest me.

Culture note

The Lion King is a musical stage show performed at a theatre in London. It is adapted from the Disney film and tells the story of a pride of lions in Africa. The actors wear elaborate animal costumes.

The second poster is for a pop punk festival featuring some well-known American pop punk bands, notably Blink-182 and Weezer, who are from California and are influential pioneers of this type of music, and Fall Out Boy, formed in 2001, which is a pop punk band from Illinois.

Exercise 2  CD1/08

- Give students a moment to read the form. Ask, *What type of missing information will you listen for?*
- Play the recording. Students listen and complete the form. Let them check in pairs.

Extra activity

As revision, brainstorm other words connected with theatre: *play, stage, actors, designers*, etc.

Audioscript

Agent	Strada Box Office, Sandra speaking. How may I help you?
Student	Yes, hello … er, I'd like to book some tickets for *The Lion King*.
Agent	Certainly, sir. On what date?
Student	12th October.
Agent	12th October … I'm afraid that day's performances are sold out – we don't have any tickets left at all. I have lots of tickets for the 13th.
Student	Er no, we're leaving on the 13th. … What about the 11th?
Agent	11th October … yes … Would you like matinee or evening tickets?
Student	Er … what's a matinee?
Agent	That's the early afternoon performance.
Student	Oh, evening tickets, please.
Agent	Right, the evening performance starts at half past seven. How many tickets do you require?
Student	Twenty, please.
Agent	Sorry, did you say 20?
Student	Yes, we are on a school trip.
Agent	OK – would you like circle or stalls?
Student	Sorry?
Agent	The seats in the stalls are next to the stage and seats in the circle are higher up.
Student	Er … stalls, please. Is there a student discount?
Agent	Yes, there is but I can also give you a group rate. That means each ticket costs £22 instead of £53.
Student	That sounds fine.
Agent	I can reserve the tickets for you and you can collect them from our office the day before … Can you give me your name, please?

Student	Yes, of course. It's Mark Dupont.
Agent	How do you spell that, please?
Student	D–U–P–O–N–T.
Agent	Right, thank you for booking with us, Mr Dupont.
Student	Thanks for your help. Goodbye.

Answers
Show: *Lion King*
Date: *11 October;
           evening*
Number of tickets: *20*
Discounts: *group; student*
Ticket price: *£22*
Name: *Mark Dupont*

Exercise 3   CD1/08

■ Play the recording again. Ask students to work in pairs to explain the words.

Answers
sold out = there aren't any tickets left
matinee = early afternoon performance
circle = seats higher up, further away from the stage
stalls = seats next to the stage
student discount = money off the price of a ticket for a student
group rate = special price for a group

> **Vocabulary note**
> *Matinee* is pronounced as in French: /'mætɪneɪ/.

Exercise 4

Extra activity

■ Ask students to work in pairs to complete the rules.

Ask students to write three things they are planning with friends and three events that are happening at the weekend. Ask them to tell the class what they wrote.

Answers
present simple
present continuous

> **Grammar note**
> The present simple is only used to talk about future events that are impersonal and scheduled. Consequently, it is a much less common way of expressing the future than the present continuous, which is used for personal arrangements.

■ Refer students to the Grammar Reference on page 146.

Exercise 5

■ Divide the class into pairs and ask them to look at their information. Tell B to prepare as many questions as they can using the ideas on page 143, and tell A to use the information on page 141.
■ When students are ready, ask them to role play the situation.
■ Monitor the students' performance closely. In feedback, correct mistakes and comment on good language use.

Exercise 6

■ Provide further practice by asking students to change roles in their pairs, and improvise a dialogue based on the posters in exercise 1.
■ You could ask different pairs to role play the situation in front of the class.
■ Monitor the students' performance closely. Correct mistakes and comment on good language use.

2

Crossing borders

UNIT OVERVIEW

Topic	NGOs and volunteering, conservation, emigration and travel
Reading	Doctors Without Borders, Earth Hour, Ellis Island and emigrating to the USA
Listening	Doctors Without Borders volunteers, an anecdote, immigration
Grammar	determiners, narrative tenses: past simple and continuous, past perfect simple and continuous, *used to* and *would*
Function	raising awareness
Vocabulary	the environment, discourse markers, compound adjectives, compound nouns
Pronunciation	weak forms
Writing	describing a place
Speaking	talking about campaigning, describing an experience, discussing films
Culture	immigration and emigration, being born into a different culture from your parents

Books closed lead-in activity

Write *Going abroad* on the board. Ask students, *Why do people go abroad?* Brainstorm as many ideas as you can (work, study, holidays, etc.).

Let's get started

Exercise 1

- Ask students, *What are the people in the photograph doing? Where are they?*
- Ask students to work in pairs to discuss the questions. Elicit several responses.

Answers
Borders are becoming less important; we are living in a globalised world. International cooperation is possible in many fields. Modern telecommunications, in particular the Internet, mean that it is easy to communicate with people all over the world. People are more knowledgeable about, and more open to, other cultures.

Vocabulary

Exercise 2

- Ask students to work in pairs to match the activities and phrases.

Answers
1 d 2 c 3 b 4 a c 5 d 6 a d 7 a d 8 d

Extra activity

Divide the class into groups of four and ask each group to make a list of at least ten ways of keeping in touch with a good friend who has left to live abroad. Find out which group has the best list.

> **Vocabulary note**
> *chat to/with* people; *work/study in* a place
> *emigrate* = leave your home country; *immigrate* = arrive in a new country to live there

Exercise 3

- Ask students to discuss the questions, sharing interesting experiences with the class.

International cooperation

Books closed lead-in activity

Write on the board the names of three well-known NGOs or charities based in the students' country. Ask, *What are these organisations? What do they do? Do you support these organisations and why? Which organisations do you support and why?*

Extra activity

Work on stress. Before doing exercise 2, read out the words in the box and ask students to mark the strong stress: *educa̲tion, environme̲ntal, glo̲bal, humanita̲rian, me̲dical, conser̲vation*

Reading

Exercise 1

■ Ask students to work in pairs to read and choose the best definition. Elicit several responses. You could ask students to describe an NGO in their own words.

Answer
A

> **Vocabulary note**
> *funded* = given money by
> Note the collocations of key verbs: *support* (a cause or work); *provide* (aid); *promote* (awareness)

Exercise 2

■ Ask students to look at the logos for the various NGOs. Ask, *How many do you know? Which ones can you guess?*

■ Divide students into pairs or small groups to match NGOs and areas. Encourage them to describe the work of the NGOs using the verbs in the definitions in exercise 1.

Answers
Amnesty International: human rights, humanitarian aid
Médecins Sans Frontières (Doctors Without Borders): medical aid
World Wide Fund for Nature: environmental protection, nature conservation, education
Greenpeace: environmental protection, nature conservation, education
Save the Children: humanitarian aid, education

Exercise 3

■ Divide students into pairs or small groups to discuss the questions.

Exercise 4

■ Ask students to read the text and write the summary individually.
■ They can then share and compare their sentences in pairs.
■ Elicit suggestions from the class and work towards a one-sentence summary as a class.

Example answer
Doctors Without Borders is an independent organisation which helps people who are in need of urgent medical care because of events such as natural disasters and armed conflict.

Exercise 5

■ Ask students to read the text again and answer the question with a partner.

Answers
an encyclopaedia entry; a mission statement

Vocabulary

Exercise 6

■ Ask students to work in pairs to choose the adjectives. Tell them to look back at the text if necessary.

■ Check understanding with concept-check questions. For example, *Which word means it makes money? Which word means it has many projects?*

Answers
1 a 2 b 3 b 4 b 5 a

> **Pronunciation note**
> Point out strong stress: <u>cha</u>ritable, <u>pro</u>fitable, es<u>tab</u>lished, theo<u>re</u>tical, <u>prac</u>tical, ex<u>ten</u>sive.

Exercise 7

■ Ask students to complete the sentences individually then check in pairs.

Answers
1 Discrimination 2 Refugees 3 Victims 4 Natural disasters 5 Crises 6 Survival
7 Vulnerable individuals 8 Humanitarian aid

Listening

Exercise 8   CD1/09

■ Encourage students to predict the listening content by asking, *What sort of work do you think Doctors Without Borders volunteers do? What are the good and bad things about doing work like this?*

■ Ask students to listen to the recording and answer the question.

Audioscript

Deepa   I work at local public events. We treat people for things like sprained ankles, to more serious problems such as, erm, heart attacks. It's quite surprising how many people need some sort of medical attention in the course of a single event. It isn't easy work, in fact it can be quite stressful, but all of us enjoy it. I think I'll enjoy it for a long time.

Liam   Doctors Without Borders is a huge international organisation but it's like being part of a global family. It's amazing. Every one of us is working towards the same goal, and without pay. There's always a bond between volunteers. It doesn't matter who you are or where you come from. If I ever left, I'd really miss that.

Amy   My mother has worked as a first aid helper at local events like music festivals and football matches for years and … er I used to go along with her, every Saturday. It was just something I always did. It seemed natural to become a volunteer too, so I got involved.

Noah   I did a first aid course at school and volunteered for a few local events. Then I was asked to join a relief operation abroad. I was part of a small team who were sent to the site of a bad flood in Albania. We helped distribute stuff like blankets, tents, emergency food items. Now I regularly take part in other relief operations abroad. No operation is ever entirely safe. We need to be careful, but I feel like I'm making a difference.

Hong   A lot of my friends go to sports training on Saturdays or hang out at the shopping centre. I'm not very sporty and I prefer to do something concrete with my time, something that is useful. I really like knowing I'm helping people. I think as a volunteer you get back much more than you give.

Answer
Speaker 4

Extra activity

Ask students to think of two recent news stories involving crime or disaster, then tell the stories using the vocabulary in exercises 6 and 7.

Exercise 9 ⊙ CD1/09

■ Ask students to talk in pairs and say which summary goes with which person. Then play the recording a second time and let students check in pairs.

Answers
Speaker 1: C Speaker 2: D Speaker 3: E Speaker 4: A Speaker 5: F

Exercise 10

■ Ask students to discuss the questions in pairs or small groups.

Grammar: determiners

Exercise 11

■ Ask students to read the rules carefully. Check understanding by asking a few concept-check and form questions: *Which words cannot be followed by* of? (no, every); *Which words have a negative meaning?* (no, none, neither); *Which words are followed by a plural verb?* (both, all, some, none).

■ Ask students to work in pairs to complete the sentences.

Answers
1 Both; enjoy 2 Neither; gets 3 Some of; have 4 Each of; has 5 None of the; are
6 either; stops

Grammar note
A visual way of showing *both*, *neither* and *either*:

Both Joe and Sue like chocolate.   ✓   ✓

Neither Joe nor Sue likes chocolate.   ✗   ✗

Does either Joe or Sue like chocolate?   ?   OR   ?

A visual way of showing *each* and *every*:

Each student works hard.

Every student works hard.

■ Refer students to the Grammar Reference on page 147.

Exercise 12

■ Ask students to work individually to write sentences, then check in pairs. Monitor and correct any errors.

■ Ask students in groups or as a class to read out their sentences.

Extra activity

Tell students to imagine they have 10,000 euros to give to charity. Ask them to decide which of the NGOs in exercise 2 they would support and why.

Extra activity

Ask students to research the NGOs in exercise 2 for homework and write about them. Their sentences should use determiners to compare the organisations. For example, *None of them make a profit.*

Global action

Books closed lead-in activity

Write on the board *Electricity*. Ask students to brainstorm all the things electricity is used for at home.

Extra activity

Ask students to look at these three phrases from the text and explain what they mean: *that may not strike you as a major event* (it may not seem to you to be very important); *high-profile landmarks* (well-known international buildings); *it doesn't take a great leap of the imagination to see* (you do not have to be very intelligent to understand).

Extra activity

Ask students to swap partners and roles and to do the role play again. Circulate, monitor and provide feedback again.

Speaking and vocabulary

Exercise 1

■ Ask students to work in groups of four and discuss the questions.

Exercise 2

■ Give students dictionaries or pre-teach unknown words.
■ Ask students to carry out the task individually, then to check in pairs.
■ Elicit answers from the whole class as complete sentences.

Answers
1 participants 2 consumes 3 emissions; global 4 initiative; backing 5 species; habitats

Pronunciation note
Note the words where the stress is on the second syllable: *parti̱cipants; consu̱mes; emi̱ssions; ini̱tiative*

Reading

Exercise 3

■ Ask students to read the multiple choice options.
■ Ask them to read the article and choose the best option.
■ They can then check their answers in pairs.
■ Elicit the answers from the class as complete sentences.

Answers
1 B 2 C 3 A 4 C 5 B 6 A

Speaking

Exercise 4

■ Ask students to get into pairs and decide who is A and who is B.
■ Read through the instructions with the class, and ask them to turn to the correct page: Student A looks at page 141 and Student B looks at page 143.
■ Ask them to do the role play. Circulate and monitor their production.
■ Provide feedback on their use of language.

Grammar: narrative tenses

Exercise 5

■ Read the grammar box with the class and ensure they understand the three tenses and their uses.
■ Then ask students to read the text in Exercise 3 again, and underline examples of the tenses.
■ Elicit answers from the whole class.

Answers
past simple: *went; was; turned off; joined in; turned into; did they do . . . ?; pointed out; went back to; made; left*

past continuous: *were putting*

past perfect simple: *had grown; had started*

Grammar note
The past simple is often shown in a timeline in this way:

Now

Past ◄────x────▲

The past continuous is often shown in a timeline in this way:

x   Now

Past ◄────────▲

The past perfect simple is often shown in a timeline in this way:

Now

Past ◄──x───x──▲

Exercise 6

Extra activity

Ask students to describe what they did last weekend using *while*, *before* and *after*.

■ Ask students to work individually to complete the text, and then check in pairs. Monitor and correct any errors.

Answers
1 joined 2 had read/read 3 was running 4 volunteered 5 was raising
6 was working 7 communicated 8 realised 9 had achieved

In 2, it is possible to use the past simple because *before* reveals which action happened first.

Exercise 7

■ Ask students to read the rules carefully and match them to the examples. Let them compare answers with a partner.

Answers
Past perfect simple = **A**. Past perfect continuous = **B**.

■ Refer students to the Grammar Reference on page 147.

Pronunciation: weak forms

Exercise 8  CD1/10

Extra activity

Ask students to write a short narrative about a time they worked with others to achieve a common goal. It could be a school project, a sporting event or a fundraising event. Encourage students to use a range of narrative tenses.

■ Ask students to listen to the recording. Point out the weak form of *had* /həd/.
■ Play the recording again. Students listen and repeat.

Exercise 9

■ Ask students to choose the correct forms, and then compare answers with a partner. Check the answers as a class.
■ Give students time to practise saying the sentences in pairs. Monitor and correct pronunciation.

Answers
1 had got 2 had decided 3 had been thinking 4 had been waiting 5 had been doing

2C Leaving home

Books closed lead-in activity

Write on the board *Leaving home*. Ask students in pairs to brainstorm pros and cons of leaving home. In feedback, build up a list of good and bad things on the board.

Speaking

Exercise 1

- Ask students to work in pairs initially to discuss the questions. Then put pairs together to make groups of four to share their ideas. Finally, ask one student from each group to tell the class what answers they came up with.

Reading

Exercise 2

- Ask students what they can see in the photos on page 23. Then divide the class into pairs to discuss the questions.

Example answers
1 Ellis Island is in New York in the USA, near the Statue of Liberty. 2 Somebody is writing down the people's names. I think the people are trying to immigrate into the USA. 3 I think the photo was taken in … I think the people in the photo feel tired/happy/worried …

Culture note
Today, **Ellis Island** can be visited on a day trip by boat from downtown Manhattan. Many American visitors go there to trace their ancestors.

Exercise 3

- Ask students to read the sentences in pairs. Tell them to guess what the paragraphs that the sentences come from might be about. For example, sentence A may come from a paragraph that describes the procedure for interviewing new arrivals.
- Ask students to read the text and match sentences to gaps. Let them check in pairs.

Answers
1 F 2 G 3 A 4 D 5 B

Exercise 4

- Ask students to discuss what the dates refer to in pairs. Tell them to look back at the text to find the answers.

Answers
1900: Ellis Island became the primary arrival place for immigrants.
1907: The peak year for immigrants at Ellis Island.
1954: The Ellis Island building was closed.
1990: The building reopened as a museum honouring immigrants to the USA.

Exercise 5

- Ask students to work with a partner to work out the meanings from the context.
- Find out which pairs can explain the words the best.

Answers
1 come in large numbers 2 strongly increase 3 annoy 4 chosen 5 limit 6 write untidily

Extra activity

Ask pairs to write new sentences that contain the words in the exercise and show their meaning.

> **Vocabulary note**
> *would-be Americans* = people who wanted to be Americans; *peak year* = year of most activity

Exercise 6

■ Ask students to discuss the questions in pairs.

Grammar: *used to* and *would*

Exercise 7

■ Ask students to find and underline *used to* and *would* in the example sentences and check the form: *used to* + infinitive, *would* + infinitive.

■ Give students time to work in pairs to answer the questions and write grammar rules. Monitor and help.

■ As a class, find out who has the best rule.

> **Answers**
> a 1, 2, 3 b 4, 5

> **Grammar and pronunciation note**
> Note that we use *used to* + infinitive for states and repeated actions that are no longer true, and *would* + infinitive for repeated actions that are no longer true (but not states). When talking about a series of repeated actions, we tend to use *would* or its abbreviated version *'d* to avoid repeating *used to*. For example, *I used to get up early, then I'd pull on my clothes and I'd run all the way to school.*
>
> Point out the pronunciation of *used to* /ˈjuːstə/.

■ Refer students to the Grammar Reference on page 147.

Exercise 8

■ Ask students to rewrite the sentences. Let them check their answers in pairs.

> **Answers**
> 1 Every day in Ellis Island, 1,200 immigrants **would eat / used to eat** lunch in the dining room.
> 2 Different nationalities **used to like** different meals.
> 3 The Scandinavians **would ask / used to ask** for dried fish.
> 4 The Chinese **used to want** rice.
> 5 But menus at Ellis Island **would usually reflect** typical American food.

> **Grammar note**
> In 2, 4 and 5 we can only use *used to* because they are states.

Speaking

Exercise 9

■ Ask students to read the questions carefully and make a few notes about what they would like to say.

■ Divide the class into groups of three or four to discuss the questions.

Extra activity

Ask students to think of a place they once knew well but no longer do. For example, a previous home or school, or a regular holiday destination. Ask students to prepare to talk about what life was like there, using *used to* and *would*. When they are ready, ask students to describe their places in groups of four.

Travel experiences

Books closed lead-in activity

Put students in groups of three. Ask students to close their eyes and think of a place that is special to them. Ask, *Where are you? What is the place like? Why is it special? How do you feel?* Tell students to open their eyes and to describe the place to the people in their group.

Extra activity

Ask students in pairs or groups to plan a trip to Australia by bus. They must choose five places in the world to visit on the way. Ask groups to present their trips and say why they chose each place to visit.

Listening: listening to an anecdote

Exercise 1

- Ask students to look at the photograph. Ask, *What can you see? What sort of holiday do you think it shows? Would you like to take this bus? Why?*
- Ask students to complete the notes, and then check with a partner.

Answers

Route: from London to Sydney (or Sydney to London) via 17 countries

Length of journey: 85 days

Method of transport: bus

Price: £4,699

> **Culture note**
> The **Taj Mahal** is a beautiful, palatial mausoleum in India. The **Himalayas** are the mountain range in Tibet, north of India. **Bangkok** is the capital of Thailand. **Bali** is a popular holiday island in Indonesia. **Uluru** is a mountain in central Australia.

Exercise 2

- Ask students to discuss the questions in pairs.
- Elicit which of the places mentioned they would most like to go to and why.

Answers

1 It is described as awesome, amazing, epic, life-affirming and unforgettable. It is for travellers who are adventurous and who want to experience a unique journey.

2 (example answer) I couldn't imagine going on a trip like this because I'm not very adventurous and I don't like travelling by bus. / I could imagine going on a trip like this because I love going to different places and meeting new people and I hate package holidays.

> **Vocabulary note**
> *truly awesome* = really amazing (*awesome* is commonly used by American teenagers as an extreme adjective); *life-affirming encounter* = a meeting (with people or cultures) that makes you feel positive and excited about life

Exercise 3 CD1/11

- Ask students to read the events with a partner. Check *towed* (pulled by a vehicle) and *tilted* (pushed a little to one side). Ask, *What can you guess about Naomi's trip from the events in the exercise?*
- Play the recording. Students listen and put the events in order. Let them check their answers in pairs.

Audioscript

Naomi Hi Emily, can you hear me?

Emily Hi Naomi! Just getting my headset on … Where are you now?

Naomi Pakistan … in a hotel. I've finally found somewhere I can use the Internet.

Emily Everything going OK?

Naomi Yeah, the last few days have been absolutely fantastic. Actually, I was a bit freaked out this morning …

Emily Really? What happened?

Naomi Well, I'd decided to go off on my own and visit this mountain village I'd read about. I booked a place on a minibus with a local sightseeing company. And I was rather tired, so I was listening to music on my mp3 player half asleep when the minibus started to tilt a bit over to the left … then there was a sort of grinding noise and suddenly the bus stopped with this big jerk. Anyway, I was thrown forward into the seat in front and when I looked up …

Emily	What?
Naomi	… we were hanging right off the edge of a mountain!
Emily	No way!
Naomi	Yeah, it was pretty scary. But to be honest, it didn't feel real. I felt, you know, as if I was in a film. At first nobody moved. Everybody was totally shocked, although luckily no one was hurt. Strangely enough, it turned out there wasn't that much damage to the bus either. Anyway, four of the guys got out then and stabilised the bus … you know, … held the bus so it wouldn't overbalance. And after that we all got out really carefully. Unfortunately, we were in the middle of nowhere, just the road and like, rocks and bushes as far as you could see. But after a while a really big lorry came past and it towed the bus onto the road again. Anyway, it all ended well, but it was a bit scary.
Emily	Wow! Well, you wanted adventure …

Answers
a 4 b 3 c 8 d 7 e 2 f 6 g 1 h 5

Vocabulary: discourse markers
Exercise 4

- Ask students to read the sentences and answer the questions. Give them time to discuss their answers with a partner.

Answers
a all except 4 b 3 c 5, 6

> **Vocabulary note**
> *Actually* is used to state something that is factually true or to correct something that is not quite true. It can go at the start of a sentence or at the end.
>
> *Well* introduces a statement. It has no real meaning – it just gives the speaker thinking time or is used to get the listener's attention.
>
> *Anyway* is used to come back to what you are talking about after an interruption or digression, or it can be used to shorten or finish what you are saying.
>
> We use *you know* in the middle of a sentence to include the listener in what we are talking about, by saying that they understand or are aware of what we are saying. Often, however, it is used redundantly with no useful meaning.
>
> *Luckily* and *unfortunately* are used in stories to evaluate events.

Speaking: describing an experience
Exercise 5

- Ask students to think of a funny, strange or frightening event that happened to them on a journey. Ask a few open questions to get students thinking.
- Give students five or six minutes to read the questions and make notes individually. Monitor and help with ideas and vocabulary. Remind students that they should try to tell their stories using discourse markers.

Exercise 6

- Divide the class into pairs to share their stories. Partners should listen carefully and prepare a question to ask at the end.
- Elicit which was the best story. You could ask the student with the best story to tell it to the class.

Writing: describing a place
Exercises 7 and 8

- Ask students to describe the photo and tell you what they know about the place. You could pre-teach vocabulary and help students predict the text by writing some key words on the board before reading: *rock, luminous, gigantic, aborigine, ancestors.*

Extra activity

Write the following in a list on the board: *At first, … Anyway, … Unfortunately, … Luckily, … In the end, …*

Divide students into pairs to make up short stories together. Student A says a sentence beginning *At first, …* B continues, starting with *Anyway, …* etc. In feedback, ask one or two pairs to act out one of their stories.

Extra activity

It is a good idea to introduce this activity by telling a short story about a trip you have taken. Keep it short and simple and try to include discourse markers. At the end, ask students if your story was funny, strange or frightening.

Extra activity

Check vocabulary from the text by writing the definitions (shown in brackets) on the board and asking students to find synonyms in the text: gigantic (huge); luminous (very bright); ancestral (belonging to your forefathers); disrespectful (insulting).

Answer
C

Exercise 9

■ Ask students to read the text again and make notes. Let them check in pairs and expand their notes together before discussing as a class.

Answers
Why the writer is writing about this place: it was the highlight of a trip through Australia

Where and what it is: a gigantic rock in central Australia

What the place looks like: water holes, caves, rock paintings; rock changes colour at different times of the day

What the function of the place is: tourist attraction and sacred site

What the writer thinks of the place: fascinating, impressive

Vocabulary: compound adjectives

Exercise 10

■ Ask students to match compound adjectives to groups then check with a partner.

Answers
1 deeply-rooted
2 long-running
3 world-famous
4 high-profile
5 346-metre high
6 reddish-brown

■ Refer students to the Grammar Reference on page 148.

Exercise 11

Extra activity

Ask fast finishers to write other sentences which contain words that could be combined to make compound adjectives. Ask them to read them out and see if others can say what the compound adjective is.

■ Ask students to make adjectives from the sentences and match the structure to those in exercise 10. Let them check their answers in pairs.

Answers
2 a last-minute flight (group 4) 3 a centuries-old tradition (group 3) 4 a dark-blue sky (group 4) 5 a three-hour walk (group 5) 6 a pyramid-shaped building (group 3)

Exercise 12

■ Ask students to write a description of a place following the instructions. Allow time for students to compare and correct each other's work.

Between two cultures?

Books closed lead-in activity

Ask students what advice they would give to someone coming to live in their country. Ask, *What do you think they would find strange? What advice would you give to help them settle in your society?*

Vocabulary

Exercise 1

■ Discuss the first pair of words as a class to get students started. Elicit several possible definitions.

■ Ask students in pairs to discuss the other words. Allow them to use a dictionary if necessary.

Answers

2 A *foreigner* is somebody who is in a country which is not their home country; a *stranger* is somebody who you do not know or who does not know a place.

3 A *refugee* is somebody who has been forced to leave their country; an *economic migrant* is somebody who goes to a new country for a better job or better living conditions.

4 *Integration* is when foreigners are able to become fully involved in the life of the new country they are living in; *assimilation* is when foreigners become part of a new culture and leave behind their own language and customs.

5 A *first-generation immigrant* is somebody who moves to a new country; a *second-generation immigrant* is the child of that person, somebody who has foreign parents but who was born in the new country.

Exercises 2 and 3

■ Ask students to look at the graph and answer the question.

■ Ask students to look at the *Useful expressions* box and check meanings. Then ask them to complete the information about the graph with phrases from the box. Let students check in pairs before discussing answers as a class.

Answers

The graph shows the rising percentage of UK citizens born outside the UK.
1 risen **2** just over 4%; just over 8% **3** doubled

Extra activity

Ask students to think about how the following have changed in the last few years: *migration to/ from their country; prices.* Ask students to make up phrases about the topics using the language in exercise 3.

Listening

Exercise 4 ○ CD1/12

■ Check the pronunciation of the countries mentioned and check students know where they are on a map. Then divide students into small groups to guess when they think each group may have started emigrating to the UK.

■ Play the recording. Students listen and complete the task. Let them check their answers in pairs before discussing as a class.

Audioscript

At the end of the Second World War, Britain needed workers for its rebuilding programme. Many men and women from Ireland worked in Britain during the war, and after the war thousands more joined the British workforce. At the same time large numbers of refugees also arrived in Britain, mainly from Central European countries. In particular, around 100,000 Poles made Britain their home. Many of these had fought for Britain in the war.

However, the first real wave of immigration began at the end of the 1940s, and continued into the 1950s and 1960s. In 1947 India became independent from Britain and was divided into India and Pakistan. In the next two decades, large numbers of economic migrants arrived from these two countries. Some took unskilled manufacturing jobs, but many took qualified medical jobs in the National Heath Service. Then in 1948, every Commonwealth citizen was given the right to live in Britain. Hundreds of thousands emigrated from the Caribbean.

In the 1960s, problems with race relations led to new immigration laws. It became more difficult to enter Britain, so the number of economic migrants fell. But Britain still continued to take in refugees from countries where there was political unrest, civil war or famine. For example, people from Uganda, Kenya, Somalia and the Balkans.

In the early 2000s the number of asylum seekers in Britain strongly increased, mainly as a result of the wars in Iraq and Afghanistan and political unrest in Zimbabwe. Then in May 2004, citizens of the ten new European Union countries got the right to live anywhere in the enlarged EU. The UK, Ireland and Sweden opened their labour market to workers from these countries immediately. This caused the biggest wave of immigration into the UK since the 1950s and 60s. Six out of every ten of the new migrants were Polish and many were highly qualified. However, at the end of the decade, the economic situation in the UK became worse and many Central European immigrants returned home.

Answers

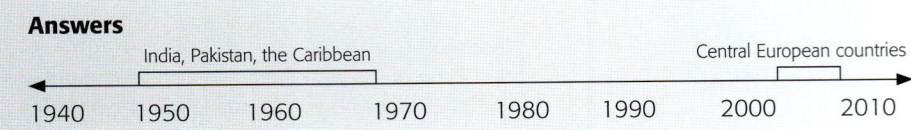

Exercise 5   CD1/12

■ Allow students a moment to read the reasons, and then play the recording again. Let students check answers with a partner.

Answers
first wave (1): immigration from a former British colony
second wave (2): enlargement of the EU; a new law for Commonwealth citizens

Exercise 6

■ Ask students to discuss the questions in pairs.

Example answers
I think it would have been very hard for the first wave of immigrants to settle in Britain. They came from totally different cultures and they must have found Britain cold and unfriendly.

I think it was easier for the second wave of immigrants: they came from other European countries, so British culture was similar in some ways. The world had also become more globalised by the beginning of the 21st century. However, I think moving to a new country is always hard.

Vocabulary: compound nouns
Exercise 7   CD1/13

Extra activity

Ask students to think of other compound nouns that can be formed using the headwords given in exercise 7.

■ Ask students to work in pairs to make compound nouns. Play the recording to check.

Answers
1 d 2 f 3 b 4 e 5 a 6 c

> **Vocabulary and pronunciation note**
> Note that compound nouns can be one word (*workforce*), two words (*civil war*) or hyphenated (*second-generation immigrant*). In general, the stress is on the first syllable, but not always (e.g. civil *war*).
> *Labour force* and *labour relations* are also possible collocations.

■ Refer students to the Grammar Reference on page 148.

Exercise 8

■ Ask students to work in pairs to make collocations and find the words that don't form a common compound with the words in capitals. Check the meaning of the compounds in feedback.

Answers
1 story 2 transport 3 problem 4 pay 5 place

Reading and speaking

Exercise 9

- Ask students to read and make notes individually, then compare their notes.
- Elicit answers from the whole class.

> **Example answers**
> Sajid: George's teenage son, a second-generation immigrant
> Sajid's mother: an English woman
> Sajid's brother: he is older, and has lived in Pakistan for some time

> **Vocabulary note**
> A *multicultural society* is a society made up of many different ethnic groups.
>
> *his father's roots* = where his father came from; *friction* = tension, bad feeling; *a victim of bullying* = a person who is mistreated by others; *the rural existence* = life in the country as opposed to the town; *his new surroundings* = the things he finds around him; *to confront the fact* = to face up to something difficult; *to sympathise with* = to feel positive emotions for and understand somebody; *Pakistani values* = ideas about how to live as Pakistani people; *to have divided loyalties* = to feel positively about two different things; *an eye-opener* = something that makes you understand something you didn't before; *to strike a chord* = to reflect your own experience

Exercise 10

- Ask students to discuss the six questions in pairs. Ask them to make short notes.
- Invite the class to discuss the questions together, and encourage them to present different opinions and challenge each other.

Artists for the planet

Lead-in

Elicit from students what they understand by the word *artist*. Try to establish that it can mean anyone who is involved in the arts in general (e.g. painting, drawing, music, literature, dance, painting, sculpture). Move on to elicit some of their favourite artists. Ask what the person does and why they like them.

Exercise 1

- Ask students to read the sentences to focus their reading, then to read the text and decide if the sentences are true or false.
- They can check their answers in pairs.
- Elicit the answers from the class, having them read a sentence and then say whether it is true or false.

> **Answers**
> 1 True 2 False 3 False 4 True 5 True

Exercise 2

- Read the words and phrases with students and check they understand them.
- Ask students to match them with the bold words in the text.
- They can then check in pairs.
- Elicit the answers from the class, having one student say the phrase/word in exercise 2, and another give the matching phrase/word from the text.

> **Answers**
> 1 subsequent 2 causes 3 commitment to 4 promote 5 landfills 6 dyed 7 high-profile
> 8 dedicated to 9 approach to 10 donates

Exercise 3

- Ask students to read the information about the people and their actions.
- They can then check in pairs.
- Elicit the answers from the class, having one student say the artist's name, and another give the matching action.

> **Answers**
> 1 g 2 e 3 d 4 b 5 f 6 c 7 a

Find out more!

Do some research about what artists are doing to highlight the planet's ecological problems, for example:

- global warming
- farming the Amazon
- Jack Johnson and the 1% for the Planet movement

Look on the Internet and in books in the library. In particular, have a look at the National Geographic website: www.nationalgeographic.com

Units 1 and 2

Unit 1 Review

Ask students to complete the exercises in class or set the review for homework. After they have completed the exercises, students should evaluate their own performance, using the self-assessment box.

Answers

Exercise 1
1 cast 2 play 3 sketches 4 portrait (or painting) 5 gig 6 venue 7 sold

Exercise 2
A Auditions B Costume C script D props E run F Special effects

Exercise 3
1 haven't been waiting 2 have sold 3 have been looking 4 has been
5 have been turning 6 have scheduled

Exercise 4
1 will often go/often go 2 see 3 will always say/always say 4 always want 5 are missing

Exercise 5
1 ∅, a 2 a, a 3 a, ∅ 4 ∅, ∅ 5 the, a

Exercise 6
1 thing 2 loved, fan 3 mood 4 reminded 5 keen, appeal

Unit 2 Review

Answers

Exercise 1
1 victims 2 emergency 3 refugees 4 relief 5 humanitarian 6 volunteers
7 charitable 8 survival 9 natural

Exercise 2
1 asylum seekers 2 civil war 3 world-famous 4 long-running 5 race relations
6 labour market 7 deeply-rooted 8 immigration law

Exercise 3
1 global 2 flocked 3 bother 4 initiative 5 singled out 6 backing 7 curb

Exercise 4
1 used to always go 2 would always spend 3 missed 4 had been waiting 5 realised
6 had forgotten 7 were running 8 closed 9 had been calling 10 hadn't heard

Exercise 5
1 Both of us love travelling. 2 Neither of us has done a trip like this before.
3 All of the holidays we have been on have been with our parents. 4 None of our trips
has included so much train travel. 5 Each of us has a huge rucksack and a sleeping bag.
6 No hotels are on our accommodation list – just hostels.

3

Living in a changing world

UNIT OVERVIEW

Topic	adapting to a changing world, getting older, nanotechnology, predicting how society will change
Reading	facts about ageing, nanotechnology, UK chef Jamie Oliver
Listening	radio programme about the future of Bhutan
Grammar	future: *will, be going to,* present simple and continuous, future perfect, future continuous and future perfect continuous
Function	making arrangements
Vocabulary	ageing, prefixes of measurement, types of meal
Pronunciation	word stress
Writing	an opinion essay
Speaking	talking about getting older, discussing population tables, speculating about the future, expressing opinions
Culture	Bhutan, technology, food

Books closed lead-in activity

Write *man-made disasters* and *natural disasters* on the board. Put students in pairs to brainstorm examples of both (man-made: war, pollution, deforestation, etc.; natural: drought, earthquake, etc.). Ask, *Which are the most significant threats to the world's environment? How can we avoid them?*

Extra activity

Divide the class into groups of optimists and pessimists. Each group must write four sentences to support their view. For example, *Millions of people now recycle their rubbish.* Or, *The population is growing out of control.* Find out which group has the best list.

Let's get started

Exercise 1

- Ask students to look at the picture. Ask, *What does it show?* Elicit several responses.
- Ask students to work in pairs to discuss the questions. Elicit responses from several students in feedback.

> **Culture note**
> **Charles Michael 'Chuck' Palahniuk** (pronounced /ˈpɑːlənɪk/) is an American novelist and freelance journalist. He is best known for the award-winning novel *Fight Club.*
>
> The statistics come from: www.theholidayspot.com/earth_day/environmental_facts.htm
>
> Some other facts from the website that you may wish to share with students:
>
> Over 40 per cent of all tropical forests have been destroyed. An acre is lost each second. 99 per cent of all the things we buy are not in use after six months.
> Americans annually use 50 million tons of paper. This is the equivalent of more than 850 million trees.
> 40,000 children in the world die every year from preventable diseases. The human population of the world is expected to rise by nearly three times by the year 2100.
> Every day 50 to 100 species of plants and animals become extinct as human activities destroy their habitats.

Speaking

Exercise 2

- Check that students know what the words in the box mean. Then ask them to work in pairs to discuss the question.

Embracing the future

Listening

Exercise 1

■ Divide students into pairs or small groups to discuss the pictures and complete the tasks. You could check the meaning of the words in the box first.

Answers

1 Bhutan is in south Asia. The country's neighbours are India and China.

2 (example answer) The photo of a Buddhist monk performing a ritual shows that religion is perhaps important in Bhutan. Many people seem to live in rural societies without modern conveniences. A man is ploughing the fields with oxen, for example, instead of modern agricultural machinery. A woman is bathing her children outside in a bowl using water from a container. So there are areas without running water and maybe without electricity.

The two photos on page 33 show young people in western dress, probably in a town or city. The photos show that teenagers in Bhutan are the same as anywhere else: they like using computers and hanging out with their friends.

Vocabulary note
plough = break up the earth in order to plant crops; *running water* = water that is easily available from a tap

Exercise 2   CD1/14

■ Play the recording. Ask students to listen and answer the questions. Let them check their answers in pairs before discussing as a class.

Audioscript

For more than a thousand years, the tiny Himalayan country of Bhutan, with a population of 635,000, has survived in splendid isolation. Closed off from the outside world both by geography and political policy, the country had no roads, no electricity, no motor vehicles, no telephones and no postal service until the 1960s. Even these days, its ancient temples and untouched rivers and forests evoke a place that time forgot.

When Bhutan's fourth king, King Jigme Singye Wangchuck, ascended the throne in 1972, Bhutan suffered from some of the highest poverty, illiteracy and infant-mortality rates in the world. The king's father had begun opening up the country in the 1960s, building roads, establishing schools and health clinics, and pushing for United Nations membership. King Jigme Singye Wangchuck wanted to continue developing the country but at the same time protect its heritage. Instead of setting goals for standards of living measured in the more usual Gross National Product, the fourth king decided to develop the economy based on the rather vague idea of Gross National Happiness.

Bhutan has pulled itself out of poverty without spoiling its landscape – nearly three-quarters of the country is still forested, with more than 25 per cent designated as national parks and other protected areas. Rates of illiteracy and infant mortality have fallen and the economy has improved dramatically. Tourism is growing too, though there are strict limits on new construction and a daily tax of up to $240 a visitor to keep out too many tourists.

In 1999, Bhutan granted its citizens access to television, the last country on the planet to do so. Then in 2006, the fourth king handed over the crown to his 28-year-old son and set in motion the country's first democratic elections in 2008.

But what happens when an isolated, deeply conservative society is suddenly exposed to rap music, violent TV shows and democracy – especially in a country where half of the population is under 22 years old? How do young and old adapt to such a situation? The real test of Bhutan's Gross National Happiness is just beginning.

Answers
1 Students' own answers 2 In the 1960s.

Books closed lead-in activity

Write *Bhutan* on the board. Tell students it is a country, then ask them to brainstorm in pairs as many questions as they can about the place in three minutes. Ask them to tell you the questions. You could try to answer them or you could tell students to see how many questions they can answer by the end of the unit.

Exercise 3

■ Divide students into pairs to match words to meanings.

> **Answers**
> 1 b 2 d 3 a 4 c 5 e

Exercise 4 CD1/14

■ This listening task tests the students' ability to hear large numbers, dates and percentages, so revise this area before doing the listening, and make sure students know how to say all the numbers and dates in the tasks.

■ Give students a moment to read through the options and think of any answers they already know.

■ Play the recording again. Let students check their answers with a partner.

> **Answers**
> 1 C 2 D 3 B 4 D 5 D 6 D

Exercise 5

■ Ask students to work in pairs to discuss the questions.

> **Culture note**
> The **Kingdom of Bhutan** (pronounced /buːˈtɑːn/) is a landlocked country located at the eastern end of the Himalayas. The state religion is Vajrayana Buddhism. The population is predominantly Buddhist, with Hinduism being the second-largest religion. The capital and largest city is Thimphu. In 2006, *Business Week* magazine rated Bhutan the happiest country in Asia and the eighth-happiest in the world.

Exercise 6 CD1/15

■ Ask students to listen to the recording and answer the question.

■ Ask students what they heard which suggested their answer.

Audioscript

Presenter … you spent several months in Bhutan as a journalist covering the elections and you're travelling back there tomorrow. What do you think will happen in Bhutan now?

Journalist Well, firstly I think the big question is how democracy will develop. Obviously it's very much in its infancy at the moment, so I'll reserve judgement for now. But the new government has already banned TV channels which it thought were harmful, including MTV and Fashion TV, so a more serious form of censorship could well develop … Experience from other countries suggests that there's going to be a difficult transitional period.

Presenter What about culture? Is there a real danger that Bhutan will lose its cultural identity?

Journalist Well, Bhutan is far from being a developed country. So right now it's mainly the younger generation in urban areas that are adapting to the new situation. In the towns kids are wearing western clothes, listening to rap music, and playing video games in internet cafés. These changes will definitely become more widespread and the older generation are obviously very concerned about the situation.

Presenter But there is also evidence to show that national culture can actually be strengthened by the introduction of new technology, isn't there?

Journalist Yeah, that's right. Television, for example, can give a country shared cultural experiences, the Internet too. This year, a new five-year plan starts and the government is going to invest heavily in broadband Internet. Once there are more computers, the people within Bhutan will also be able to communicate more easily with *each other* – not just with the outside world. There's also the Bhutanese feature-film industry. Many of the films explore Bhutanese culture and how tradition and modernity come together. So, that's all very positive, actually, in terms of cultural heritage.

Presenter Have there been any negative social problems as a consequence of all the changes?

Journalist Well, inevitably there have been and I'll give you some examples … youth unemployment, for instance – many high-school graduates have come to

Thimphu, the capital city, hoping for jobs with the new government. But the jobs simply haven't happened and youth unemployment in Thimphu is now running at about 30 per cent. Theft, which previously didn't exist, is becoming more common – people are starting to steal their neighbours' new mobile phones and CD players.

Answer
He seems more pessimistic.

Exercise 7 CD1/15

- Listening and note-taking is difficult. Prepare students by suggesting some of the following techniques: 1 Write in lists with bullet points and dashes to separate information. 2 Miss out articles, auxiliaries, etc. 3 Use symbols (->, ☺, &, etc.) and abbreviations (e.g. *min* not *minute*).
- Give students a moment to look at the headings and prepare to take notes. They can start by writing anything they remember from the first listening in note form under the four headings.
- Play the recording again. Ask students to write notes, and then compare answers in pairs. You could play the recording a third time if students find note-taking difficult.

Speaking

Exercise 8

- Ask students to discuss the questions in pairs or small groups.

Grammar: the future

Exercise 9

- Ask students to read the rules carefully. Check understanding by asking a few concept-check and form questions: *Which verb form do we use if we have already made a plan?* (going to).
- Ask students to work in pairs to complete the sentences.

Answers
1 are travelling / are going to travel 2 will happen / is going to happen 3 will reserve 4 is going to be / will be 5 will definitely become 6 starts / is starting / is going to start 7 is going to invest 8 will give

> **Grammar note**
> The choice of tenses depends on what the speaker wants to express. So, in 1, *are travelling* is preferable if the speaker is talking about an arrangement. In 2, *will* future is preferable if it is a personal opinion, but *going to* is preferable if it is based on evidence. In 4, *going to* is the best answer because there is evidence (but *will* is possible). In 6, the fact that this is an impersonal, timetabled event suggests the present simple is the best choice of tense (but the other suggested answers are possible).

- Refer students to the Grammar Reference on page 149.

Exercises 10 and 11

- Ask students to work individually to write sentences about the future. Then put them in pairs to compare ideas. Find out which pair has the best ideas.

Extra activity

Provide practice of the present continuous by asking students to interview each other about their weekend plans.

Provide practice of *going to* for predictions by asking students to predict Bhutan's future from evidence in the listening text.

3B Getting older

Books closed lead-in activity

Write or elicit the following words onto the board: *adult, teenager, child, pensioner, middle-aged person, youth, baby, girl.* Tell students to work in pairs to put the words in order of age and say approximately what ages these people are.

Extra activity

Ask students to work in small groups to make a list of *dos* and *don'ts* for being healthy. For example: *Do eat vegetables.*

Speaking

Exercise 1

■ Divide students into pairs or small groups to discuss the questions.

Exercise 2

■ Build up a list of positives and negatives on the board.

Exercise 3

■ Ask students to look at the graph and the *Useful expressions* box. Elicit one or two expressions from the students to describe the graphs in order to get them started. Then put them in pairs to discuss the graphs. Ask a few pairs to share their findings.

Example answer

Both graphs show that people are getting much older.

The first graph shows that, at the moment, the 80-or-over age group is growing by over four per cent. This is twice as high as the growth rate of the 60-or-over group. The number of people over 60, 65 and 80 is going to increase steadily until 2025. Then the growth rate of all three age groups is expected to decrease. But in 2050 the growth rate of the over-80s will still be almost double that of the over-60s (about 3 per cent compared to about 1.5 per cent).

The second graph shows what this means in actual numbers. In 1950 there were 13.8 million people aged 80 or over in the world. In 2000 it was 69.2 million. By 2050 it will be 379 million.

Vocabulary note

69.2 = sixty-nine point two; *or over* = or more

You could revise a wider area of vocabulary to describe statistics here: *is rising/growing; is falling; fewer than; greater than; a rapid/large increase or rise.*

Exercise 4

■ Put pairs into groups of four to discuss the consequences of an ageing population.

Reading

Exercise 5

■ Ask students to read the questions carefully. Then put them into pairs to predict what they think the answers might be.
■ Ask students to read the text quickly and find the answers.

Answers

1 A sharp drop in the birth rate and higher life expectancy.

2 Between 0.7 and 0.9 children. Possible reasons: more working women, better choice of jobs for women, increasing cost of bringing up children, uncertainty about the future.

3 Two

4 80+

5 Pension funds and health services will be under pressure.

Vocabulary note

You could point out phrases in the text that are used to describe statistics: *steadily older; sharp drop* (or *fall*); *double; two thirds; increased to; ratio of … to …*

Grammar: future perfect, future continuous and future perfect continuous

Exercise 6

- Ask students to read the examples and rules carefully. Let them work in pairs to match them.
- In feedback, you could check the form and draw timelines on the board to show the different tense uses (see Grammar note below).

Answers
Future perfect: C Future continuous: A Future perfect continuous: B

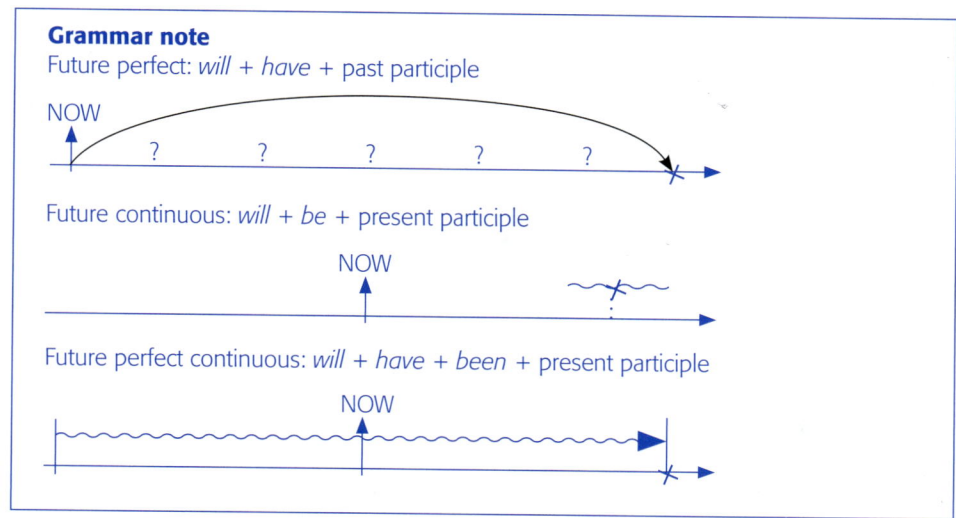

Grammar note
Future perfect: *will + have* + past participle

NOW

Future continuous: *will + be* + present participle

NOW

Future perfect continuous: *will + have + been* + present participle

NOW

- Refer students to the Grammar Reference on page 149.

Exercise 7

- Ask students to work in pairs to research the text for other examples.

Answers
Future perfect: In forty years' time this will have increased to 80 per cent by 2050 the number of older people will have become double the number of children.

Future continuous: In 2050 the biggest number of 'oldest old' people will be living in developing countries.

Future perfect continuous: Social insurance contributions will have been decreasing for several years.

Future perfect: *will + have* + past participle
Future continuous: *will + be* + present participle
Future perfect continuous: *will + have + been* + present participle

Exercise 8

- Ask students to choose the correct form. Let them check their answers in pairs before discussing as a class.

Answers
1 will have been living 2 will be doing 3 'll have finished 4 'll have saved 5 will have been working 6 'll be doing

Grammar note
The use of time phrases dictates which tenses to use in exercise 8. So, *for X years* demands future perfect continuous to show a period of time up to a point in future time. *This time next week* is a certain time in the future. *By next month* or *In X months* (= X months from now) demands the future perfect simple to show an action completed before a certain time.

Extra activity

You could introduce phrases to express addition (*moreover, in addition, what's more*) and contrast (*whereas, while, however, on the other hand*), then ask pairs to prepare a presentation of the figures from exercise 9. Ask them to draw conclusions. Ask one or two pairs to read out their presentation to the class.

Speaking

Exercise 9

- Ask students to look at the figures carefully and to think how to interpret and pronounce the statistics. Then put them in pairs to prepare sentences using future forms to express the figures.

Answers
By 2050 the population of France will have risen from 61.8 million to 71 million.
By 2050 the population of Germany will have fallen from 82.2 million to 74.4 million.
By 2050 the population of Hungary will have fallen from 10 million to 9 million.
By 2050 the population of Ireland will have risen from 4.4 million to 6.5 million.
By 2050 the population of Poland will have fallen from 38.1 million to 33.2 million.
By 2050 the population of Romania will have fallen from 21.4 million to 18.1 million.
By 2050 the population of Spain will have risen from 45.2 million to 53.2 million.
By 2050 the population of the UK will have risen from 61.2 million to 74.5 million.

Exercise 10

- Ask students to discuss the questions in pairs. Then have a whole-class discussion.

Example answers
1 Most people live in Germany now. In 2050 most people will be living in the UK. This is probably because the birth rate is falling in Germany and rising in the UK. It could also be because the UK has a greater number of older people. It might also be due to immigration into the UK.

2 By 2050 the population will have fallen most in Germany and Poland. This will probably be due to the falling birth rate.

Exercise 11

- Ask students to prepare the questions individually. Monitor and make sure students have correct answers.
- Mix pairs or divide the students into small groups to interview each other. Monitor for errors.
- Ask students to make their own questions, and to ask and answer them.

Answers
1 Will you still be living in this country in five years? 2 What will you be doing in five years' time? 3 Do you think you'll have found your dream job by the time you're 25?
4 What will you have achieved in 20 years' time? 5 How long will you have been working by the time you retire?

Nanotechnology

Reading

Exercise 1

- Ask students to discuss the questions in pairs. Ask students to look at the headline, background picture to the text, and the stand out quotation. Ask them what these things say about nanotechnology.

> **Vocabulary note**
> Nanotechnology /ˈnænəʊtekˌnɒlədʒi/, often shortened to nanotech, is the study of how to control matter on a molecular or atomic scale. It can be used for many purposes, particularly in fields such as medicine and electronics.

Exercise 2

- Check the meanings of the adjectives, and ask students to guess which ones might be used to describe nanotechnology.
- Ask students to read the text on page 37 and check their answers.

> **Answers**
> widespread; versatile; tiny; energy-saving; time-saving; life-saving

> **Vocabulary and pronunciation note**
> versatile /ˈvɜː(r)sətaɪl/ = easily adapted to many purposes; widespread = in many areas or fields

Exercise 3

- Ask students to read the sentences carefully. Then ask them to read the sentences around each gap carefully and to guess where each sentence goes. Ask students to work individually then discuss their answers in pairs.

> **Answers**
> 1 E 2 C 3 F 4 A 5 D

Exercise 4

- Ask students to match words and definitions. Tell them to look back at the text to see the word in context if they are not sure of its meaning.

> **Answers**
> 1 f 2 g 3 a 4 d 5 c 6 e 7 b 8 h

Exercise 5

- Ask students to work in pairs or small groups to discuss the questions.

Books closed lead-in activity

Write a list of firsts on the board: *the first mobile phone; the first SMS; the first home computer; the first email.* Ask students to guess which year each happened then have a small quiz. The pair that guess the year closest to the correct answer get a point. The answers (in order): 1983, 1993, 1970, 1971.

Extra activity

Ask students to look back through the text and find as many positive applications of nanotechnology as they can. Tell them to discuss their findings with a partner before telling the class.

Vocabulary: prefixes of measurement

Exercise 6

■ Ask students to search the text for the words.

Answers
nanotechnology (nanotech), nano-scientist, nanotubes, nanosize, nanofilters, nanoparticles
The prefix is used with nouns to make both nouns and adjectives.

Exercise 7

■ Ask students to work in pairs to find the meanings of the prefixes. Then discuss answers as a class.

Answers
hyper = more than normal; micro = small; semi = half; ultra = extremely

Exercise 8   CD1/16

■ Ask students to match prefixes to words. Let them check in pairs. Then play the recording.

Answers
1 hyperlink 2 microscope 3 ultra-violet 4 semi-circle 5 ultrasound 6 microwave
7 semi-colon 8 hyperactive 9 microchip 10 hypermarket 11 ultra-modern
12 semi-skimmed

Pronunciation: word stress

Exercise 9   CD1/16

■ Ask students to listen and mark the word stress. Discuss the stress pattern in feedback.
■ You could play the recording again and ask students to listen and repeat.

Answers
For nouns, the stress is on the prefix; for adjectives, the stress is on the main word.

> **Pronunciation note**
> Compare *hyperactive* /ˌhaɪpərˈæktɪv/ to *hypermarket* /ˈhaɪpə(r)ˌmɑː(r)kɪt/.

Exercise 10

■ Ask students to complete the text. Let them check answers in pairs before discussing as a class.

Answers
1 ultra-modern 2 semi-circle 3 microscope 4 microchips 5 ultra-violet

Extra activity

Ask students in small groups to design a poster or advertisement to promote a brand new product using nanotechnology. It could be a product already mentioned such as sun cream or clothing.

Predicting the future

Speaking: speculating about the future

Exercise 1

- Ask students to work in groups of four to discuss the issues.
- Ask one of them to act as secretary and make short notes.
- Elicit responses from all the secretaries and open the discussion to the whole class.

Exercise 2

- Ask students to match the sentences individually and then compare their answers in pairs.
- Elicit answers from the whole class.

Answers
Extremely likely to happen 5; 7
Likely 6; 1
Possible 2; 10
Unlikely 4; 8
Impossible 3; 9

Exercise 3

- Read the *Useful expressions* box with the students and make sure they understand their meanings and how to use them.
- Ask students to do the activity individually, and then share their ideas in pairs using the useful expressions.
- Elicit ideas from the whole class, and monitor their use of the expressions.

Exercise 4

- Read through the examples with the class.
- Ask students to write their predictions.
- Ask students to swap predictions and make comments. Students then discuss their feedback in pairs.

Writing: an opinion essay

Exercise 5

- Ask students to look at the photos and the title of the essay. Ask, *What do you think the text will be about?*
- Ask students to read the essay quickly and match the paragraph plan to the different sections. Let students check their answers in pairs.

Answers
1 C 2 E 3 B 4 D 5 A

Books closed lead-in activity

Write on the board *Change*. Ask students to think about their school and brainstorm the things that have changed since they became students there.

Exercise 6

■ Ask students to read and list arguments. Let them check answers in pairs.

> **Answers**
> clean source of energy (no carbon emissions, doesn't contribute to global warming); renewable source (won't run out); plentiful: available in all corners of the globe; cheap to harvest, efficient; wind turbines take up little space; can be used in remote areas; potential to convert excess wind power into a fuel of some kind

> **Vocabulary note**
> *safeguard* = protect; *harvest* = here, collect and use; *national grid* = the way all electricity is provided across a nation; *spoil* = ruin, make something look unattractive.

Exercise 7

■ Ask students to work in pairs to complete the table.

> **Answers**
>
> | Adding similar opinions | Introducing contrasting opinions | Concluding |
> |---|---|---|
> | In addition
Moreover
What is more | In contrast
On the other hand
However | Therefore
To sum up |

> **Vocabulary and grammar note**
> Point out that *In addition*, *Moreover* and *What is more* are formal expressions, usually used when writing. They go at the start of a sentence and are followed by a comma.
> *However* also starts a sentence and is followed by a comma. *Although* and *Even though* link two contrasting clauses when the contrast is surprising. *In spite of* (like *despite*) is followed by a noun or *-ing*.

Exercise 8

■ Give students a moment to read the notes and check any unknown words.
■ Students work in pairs to divide the notes into arguments for and against and to discuss the question.

> **Vocabulary note**
> *dismantling* = taking apart into sections

Exercise 9

■ Ask students to choose a title and plan their essay. Ask them to write notes individually under each of the five headings in the paragraph plan. Then ask them to work with a partner who chose the same title to compare their ideas.

Exercise 10

■ Ask students to write an opinion essay following the instructions. Allow time for students to compare and correct each other's work.

Extra activity

Ask half the class to write an essay in favour of nuclear power and the other half to write against it. Pin the 'in favour' essays to one classroom wall, and the 'against' essays to another. Ask students to design a poster to go with their essays. Then ask students to read the essays on the walls and say whether they have changed their opinions as a result. This could lead to a class debate about nuclear power.

Changing food culture

Books closed lead-in activity

Write on the board *British food*. Elicit types of food and adjectives to describe food.

Listening and speaking

Exercise 1

- Ask students to work in pairs to discuss the questions.

Exercise 2   CD1/17

- Ask students to predict what the speakers might say. For example, under *Where*, they might mention *café*, *canteen* or *park*.
- Play the recording. Students listen and make notes. Let students check their answers in pairs before discussing as a class.

Audioscript

Speaker 1 I eat breakfast and lunch at work. I usually have breakfast in the canteen, and then at lunchtime I'll grab a sandwich at my desk while I check my emails or carry on with work. I don't usually have time to sit and eat with colleagues – most of them eat at their desks anyway or use their lunch hour to go shopping. On Fridays, we usually eat out. We might go to a pub or a sushi bar, or sometimes we go to an Indian or Chinese restaurant.

Speaker 2 Well, I must admit I'm a bit of a foodie. I don't like to eat on the go. I think it's important to savour food. I work from home, so I usually make myself a salad or an omelette for lunch. If I'm really busy, I'll fetch something from the deli round the corner but I always make time for a proper lunch break.

Speaker 3 I'm at college and in the week I generally skip lunch. Food is too expensive on campus and I can't be bothered to make a packed lunch. I eat a good breakfast in the morning and then I really just snack between lectures throughout the day, usually fruit and cereal bars. I chew a lot of gum as well! At lunchtime I go to the library or have a coffee with friends.

Speaker 4 The food in our school canteen used to be disgusting – cold pizza and chips every day – but it's got a lot better recently. There's been a big healthy eating campaign at our school and now they serve things like fish and pasta. So I usually have something to eat in the school canteen now. Some of the kids in my class go out to the baker's or to a fast food place and then eat their lunch on the way back to school, but I like to sit down and eat.

Answers

	Where	What	Why
Speaker 1	at desk at work	sandwich	no time
Speaker 2	home	salad or omelette	doesn't like to eat on the go
Speaker 3	at college	nothing	too expensive, can't be bothered
Speaker 4	school canteen	fish or pasta	likes to sit down and eat

Exercise 3   CD1/17

- Ask students to look at the words from the text, and point out difficult pronunciations (*chew* /tʃuː/; *savour* /ˈseɪvə(r)/).
- Ask students to work in pairs to complete the sentences. Then play the recording so that students can check.

Answers
1 grab 2 eat out 3 foodie 4 on the go 5 savour 6 skip 7 snack 8 chew 9 school canteen

> **Vocabulary note**
> A *foodie* is someone who really enjoys trying lots of different types of food. Here, *grab* means eat quickly and *skip* means miss or not have.

■   Ask students to work in pairs to talk about their lunch habits.

Reading
Exercise 5

■   Ask students to look at the picture. Ask, *Do you know him? Why do you think he is famous?* Ask students to predict the content of the text from the title.

■   Give students a moment to read through the options. Then ask them to work individually to complete the gaps. Let students check their answers in pairs before discussing as a class.

Answers
1 B 2 C 3 B 4 D 5 B 6 B

Culture note
Jamie Oliver, who was born in 1975, is a British chef and restaurateur well known for his food-focused television shows, cookbooks, his role in campaigning against the use of processed foods in national schools, and his campaign to change unhealthy diets and poor cooking habits in both the UK and the USA.

Exercise 6

■   Ask students to work in pairs to explain the words. Tell them to find the phrases in the text for context, and to use dictionaries to check what they think the words mean.

Answers
home-cooked meal: a meal which is made by somebody at home and not bought
low-calorie meal: a meal which only contains a limited number of calories, for people who want to lose weight
takeaway meal: a meal which is bought from a restaurant to be eaten at home
meal cooked from scratch: a meal that is prepared from basic ingredients and not using processed foods
ready meal: a meal that is already prepared and that you can just heat up
sit-down meal: a meal where you sit down at a table
three-course meal: a meal which has three different parts (starter/appetiser, main course and dessert)

Exercise 7

■   Ask students to discuss the questions in pairs or small groups.

Answers
1 ready meals and takeaway meals 2 lack of interest in food, lack of skills 3 Students' own answers

Speaking
Exercise 8

■   Ask students to read the questions carefully and make notes to answer them if they wish. Then divide the class into groups of three or four to discuss the questions. Ask all students to make notes.

Exercise 9

■   Ask students to look at the *Useful expressions* box, and to think about how they can present the results of the discussion using the expressions.

■   When they are ready, match one group with another to compare opinions.

Vocabulary note
Note the expressions used to make generalisations: *on the whole* = in general; *tend to* = usually, most of the time.

Extra activity
You could extend this into a survey. Ask pairs to design a simple questionnaire about breakfast, lunch and dinner. Then ask them to interview other students, collate their results, and present findings to the class.

Extra activity
Ask students to research food from other European countries under the following headings: *Types of food; Ways of cooking; When and how they eat; Changes in eating habits.* Ask students in threes to choose a country, research it for homework, compare ideas in class, then make a presentation to the rest of the class.

Making arrangements

Reading and speaking

Exercise 1

■ Ask students to work in pairs to predict the topic from the headline and then to discuss the questions.

■ Follow up by asking whether they think the statement is true for them and their generation.

> **Example answers**
>
> The headline means that teenagers today have more ways of communicating with each other than in the past. Teenagers today mostly communicate using technology instead of face-to-face. They talk to each other on their mobiles or send each other text messages or instant messages.
>
> Face-to-face communication is best in some situations because you can use your partner's body language and facial expressions to help you understand what they are trying to say. Sometimes, though, you don't want the person you are speaking with to see your emotions (perhaps if you are upset), so then text messages, instant messages or email are better. You can add emoticons to your messages, but nobody knows if they are true! Communicating by mobile phone or SMS is the easiest way when you are on the move. But it can be very expensive. Emailing is cheaper.

Exercise 2

■ Ask students to read the conversations and messages quickly and answer the questions. Let them check in pairs, then discuss the language used as a class.

> **Answers**
>
> 1 formal (formal phrases like *just one moment please*, *thank you for calling*)
> 2 informal (abbreviations and acronyms) 3 formal (formal phrases like *We would like to invite you*, *Yours sincerely*) 4 informal (informal phrases like *Hi*, *OK*, *see you*)

Exercise 3

■ Ask students to work in pairs to decide whether the phrases are formal or informal.

> **Answers**
>
> 1 I 2 F 3 B 4 F 5 I 6 F 7 F 8 F 9 B 10 I 11 I 12 I

Exercise 4

■ Divide the students into pairs. Ask each pair to decide on their role and read the relevant information.

■ With lower-level classes, give students time to prepare or write their dialogues, then ask a few pairs to act them out. With higher-level classes, get students to improvise the dialogues and change roles when they have finished. Monitor for errors and good language use.

■ Students then repeat for situation 2.

Books closed lead-in activity

Ask students how they communicate with friends and family. Brainstorm *mobile phone, texting, emails,* etc. writing ideas on the board. Ask students in pairs to discuss when, how and with whom they use each mode of communication.

Extra activity

Ask students to write mini-dialogues using the phrases in exercise 3 (e.g. *Hi Jan. What are you doing tomorrow?–Oh, nothing special.*) Then get the students practising them, paying attention to their pronunciation and intonation.

4

Reaching for the stars

UNIT OVERVIEW	
Topic	science fiction, space travel
Reading	science fiction films and books, history of human space travel, UFOs, Professor Brian Cox
Listening	the merits of reading science fiction, the effects of a long stay in space, SETI
Grammar	time conjunctions, speculating about the past
Function	talking about science
Vocabulary	synonyms, verbs of achievement, the universe
Pronunciation	/e/ or /iː/
Writing	telling a story
Speaking	predicting, talking about space tourism and exploration
Culture	science fiction, astonomy

Books closed lead-in activity

Write on the board *In a perfect world there would/ wouldn't be …* Ask students to complete the sentence in their own words. Elicit a few ideas and discuss interesting ideas as a class.

Extra activity

Ask students to work in groups to develop a five-point plan to make the world a better place. Ask them to deliver their plan in a presentation to the class.

Let's get started

Exercise 1

- Discuss the photo. Elicit topic words: *space*, *stars*, *planets*, *galaxies*.
- Ask students in pairs to discuss the question. Have a class discussion.

Exercise 2

- Ask students to read the quotations and say which one they agree with the most.

> **Culture note**
> Anatole France was a French writer. He won the Nobel Prize for Literature in 1921.
> Kurt Vonnegut is most famous for the novel *Slaughterhouse-five* (1969).

Vocabulary and speaking

Exercise 3

- Ask students to work in pairs to match the words to the phrases.
- Ask students to say which are most important in terms of creating a perfect world.

> **Answers**
> 1 c 2 e 3 f 4 b 5 a 6 d

> **Vocabulary note**
> *put an end to* = stop or eliminate; *treat* = deal with or behave towards

Exercise 4

- Ask students to discuss the questions in pairs or small groups.

Science fiction 4A

Books closed lead-in activity

Reading
Exercise 1
- Ask students to work in pairs to discuss the questions. Elicit key themes and note them on the board.

Exercise 2
- Ask students to read the texts quickly and note which themes are mentioned.
- As a class discussion, ask students if they know any other science fiction stories or films with the same themes as those mentioned.

> **Answers**
> The themes mentioned are: intelligent robots; humans being slaves to machines (also virtual reality); living longer, immortality; a single world state.

Exercise 3
- Ask students to read the texts carefully and answer the questions. Let students compare their answers in pairs before discussing as a class.

> **Answers**
> 1 The robots rebel against their masters. 2 All the people in the world. 3 That he will live forever but will keep growing older. 4 No – it is 'far from the Utopia that it seems to be'.

Speaking
Exercise 4
- Ask students to tell you what the text predicted about each of the themes in the headings.
- Then ask students to work individually to answer the questions and prepare things to say under each heading.

Exercise 5
- Divide the class into groups of three or four. Ask students to discuss their ideas. In feedback, ask a spokesperson from each group to summarise the discussion.

Listening
Exercise 6
- Ask students to describe the picture. Ask, *If you could travel in time, where would you go and why?*

> **Answer**
> A time machine.

> **Culture note**
> The photo shows a still from the 1960s film version of H G Wells' classic science fiction story **The Time Machine**. The book was first published in 1895.

Books closed lead-in activity
Ask students to think of the last science fiction film they saw or book they read. Ask them to think of setting, time, plot and characters. Divide the class into threes to tell each other about their film or book.

Extra activity
Ask students to work out the meaning of the following words in the text from context (answers in brackets): *drudgery* (hard, boring work), *shrivelled* (reduced to a small dried up thing), *recurring* (happening again and again).

Extra activity

Discuss the following as a class: *Do you think science fiction has important messages for us all? Why (not)? What science fiction stories do you know that have a message? What are the messages?*

- Ask, *What reasons do you think the speaker might give for encouraging people to read more science fiction?* Elicit a few ideas from students to help them predict the content of the text.
- Play the recording. Give students time to check the answer to the focus question in pairs before discussing as a class.

Audioscript

Interviewer	So, Gerald, you're a big fan of science fiction and you're here to tell us why we should be reading more of it …
Gerald	Yes, thank you, Sarah. I'm very glad to have the opportunity. I'm afraid that science fiction isn't taken very seriously by most critics, as if it were a second-rate type of literature. I think people generally believe it offers a rather simplistic view of the world – the kind of good versus evil scenario that you get in *Star Wars,* for example, with the Force and its dark side. But in fact it's often much more thoughtful than that. You find a lot of very interesting political and social ideas in science fiction.
Interviewer	For example …
Gerald	Well, take H G Wells' *The Time Machine*, which was published in 1895. His time traveller takes a journey forward in time to find that mankind has evolved into two groups: a group of small, childlike people called the Eloi, whose lives are peaceful but who don't work or have any real interests. They have mastered technology so that they can take it easy and live a life of comfort and leisure. The other group are the brutish Morlocks who live underground because they are afraid of the light. They operate the machines that make the Eloi's life possible.
Interviewer	And what social message, or point, was *The Time Machine* making?
Gerald	Well, it's clearly a warning not to allow society to become divided by class: a rich leisure class and a downtrodden working class. But it's more than that: it's also saying that a life of comfort without work is a false utopia. People must have a goal and must struggle to achieve that goal in order to be happy.
Interviewer	I see. And can you give us a more modern-day example of thought-provoking science fiction?
Gerald	Mm, easily. Kim Stanley Robinson's *Science in the Capital* trilogy. The story is basically one of a climate catastrophe caused by global warming and … um … some scientists' efforts – including things like shutting down the Gulf Stream – to combat it. The science in it is really interesting, actually, but the political message also. Robinson is saying that big business – the capitalists – have no interest in the long-term survival of the Earth's bio-systems. Their only target is profit. It's up to politicians and law-makers to regulate this activity. That's why the story is based in Washington DC – hence the title – *Science in the Capital*. There's also the scientist hero, Vanderwal, who lives a kind of Stone Age lifestyle, hunting and sleeping in the open. The point of this is to show how simple man's needs can be and in fact how much we take for granted the satisfaction and pleasure that nature brings us. I think that's very true. When bits of nature start to disappear – certain rivers or species of animal – people *will* finally wake up and realise just how much we need them.

Answer
There are a lot of very interesting political and social ideas in science fiction.

Exercise 8   CD1/18

- Give students a moment to read through the options and choose any that they think they already know the answer to.
- Play the recording. Ask students to choose the correct option then check with a partner before discussing as a class.

Answers
1 A 2 D 3 B 4 B 5 A 6 C 7 B

> **Vocabulary note**
> *brutish* /ˈbruːtɪʃ/ = ugly and animal-like; *downtrodden* = poor and oppressed; *take for granted* = not treat with respect because you think it will always be there.

Pronunciation: /e/ or /iː/

Exercise 9   CD1/19

- Ask students to work in pairs to decide on the correct pronunciation.
- Play the recording. Ask students to listen, check their answers, and repeat.

> **Answers**
> /e/ as in 'bed': leisure, hence, regulate, efforts, pleasure, catastrophe
> /iː/ as in 'we': believe, achieve, evil, species

Vocabulary and speaking

Exercise 10

- Ask students if they have seen *Avatar*. Encourage students to tell you about the plot and characters. Then ask students to read the text quickly and say what they found out about the plot.
- Ask students to work in pairs to match the synonyms.

> **Answers**
> 1 population 2 peaceful 3 people 4 wicked 5 plentiful 6 valuable 7 task 8 ally

> **Culture note**
> *Avatar* was directed by James Cameron and released in 2010. It was notable for its expensive, state-of-the-art, 3D special effects.

Exercise 11

- Ask students to match words to opposites. Let them check in pairs before discussing answers as a class.

> **Answers**
> 1 g 2 c 3 f 4 d 5 e 6 a 7 b

> **Pronunciation note**
> Note the trickier pronunciations: *cruel* /ˈkruːəl/; *scarce* /skeə(r)s/

Exercise 12

- Lead in by eliciting setting, time, characters and plot from students, and asking them to give examples of each.
- Ask students to work in pairs to plan their own synopsis. Monitor and help with ideas and vocabulary.
- Ask each pair to present their synopsis to the class.

4B Life on the Space Station

Books closed lead-in activity ────────→

Books closed lead-in activity

Tell students to close their eyes and imagine they are an astronaut floating in space. Ask, *What can you see? How do you feel? What will you remember most about this experience?* Pause between each question so students have time to think. Ask students to open their eyes and tell a partner about what they saw and how they felt.

Listening

Exercise 1

- Ask students to look at the photo. Ask, *What do you know about the Space Station?*
- Ask students to work in pairs to discuss how life on a space station might be different from life on earth. As a class, build up a list of differences on the board.

Exercise 2   CD1/20

- Play the recording. Ask students to listen and note what the expert says.

Audioscript

Expert	… so astronauts sleep near a ventilator to avoid waking up in a bubble of their own carbon dioxide.
Interviewer	And what are the psychological effects of living in space for such long periods of time?
Expert	Well, when an astronaut comes to live on the Space Station, he or she will find conditions that are very different to those on Earth: the weightlessness, as I've already mentioned, and the lack of a real day and night. You can see the sun rise 15 times in a 24-hour period, which can be disorientating to say the least. But they have been prepared for these things, and also every attempt has been made to recreate 'normal' conditions as far as is possible – in other words, a working day and a night of sleep.
Interviewer	So, they don't really suffer from disorientation. Do they get depressed? I think I might after five months away from home.
Expert	Well, there seem to be three, or maybe four phases, psychologically. Let's imagine you were to go out there as a research scientist …
Interviewer	That does take some imagining …
Expert	Well, when you arrive, the first thing you will experience is space sickness, which affects everyone. This is a kind of motion sickness (umm … nausea and dizziness) that you get from being in a non-gravity environment. But once you've got over that, you'll get a feeling of great exhilaration from being weightless. It makes everyday chores like washing and eating difficult, but in another sense, it's very liberating.
Interviewer	Indeed …
Expert	Also, while you're adapting to life in space, you will be very preoccupied with all the jobs you have to do, and motivated by the challenges it brings. After this period of adaptation is over – usually about two months later – you will, I'm afraid, begin to feel mentally tired and your motivation will drop.
Interviewer	But this happens to people engaged in any new task, doesn't it?
Expert	Yes, but it's probably more acute in space travel. And finally, when you enter your last two months or so, you may well become bad-tempered and over-sensitive. Living in a confined space with the same people for a protracted period tends to have that effect anyway …
Interviewer	Mmm, I know that syndrome. Is there any cure for that?
Expert	Well, apart from coming home, not really. Lots of opportunities to keep in touch with friends and family by email is a help of course and …

Answers

weightlessness: makes everyday chores like **eating and washing** difficult

lack of a real **day and night:** you can see the sun rise 15 times in 24 hours – disorientating

space sickness: affects everyone – a kind of motion sickness (nausea and dizziness)

living in a confined space: become bad-tempered and over-sensitive

contact with home: keep in touch with friends and family by email

---

Vocabulary and pronunciation note
disorientation /dɪsˌɔːriən'teɪʃ(ə)n/ = losing a sense of where you are; *nausea* /'nɔːziə/ = feeling sick; *exhilaration* /ɪɡˌzɪlə'reɪʃ(ə)n/ = feeling of excitement; *preoccupied* /priˈɒkjʊpaɪd/ = busy doing things

Exercise 3 CD1/20

- ► ■ Give students time to read through the statements. Check any unknown words.
  - ■ Play the recording. Ask students to listen then check their answers in pairs.

Answers
1 False 2 True 3 False 4 True 5 False 6 True

Grammar: time conjunctions

Exercise 4

- ■ Ask students to read the examples carefully then discuss what they notice with a partner. Elicit suggestions, but do not deny or confirm at this stage.

Answers
The verb in the time clause (when, after, etc.) is always a present tense, when you might expect a future tense, as in the main clause.

Exercise 5

- ► ■ Ask students to read the explanation carefully then talk to a partner to check whether they 'noticed' how the conjunctions worked in the examples.
  - ■ Refer students to the Grammar Reference on page 150.

Exercise 6

- ■ Ask students to complete the gaps. Do the first as an example.

Answers
1 sleep / are sleeping 2 is 3 was / had been 4 were 5 became / had become
6 launch / have launched

Exercise 7

- ■ Ask students to read the explanation. You could check understanding by doing another example on the board. For example, write up number 5 from exercise 6 on the board, and elicit *After becoming president, Obama said he would …*
- ■ Ask students to complete the sentences then check their answers in pairs.

Answers
1 On 2 During 3 Following 4 Prior to 5 Within

- ■ Refer students to the Grammar Reference on page 150.

Exercise 8

- ■ Ask students to read the text through quickly. Ask, *When do astronauts feel most nervous during take-off?* (At T minus 90 seconds. T = take-off.)
- ► ■ Ask students to choose the correct option and check their answers in pairs.

Answers
1 before 2 during 3 once 4 until 5 as soon as 6 moment 7 Following 8 On

Exercise 9

- ■ Ask students to complete the sentences. Monitor, prompt and correct, making sure students are using the correct tense forms after conjunctions.
- ■ Ask students to read out sentences in pairs or groups.

Example answers
1 I have got a garden. 2 I was at primary school / primary school. 3 I will look for a job.
4 I heard I had got a place at Oxford University. 5 I will buy a car. / I bought a car.
6 I have nothing else to do. 7 make a big decision. 8 my exams are finished.

Extra activity

Ask students in groups to prepare and present a list of good advice for somebody who is about to go and spend three months living on a space station.

Extra activity

Check that students understand the difference in meaning between the words by writing the following sentence on the board and asking students to insert different conjunctions and say how they change the meaning:

We played football in the park _____ John arrived.

Extra activity

Write the following story prompts on the board:

we had breakfast / we set out for the station / we were walking / it started to rain heavily / we waited under a tree / the rain stopped / we carried on / we were running late now / we arrived at the station / we still had to buy our tickets / we bought the tickets / we rushed to the train / we got on / the train pulled out of the station / we arrived at the next station / we realised we had got on the wrong train!

Ask students in pairs to rewrite the story using time conjunctions.

4C Science fact

Books closed lead-in activity

Write on the board *My greatest achievement*. Ask students to think for a moment what their greatest achievement is. Then ask them to tell their partner. Elicit some interesting examples.

Extra activity

Ask students to think of times when they have fulfilled a dream, tested or discovered their limits, accomplished a demanding task or failed to justify the time and effort they have spent on something. Give them time to think of what to say. Put them in groups to discuss.

Vocabulary and speaking

Exercise 1

- Ask students to work in pairs to discuss the quotation.

> **Culture note**
> Robert Browning was a poet and playwright. He was born in London, and became one of the greatest writers of the Victorian era, most famous for his dramatic monologues.

Exercise 2

- Ask students to choose the correct option. Do the first as a class to get students started. Let students check answers in pairs before discussing as a class.

Answers
1 B 2 A 3 B 4 C 5 A 6 C 7 B 8 B 9 C

> **Vocabulary note**
> You could encourage students to make a list of common collocations: *have/fulfil a dream*; *take on/accept a challenge*; *test/discover your limits*; *justify cost/effort/hard work*; *accomplish a task*; *attain a goal*.

Exercise 3

- Ask students to work in pairs to discuss the question. Encourage them to use verb/noun collocations from exercise 2. Elicit a list of reasons and note them on the board.

Example answers
to advance the causes of science and make new discoveries; to gain status in the world; for reasons of national pride and prestige; to potentially find new materials

Reading

Exercise 4

- Lead in by asking students what they know about the history of space travel.
- Ask students to read the questions carefully. You could brainstorm a few possible answers to question 1 in order to help students try and predict the text.
- Ask students to read the text quickly and answer the questions. Let them check their answers in pairs.

Answers
1 to fulfil our dreams 2 sending robots into space; building telescopes to photograph the cosmos

> **Vocabulary note**
> The *space age* was ultimately a race for prestige and military superiority between the USA and the Soviet Union. Key events included the first artificial satellite (Sputnik 1) and the first animal in space (a dog, Laika, in Sputnik 2), both sent up by the USSR in 1957; the first human in space (Yuri Gagarin of the USSR in 1961), and the first human on the moon (Neil Armstrong of the USA in 1969).

Exercise 5

■ Give students a moment to read through the statements and see if they can answer any questions. Check any unknown words in the questions.

■ Ask students to read the text more carefully and decide if the answers are true or false. Let students check answers in pairs.

Answers
1 False (it was the first man-made object to orbit Earth) 2 True 3 False (public interest in human spaceflight waned) 4 True 5 False 6 True 7 False 8 True

Vocabulary note
pressing ahead = going forward with plans without delay; *incidental benefit* = an extra benefit, not the main reason for doing something

Exercise 6

■ Ask students to match the definitions to words in the article. Let them check answers in pairs.

Answers
1 epoch 2 plagued by 3 wore off 4 withstanding 5 a snapshot 6 extract 7 bother

Vocabulary note
streaked = moved very fast; *waned* = became smaller or lesser; *triumphs* = achievements; *compelling* = powerful and persuasive

Speaking

Exercise 7

■ Ask students to discuss the questions in small groups.

Extra activity

Prepare and distribute handouts with the following comments and ask students to express their opinion about each comment:

We should fulfil our dreams and exploring space is one of man's greatest dreams.

It is irresponsible to waste money and resources on space travel when there is poverty and hardship on our own planet.

Have a class debate on the subject of space travel.

4D Unexplained events

Books closed lead-in activity

Draw on the board a simple but mysterious diagram. For example:

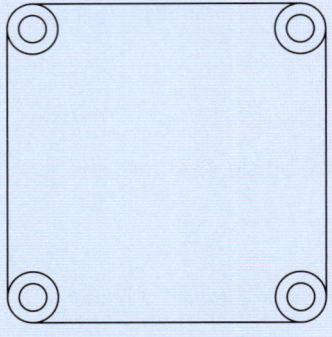

Ask students to guess what the drawing represents. Elicits lots of ideas then reveal the answer.

Reading

Exercise 1

- Ask students to look at the pictures. Ask, *What can you see?*
- Ask students to work in pairs to discuss the images.

Exercise 2

- Ask students to read the text and check their answers.

> **Example answers**
> Picture 1: The photographer may have kept the camera shutter open too long and that may have caused the illusion.
> Picture 2: It must have been an unusual cloud formation.
> *Hoax* means a deliberate attempt to deceive somebody.

> **Vocabulary note**
> *shutter* = the part of the camera that opens to allow light in when taking a photo;
> *die-hard* = used to describe people who support or believe something no matter what happens

Grammar: speculating about the past

Exercise 3

- Lead in by brainstorming phrases students know to speculate about the past.
- Ask students to work in pairs to match phrases to lists.

> **Answers**
> Perhaps she was … **C**   It can't have been … **A**   He may well have been … **B**

> **Grammar note**
> Note the use of *must* and *can't* when there is a logical reason to deduce that something is true. For example, *The volcano was dormant, so it can't have been caused by heat rising.* Here, there is a logical reason that allows the speaker to use *can't* to deduce something.

- Refer students to the Grammar Reference on page 150.

Exercise 4

- Ask students to complete the sentences with words in the box. Do the first as a class to get students started. Let students check their answers in pairs before discussing as a class.

> **Answers**
> 1 believe 2 sure 3 likely / possible 4 possible / likely 5 probably

Extra activity

Extend the discussion by getting students to think of their own situations, or by writing up some of the following on the board:

You arrive home from school, and the front door is open.

You think you have done your homework really well, but it is returned with a low mark.

You meet your friend and he or she is soaking wet even though it is a sunny day.

Exercise 5

- Divide students into pairs or small groups. Give students a couple of minutes to read the situations and to think of things to say. Tell them to refer to the phrases in exercises 3 and 4 when formulating sentences.
- Monitor the discussion carefully and listen for errors and good language use.

> **Example answers**
> 1 Someone must have stolen it. 2 He can't have forgotten. 3 It might have been a firework.

Vocabulary: synonyms

Exercise 6

- Ask the students to brainstorm lists in pairs, then build up a list on the board.

Answers
weird, odd, bizarre, unusual, uncommon

Exercise 7

Extra activity →

- Ask students to match the adjectives to their synonyms. Let them check their answers in pairs before discussing as a class.

Answers
1 d 2 f 3 a 4 c 5 h 6 b 7 g 8 i 9 e

Extra activity

Ask students to brainstorm synonyms of other common adjectives: *big, small, happy, sad,* etc.

> **Vocabulary and pronunciation note**
> *Creepy* describes a feeling when you are uncomfortable and a little afraid because something or someone is strange.
> Note the stress: <u>fright</u>ening, a<u>ston</u>ishing, un<u>sett</u>ling, <u>mys</u>tifying, di<u>stressed</u>.

Writing: telling a story

Exercise 8   CD1/21

- Lead in by asking students to read the four situations A to D, then to guess what strange experience each speaker may have had.
- Ask students to listen and match speakers to statements. Let them check their answers in pairs.

Audioscript

Speaker 1   I like to think that I am a relatively cool and rational person, but what happened a few years ago is something that still upsets me. Anyway, when I was younger we lived near a big park, a really beautiful place with tall trees and a lake. There was a particular line of trees, about four of them, poplars I think they were, that I always kept away from. Whenever my sister and I were playing near them, I would call her away if she got too close and I would get quite distressed. Then about ten years later, I went back there with a friend to show her where I had grown up. We took a picnic down to the lake and she suggested sitting in the shade under the same group of trees because it was too warm in the sun. However, I still had the same intense, rather creepy feeling about them, so we sat further up the slope and ate our lunch. Suddenly, there was this incredible cracking noise. One of the trees swayed for a moment before crashing to the ground … right where we would have been sitting. It was really creepy.

Speaker 2   I had this really scary dream when I was camping one summer in France. I dreamt that someone was trying to get a splinter out of my arm with a rusty penknife and was cutting me. I woke up in a sweat, and when I looked at my arm there were lots of little red marks all down it. There was no one else in the tent with me …

Speaker 3   I'm a very sceptical person normally when it comes to paranormal phenomena. But sometimes things happen that you just can't explain. One evening I was sitting in the garden with some friends. It was just getting dark and we were gazing at the sky, which had turned a beautiful colour. Suddenly six or seven lights appeared in the sky, one after the other, in a kind of procession, moving very slowly and steadily in a straight line. They passed very serenely over our heads. They were too low and too bright to be satellites. I looked in the local newspaper the following day to see if there was a report … if others had seen some UFOs too, but nothing. All very puzzling really.

Speaker 4   We moved to a new house when I was about eight and I remember some very weird things happening. They didn't seem that remarkable at the time, but now I look back on them … Some of my toys used to do things by themselves. My radio-controlled car would suddenly just set off by itself around the room without me doing anything. Also, I used to find things in odd places. Books would turn up on top of cupboards, toys in the washing machine, when none of us could remember putting them there …

Answers
A 2 B 4 C 1 D 3

Exercise 9   CD1/21

- Ask students to work in pairs to reconstruct the stories. You could replay the recording to check.

Answers
I C E G A D F B H

Exercise 10

- Ask students to notice the sequencing words in exercise 9. Check their meaning.
- Ask students to work in pairs to compare the sentences.

Answers
1 When = on one occasion; Whenever = on every occasion 2 Then = next; Just then = at that precise moment 3 Suddenly = very quickly; Gradually = little by little

> **Vocabulary note**
> *it dawned on me* = it gradually occurred to me

Exercise 11

- Divide students into small groups to speculate. Start by eliciting two or three suggestions about the first story.
- Once the students have finished, find out which group had the best explanations.

Exercise 12

- A good way of introducing this activity is to briefly tell your own story – it could be true or one you make up. Try to include information that could go under each heading.
- Give students a few minutes to prepare what they are going to say, and monitor closely to help with ideas and vocabulary.
- Ask students to tell their partners their story. Ask partners to make comments about how to improve the stories.

Exercise 13

- Ask students to read the final sentence. Then elicit what type of story might have such an ending.
- Ask students to think of a story and to write detailed notes under each ending. It could be the story they told in exercise 12, or a different story. Monitor and help with ideas and vocabulary.
- You could ask students to write up a final version of the story for homework.
- Refer students to the DVD about mysterious crop circles. Video worksheet on page 137.

Extra activity

Write a list of sequencers on the board (*suddenly, gradually, whenever*, etc.). Then ask students in pairs to try to recall and tell part of one of the stories from the listening in exercise 8 using the sequencers.

Extra activity

Once students have completed their stories, pin them on classroom walls, or pass them round the class, so that other students can read them. Ask students to write positive comments about the stories, at the bottom of each.

Alternatively, ask students to exchange stories with a partner. They must read each other's work then make comments, finishing with, *What I really liked was* … and *I think you could have* …

Books closed lead-in activity

Write *Universe* on the board and brainstorm as many words as you can from the students about the subject.

Vocabulary and speaking

Exercise 1

- Ask students to work in groups of four to discuss the words.
- Elicit their answers as a class.

Answers

our Sun is a *star*, and the Earth are one of the *planets* which move around it; *moons* move around planets

mass is a related body of matter with no definite shape; *gravity* is the force which keeps things on the ground on Earth

a *solar system* is a group of planets which orbit a particular star (sun); a galaxy is a set of solar systems held together by gravitational pull; the *universe* is the whole of space and matter and energy

asteroids are small planets which move around the sun; a *meteor* is a small celestial body which orbits the Sun; when a *meteorite* enters Earth's atmosphere it burns brightly as a meteor

a *physicist* studies physics; an *astronomer* studies space; an *astrologer* studies stars and planets to understand human behaviour

a solar *eclipse* is when the moon goes across the Sun (there can be other eclipses); an *orbit* is the path a planet takes around a star, or a moon (or satellite) around a planet

an *element* is any of the 118 known substances which consist of atoms with the same number of protons in their nuclei; an *atom* is the smallest quantity of an element that can take part in a chemical reaction

a *fraction* is a part of something whole; a *particle* is an extremely small piece of matter

Exercise 2

- Ask the whole class to consider the questions and to make comments on them.
- Encourage discussion of the issues, pointing out that there is no definitive answer to any of them.

Reading

Exercise 3

- Ask students to read the words to focus their reading of the text.
- Ask them to read the text and choose the meanings individually.
- They can check their answers in pairs.
- Elicit the answers from the whole class.

Answers

1 communicate 2 easily understood 3 understand 4 natural ability 5 caused 6 led to

> **Pronunciation note**
> Note the stress on these words: impart; accessible; potential; communicate; considered; understood; understand; explain; ability; possibility.

Exercise 4

- Ask students to read the text again and to answer the questions individually.
- They can check their answers with a partner.

Answers
Paragraph 1: b
Example answers:

Paragraph 2:
a he got many qualifications and became a professor

b can help everyone to understand science

c the human mind could not understand the dimensions of space and time

Paragraph 3:
a his youth, smile and uncomplicated way of explaining things
b more people study physics at university, and telescope sales increased

Culture note
Professor Brian Cox was born near Oldham, Lancashire in 1968. Despite not doing particularly well at school, he went to Manchester University to study physics. During the period 1988–1997, while studying for his M.Phil and PhD degrees in physics, he was also the keyboard player in the bands Dare and D:Ream. His particular professional area of expertise is high energy particle physics. He is currently a Professor at Manchester University, and is involved in the ATLAS experiment at the Large Hadron Collider at Cern, near Geneva, Switzerland. He is also nationally and internationally famous for the TV and radio shows that he presents, and has won various awards for popularising science.

Exercise 5

- Ask students to read the sentences first.
- Ask them to read the text and order the sentences individually, then check with a partner.
- Elicit the answers from the class as sentences given in the correct order.

Answers
1 d 2 h 3 b 4 g 5 c 6 f 7 i 8 j 9 a 10 e

Listening and vocabulary

Exercise 6

- Read the words with the class. Check that they understand the meanings.
- Ask the class to suggest answers using the words in the box.

Exercise 7 CD1/22

- Ask students to read the sentences to focus their listening.
- Play the recording while they just listen and follow.
- Play it again for them to complete the answers.
- Play it once more for them to check and correct.
- Students compare their answers with a partner. Then elicit the answers from the class as complete sentences.

Audioscript

Presenter	I have somebody in the studio today who has spent the last ten years listening – not to the radio or to music. Not even to other people. But listening for something very particular. David Hughes, tell us what you do.
David	Well, you make it sound as though I've been sitting at home with headphones on. It's not exactly like that! I'm a participating member of the seti@home project.
Presenter	OK, you've lost me already. What is that exactly?
David	SETI stands for the Search for Extraterrestrial Intelligence – alien life if you want to put it another way. You've probably seen pictures of giant radio telescopes in various places in the world. Well some of these are pointing at various parts of the sky and collecting information about the sounds that they receive.
Presenter	So you're listening for aliens?
David	Yes – to put it simply. Many scientists believe that if there is intelligent life somewhere else in the universe, they could well be trying to contact us. And, because they are so far away, their message will be in the form of some kind of radio signal that they are transmitting.
Presenter	Like the radios signals we listen to music on?
David	Yes, kind of. The problem is that there is already a lot of noise out there. Some of it is just background noise, and a lot of it is noise that we've created, from radio stations, television broadcasts and satellites. So what the radio telescopes do is they listen for anything unusual.
Presenter	And where do you fit in?

David	Well to analyse all of the information that is picked up, we would need the biggest computer in the world – something that nobody can afford – or to spend years doing it. But back in the 1990s, someone suggested that this could be done virtually – by using the computers in our homes when we are not using them. And in 1999, the seti@home project began, using the computing power of ordinary home computers like yours and mine.
Presenter	So, do they do this without our knowledge?
David	No, not at all. You volunteer for the project. You simply download a small programme, which is a screensaver actually, and it analyses a small piece of information at a time. Multiply this by thousands of computers whose owners have all joined the project, and you have enormous computing power.
Presenter	And it doesn't interfere with your computer in any way?
David	No. Let's say you're working or playing games on your computer and you stop for lunch. That's when the SETI program starts working. It only uses your computer when you don't need it … and when you come back to your computer, it stops working and lets you carry on what you were doing.
Presenter	Why did you volunteer for the project?
David	Well, some people believe that there is life out there and some people don't. I just happen to be one of those who believe. So when I heard about the project, I thought it would be a good idea.
Presenter	And what if you do discover a strange message?
David	Well the people at SETI are best qualified to deal with that. They know that computers make mistakes sometimes, so they would thoroughly check any interesting signals.
Presenter	But if we discover intelligent life, it could be thanks to your computer, David!
David	Yes, it could. Or yours. Or any of the thousands of others. And imagine how you would feel if you volunteered the use of your computer and you were part of the biggest scientific discovery ever!
Presenter	Now that would be something to be proud of!

Answers
1 ten 2 collect information; receive 3 pick up; stations; broadcasts 4 download; program
5 check; make mistakes 6 scientific discovery

Speaking

Exercise 8

- Ask students to discuss the questions in groups of four.
- Ask one student in each group to act as secretary and make short notes of the answers.
- Elicit ideas from the secretaries and encourage the whole class to discuss them.

The end of the world

Lead-in

Ask the class to discuss some possible things which they think could end the world (e.g. nuclear war, meteor strike).

Exercise 1

Ask students to read the text and note the predictions individually. Then they check in pairs, and sort their answers into *natural causes* and *man-made*. Elicit answers from the whole class.

> **Answers**
> **Natural causes**
> the Earth will enter a new ice age
> supervolcano eruption
> planet being hit by an asteroid / meteorite
> death of the sun
>
> **Man-made**
> climate change caused by pollution

Exercise 2

- Ask students to choose the meanings individually, then compare their answers in pairs.
- Elicit answers from the whole class.

> **Answers**
> 1 a 2 a 3 a 4 b 5 a 6 a

Exercise 3

- Ask students to read the questions to focus their reading. Then they read the text and answer the questions.
- They can check their answers in pairs.
- Elicit the answers from the class, having one student ask the question and another give the answer.

> **Answers**
> 1 That we have used up the planet's resources and therefore destroyed it.
> 2 Yes, because we have overused fossil fuels, which cause global warming.
> 3 The eruption of a volcano could cover the sun so nothing would grow.
> 4 The sun will get hotter and kill everything on Earth.

Find out more!

Do some research about an aspect of this topic which interests you, for example:
- global warming
- the Maya prophecy
- how the Earth could end

Look on the Internet and in books in the library. In particular, have a look at the National Geographic website: www.nationalgeographic.com

Units 3 and 4

Unit 3 Review

Ask students to complete the exercises in class or set the review for homework. After they have completed the exercises, students should evaluate their own performance, using the self-assessment box.

Answers
Exercise 1
1 illiteracy 2 predict 3 huge 4 source 5 in addition 6 inspire

Exercise 2
1 06.02; 08.10 2 get an entry permit; is going to take the bus to Thimpu 3 will / is going to be; will / is going to take about six hours 4 is staying / going to stay at the; two nights 5 is meeting / going to meet a guide at the Heritage Museum for a tour 6 he is going to walk to the monastery 7 will visit the market 8 leaves at 08.00

Exercise 3
1 will have been constantly rising 2 will have increased 3 will have been waiting 4 will have turned into 5 will have become 6 will be looking for 7 will have died 8 will be fighting

Exercise 4
b 2 e 3 c 5 a 1 4 d

Unit 4 Review

Answers
Exercise 1
1 scarce 2 discovered 3 justify 4 hero 5 takes on 6 fulfil

Exercise 2
1 When you arrive, please report to reception.
2 Before she worked as an actor, she had been / was a primary school teacher.
3 After the head teacher retired / had retired, the school went downhill.
4 While we were eating / having dinner, a live band played.

Exercise 3
1 were riding 2 returned 3 begin 4 have done 5 dries/has dried 6 pump
7 fitted / had fitted

Exercise 4
1 must 2 likely 3 may 4 unlikely 5 can't

5

Higher education

UNIT OVERVIEW

Topic	education systems in Britain and America, career choices and paths, university life
Reading	university prospectus, a herpetologist and explorer, Erasmus exchange students
Listening	a student comparing British and American universities, people describing their unusual career paths, students giving advice to new students
Grammar	question tags, conditionals (zero, first, second, third, mixed)
Function	obligations and requirements, applying for a student loan
Vocabulary	university, specialists, life experiences
Pronunciation	question tags, stress on nouns with *-er, -ist* or *-ian*
Writing	applying to a British University (writing a personal statement)
Speaking	talking about the merits of vocational degrees, talking about student accommodation, talking about bar charts
Culture	university life

Books closed lead-in activity

Write *Higher education* on the board and brainstorm as many words as you can from the students about the subject. For example: *university, degree, study, subject, arts, masters*, etc.

Let's get started

Exercise 1

■ Ask students to work in pairs to discuss the question. In feedback, have a whole-class debate.

> **Culture note**
> University students in England are entitled to take out **student loans** to pay for tuition fees and living costs. These have to be paid back gradually once the student is in full-time work. Students from poor households are entitled to a grant for their tuition fees that does not have to be paid back.
>
> The current system is controversial. Loans replaced grants for the majority of students in 1998, and as a result the debt faced by many students has risen. In Scotland and Wales, most students are entitled to claim a grant from the state.

Vocabulary and speaking

Exercise 2

■ Ask students to work in pairs to discuss the words.

> **Answers**
> 1 loan = money you borrow to pay for your education; grant = money the state gives you to pay for your education
>
> 2 undergraduate = someone who is studying at university to get a bachelor's degree; postgraduate = someone who has completed a bachelor's degree and is studying a postgraduate course
>
> 3 academic = study that involves intellectual study, for example, literature, history or science; vocational = study that involves practical application of knowledge, for example, electrical engineering or carpentry
>
> 4 degree = a qualification awarded by a university; qualification = a general word to describe what you are given for successfully completing a course of study
>
> 5 scholarship = a financially-supported place at a college or university; prize = here, it refers to an award of money given for winning a competition or achieving something

Divide students into groups of three. Each student is responsible for leading the discussion on one of the questions. Tell them to think of follow-up questions to ask, and tell them to take notes on the discussion so that they can summarise in feedback.

Exercise 3

- Give students a couple of minutes to read the questions and think of things to say. Tell them to take notes if they like.
- Ask students to work in pairs or small groups to discuss the questions.
- Ask a student from each group to summarise the discussion.

5A Education systems

Books closed lead-in ──▶
activity

Write on the board: *Are you
planning to go to university?
Why?/Why not?*

Put students in pairs to
discuss the questions.

Vocabulary and speaking

Exercise 1

■ Ask students to work in pairs to discuss the questions.

Exercise 2

■ Ask students to work in pairs to choose the correct collocations.
■ Check the answers then encourage students to ask and answer the questions in pairs. Ask a few students to summarise their discussions.

Answers
1 campus 2 fees 3 activities 4 course 5 requirements 6 specialisation

Vocabulary note
You pay *fees* to attend an institution. You pay *bills* for your use of electricity, gas, etc. *Hobbies* are what people do in their own personal free time. A *term* is part of a year – there are three terms in an academic year.

Reading

Exercise 3

■ Ask students to look at the brochures briefly without reading the text. Ask, *What can you see? Where are these universities? What differences do you think there are between universities in Britain and the USA?*
■ Put students in pairs to discuss differences.

Exercise 4

■ Ask students to work in pairs. Tell them to decide which text to read, then give them three minutes to read and find answers.
■ Ask students to tell each other about their universities. Have a brief class discussion.

Answers
1 Birmingham is looking for students with an analytical mind who want to focus more on a single subject. UCLA is looking for students who have diverse interests and want to combine studies for their career with studies for interest.

2 Birmingham offers single-subject courses or two-subject courses. UCLA offers a huge range of courses and combinations.

Vocabulary note
enquiring = asking questions; *fit in well* = be similar to other students; *vibrant* = lively; *major* = your main degree or course of study (US English)

Exercise 5

■ Ask students to discuss the questions in pairs then as a class. Encourage students to give reasons for their answers.

Listening

Exercise 6 CD1/23

■ Ask students to read through the list of topics. Ask, *What information do you expect to hear about each topic?* Encourage students to predict content as much as possible.
■ Play the recording. Ask students to listen and tick the topics. Let students check their answers in pairs before discussing as a class.

Extra activity ──────▶

Ask students to discuss how
universities in their own
countries differ from those
in Britain and/or the USA.

You could get students to
design a brochure for a
university in their country.

Audioscript

Interviewer	I have with me in the studio James Richards, who is a recent graduate. He has a rather unique perspective on the British university system, having studied both at an American and a British university. James, what were the main differences?
James	I suppose the biggest difference is the number of subjects you study, at undergraduate level, that is. In Britain, we tend to focus on just one or at most two subjects, whereas the idea in the United States is to expose students to a range of things. It's not unusual for someone who's majoring in History to take courses in science, art, literature … You name it.
Interviewer	But the danger of that is that by the end of your studies, you aren't really expert in anything, are you?
James	Yeah, well that *is* the common criticism. But you do actually become an expert in academic learning, and also I think you become a more rounded individual. My programme in the States was much fuller than it was here. In London I only had 12 contact hours per week. The rest of the time I was expected to get on with reading and essay writing on my own.
Interviewer	So I imagine studying here takes a lot more self-motivation, doesn't it?
James	You're not kidding. There were periods in London where I had very little to do, followed by periods where I was up all night for several days in a row, trying to get work finished. The workload in the States was constant – we had lectures every day and assignments every day.
Interviewer	And what about student life in general? Students here have a reputation for partying pretty hard. Is it the same in America?
James	Not at all. Of course students do relax and enjoy themselves, but because it's more full-time and more structured, as I just explained, *and* a lot more expensive, people tend to take it more seriously.
Interviewer	Could I be rude and ask you how much your year in America cost you?
James	The normal fees would have been $35,000. But I was lucky. I had a scholarship.
Interviewer	That isn't just for tuition, is it?
James	No, that does include your room and meals as well.
Interviewer	Still, it's a lot of money, as you say …
James	It really is, but it's a private college and they can charge what they like. Mind you, they put it to good use – the facilities were fantastic. But the point I was trying to make is that most students have part-time jobs to help pay some of their costs. They also take out student loans if they're not eligible for any financial aid. The result is people are busy, you know, and pretty motivated … more than their British counterparts, I'd say. They're very focused on getting good grades so that they'll be able to get a good job and pay their debts off.

Answers
Ticked topics: status of university (private or public); extent of subject specialisation; intensiveness of courses; cost of studying and living; social life

> **Vocabulary note**
> *rounded* = having a broader personality; *you're not kidding* = you're not joking; *eligible* = allowed to get something; *counterparts* = similar people in a different situation; *fund* = pay for

Exercise 7 CD1/23

- Ask students to read through the statements carefully and answer any they can.
- Play the recording. Ask students to listen again and choose true or false.

Answers
1 True 2 True 3 False (lectures every day in the USA) 4 True 5 False (British students do) 6 False (he had a scholarship) 7 True 8 False

Grammar and pronunciation: question tags

Exercise 8   CD1/24

- Ask students to look at the example sentences and check the way they are formed.
- Ask students to work in pairs to discuss the first question. In feedback, answer any questions about use.
- Play the recording. Ask students to listen and mark whether the intonation rises or falls in the three examples.

Answers
1 To check information or request agreement with an opinion (see box in exercise 9).
2 The intonation falls on sentence a, and rises on b and c. So, in a the speaker is expecting agreement, but in b and c the speaker has doubt.

Grammar note
Tag questions
The subject becomes a pronoun: … _studying_ takes …, doesn't _it_?
The subject and verb invert: … _you aren't_ …, _are you_?
With the verb _to be_, the verb changes from positive to negative (or negative to positive): … _that isn't_ …, _is it_?
With other verbs, the auxiliary or modal verb is used. It changes from positive to negative (or negative to positive): … _takes_…, _doesn't it_?

Exercise 9

- Ask students to read the information about use and intonation and check their answers.
- Refer students to the Grammar Reference on page 151.

Exercise 10

- Ask students to complete the statements. Let them check their answers in pairs before discussing as a class.

Answers
2 isn't it 3 have you 4 doesn't she 5 didn't they 6 hasn't he 7 didn't you 8 aren't I
9 isn't he 10 shall we

Exercise 11   CD1/25

- Ask students to listen and check answers.
- Ask them to listen again, note whether the intonation is falling or rising, and practise saying the sentences.

Answers
1 falling 2 falling 3 rising 4 rising 5 falling 6 rising 7 falling 8 falling 9 falling 10 rising

Speaking
Exercise 12

- Ask students to follow the instructions to prepare and practise tag questions.

Extra activity

Ask students to write five facts they know about their partner (e.g. _She's Italian_). Tell them to make the facts into sentences with tag questions and to interview their partner.

Change partners. Ask students to write five things that may be true about their new partner, but they are doubtful of. Make sentences with tag questions and ask. Monitor and make sure students are attempting falling and rising intonation appropriately.

Making the right choice

Speaking

Exercise 1

- Ask students to work in pairs to guess answers to the questions. Then ask them to check answers on page 141.
- Find out which pair got most correct answers, and discuss the question.

> **Answers**
> 1 d 2 c 3 All of them 4 c 5 d

Listening

Exercise 2 CD1/26

- Ask students to listen to the recording and complete the table. Let students check their answers in pairs before discussing as a class.

Audioscript

Interviewer	Lucy, did going to university help you or was it a waste of time?
Lucy	Not at all. If I hadn't gone to university, I certainly wouldn't be doing what I am now. I studied politics in fact, but in my first year I got involved in the student radio station. It was really good fun, so the next summer I applied to the local BBC station and got a job as a research assistant. The guy I was working for then got me a slot on a Sunday show, and when I graduated I became a full-time DJ there. I think that's the great thing about university: there are so many opportunities to explore different interests, and if you don't take advantage of them, you probably won't find out what it is you really want to do in life.
Interviewer	Edward, you trained and qualified as a doctor. How on earth did you go from that to being a comedian?
Edward	Well, I was doing my rounds in the hospital and a TV producer, who happened to be a patient, heard me crack a joke. He laughed so much, it made him better instantly and he signed me up for a TV series there and then … No, I can see you want a serious answer. It would have been nice if it had happened that way. What actually happened was that I kind of lost my confidence as a doctor. If I had carried on, I would probably be still working in a hospital, but I'd be very unhappy. So, I just stopped and started doing stand-up comedy in clubs. It was very tough at first.
Interviewer	So, Andrew, what did you study at college and how did it help you in what you do now?
Andrew	A lot of entrepreneurs like me tend either not to go to college, or if they go, then they drop out before they graduate. I think that's because, well, certainly it's true in my case, if they were more academic types, they would probably have followed a more conventional career path and be doctors or lawyers or something like that now. I wasn't very successful at school and never made it to university. I had to prove my worth in some other way. So, I started my own publishing company and I've never looked back.

> **Answers**
>
> | | University degree | Current job |
> | --- | --- | --- |
> | Susan | Politics | DJ at local (BBC) radio station |
> | Edward | Medicine | Comedian |
> | Andrew | didn't go | Entrepreneur/Director of a publishing company |

Exercise 3 CD1/26

- Play the recording again. Ask students to complete the sentences.
- Check the meaning and pronunciation of the missing words.

Books closed lead-in activity

Write on the board *If you could study anywhere in the world, where would you go and why?* Ask students to think of their answer, tell a partner, then tell the class. Discuss interesting responses.

Extra activity

Ask students if they can guess what the following superstars studied at college (answers in brackets): Brad Pitt (journalism); Tiger Woods (economics); Julia Roberts (veterinary science); Madonna (modern dance).

Answers
1 first; got involved 2 applied to; research assistant 3 graduated; full-time 4 actually; lost; confidence 5 stopped; started; tough 6 successful at; made it 7 own publishing; looked back

Exercise 4

■ Ask students to work in pairs to discuss the questions. Discuss as a class.

Answers
1 There are so many opportunities to explore different interests. 2 He realised he had lost his confidence as a doctor and would be unhappy if he continued. 3 They tend not to go or drop out, probably because they are not academic.

Grammar: conditionals

Exercise 5

■ Ask students to read the rules, complete the examples and check in pairs.

Answers
boils; will give; would buy; won; had passed; would be

Grammar note
Point out that choosing between first and second conditional is often about whether you see the possibility as real/likely or unreal/unlikely (for example, *If I see him, I'll give him the message* = there's a good chance of seeing him because he goes to my school, whereas, *If I knew Paul, I'd give him the message* = there's no real chance of giving him the message because the speaker has no idea who Paul is).

Mixed conditionals are used when the condition is past (*If I'd worked hard when I was young, …*) but the result is present (*… I'd have a good job now*), or when the condition is present (*If you were a better player …*) but the result is past (*… you would have been on the team*).

■ Refer students to the Grammar Reference on page 151.

Exercise 6

■ Ask students to work in pairs to identify form and meaning.
■ In feedback, ask students to say what use each sentence is expressing.

Answers
1 Mixed 2 First 3 Third 4 Mixed 5 Zero 6 Mixed

Exercise 7

■ Ask students to complete the sentences then check their answers in pairs.

Answers
2 you were not so; would not have got 3 I hadn't sold; wouldn't have to travel 4 he hadn't saved; wouldn't be able to afford 5 wouldn't be; hadn't won

Speaking

Exercise 8

■ Give students a moment to read through the questions and think of things to say. Tell them to make notes if they wish.
■ Ask students to discuss the questions in pairs or small groups.

Extra activity

Extend exercise 7 by getting students to write other situations which they then hand to a partner to change into a mixed conditional.

Or, write these situations on the board for students to write conditional sentences about: *I always want to succeed so I was upset when the university rejected me. (If I didn't always want to succeed, I wouldn't have been so upset when the university rejected me.); I broke my leg when I was 14 so I am not playing football now. (If I hadn't broken my leg when I was 14, I would still be playing (or play) football now.); You still feel sick because you haven't taken the medicine. (If you had taken the medicine, you wouldn't still feel (or be feeling) sick.)*

Career paths

Vocabulary and pronunciation: specialists

Exercise 1

- Ask students to work in pairs to add the suffixes.
- Check meaning by asking, e.g., *Who studies animals/ideas/old facts, etc?*

Answers
1 scientist 2 geographer 3 historian 4 biologist 5 psychologist 6 mathematician
7 philosopher 8 musician 9 zoologist

Exercise 2 CD1/27

- Ask students to listen and check. Then ask them to work in pairs to mark the strong stress in the words.
- Play the recording again for students to check where the stress is and answer the question. You could ask students to repeat the words.

Answers
Adding the suffix *–er* or *–ist* doesn't usually change word stress. Adding the suffix *–ian* moves the stress onto the syllable that goes before *–ian*.

Pronunciation note
Note the stress on these words: science scientist; geography geographer; biology biologist; psychology psychologist; philosophy philosopher; zoology zoologist

Note the shifting stress on words ending with *–ian*: history historian; mathematics mathematician; music musician

Reading

Exercise 3

- Ask students to look at the photo and answer the questions. Then ask students to read and check answers. Let students check in pairs before discussing as a class.

Answers
1 A herpetologist studies amphibians and reptiles, e.g. snakes, frogs and crocodiles.
2 For the job you need a BSc and a PhD in zoology and some practical training.

Pronunciation note
Note the pronunciation: *herpetologist* /ˈhɜː(r)p/ˈtɒlədʒɪst/

Exercise 4

- Ask students to read through the options carefully and answer any questions they are sure of. Check unknown words in the task.
- Ask students to read the text again and choose the correct options. Let students check their answers in pairs before checking as a class.

Answers
1 B 2 D 3 C 4 A

Vocabulary note
slash = cut (forest); *slither* = move like a snake; *virulent* = powerful, spreading quickly; *unspoilt* = unchanged by humans; *accumulated* = gradually collected; *a pit* = a deep hole

---

Books closed lead-in activity

Ask students to think about what qualities, skills and knowledge are required to do their dream job. When they are ready, ask students to tell their partner. Then ask a few individuals to tell the class.

Extra activity

Ask students to think of other jobs ending with these suffixes: *geology – geologist; statistics – statistician; physics – physicist; chemistry – chemist; engineering – engineer.*

Extra activity

Practise collocations and idioms from the text by asking students to think of personal examples for the following: *an unspoilt place, a passion that bloomed early, something that isn't your cup of tea, an endangered species, something you have never grown out of.*

Speaking

Exercise 5

■ Ask students to work in pairs or small groups to discuss the questions.

> **Example answers**
> She uses her university education for knowledge about different species and their habitats and behaviour.
>
> Through experience she has probably learned how to handle reptiles, how to travel and behave in different countries and habitats, and what to do in a difficult situation.

Exercise 6

■ Ask students to work in pairs to choose a vocational job and discuss it. You could elicit and list some jobs on the board first to get students started (electrical engineer, plumber, carpenter, care assistant, etc).

> **Example answers (hairdresser)**
> **Knowledge:** different types of hair, how it grows, why it falls out
> **Hard skills:** cutting hair, washing hair, hygiene
> **Soft skills:** talking to customers (making small talk, sympathising, showing interest), persuading customers to buy products

Exercise 7

■ Ask students to read the text and answer question 1. Let them check their answer in pairs before discussing as a class.

■ Discuss questions 2 and 3 as a class. Encourage students to talk about their plans and aspirations.

> **Answers**
> **1** Vocational degrees are necessary for a wide range of serious jobs; the economy needs people with these skills; vocational students often establish their own businesses; employers want employees with practical skills **2** and **3** Students' own answers

> **Vocabulary note**
> *look down our noses at* = consider something to be of less value or importance; *the job at hand* = the job currently available

Extra activity

Write on the board: *explorer in the Amazon; astronaut; deep sea diver; fire fighter.* Ask students in pairs to decide which of these jobs they would like to do and what knowledge and skills they would need.

Talking about obligations

Books closed lead-in activity

Write on the board *Living at home* and *Living away from home*. Ask half the class (in pairs) to think of good things about living at home, and half the class to think of good things about living away. Find out which half has the longer list.

Speaking: discussing student accommodation

Exercise 1

- Ask students to read the fact and discuss the question as a class.

> **Culture note**
> Most students in the UK choose the university that offers the course they would most like to do, or choose a university like Oxford because of the prestige it brings from studying there, or choose a big city university because of the lifestyle it offers. Living close to home is often low on the list of priorities. However, in recent years, the number of students choosing to live at home in order to have less debt has been rising.

Exercise 2

- Ask students to look at the photo and discuss the question in pairs. Build up a list of impressions on the board.

> **Example answers**
> The kitchen looks as if it's a good place to meet and talk to other students. I think I'd enjoy living there because I think it's important that you have the chance to be with other students and not just spend all your time alone in your bedroom.

> **Culture note**
> **Halls of residence** are purpose-built blocks where students can live together. They are usually on a campus with facilities such as a sports hall and shop nearby. Rooms may be individual or shared between two. There are separate shared kitchens and shower blocks and, often, a communal dining area where regular meals are served.

Listening: giving advice to students

Exercise 3 CD1/28

- Ask, *What is Freshers' Week? What sort of events take place during Freshers' Week, do you think?*
- Ask students to look at the headings in pairs and predict what the students might say for each.
- Play the recording. Students listen and match speakers to headings. Let students check their answers in pairs before discussing as a class.

Audioscript

Student 1	Hello to you all. Welcome to the university and welcome to Freshers' Week. As you know, Freshers' Week is the week when you get acquainted with the university and its facilities, and of course, with your fellow students. It's your chance to settle in and find your feet without the distraction of having to go to lectures or study. So, please make the most of it – you won't get a week like this again.
Student 2	… Now, first, I'd like to say a few words about university life in general. Now for most of you this will be the first time you've left home and you'll no doubt be feeling a bit nervous. But what you ought to remember is that everybody is in the same boat. This is your big chance to make new friends. So it's up to you to get out there and join in with the activities on offer.
Student 3	I'd like to say a few words about joining in with communal life in the halls of residence: for many of you, this week will be the first time that you have to cook for yourself, where you're expected to do your own shopping and washing. Most of you are probably not used to living with people outside your own family. So some advice here: you will find it easier to get along with your flatmates if they don't have to constantly wash up your dirty dishes, tidy up your mess or throw your mouldy food out of the fridge. And they will find it easier not to fall out with you if you don't play your favourite music at full blast when they're trying to study. I'm sure that most of you will settle in really

quickly, but with communal living, it requires a bit of give and take: it's your job to ensure that you behave correctly, but you should also try to put up with certain things within reason.

Student 4   Now on the subject of studying … Unlike school, you won't have a full timetable and you won't be required to go to lectures all the time. On the contrary, there will be mornings or afternoons, even days in some timetables, where you won't have to attend lectures. This is the time when you're supposed to be studying, of course. But experience tells us that many students find it difficult to plan their time and use it effectively. As you might know it can be very easy to waste a whole day playing games on the internet. But it's up to you to organise your time. If you find you can't do that alone, then you must contact a member of staff or somebody in the students' union for help.

Student 5   Right, I think that's all we have to say on the practical stuff, so let me come now to what you've all been waiting for – what's happening this week during Freshers' Week. Well, let me start with tonight and . . .

Answers
1 D 2 F 3 C 4 A 5 E

Exercise 4    CD1/28

- Ask students to read through the sentences and see if they can work out or remember which words go in which spaces.
- Play the recording again. Students listen and complete the sentences. Let them check in pairs before discussing as a class.

Answers
1 ought to 2 it's up to you to 3 have to 4 expected to 5 don't have to 6 it's your job to
7 should 8 required to 9 supposed to 10 must

> **Grammar note**
> Expressing obligation: *have to, must, it's your job to, be required to*
>
> Expressing advice: *ought to, expected to* = this is what always happens, so it is almost an obligation in that people will be surprised or annoyed if you don't do this; *supposed to* = this is what most people do, so it implies you are strongly advised to do it
>
> Expressing no obligation: *it's up to you* = it's your choice; *don't have to*

Pronunciation: *to*

Exercise 5    CD1/29

- Play the recording. Ask students to listen and choose the correct option.

Answers
1 /tə/ 2 It is pronounced /tuː/ before a vowel – here it links to the vowel with a /w/ sound.

Exercise 6    CD1/29

- Ask students to listen and repeat, paying attention to the weak pronunciation of *to*.

Speaking
Exercise 7

- Divide students into pairs. Ask them to decide which role to play and to find and read the relevant information in the back of the Student's Book.
- Give students time to prepare what to say. When they are ready, ask students to act out the conversations. Monitor and listen for errors and good use of the language of advice and obligation.

Extra activity

Ask students to categorise the phrases in the box into three sections: obligations, advice and no obligations (see Grammar note).

Extra activity

Ask students in pairs to write a list of advice and obligations for students in one of the following university situations: 1 In a lecture hall; 2 In a gym or sports hall; 3 In a swimming pool; 4 In a canteen or dining hall.

Ask some pairs to read out their list or share their list with a different pair.

Writing: applying to a British university

Exercise 8

- Lead in by asking, *When applying for a university place what do you have to do?* Elicit *fill in an application form, take an entrance exam, write a personal statement,* etc.
- Ask students to read the guidelines carefully. Ask, *What could you write under each heading? What do international students have to write?*
- Ask students to read the personal statement quickly and tell a partner what they think of it. Have a brief class discussion.

> **Example answers**
> I think it's a good statement. The writer includes all of the things listed in the tips and he relates his experiences to the things they have taught him. The last paragraph is a bit abstract, though. I think he could give more concrete reasons.

> **Vocabulary note**
> *keen interest* = very enthusiastic interest

Exercise 9

- Ask students to work in pairs to categorise the expressions.

> **Answers**
> **1 Talking about interests and skills:** I have a keen interest in; I consider myself to be; I find the sport very rewarding; I enjoy meeting people
>
> **2 Talking about past experiences:** My A level history has allowed me to; I was required to; For this I had to be; This has improved; I have learned to
>
> **3 Talking about future plans and expectations:** I would very much like to; I am looking forward to; I am optimistic that; I believe that; I am confident that

Exercise 10

- Lead in by asking students to make notes under each of the headings in exercise 9. Elicit a few ideas to get students started. Then let them work in pairs to come up with ideas. However, make sure students are writing their own personal notes.
- Ask students to follow the instructions to write their own personal statements.

Exercise 11

- Ask students to exchange and comment on each other's statements.

Extra activity

Tell students in pairs to exchange their personal statements, then to think about questions they can ask about the information in the statements.

Students then role play an interview between a university admissions officer and a prospective student.

Books closed lead-in
activity

Write on the board
University life. Ask students
in pairs to think of as
many different aspects of
university life as they can.
Brainstorm the ideas, writing
them on the board.

Speaking

Exercise 1

- Ask students to read the information in the graph carefully. Then ask them to work in pairs to discuss the questions.

Answers
1 The most important aspects are meeting new friends and improving their career prospects. The least important aspects are getting away from their parents and having their own money. **2** Students' own answers **3** Students' own answers

Vocabulary note
stretch oneself intellectually = try to do difficult and demanding intellectual things; *mix with people* = meet lots of different people socially

Reading

Exercise 2

- Ask students, *What do you know about the Erasmus programme?* Elicit any general knowledge from the class.
- Ask students to read the text and answer the questions. Let them check their answers in pairs before discussing as a class.

Answers
1 The Erasmus programme is an exchange programme for higher education.
2 Teachers and students. **3** It allows students to study at a different European university/ gives many EU students their first chance to live and experience life abroad.

Vocabulary and culture note
flagship = most important, leading or high profile

Erasmus stands for **E**uropean **R**egion **A**ction **S**cheme for the **M**obility of **U**niversity **S**tudents. The programme began in 1987 and forms a major part of the EU lifelong learning programme.

Erasmus was a Dutch classical scholar of the late 15th and early 16th centuries.

Exercise 3

- Ask students to work in pairs to discuss the questions and complete the notes. In feedback, build up a list of benefits and problems on the board.

Answers
Benefits
Career: experience abroad looks good on CV; Personal development: chance to be independent, meet new people and learn new skills; Friends and contacts: new friends, future work contacts; Other: learn a new language
Problems
University system: different system, possible paperwork; Language: difficult to study in a foreign language and to make friends when you don't speak the language properly; Cultural differences: ways of doing things may be different; Things you might miss: family, friends, food

Exercise 4

- Ask students to work in pairs. Tell them to decide which of the two texts they would each like to read. Then ask them to read the texts and complete the notes.

Answers

A

Name: Aldo Keller **Home university:** University of Munich, Germany

Exchange university: Liverpool University, UK **Subject:** computer science

Positive aspects of exchange: new challenges, responsibility, will open lots of doors in future career, life experience (adapting to new culture, meeting people)

Negative aspects: not enough support and personal contact with tutor, missed family and friends, felt homesick, high cost of living

B

Name: Ellen Jameson **Home university:** Dublin City University, Ireland

Exchange university: Academy of Fine Arts, Milan **Subject:** graphic arts

Positive aspects of exchange: people at university very helpful, made lots of useful contacts, helped to get a better degree, positive factor in job interviews, helped her grow up and become more independent

Negative aspects: course in Italian (difficult, struggled with language), spent a lot of time with other British students (not good for language)

Vocabulary note
hands-on approach = practical approach; *all in all* = when you consider everything; *struggled with* = found it difficult to do

---

Exercise 5

■ Ask students to work in pairs to exchange information and answer the questions.

Answer
1 Hard to say – both experiences were largely positive 2 Students' own answers

Vocabulary
Exercise 6

■ Ask students to research the texts and find the verbs. Let them compare answers in pairs before discussing as a class.

Answers
1 getting 2 experienced 3 taking 4 gained 5 adapt 6 made 7 draw 8 put

Exercise 7

■ Ask students to discuss the questions in pairs or small groups.

Extra activity

Ask students to role play interviews with Aldo and Ellen about their experiences.

Extra activity

Ask students to find collocations with *do*, *make*, *get* and *take* in the text related to studying at university. Then ask them to think of other collocations for the same verbs. For example: *do a course, get a degree, take a degree in, get to know people, make friends, do homework,* etc.

Applying for a student loan

Books closed lead-in activity

Ask, *How much does it cost to maintain you for a week?* Ask students to work in pairs to work out how much money is spent by themselves (on clothes, books, etc.) and by their parents (on food, school, etc.) in a week.

Extra activity

Ask students to find or think of other words connected with money: *fee, bill, cash, change, waste, wallet, purse, cost, broke, rich, poor, wealthy*.

Listening and speaking

Exercise 1

■ Ask students to look at the picture, and ask what the two different meanings of *afford* are in the questions. Ask students how they would answer the questions.

■ Ask students to work in pairs to make a list. Build up a list of costs on the board.

Example answers
tuition fees, rent, food, travel, books, stationery, clothes, computer or laptop

> **Vocabulary note**
> *I can't afford it* means *I don't have enough money to study*, but *I can't afford not to study* means *If I don't study, I will lose out financially or in other ways in the future*.

Exercise 2

■ Ask students to complete the sentences. Do the first as a class to get students started. Let them check answers in pairs before discussing as a class.

Answers
1 loan 2 money 3 savings 4 credit 5 charge 6 debt 7 repayments 8 income 9 expenses

> **Vocabulary and pronunciation note**
> Note: you *lend money **to** someone* (a loan); but you *borrow money **from** someone* (a debt).
> Note the pronunciation: *debt* /det/; *income* /'ɪnkʌm/; *expenses* /ɪk'spensɪs/

Exercise 3 CD1/30

■ Give students a moment to read through the statements. Check vocabulary.

■ Play the recording. Ask students to listen and choose true or false. Let students check their answers in pairs before discussing as a class.

Audioscript

Student	I've read the literature and I think I understand most of the terms. But there are a couple of things I'm still unsure about.
Bank adviser	Please, go ahead. I'll do my best to answer.
Student	Well, firstly, is there a limit on what I can borrow? For, example if we agree a loan for a certain amount and then find I can't cover all my expenses, can I come back and borrow more?
Bank adviser	That depends on how much you've borrowed in the first place. There is an overall limit. For tuition fees, it's whatever your university is charging, and for living costs, it's fixed at £4,000 a year.
Student	OK, that's clear enough. And when do I have to start repayments?
Bank adviser	You start in April of the year following graduation. But you only start paying the loan back if you are earning more than £15,000 a year.
Student	And how much interest will I pay on the loan?
Bank adviser	Interest is fixed at four per cent.

Answers
1 True 2 False (for living costs) 3 False (April following graduation) 4 True 5 False (four per cent)

> **Vocabulary note**
> Note the collocations: *charge fees, cover expenses, pay back a loan, earn a salary*.

Exercise 4

- Divide students into pairs and ask them to decide who is to play which role.
- Give students a few minutes to prepare. When they are ready, ask students to act out the role play. Monitor and note errors and good language use.
- Ask fast finishers to change roles and repeat the role play.

Extra activity

Ask students to prepare in pairs: two bank managers together, and two students together. Then ask the 'students' to stand up and visit three different 'banks'. At the end, ask the bank managers if they are prepared to lend money to the students they interviewed, and ask the students which bank they have decided to borrow from.

6

Learning from the past

Books closed lead-in activity

Write the word *History* on the board and ask students to offer comments. Encourage them to speak about whether they find it interesting and, if so, what periods in particular. Ask why they do or don't find history interesting.

Let's get started

Exercise 1

■ Ask the students to read the four quotations and comment on them. Encourage them to discuss their different points of view in groups

Vocabulary and speaking

Exercise 2

■ Ask students to match the periods and dates in pairs.
■ Elicit answers and any information they know about each period.

> **Answers**
> 1 The Stone Age 2 The Bronze Age 3 The Iron Age 4 First agricultural settlements
> 5 Earliest civilisations

Vocabulary and listening

Books closed lead-in activity

Ask students to describe some of the natural features of the Earth (e.g. mountain ranges, deserts, oceans, ice, volcanoes, lakes) and to say if there are any in their country.

Exercise 1

- Ask students to discuss the questions in pairs.
- Elicit responses from the whole class and discuss the answers given.

Answers
Continents: Europe, Asia, Australasia, Antarctica, Africa, North America, South America

Exercise 2

- Ask students to make sentences individually, then check in pairs.
- Elicit sentence answers from the whole class. You could write some or all of them on the board in preparation for Exercise 3.

Example answers
The Earth was bombarded by meteorites.
The pieces of land made up a supercontinent.
The whole planet was covered with ice.
The land split into several pieces.

Exercise 3  CD2/02

- Play the recording while students listen and check their sentences.
- Ask for comments and corrections from the class.

Audioscript

The story of how the Earth became the way it is today is a very dramatic one. The geological history of our planet is very violent, and many of the events that happened in prehistoric times are impossible to imagine – far more catastrophic than anything we humans have ever witnessed. The newly-formed Earth was constantly bombarded by meteorites. Some scientists believe that a very large object from space – possibly a young planet very much like our own – hit the Earth, breaking off a large part of the crust to create the moon. The Earth itself was constantly changing due to volcanic activity. Much of the Earth was made up of molten rock at this early stage, and temperatures were immense. There was, of course, no life on the planet at this time. Many of the events that took place in the Earth's first billion years would have destroyed all life anyway.

Over the next three or four billion years, the planet cooled, developed oceans, got hotter, got colder … the whole planet was covered with ice, it got hotter again, and was covered with ice again … several times. We also gained an atmosphere, lost it, and gained another one. Slowly, over time, the surface of the Earth was roughly divided between a giant ocean and one huge land mass, or supercontinent. Then the movement under the surface of the Earth created what we call rifting. Rifting is what happened when the land separated. It split into two, three, four pieces … and more. And it formed something similar to the continental land masses we know today. But the movement continued and we know that the land was re-formed as a supercontinent several times. This is the process we call continental collision. When the land masses were pushed back together, there was so much force that they often created mountains at the point where the two coasts met. Now, I mentioned that this happened several times, and we have names for the supercontinents that were formed by the collisions – Rodinia, Columbia and Pannotia are three examples that we know most about. The last time this happened was about 300 million years ago and the supercontinent was called Pangaea. Pangaea broke up and rifted into Laurasia, which then became North America and Eurasia, and Gondwana, which became the other continents.

Exercise 4  CD2/02

- Ask students to read the sentences carefully to focus their listening.
- Play the recording twice while they complete the sentences.
- Ask them to check in pairs.
- Elicit the answers as complete sentences from the whole class.

Example answers
1 violent 2 changing 3 destroyed 4 an atmosphere 5 splits 6 pushed 7 supercontinents
8 North America

Exercise 5 CD2/03

- Ask students to examine the diagram very carefully so that they understand what they need to write.
- Play the recording twice to allow them to complete the timeline.
- Ask them to check their answers in pairs.
- Elicit answers from the class.
- Play the recording once more for students to check their answers again.

Audioscript

Of course, tracking the movements of early humans is an almost impossible task, and don't forget that there is still some doubt that Homo sapiens began in just one place … But here is what we believe at the moment. We think that Homo sapiens – the modern human species – originated around 200,000 years ago in Africa. We now think that there were two major waves of migration out of Africa. The first big one seems to have been about 125,000 years ago, but we know more about the migration of 70,000 years ago. And what else do we know? We know that the route chosen out of Africa was probably across the Red Sea into the modern-day Arab World. These first migrants went to the Near East and eventually, after many years, went on to South Asia by about 50,000 years ago and Australia by 40,000 years ago. I should point out here that the world didn't quite look the way it does today. We believe that the crossing of the Red Sea would have been a lot easier due to the much lower sea levels. And the passage into Australia was a lot easier than it would be today because the low sea levels meant that there was a large land mass – sometimes known as the lost continent of Sunda – which helped close the distance across the sea. Anyway, at the same time – that is, 40,000 years ago – a separate group reached Europe. Here again, the lower sea level meant that Great Britain was a part of continental Europe – joined by what we call a land bridge. And it was another land bridge, this time joining Siberia and Alaska, that allowed people to travel to North America. We can't be sure of the date, but we believe this was around 15,000 years ago and that they travelled down, quite slowly, through the continent of North America and then South America, until they reached the furthest point south around 11,000 years ago.

Answers
1 200,000 2 Africa 3 70,000 4 Asia 5 40,000; Europe 6 North America 7 11,000

Reading
Exercise 6

- Ask students to guess the meanings of the highlighted words individually, then check in pairs.
- Elicit answers from the whole class.

Answers
evidence: information that leads you to understand something
settlers: people who moved to an area to live there
succession: a series, one after the other
trace: find by looking carefully
via: by way of, across
ascertain: understand and know
jigsaw puzzle: a puzzle where you put small pieces together to make a picture
genetic make-up: the elements that complete the genetic character of someone
chromosome: one of the elements that determine our sex
re-evaluate: to think about something again in a different way

Exercise 7

- Ask students to complete the sentences individually, then check in pairs.
- Elicit some answers from the class.

Example answers
1 of the succession of ice ages 2 present-day Spain and Portugal or the Middle East
3 were the ones who had been driven out by the Ice Age 4 the Romans, the Angles, the
Jutes, the Saxons, the Normans and the Vikings 5 help scientists to understand the history
of the British Isles

Pronunciation note
Note the stress: suc<u>ce</u>ssion, ascer<u>tain</u>, ge<u>ne</u>tic, e<u>va</u>luate, o<u>ri</u>ginating, i<u>den</u>tity, de<u>scen</u>dents, in<u>va</u>sion

Grammar: gender-neutral pronouns

Exercise 8

- Ask students to complete the rule individually, then check in pairs.
- Elicit answers from the class.

Answers
their, they, them

- Refer students to the Grammar Reference on page 152.

Speaking

Exercise 9

- Ask the whole class to have a discussion about each of the questions.

Books closed lead-in activity

Ask students what they know about the Roman Empire. Elicit any information you can from the class about when it existed, why it declined, why it was important, what area it covered, and so on.

Speaking and vocabulary

Exercise 1

■ Discuss the questions as a class. List their answers on the board.

Example answers
Aztecs, Maya, Persians, Chinese, Japanese, Egyptians, Romans, Greeks, Indian

Exercise 2

■ Ask students to complete the table individually, then check in pairs. Encourage them to explain their answers to each other.
■ Elicit answers from the whole class.

Reading

Exercise 3

■ Ask students to read the questions before they read the texts to focus their reading.
■ They should then write 1 or 2 in each box, depending upon which civilisation it refers to.
■ They should do this individually, and then check in pairs.
■ Elicit answers from the whole class.

Answers
1 1 2 2 3 1 4 2 5 2 6 1 7 2

Vocabulary note
devise = have an idea for something and design it; *irrigate* = water land in order to help crops grow; *adopt* = begin a new plan or attitude; *cultivate* = prepare land and grow crops on it; *surplus* = more than is needed; *sophisticated* = refined and complex; *bizarre* = odd or unusual

Grammar: verb patterns with gerund and infinitive

Exercise 4

■ Ask students to read the passage and answer the question individually, then check in pairs.
■ Elicit answers from the whole class.

Answers
liked (to wrestle), weren't allowed (to sleep)
liked (sailing), don't mind (doing), go (riding)
expected (women to carry out), help (their wives to do)
made (the slaves do)
Like can be used with the infinitive with *to* and the gerund

Exercise 5

■ Ask students to complete the sentences individually, then check in pairs.
■ Elicit the answers from the class, having one student read the original sentence and another the paraphrased version.

Answers
1 me help with the cooking 2 me to sew 3 nagging about tidying up 4 me to learn to cook

■ Refer students to the Grammar Reference on page 152.

Exercise 6

■ Read the sentences with the class and have them answer the questions.

> **Answers**
> 1 is about a memory in the past 2 is about (not) forgetting to do something

Exercise 7

■ Ask students to choose the meanings individually, then check in pairs.
■ Elicit the answers from the class.

> **Answers**
> 1 b 2 b 3 b 4 b

Exercise 8

■ Ask students to complete the sentences truthfully.
■ Elicit different answers for each one from the class.

Listening and grammar: *have/get something done*

Exercise 9   CD2/04

■ Ask students to read the sentences first, to focus their listening.
■ Play the recording once or twice for them to complete the sentences.
■ They can check their answers in pairs.
■ Elicit the answers from the class as complete sentences.

Audioscript

Of course, like today, society in ancient Greece was not the same for everybody, and a lot of facts might be blurred by time, but we are able to say some things with a fair amount of certainty. At home, the men were treated with great respect – they didn't need to do much. For example, during dinner, they had their food brought to them by slaves – and they just enjoyed themselves, really! But the women often had an easy life too – they had all the household jobs done by the slaves. They even had the water brought to the house by slaves – a job that women and young girls had to do in other civilisations. For some of the time in Ancient Greece, men didn't have their hair cut if they were going to go into battle. Long hair was considered fashionable and a sign of power. Slaves, on the other hand, usually had their heads shaved.

> **Answers**
> 1 their food 2 done; brought 3 cut 4 their heads

Exercise 10   CD2/04

■ Read the gapped rules with the class, so they understand what to listen for.
■ Play the recording again.
■ Elicit answers from the class.

> **Answers**
> something; done
> by

■ Refer students to the Grammar Reference on page 153.

Exercise 11

■ Refer students to the Grammar Reference on page 153.
■ Ask students to discuss the questions in pairs.
■ Elicit answers from the class, and discuss them more widely.

Unlocking the secrets of the past

Books closed lead-in activity

Ask students what they know about archaeology. Ask what archaeologists do and if students can think of any examples of archeological work locally, nationally or internationally.

Vocabulary and pronunciation: prefixes

Exercise 1

■ Ask the class to read the words in the box and answer the question.

> **Answer**
> It makes them have the opposite meaning.

> **Pronunciation note**
> Note the stress: interesting – uninteresting, moral – immoral, proper – improper, responsible – irresponsible, logical – illogical, possible – impossible, replaceable – irreplaceable, direct – indirect

Exercise 2   CD2/05

■ Ask students to repeat all the words in the list chorally and individually and to note where the syllable stress is.
■ Then ask them to work individually, adding the correct prefix to make each word negative.
■ Let them check in pairs.
■ Elicit the answers from the class, without saying which is correct. You could list their suggestions on the board.
■ Play the recording for them to listen and check.
■ Then play it again for them to repeat chorally and individually.

> **Answers**
> 1 illegible 2 unpredictable 3 impolite 4 illegal 5 unbelievable 6 immature 7 insufficient 8 inadequate 9 irregular 10 irrelevant

Exercise 3

■ Ask students to complete the text individually, then check in pairs.
■ Elicit the answers as complete sentences.

> **Answers**
> 1 uninteresting 2 improper 3 illegal 4 irresponsible 5 impolite 6 unbelievable

Reading

Exercise 4

■ Ask the students to find the words and suggest meanings as a whole class.

> **Answers**
> **impractical:** difficult to do in some way
> **inadequate:** not suitable, or without enough quality to do something
> **imprecise:** not precise enough
> **incapable:** unable to do something
> **inaccurate:** not accurate enough, wrong
> **unlikely:** surprising, unusual
> **irreparable:** destroyed so badly that it cannot be repaired
> **undiscovered:** not found yet

Extra activity

Ask students to choose five different words from exercises 1 and 2, and make a sentence for each one. They should exchange these with a partner to see if they are using the words correctly. Discuss some of their sentences with the whole class.

Exercise 5

■ Ask students to read through the questions then read the text.
■ When they have answered the questions individually and noted down their answers, ask them to discuss them in pairs.
■ Elicit ideas from the whole class and encourage further discussion.

Example answers
1 It relied on human judgement and random sampling. 2 shapes underground caused by human activity, such as building 3 they cannot say precisely which metal is underground 4 the fact that it decays at a fixed rate 5 It can only be used on organic material, and cannot be used on anything older than 60,000 years. 6 It is used to see what lies below the surface, without damaging the object or painting. 7 The ruins absorbed more water in winter and so were more visible. 8 that new technology will help us discover many new sites of archaeological interest in the future

Exercise 6

■ Ask students to choose the best meanings individually, then check in pairs.
■ Elicit answers from the whole class.

Answers
1 B 2 A 3 A 4 B 5 B 6 B 7 A 8 B 9 A 10 B

Books closed lead-in activity

Ask students what historical programmes they have watched on television in the past six months. Ask them if they like them and why, and what the best one they have ever seen was and why.

Extra activity

Ask students to discuss their notes from Exercise 2. Then elicit answers from the whole class.

Speaking

Exercise 1

- Ask students to read the three programme previews individually.
- Ask the class to comment on the questions.

> **Vocabulary note**
> *listed buildings* = buildings protected from demolition or alteration because of their special historical or architectural interest; *disturb* = disarrange or muddle; *struggle* = work or strive; *labour-saving devices* = equipment reducing the amount of work or effort needed to carry out a task; *spectrum* = a range or scale

Listening

Exercise 2   CD2/06

- Play the recording and ask students to listen and make short notes on the four areas.

Audioscript

Man 1	As a history teacher myself, I have to say that anything that takes us away from the old-style teaching that we suffered … well it has to be a good thing.
Woman 1	I think 'suffered' is the word … I remember hating history at school. But more significantly, I don't remember much else. All that memorising … all that agonising over dates and dry, boring facts … and for what? I'm sorry to say that I really remember very little about what they taught us.
Man 2	I agree with you both. I think I learned more from an hour-long documentary on television than from anything I learned in school.
Woman 1	It's true, I think. There's an immediacy to television. And it's what children relate to. Programme makers know how to engage the viewer. It's what they're paid to do. So they do a good job.
Man 1	Well, don't get me wrong, but it's what history teachers are paid to do as well.
Woman 1	And I'm sure you do an excellent job. But times have changed. We've had good-quality television for decades now. And besides, it's what children want – so they're bound to show more interest.
Man 2	I think things have moved on even further. I think the Internet is now the preferred medium for young people. And there's an awful lot of information out there. Just with the click of a mouse.
Woman 2	I'm a bit concerned about the standards of what's on the Internet. I mean anyone can post information on a site. That doesn't make it accurate. In my experience, there's a lot of rubbish written on the Internet about history.
Man 1	Sad but true. I often find that students have been misinformed because a website's inaccurate.
Woman 2	If you ask me, it's a great resource but you need to know where to look. I think students could use it as long as they've got guidance, you know, from their teacher, about where to look.
Man 2	That's a good point. And I think we could apply the same to museums. I mean, museums are great but you need to know what to look at or you won't get anything out of the experience.
Woman 2	Well I think museums are beginning to realise that for themselves. I went to the new archaeological museum last week and I was really impressed. You know, you go in there and they offer you an mp3 player as your own personal guide … You can still hire a real living human guide if you want, but who needs them now?
Man 1	Well, if you wanted to ask a question …
Woman 2	Yes, good point. But what I wanted to say was … it really is a different experience these days. You have interactive exhibits and touch-sensitive screens … OK, we've had those for years … but you know what I mean.
Man 2	I went to a museum in Athens and it was very contemporary. You could take a kind of virtual reality tour of an ancient city … It was in Asia Minor … I mean I wouldn't say it was just like being there, but it was a good experience. I think it brings history to life when they use technology in that way.

Exercise 3 CD2/06

- Ask students to read through the sentences, to focus their listening.
- Play the recording once or twice while students complete the sentences.
- Ask them to check their answers in pairs.
- Elicit the answers as complete sentences.

Answers
1 I have to say that 2 I'm sorry to say that 3 Well, don't get me wrong, but 4 I'm a bit concerned about 5 In my experience 6 I often find that 7 If you ask me 8 I think

Speaking

Exercise 4

- Ask students to think about the three statements individually, then discuss them as a class.

Exercise 5

- Read the instructions and ideas with the class and make sure they understand the task.
- Ask them to work in groups of four to plan their course.

Writing: a review of a book or television programme

Exercise 6

- Read through the book types in the box with the class and elicit the differences between them.
- Ask students to answer the questions in pairs.

Exercise 7

- Ask students to match the parts of the book and descriptions individually, and then check in pairs.
- Elicit the answers from the class, having one student read the part of the book and another student give the definition.

Answers
1 d 2 f 3 a 4 b 5 c 6 e

Exercise 8

- Ask students to do this individually, then check with a partner.
- Elicit the answers as complete sentences.

Answers
1 series 2 aims 3 designed 4 present 5 appeal 6 aspects 7 style 8 make 9 engage
10 educate

Exercise 9

- Ask students to discuss the questions in pairs.
- Elicit ideas from the whole class and compare them.

Answers
1 a series of books called Horrible Histories 2 to teach young people history in an interesting and enjoyable way 3 the books deal with different aspects of history, the language is easy to understand, there are jokes, they engage and educate students
4 no 5 paragraph 1 – introduction; paragraph 2 – details about the books; paragraph 3 – TV series 6 yes

Extra activity

When students have completed their plan, have the groups make a presentation to the class about it. Each member of the group should present a part.

Exercise 10

- Read the instructions and the *Useful expressions* box with the class.
- Ask students to choose an educational book or television programme and write their reviews individually.
- When they have finished, ask them to swap reviews and give comments.
- Students amend their reviews based on the comments (this could be a homework activity).

Speaking and listening

Exercise 1

■ Ask the class to read the texts and answer the questions.

Exercise 2 🔊 CD2/07

■ Ask students to read the table and see what information is required.
■ Play the recording once or twice while students complete the details.
■ Let them check in pairs.
■ Elicit the answers from the whole class.

Audioscript

Speaker 1 I remember my dad struggling to get the car going in the mornings. He had one of those crank-handle things to get it started. Well it must have been hard work because I remember him being tired after doing that for a few minutes – and that's before he went to work! This would have been around 1960. He had a motorcycle too, and I remember that he spent a lot of time working on it. I have a very clear memory of the motorbike engine on the kitchen table because it was too cold and dark to work outside! I think he had to take the bus more than we would have liked!

Speaker 2 I remember my mother talking about life in the 1940s. She said she really loved living in a small town where everyone pretty much knew everyone else. She often told me that she used to like doing the shopping because it got her out of the house. She used to walk everywhere of course – they didn't have a car in those days, and anyway, my dad would be at work. She'd walk about two miles on a Friday to the grocer's. She always used to go to the same one because they used to deliver, which meant she could go and have her hair and her nails done and still be home before the groceries arrived! All that changed when she had us children, of course!

Speaker 3 I remember some time around the early 70s or perhaps the late 60s … the first colour television in our street was at my friend's house – everyone else still had a black and white one. So I used to be there all the time – I would watch everything with wide eyes because it was in colour and that was so new – it was magical! I remember a couple of trips to the theatre to see pantomimes or shows like that. And I remember going to the cinema very young too – in the mid 60s. But there was this thing called Saturday Morning Pictures. And all the kids in our neighbourhood used to go. We could pay a small amount of money or we got in to the cinema free if we took a bag of milk bottle tops made of aluminium foil. So we collected all our bottle tops so we didn't have to pay! I don't remember much about what we saw but I do remember shouting at the screen, so it must have been exciting!

Speaker 4 Well, I was a housewife in the 1960s and, really, it was a very nice life. My friends used to come round for coffee or I would go to their houses. We were a long way out of town so we had all these services. There was a mobile shop which came round twice a week … and a fishmonger who sold fresh fish out of the back of his van on a Friday. Of course, the milkman brought milk to the doorstep every day … oh and your newspapers were delivered by the paper boy. Then, there was a greengrocer who used to come round and sell fresh fruit and vegetables from the back of his lorry. We even had a mobile library which came round once a week. That meant you could change your books without going into town.

Speaker 5 Growing up in the fifties was not such a bad thing, I suppose. There wasn't a huge amount of money to go round, but I don't remember being hungry. I don't remember being bored either, which is strange because … well … compared to kids today, we had nothing in the way of toys to play with! I had a bike, which was my outdoor toy, I suppose. I certainly spent all my time on it in the summer. In the house, I just remember a few toy cars and an old train set – it really was old and I don't think it ever worked properly! I was allowed a comic a week, which I read from cover to cover. And I read books too … stories, encyclopaedias … anything I could get my hands on. But I have fond memories of my childhood.

Books closed lead-in activity

Ask students to get into pairs and tell each other something about their parents and their grandparents. Elicit a few things from the class.

Answers

	Period(s) discussed	Subject(s) discussed	Other key points
Speaker 1	around 1960	transport	his dad used a crank-handle to start the car; had a motorcycle; fixed it in the kitchen
Speaker 2	the 1940s	shopping	everyone knew each other; no car; got the groceries delivered
Speaker 3	the mid 60s the late 60s the early 70s	television cinema theatre	got in free with a bag of bottle tops
Speaker 4	the 1960s	services	had everything brought to the house, including milk, newspapers, groceries, fresh fruit and vegetables, fish and library books
Speaker 5	the 1950s	toys and childhood	had a bike and a train set and a few toy cars; used to read comics/anything

Exercise 3  CD2/07

- Ask students to read the sentences to see which parts they need to focus on when listening.
- Play the recording and let them answer. Then they check in pairs.
- Play it again, if necessary, for them to complete and correct their answers.
- Elicit answers from the whole class as complete sentences.

Answers
1 him being tired 2 working on it 3 got her out of the 4 used to go to 5 wide
6 shouting at the screen 7 were a long way out of 8 had a mobile library 9 to go round
10 nothing in the way of

Grammar: comparatives
Exercise 4

- Ask students to read the sentences to focus their reading, then to read the three texts to find the answers.
- They can then check in pairs.
- Elicit answers from the whole class.

Extra activity

Ask students to talk about some of the changes they have seen in media (e.g. TV, radio, music) in their lifetimes.

Answers
1 adventure stories and science fiction programmes on the radio 2 3D television programmes 3 television programmes 4 colour on television 5 comedies

Exercise 5

- Ask students to complete the rules individually, then check in pairs.
- Elicit the answers from the whole class as complete sentences.

> **Answers**
> -er
> more; less
> than
> as; as
> not
> better; worse
> nice; hotter

- Refer students to the Grammar Reference on page 153.

Speaking

Exercise 6

- Read through the questions and the *Useful expressions* box with the class, making sure they understand the task and the language.
- Ask students to work in pairs to complete the task.
- Circulate and monitor their production and give feedback at the end, with pronunciation practice and grammar work as necessary.

Writing

Exercise 7

- Ask students to do stages 1 and 2 of this exercise in class.
- For homework, students do stages 3 and 4.
- Students should then read their reports in groups and discuss what they found.

Putting the world on the map

Lead-in

Ask students when they last used a map. Ask what it was a map of and why they used it. Ask if they have an atlas at home and, if so, how often they use it.

Exercise 1

- Ask students to read the four sentences before they read the text.
- They can check in pairs when they have finished.
- Elicit answers from the class.

Answers
1 Mercator 2 Tharp 3 Vespucci 4 Ptolemy

Exercise 2

- Ask students to make sentences individually, then check in pairs.
- Elicit answers from the class as complete sentences.

Answers
1 c 2 d 3 b 4 a

Exercise 3

- Ask students to discuss the words in pairs or small groups and to guess which area is closest to Geography. Check answers as a class.
- Then students decide which area interests them most and why.

Find out more!

Do some research about an aspect of this topic which interests you, for example:
- mapping the sea floor
- geoliteracy
- plate tectonics

Look on the Internet and in books in the library. In particular, have a look at the National Geographic website: www.nationalgeographic.com

Units 5 and 6

Unit 5 Review

Ask students to complete the exercises in class or set the review for homework. After they have completed the exercises, students should evaluate their own performance, using the self-assessment box.

Answers
Exercise 1
1 best 2 campus 3 adapt 4 experiencing 5 practice 6 contacts 7 course
8 requirements

Exercise 2
1 Zoology; zoologist 2 Music; musician 3 Philosophy; philosopher

Exercise 3
1 The cafeteria is next to the main lecture hall, isn't it? 2 We don't have to give in our essay tomorrow, do we? 3 She asked us to read the whole chapter, didn't she? 4 The lecture hasn't already started, has it? 5 We'll get more information about the exams, won't we?

Exercise 4
1 wouldn't be; hadn't 2 would have got; would never have gone; hadn't 3 were; wouldn't have 4 wouldn't be; hadn't travelled 5 finds; will be

Exercise 5
1 loan 2 fees 3 expenses 4 afford 5 borrow 6 debts 7 owe 8 repayments
9 interest 10 income

Unit 6 Review

Answers
Exercise 1
1 bombarded 2 meteorites 3 continent 4 settlements 5 Stone 6 civilisations

Exercise 2
1 crops 2 invasion 3 monument 4 surface 5 destroyed 6 finds

Exercise 3
1 them 2 their 3 they 4 they 5 their 6 they 7 them 8 them

Exercise 4
1 doing 2 making 3 to take 4 to take 5 empty 6 being

Exercise 5
1 interesting than 2 more important 3 difficult as 4 better 5 nicer than

7

Important events

UNIT OVERVIEW

Topic	coming of age, special occasions, traditions and festivals
Reading	large families, traditions, national days, Dragon Boat festival
Listening	coming of age celebrations, people describing significant moments in growing up, important birthdays in the UK, describing traditions
Grammar	passive gerund and infinitive, passive reporting verbs
Function	choosing a present
Vocabulary	festivals, stages of life
Pronunciation	weak forms
Writing	attaining various legal rights, description of an event
Speaking	talking about important personal events, talking about weddings and marriage, comparing relationships in the past with nowadays, talking about the significance of festivals, presenting a proposal
Culture	how people celebrate

Let's get started

Books closed lead-in activity

Write *Important annual events* on the board and brainstorm as many events as you can from the students. Ask students to say which event in the year is most important for them.

Exercise 1

■ Ask students to work in pairs to discuss the questions. In feedback, have a whole-class debate.

> **Culture note**
> **Camarinas** is a coastal town, famous for fishing and lace-making, on the coast of Spain's north-western province, Galicia.

Exercise 2

■ Ask students to work in pairs to discuss the quotations.

> **Culture note**
> **Mark Twain** is one of America's greatest novelists, famous for *The Adventures of Tom Sawyer* and *Adventures of Huckleberry Finn*.
> **Amanda Bradley** is an American writer of inspirational poetry.

Vocabulary and speaking

Exercise 3

■ Give students a moment to read through the words. Then put them in pairs to complete the table.
■ Check words that students aren't sure of.

Answers

Decorations	Clothing	Actions	Entertainment
garland	mask	clapping	acrobats
streamers	sash	making a speech	fireworks
banner	hat	singing	parade

> **Vocabulary note**
>
> A *garland* (of flowers, for example) goes round the neck. A *streamer* is a long paper decoration. A *banner* is a big sheet of cloth or paper with a message on it, such as WELCOME HOME. A *mask* is worn on the face. A *sash* is a stretch of cloth, worn from shoulder to hip. *Acrobats* are performers whose show involves jumping, balancing, etc.

Exercise 4

Extra activity

■ Ask students to work in pairs or small groups to discuss the questions. You could ask different groups to think of how to describe just one of the types of party and then present their findings to the class.

Example answers
Street party: a community party, usually to celebrate a public holiday – residents eat together; **Housewarming party:** to celebrate moving into a new flat/house – friends and new neighbours; **Fancy dress party:** it could be a birthday or any other occasion – people wear costumes to look like well-known characters; **Farewell party:** someone leaving (to go abroad or to a new job) – at the office at the end of the day, someone will make a speech.

> **Culture note**
>
> In the UK, **street parties,** in which people sit at long tables, eating sandwiches and other picnic food, with hats, streamers, balloons and banners, are a popular way to celebrate national events such as royal jubilees and weddings.

Extra activity

Ask students to describe in groups a party that they recently attended. Tell them to describe what sort of party it was, who attended, what happened and what was special about it.

Books closed lead-in activity —————→

Books closed lead-in activity

Ask students, *If you could be any age now, what age would you choose to be and why?* Ask students to discuss in pairs then tell the class.

Extra activity ————————→

Extra activity

You could introduce words used to describe people at these different stages: *baby, toddler, kid, youth, teen, grown-up, pensioner,* etc.

Vocabulary

Exercise 1

■ Ask students to read the extract and answer the question.

> **Answer**
> The speech compares the world to a stage and life to a play.

> **Culture note**
> This speech is made in the opening monologue of Shakespeare's comedy *As You Like It* by the melancholy character, Jaques.
>
> Shakespeare's seven ages are: the infant, the schoolboy, the lover, the soldier, the justice, the pantaloon (an old man), and 'second childhood' (i.e. senile old age).

Exercise 2

■ Ask students to work in pairs to order the stages. Discuss when different stages of life start and finish.

> **Answers**
> 1 birth 2 infancy 3 childhood 4 adolescence 5 adulthood 6 middle age 7 old age
> 8 death

Speaking

Exercise 3

■ Lead in by asking students what key events in life could be placed on a timeline. Elicit a few examples.

■ Ask students to complete their timelines. Tell them to use a large, blank sheet of paper to allow them space to write plenty of events. Monitor and help with ideas and vocabulary.

Exercise 4

■ Give students a couple of minutes to prepare to describe their memories using the useful expressions in the box.

■ Ask students to work in pairs to describe their timelines.

> **Vocabulary note**
> Remind students that *remember*, *recall* and *forget* are followed by *-ing*.

Listening

Exercise 5

■ Ask students to work in pairs to discuss the questions.

> **Culture note**
> In the UK, people come of age at 18. In the past, it was 21, so this is also celebrated as a special birthday.

Exercise 6   CD2/08

■ Ask students to read through the table to focus their listening.

■ Play the recording once or twice, then students check their answers in pairs.

■ Elicit the answers from the class.

Audioscript

Presenter Back with us today is John Harkness, who you may remember from last week has written a book on celebrations and rituals around the world. John, I'd like to talk some more about the book later, but to begin with, would you like to introduce today's topic?

John Yes. Today I want to tell you something about the different 'coming of age' rituals that we find around the world. You know, when young people are introduced into the adult world and become part of it.

Presenter OK, John. Where are we going to start?

John Well, I thought we'd start in Africa and something called the mukanda, which is practised by people in Angola, the Democratic Republic of Congo, and Western Zambia.

Presenter And what happens with the mukanda?

John Well, in common with such traditions in many parts of Africa, a special camp is built outside the community. The young boys – they're usually aged between eight and twelve – are then taken to the camp for a month. It used to be much longer, by the way. While they are at the camp, the boys learn about discipline and the things they need to know in order to become useful members of the community, as well as practical skills … like hunting. What I find fascinating are the costumes and masks associated with this ritual. The boys each spend the whole time with a masked character who represents an important member of society. Some of the masks represent their ancestors, so the boys are being introduced to the past. In a way, they are being asked to kill off the boy in them and let the man grow so they can continue the tradition of their ancestors – that's one aspect of it at least.

Presenter And are they then brought back to their community as men?

John Yes. After the mukanda everybody in the village attends a dance and the boys are reintroduced to their families as men. The camp and many of the things in it are then burned as if to say a final goodbye to boyhood.

Presenter Fascinating stuff. You've got something to tell us about girls too, haven't you?

John Yes. I wanted to mention the celebration of the Quinceañera in South America.

Presenter And what's that?

John Well, it's a celebration of a girl turning fifteen.

Presenter And is that a special birthday?

John It is in South America, although I should point out that the celebration varies a lot from country to country. I'll give you a general idea of what happens though.

Presenter Yes, go on.

John Well, it can be called Quinceañera or just Quince, or sometimes a Fiesta Rosa. The girl whose birthday it is gets to choose special friends to spend it with. This might mean seven young couples – to add up to the number fourteen – one for each year of her life. Or it could be fourteen girls. In the ceremony, there is emphasis on the high-heeled shoes that the girl will change into … actually, her father will place these on her feet … and the crown that she will wear on her head, which her mother puts there. These symbolise the change from a girl to a woman. And she dances with her father – that's very important because that father is accepting that he's having the last dance with his daughter as a child, and the first dance with her as a woman. And of course, there is food and music and dancing, and the decorations for the party are bright and cheerful, and the girl carries a bouquet of flowers. Much like a wedding in the west, in fact. There is a lot of importance placed on both the girl's dress and the cake, both of which can be really elaborate, and which usually match in some way.

Presenter John, we don't really do much like this here in the UK. Why do you think that is?

John Well, we do mark certain birthdays here, don't we? And we often have big birthday parties with music, dancing, food and drink – that kind of thing. As for reasons to celebrate at a certain age … Well, at 16 you can get married without your parents' consent in England and Scotland, and you can drive at 17, but you can't vote until you are 18. There's nothing much that turning 21 allows you to do, but people still see that as a major turning point. I think any one of these milestones in your life can be seen as a coming of age. But, you know, times have changed. There are people who get married at 16, just as there are people who leave home at 18, but in recent years we find that more and more people tend to live with their parents until they are older. Compared to the past, I'd say that the average 16-year-old and even, dare I say it, the average 18-year-old, is not very well equipped to start out on their own. You could say that leaving home to go to university at 18 is probably the time when many people learn to stand on their own two feet. But I think a lot of people find this a confusing and very difficult time.

Presenter John, I'm going to play a piece of music now, but when we come back, I'd like to talk a little more about … [fade]

Answers

Culture or society	Age of young person	Name of festival	What happens?
Angola, Democratic Republic of Congo, Western Zambia	8—12	Mukanda	boys taken to special camp; learn about discipline and how to become useful members of the community; masked characters represent important members of society/their ancestors; boys reintroduced to their families as men; camp is later burned
Latin America	15	Quinceañera / Quince /Fiesta Rosa	girls celebrate their 15th birthday; they choose 14 friends to spend it with; father places shoes on his daughter's feet; mother puts crown on daughter's head; girl dances with her father; these rituals symbolise the change from girl to woman; there is food, music, dancing, decorations, flowers, elaborate dress and cake
Modern western society	16, 17, 18, 21	NA	young people often have a big birthday party with music, dancing and food

Exercise 7 ⊙ CD2/08

■ Play the last part of the recording again and ask students to answer the questions.
■ Elicit answers from the whole class.

Answers
1 get married without parents' consent 2 drive 3 vote

Exercise 8

■ Ask the class to discuss the questions together.

Writing
Exercise 9

■ Start by eliciting some legal rights for students to think about.
■ Ask students to work in pairs to prepare a few ideas. Monitor and help.
When they are ready, ask students to write a paragraph using the expressions in the box.

Listening and vocabulary
Exercise 10

■ Brainstorm a few significant growing-up moments from the class and write them on the board.
■ Ask students to tell their partner the most significant moment for themselves.

Extra activity

Ask students to say at what age people can get married, drive and vote in your country.

Exercise 11 CD2/10

■ Play the recording. Ask students to listen and answer the question.

Audioscript

Speaker 1 I think the closest thing we have to a rite of passage in the UK is when we leave home to go to university. It's a bit different to other European countries where people often stay in the same town to study. In England you generally go as far from your home town as possible. So, if you live in the north, you'd probably pick a university somewhere in the south, like London. And if you live in the south, you might go to Manchester or Edinburgh. You go home in the holidays, of course, but most of the time, you're finding out how to fend for yourself – cooking, washing, meeting your work deadlines. When you're used to being looked after by your parents, it's quite a sharp learning curve.

Speaker 2 I guess it kinda depends on your parents and how much they trust you to be an adult. Mine were pretty cool. I knew they expected me to get good grades at high school, so I always worked hard. I felt a responsibility to. If I'd gone off the rails, my parents would probably have been stricter with me, but I think the moment I really felt grown up was at the High School prom – you know, the end-of-school party. I went with my best friend and I remember we said to each other, 'Well, this is it – it's like goodbye to being school kids. We're on our own now.'

Speaker 3 It's difficult to pinpoint any single moment when you feel you've become an adult. You know, for me … I kept making statements of independence throughout my teens. I dyed my hair bright red – against my parents' wishes, needless to say – when I was only 13. Then when I was 15 I got a part-time job. I suppose the biggest thing was leaving school at 16. I applied to a local motorcycle repair shop to train as a mechanic because I was mad about motorbikes. My parents were dead set against that – they wanted me to go to university. But as it happened, it worked out really well. I worked for them for four years and then a year ago I set up my own business with a friend … Touch wood, it's all going really well so far.

Answers
1 when she went to university in another town 2 at the High School prom (a farewell dance) 3 leaving school at 16 years old

Exercise 12 CD2/10

■ Ask students to complete the phrases and check with a partner. Play the recording again so that students can check their answers.

Answers
1 rite of passage 2 fend for yourself 3 gone off the rails 4 grown up 5 independence; teens 6 dead set

> ### Vocabulary note
> *rite of passage* = an action or ceremony that symbolises a change from one period of life to another; *gone off the rails* = behaved in bad ways (from the idea of a train going off the rails and taking the wrong route); *dead set against* = very strongly against; *touch wood* = a saying for good luck

Pronunciation: weak forms
Exercise 13 CD2/11

■ Ask students to read the phrases first, and predict the pronunciation of the prepositions.
■ Play the recording. Ask students how the prepositions are pronounced.
■ Put students into pairs to practise saying the phrases.

Answer
The vowel sound in the prepositions has a weak schwa /ə/ sound.

Speaking
Exercise 14

■ Ask students to work in pairs to discuss the questions.

Extra activity

Ask students to research on the Internet the rites of passage of people in other countries (e.g. India, China, Latin America, parts of Africa) and present their findings to the class in a later lesson.

Wedding traditions

Books closed lead-in activity

Ask students to talk about a wedding they have been to. Ask, *Whose wedding was it? Where was it? What happened? What did they do?*

Speaking and vocabulary

Exercise 1

- Ask students to work in pairs and to guess the answers to all the questions.
- Elicit ideas from the whole class, and discuss which seems the most likely.
- Ask students to check their answers on page 144.

Grammar: passive gerund and infinitive

Exercise 2

- Read the grammar box with the class.
- Ask students to transform the sentences individually, then check in pairs.
- Elicit answers from the class as complete sentences.

> **Answers**
> 1 being included in the group photograph. 2 to get married by law. 3 being kept waiting
> 4 to be taken to the ceremony by Rolls-Royce.

- Refer students to the Grammar Reference on page 154.

Reading

Exercise 3

- Ask students to get into pairs and decide who is A and who is B.
- They should then read their passage and tell their partner about it.
- Reassure them to not worry about unknown vocabulary.

Grammar: passive reporting verbs

Exercise 4

- Ask students to discuss the text and highlighted words in pairs.
- Elicit suggestions from the whole class.

> **Answers**
> *civil ceremonies* = non-religious
> *in decline* = decreasing
> *dowry* = the bride gives money or goods to the groom's family
> *elaborately-embroidered* = decorated with sewing

Exercise 5

- Ask students to complete the sentences individually, then check in pairs.
- Elicit answers from the whole class

> **Answers**
> 1 are believed to be 2 was

- Refer students to the Grammar Reference on page 154.

Exercise 6

- Ask students to write the sentences individually, then check in pairs.
- Elicit answers from the whole class as complete sentences.

> **Answers**
> 2 are expected to pay half the bill 3 was always supposed to propose to the woman
> 4 is reported to have increased every year

Speaking

Exercise 7

- Ask students to discuss the questions in pairs.
- Circulate and monitor their production.
- Take notes and feedback as a class.

Books closed lead-in activity

Ask students to discuss the following questions in pairs or small groups: *When was your last birthday? What did you do for your birthday? Was it special in any way?*

Speaking and listening

Exercise 1

- Ask students to work in pairs to read and share their birthday facts.
- Find out whether any student shares a birthday with another student in the class.

> **Culture note**
> The music for *'Happy Birthday to you'* was written by two Americans, Patty and Mildred Hill, in 1893. The words were added by 1912. The song was registered for copyright by the Summy Company in 1935, a copyright that Warner acquired in 1990. It is the most recognised song in English and has been translated into many languages.

Exercise 2

- Ask students to discuss the question in pairs.

> **Culture note**
> **Important birthdays** in the UK include: 18 (legal adulthood); 21 (traditionally seen as coming of age); birthdays ending with '0', particularly 40 because it is the onset of middle age; 65 (retirement age); and 100 (UK citizens are sent a telegram by the Queen if they reach this landmark).

Exercise 3  CD2/12

- Play the recording. Ask students to listen and answer the questions. Let students check their answers in pairs before discussing as a class.

Audioscript

In the UK, people definitely make more of their important birthdays than they did in the past. In fact there's a whole industry that's grown up around it. Twenty-one-year-olds usually have a big party. Often it's fancy dress. They might dress up in 1980s fashion or go as characters from films.

If their party is at a nightclub, they hire a big limousine to take them there. Sometimes they just hire one to drive around for an hour just to feel like celebrities. It's quite a common sight to see these big white cars with blacked out windows cruising down a UK high street on Friday or Saturday night.

But it's not just the younger generation that go in for big celebrations: people seem to want to mark all the big birthdays nowadays … 30, 40, 50. (Well, perhaps, not so much 30 – that's one people try to play down more.) But I certainly don't remember my parents doing anything particularly special for theirs.

For 40th birthdays you get things like adventure weekends, for those who want to feel they are still young and daring, like going up in a hot-air balloon or doing a parachute jump or learning how to drive a racing car. Surprise parties are also popular, where old friends and family that you don't see very often all turn up for a big celebration.

> **Answers**
> 21, 30, 40, 50; 21st a big party; 40th something adventurous, a weekend away, a party with family and old friends

Extra activity

Practise the phrasal verbs by asking students to discuss the following questions in pairs: *What sort of parties do you like? Do you like dressing up for parties? Do you prefer to play down your birthday?*

Exercise 4  CD2/12

- Ask students to work in pairs to see if they can remember and write the missing phrasal verbs.
- Play the recording. Students listen, complete the gaps, then discuss meaning with a partner.

Answers
1 dress up 2 go in for 3 play down 4 turn up

> **Vocabulary note**
> *mark a birthday* = do something to make it significant; *play down* = to make something seem less important

Reading
Exercise 5
- Ask students to work in pairs to discuss the questions. Find out who has the most brothers and sisters.

Exercise 6
- Ask students to work in pairs to carry out the tasks. Monitor and help pairs with ideas for questions. You could elicit one or two answers as a class first to get students started.
- Elicit answers students found as well as potential answers to questions that weren't answered in the text.

> **Vocabulary note**
> *have/suffer a miscarriage* = lose a baby early in pregnancy; *home-schooled* = educated at home; *buddy system* = a system often used in schools where an older child supports and advises a younger one; *make ends meet* = earn enough to pay for the basic necessities of life; *thrift stores* = shops that sell products at very low prices

Exercise 7
- Give students time to read through the options and choose any that they can remember the answer to.
- Ask students to read the text and choose the correct options. Let students check their answers in pairs before discussing as a class.

Answers
1 D 2 C 3 D 4 A 5 A 6 D

Exercise 8
- Ask students to discuss the questions in pairs or small groups.

Extra activity

Ask students in pairs to brainstorm a list of advantages of being an only child and a list of advantages of having siblings. Have a class discussion as to which is best.

Books closed lead-in activity

Write on the board *Festivals*. Ask the class to name festivals they know and write these on the board. Then elicit additional details. Ask, *Where does this festival take place? What does it celebrate? What happens at this festival?*

Reading

Exercise 1

- Ask students to look at the picture and read the information.
- Elicit ideas from the class about where it is and what happens. Do not give any answers; just collect ideas and write them on the board.

Exercise 2

- Ask students to read the text and check which ideas are correct.

> **Answers**
> It is in Venice, Italy, and there is a race over the bridges in the city.

Listening

Exercise 3    CD2/13

- Ask, *Have you heard of the Edinburgh Festival?* Students look at the table to focus their listening.
- Play the recording while students complete the table.
- Let students check their answers in pairs before discussing as a class.

Audioscript

Presenter	Janice, you've just come back from the Edinburgh Festival, haven't you?
Janice	I have, yes.
Presenter	What was that like? Would you tell us about it?
Janice	Ooh! Where do I start?! It is unique, Edinburgh. I mean, they have the best of international arts all in one place – opera … theatre … dance … visual arts …
Presenter	It is, of course, more than one festival, isn't it?
Janice	Yes. People forget that. There's the Fringe festival, which probably attracts the most attention. But there's also the Edinburgh Art Festival and the Royal Edinburgh Military Tattoo. Then there's the Edinburgh International Festival and Edinburgh Book Festival … the People's Festival, the Festival of Politics and more besides. All these festivals come together, and for a few weeks starting in August, it's all happening!
Presenter	That's a lot to see!
Janice	In all, over 40,000 performances of different kinds, more than 2,500 shows, and … and this is one of the big attractions … 600 of the shows are free. All this takes place in a huge number of venues – this year, there were 258, including tents and ordinary buildings, like shops.
Presenter	And there are street performers too, I understand.
Janice	Yes, it seemed like everywhere you went, there was someone doing something unusual!
Presenter	There was a kind of theme this year, wasn't there?
Janice	Yes, the theme was Asia, and there were artists from many Asian countries taking part.
Presenter	And what did you see?
Janice	Well, like most people, I suppose, I tried to see as much as I could. But you just can't do it all – there's too much! I went to a few new and interesting theatrical productions. I saw some very talented young musicians … and some great dance performances. I also saw some really funny stand-up comedians.
Presenter	Just before we take a short break, Janice, would you be good enough to tell us about your favourite experience from the whole festival?
Janice	I suppose it was in the second week. I had gone into a café where there were works of art hanging on the walls. I'd seen the paintings and I was sitting down having a coffee, when a complete stranger came over and invited me next door, where they were showing a short film … which I really liked … and just then, another stranger approached me and took me to a dance show nearby … which was also wonderful.
Presenter	All the arts in one day!
Janice	Yes, there was an incredible variety of things to see.

Presenter	Why does that day stand out, do you think? Why was it special?
Janice	The fantastic thing about the whole experience was that it was so relaxed … and so friendly – I mean, I had no hesitation in trusting these people – and I got to see things I wouldn't perhaps have chosen, but I was so glad I went to them.
Presenter	Well, Janice, I'd like to talk to you about your favourite artists and performers from those you saw. So when we come back perhaps you'd be good enough to tell us [fade]

Exercise 4 CD2/13

- Play the recording. Ask students to listen and complete the sentences.
- Students check their answers in pairs, then elicit answers from the class.

> **Answers**
> 1 all in one 2 attracts 3 street 4 everywhere you went 5 theme 6 as I could 7 interesting; talented 8 invited me 9 variety 10 have chosen

Speaking

Exercise 5

- Ask students to think of a festival then fill in the table. Monitor and help with ideas and vocabulary.
- Once students have enough notes, tell them to prepare things to say using the useful expressions. Then ask them to take it in turns to tell their partner.
  Ask a few students to tell the class about the festival their partner described.

Writing: a description of an event

Exercise 6

- Ask students to read the two questions to focus their reading.
- They should then read through the article quickly to find the answers.

> **Answers**
> 1 The annual town carnival celebration. 2 He enjoyed it and felt proud of his town. Also, he hadn't wanted to go but enjoyed it, which taught him to have an open mind.

Exercise 7

- Ask students to search the text and find adverbs and adverbials to match the words in the box. Do the first as an example. Let students check their answers in pairs before discussing as a class.

> **Answers**
> frankly = to be honest; funnily enough = oddly; in fact = actually; of course = naturally; thankfully = fortunately

Exercise 8

- Ask students to work individually to complete the sentences. Let students check their answers in pairs before discussing as a class.

> **Answers**
> 1 Thankfully 2 In fact 3 Frankly 4 Funnily enough

Exercise 9

- Ask students to find and underline tenses used in the essay. Then ask them to discuss which ones are used and why with a partner. In feedback, you could draw timelines to show the different tenses.

> **Answers**
> 1 present simple 2 past perfect 3 past simple

Exercise 10

■ Ask students to work individually to rewrite the sentences. Do the first as an example to get them started. Let them check their answers in pairs before discussing as a class.

Answers
1 It was a memorable occasion. 2 It is traditional to celebrate with a big meal. 3 I always get excited about this kind of event. 4 It was the first time I had been to a wedding.
5 Usually I find these kinds of occasions boring. 6 It was noisy in the room. 7 We had a really good time.

Exercise 11

Extra activity

Write *What? When? Where? Who with?* and *What happened?* on the board as focus questions, then tell a story of a memorable event from your life. Ask students to answer the questions and ask any follow-up questions.

■ Ask students to think of a memorable event and make notes. You could write *What? When? Where? Who with?* and *What happened?* on the board as prompts to help them prepare.
■ Ask students to tell their partner about the event. Monitor and help with ideas and vocabulary.

Exercise 12

■ Ask students to follow the structure to write their descriptions. Tell them to make brief notes under each heading first. Encourage them to incorporate adverbs and adjectives from the lesson into their descriptions.

How people celebrate

Books closed lead-in activity

Write *dressed up* on the board, and elicit its meaning (wearing your best clothes because there's a party or special occasion to go to). Ask, *When was the last time you dressed up? What was the occasion? Where did you go and what did you do?* Ask students to talk in pairs then tell the class.

Extra activity

Write *National Day* on the board and elicit the sort of things that different countries do to celebrate their National Day. Elicit words like *parade, fireworks, party, flags, songs, music, dance*.

Speaking

Exercise 1

- Give students a moment to read through the options and choose which ones they would prefer to do. Then ask students to work in pairs to say what they chose and why.

Exercise 2

- Ask students to discuss the question in pairs or small groups. You could ask different groups to brainstorm ideas about just one of the days then share their ideas with the class.

> **Culture note**
> New Year's Eve (31st December) is an evening when people have big parties at home or go out. At midnight, everybody holds hands and sings an old Scottish song called *Auld Lang Syne.*
>
> In the UK, **Mother's Day**, or Mothering Sunday, is in March or April. It is a day to honour your mother, perhaps by giving cards or flowers, or by helping her or taking her for dinner.

Reading

Exercise 3

- Lead in by asking students what a National Day is.
- Ask students to look at the texts quickly and find the names of the national days and the countries that celebrate them.
- Give students time to read the questions, and then ask them to read the texts carefully and find answers. Let them discuss their answers in pairs before discussing as a class.

> **Answers**
> 1 B (flags, parades) 2 A (native Aborigines feel it marks the end of independence)
> 3 A (sporting events like cricket matches) 4 A B C 5 C 6 B

Exercise 4

- Ask students to find and match the words to the definitions. Do the first as a class. Let them discuss their answers in pairs before discussing as a class.

> **Answers**
> 1 crazy about 2 controversial 3 pushed 4 diverse 5 extended 6 dye 7 convivial

> **Culture note**
> **Cricket** is a game played on a large pitch with a bat and a hard ball. It is the national sport of Australia.
>
> **Sydney** is Australia's largest city and has a large harbour, spanned by a famous bridge. The picture shows the **Sydney Opera House** with the harbour in the foreground.
>
> American **Independence Day** celebrates the signing of the Declaration of Independence on the 4th July 1776. American colonists declared independence from the British crown. This led to war and, eventually, the founding of the USA.
>
> **St Patrick** is the patron saint of Ireland. The potato famine of the mid-19th century led to large-scale immigration of Irish people to Britain and, notably, to the USA. Cities like Boston, New York and Chicago have large numbers of inhabitants of Irish descent.

Exercise 5

■ Ask students to work in pairs or small groups to discuss the questions.

■ Ask students if their family has any more unusual activities that they do for their National Day.

Reading and listening

Exercise 6

■ Ask students to work in pairs to discuss the questions.

Exercise 7

■ Ask students to read the two questions first to focus their reading.

■ Ask them to read the text quickly to find the answers.

■ Elicit answers from the whole class.

Answers

1 2000 years ago people went out in boats to look for the body of the poet Qu Yuan.

2 They eat rice cakes or rice dumplings, because it is said people threw rice on the water to distract the fish from the poet's body.

Exercise 8   CD2/14

■ Ask students to read through the table to focus their listening.

■ Play the recording once or twice while they complete the task.

■ They can then check in pairs.

■ Elicit answers from the whole class.

Audioscript

Presenter   My two guests today have been lucky enough to experience the Dragon Boat festival at first hand. Let's start with Wendy. What is it like?

Wendy   Well, there is a lot of preparation and ceremony involved. People see this as an important day for the family. Probably the most significant thing is the making of the zongzi. These are a kind of dumpling with sticky rice and other fillings, like meat or nuts, which are wrapped up in bamboo leaves to be boiled. Some places actually have a zongzi-making competition. It's not as easy as it looks – I tried it … and failed! In the house people hang up mugwort, which is a special kind of plant said to give them protection. The children are given small pouches which are perfumed and are supposed to protect them from disease. There is also a belief that if you can make an egg stand on its end at exactly midday, you will have good fortune for a year, so a lot of people attempt this. It really is a fascinating day!

Presenter   It sounds it! Harry, what were your impressions?

Harry   Well, it was definitely a unique experience. A lot of people go to the river or to the sea – wherever the competition is taking place. Some people even jump into the sea! Other people use the holiday as an opportunity to go for a relaxing walk by the river, just to be together with their family. The boats are like long, thin canoes and they are brightly painted to look like dragons with a big, scary head at the front and a tail at the back. I heard that the eyes of the dragon are painted on last as this is said to bring the dragon to life. Each boat has someone at the front playing a drum. This is to encourage the oarsmen and to help them keep time. Any number of boats can race, and a boat can hold over 50 rowers, but there's usually ten or twenty. The race begins when someone fires a gun, and to win the race, someone on one of the boats has to reach out and touch the flag at the finishing line. I thought the race was incredibly exciting!

Answers

	Wendy	Harry
a drummer		✓
important family gathering	✓	✓
firing a gun		✓
jumping in the sea		✓
a flag		✓
a competition	✓	✓
hanging something up	✓	
different fillings	✓	
rowers/oarsmen		✓
bamboo leaves	✓	
a good-luck ritual	✓	✓
family walks		✓

Exercise 9 CD2/14

■ Read through the rubric with the class and ensure that they are clear about the task.
■ Play the recording while they take notes. You may need to play it twice.
■ Students then discuss the adjectives they heard and the nouns they describe.
■ Elicit answers from the whole class.

Answers
Wendy: important, significant, sticky, (not) easy, special, small, perfumed, good, fascinating
Harry: unique, relaxing, long, thin, brightly painted, big, scary, exciting

Speaking

Exercise 10

■ Check that students know all the holidays. Ask, *What do they celebrate? When are they?*
■ Divide students into small groups to discuss the holidays.

Exercise 11

■ Ask students in their groups to invent their own public holiday. You could start them off by eliciting two or three ideas as a class (for example, *World Peace Day* or *World Switch Off Your Mobile Day*).

Exercise 12

■ Ask groups to follow the procedure to prepare to speak, and choose two or three people to make the presentation.
■ Each group makes its presentation. At the end, ask students to vote for one of the new public holidays.
■ Refer students to the DVD about the great kite fight. Video worksheet on page 138.

Choosing a present

Listening and speaking

Books closed lead-in →
activity

Exercise 1

- Ask students to work in pairs to read and discuss the saying. Ask students whether they like buying presents or not.

Ask, *Who do you buy presents for? When? What sort of things do you buy?* Ask students to discuss the questions in pairs then tell the class.

Exercise 2

- Give students a moment to read through the comments. Check any unknown words. Ask students to discuss the comments in pairs, then have a whole-class discussion.

Exercise 3

- Ask students to work individually to choose the correct words. You could do the first as a class to get students started. Let students check their answers in pairs before checking as a class.

> **Answers**
> 1 thoughtful 2 tag 3 spoil; fortune 4 shouldn't 5 wrap

> **Vocabulary note**
> *Considerate* is a synonym of *thoughtful,* not *considered* (which means 'thought about carefully for a long time', e.g. *a considered opinion*); *a price tag* is a small piece of card or cloth showing the price; it *cost a fortune* (very expensive) but It *was a bargain* (good value); *wrap* a present (with wrapping paper) but *pack* a box or a suitcase (with clothes).

Exercise 4   CD2/15

- Give students a moment to read the questions. Play the recording. Ask students to listen then discuss the questions in pairs.

Audioscript

Assistant	Can I help you?
Customer	Oh, yes, thanks. The thing is I'm looking for something for my little sister and I'm a bit stuck.
Assistant	OK. How old is she?
Customer	She's 14. I've got some ideas. I know she'd like a bag, but I don't usually shop for girls.
Assistant	Did she say what kind of bag?
Customer	Yes, something called a clutch bag, whatever that is.
Assistant	It's a small evening bag that you take out to a party or some other occasion, quite smart usually.
Customer	Can I have a look at what you've got?
Assistant	Sure, there are three or four over here. What about this one?
Customer	Oh, that's really nice. What's it made of?
Assistant	This one is one hundred per cent leather, and the clasp is brass, I think.
Customer	OK, and how much is it?
Assistant	One second, I'll just find the tag. This one's £40.
Customer	Ouch. That's a lot. Have you got anything cheaper?
Assistant	There's this blue one, but it's imitation leather.
Customer	Mmm, that one doesn't look quite so nice. Perhaps I should go with the first one. Then again, she's only 14. There's no point spending a fortune. She'll probably want something different next month. What happens if she doesn't like it? Can I bring it back?
Assistant	I can give you a gift receipt. That way she can buy something for a similar value here, anywhere in the department store in fact.
Customer	And how much is the blue one?

Assistant	It's £17.99.
Customer	OK. Let's go with that then. Can you wrap it?
Assistant	Of course.
Customer	And take the price tag off, if you don't mind.

> **Answers**
> 1 His younger sister 2 A blue clutch bag (evening handbag) 3 She said she wanted a bag, but he didn't want to spend too much on a fashion item.

Exercise 5   CD2/15

- Ask students to read the phrases and see if they can remember or guess the missing words.
- Play the recording. Ask students to listen and fill in the gaps. Let them discuss their answers in pairs before discussing as a class.

> **Answers**
> 1 for; a bit 2 called; whatever 3 look at 4 really; of 5 lot; cheaper 6 bring it back 7 much; one 8 go with; wrap

Exercise 6

- Divide students into pairs and ask them to decide who is to play which role.
- Give students a few minutes to prepare. When they are ready, ask students to act out the role play. Monitor and note errors and good language use.

Exercise 7

- Ask students to change roles and repeat the role play. Note that this time Student A is the customer and has a different shopping task to Student B.

Extra activity

Ask students to work in pairs to think up three new 'characters', their hobbies or interests, and why they are buying a present. They swap their three characters with another pair then role play the conversation with one student playing the three characters one at a time, and the other student as the shop assistant.

8

Get to work

UNIT OVERVIEW

Topic	psychometric personality tests, working animals, vocational jobs, work culture
Reading	extract from *The Horse Boy*, fisherman in Bangalore, working conditions in the UK
Listening	description of psychometric tests, interview about animal therapy, people talking about problems at work and work culture, a job interview
Grammar	relative clauses, double *the* + comparative, participle clauses, inversion
Function	talking about work culture
Vocabulary	describing jobs, personality traits
Pronunciation	short pauses in non-defining relative clauses
Writing	a good or bad experience with animals, a CV, an information sheet for people doing business in a different country
Speaking	talking about a problem at work
Culture	work culture

Books closed lead-in activity

Write on the board *The world's most boring job*. Ask students to talk with a partner and decide which job must be the most boring. Elicit a few ideas and reasons in class discussion.

Let's get started

Exercise 1

- ■ Ask students to look at the photo. Ask, *What is his job? What does he do?*
- ■ Point out that *not-so-glam* is short for not-so-glamorous. Ask students to work in pairs to discuss the questions.

Example answers
1 Many people think the job of flight attendant is glamorous and exciting because they travel around the world. The article is suggesting that the reality is very different from the image that the job has. The photo shows a flight attendant giving out meals and drinks. The main part of a flight attendant's job is to serve passengers, and air passengers can often be tired, irritable and demanding.

2 To be a good flight attendant I think you have to be cheerful, patient and hard-working.

3 I wouldn't like to do this job because I think there is a lot of routine. I'd also prefer to have a job on the ground.

Vocabulary and speaking

Exercise 2

- ■ Ask students to read through the words in the box in pairs and decide which ones are positive and which negative. Check that students understand all the words.
- ■ Ask students to work in pairs to decide which words best describe a flight attendant's job.

Example answers
I would describe this job as <u>stimulating</u> because you are working with people, but also <u>stressful</u>. I think it's probably <u>physically demanding</u> because you have to stand for much of the time. I think it's probably quite a <u>low-skilled</u> job and probably quite <u>badly-paid</u>.

Vocabulary and pronunciation note

Negative words (and stress): <u>ba</u>dly-paid; <u>low</u>-skilled; mo<u>no</u>tonous; <u>phy</u>sically de<u>ma</u>nding; <u>stress</u>ful

Positive words (and stress): pres<u>ti</u>gious = having high social value; re<u>war</u>ding; se<u>cure</u>; <u>sti</u>mulating = very interesting; <u>high</u>ly-skilled

Exercise 3

Extra activity

Elicit or write a list of jobs on the board. Ask students in pairs to choose one job and write down ten adjectives to describe the job. They read out their list of adjectives. The rest of the class must listen then guess which job on the board they are describing with the adjectives.

■ Ask students to work in pairs or small groups to discuss the list. Elicit a list of other jobs that are never boring.

Example answers
buyer; event planner; waiter/waitress; non-profit fundraiser; journalist; hospital nurse; public relations manager

Vocabulary note
buyer = a purchasing agent (e.g. for a department store)

An *event planner* organises major events such as celebrity weddings or corporate dinners.

Books closed lead-in——→
activity

Ask, What qualities do
employers look for in a job
applicant? Brainstorm ideas
and adjectives and write them
on the board. Ask, *How do*
employers find out whether
a job applicant has the
qualities they are looking for?

Extra activity ————————→

Try this numerical reasoning
test with students:

Write the missing number.

a) 1   4   9   ?   25 (16)

b) $45 \div 9 = 12 - ?$ (7)

c) $83 - 17 = 56 + ?$ (10)

Speaking

Exercise 1

■ Ask students to work individually to do the test. Give them no more than
a minute. Let them compare answers in pairs before revealing the correct
answer.

Answers
1 c 2 9

> **Culture and pronunciation note**
> This is an example of an abstract reasoning exercise from a psychometric /ˌsaɪkəʊˈmetrɪk/
> test. Other types of test include verbal reasoning and numerical reasoning (see the extra
> activity idea below).

Exercise 2

■ Ask students to discuss the questions in pairs.

Vocabulary and listening

Exercise 3

■ Ask students to work individually to try to match the main areas to the definitions.
Let them check their answers in pairs. Check any words students are not sure of.

Answers
1 f 2 g 3 e 4 a 5 h 6 c 7 d 8 b

Exercise 4   CD2/16

■ Play the recording. Ask students to listen and underline the stress. Let students
check their answers in pairs before discussing as a class.

Answers
1 numeracy 2 literacy 3 logic 4 problem-solving 5 motivation 6 attitude 7 teamwork
8 social skills

> **Pronunciation note**
> Note the pronunciation: *numeracy* /ˈnjuːmərəsi/; *literacy* /ˈlɪt(ə)rəsi/

Exercise 5   CD2/17

■ Ask students to work in pairs to predict which areas might go under Skills tests,
and which might go under Personality tests.
■ Play the recording. Ask students to listen and match areas to types of tests.
Let students check their answers in pairs before discussing as a class.

Audioscript

When you apply for a job, you'll probably have to sit a psychometric test. What is a
psychometric test? Well, there are two main kinds: skills tests and personality tests. Some
employers will only use one kind, some will use both, depending on the situation.

Skills tests measure your ability and aptitude to do something. A bank looking for a bank
cashier would obviously want to know if you are the sort of person who's good at working with
numbers. An advertising agency looking for a copywriter would want to know if a job candidate
is good with words. So skills tests measure numeracy, literacy, logic, problem-solving skills and
the ability to identify mistakes accurately. They measure **what** you can do.

Personality tests, which are very different kinds of tests, measure **how** you do things, your behaviour. So these are tests that tell the employer something about your motivation, your general attitude and how you prefer to work. Do you prefer to work in a team or on your own? Are you very organised or are you perhaps rather chaotic but very creative? Do you have good social skills?

Employers often look for somebody who has a particular profile and they want to find a candidate whose personality matches it. These tests might include things like answering a questionnaire about yourself, agreeing or disagreeing with statements about a course of action in a job situation, giving a presentation, or doing a role play or simulation in a work context.

Now, the main thing is not to be nervous about these tests. As far as skills tests are concerned, the good news is that like all tests, if you practise, then you can get better. So if you find out that you have to do a skills test, then it's a good idea to go on the Internet, do a free test and see how well you do. If you find you didn't do as well as you hoped, then you can buy books which train you for these particular exercises. You can also review the basic skills you usually need in these tests such as times tables, working out percentages and spelling.

Personality tests, which have no right or wrong answers, are more difficult to prepare for. The best thing is to be natural, which isn't easy I know. And if you don't get the job, then look at it positively – you probably wouldn't have been happy in that job anyway.

Answers

Skills tests	Personality tests
numeracy	motivation
literacy	attitude
logic	teamwork
problem-solving	social skills
ability to identify mistake correctly	

> **Vocabulary and pronunciation note**
> *aptitude* /ˈæptɪˌtjuːd/ = whether you are particularly suited to something; *simulation* = like a role play, but you play yourself when doing the role

Exercise 6    CD2/17

- ■ Give students time to read through the options and choose any that they think they already know the answer to.
- ■ Play the recording again. Ask students to listen and choose the correct options. Let students check their answers in pairs before discussing as a class.

Answers
1 D 2 A 3 B 4 D 5 C

Exercise 7   CD2/18

- ■ Ask students to read the questions then play the last part of the recording again. Put students in pairs to discuss the questions before having a whole-class feedback.

Answers
Don't be nervous about the tests. Practise skills tests: do a free test on the Internet and then train for the exercises. Review basic skills such as percentages and spelling. In interviews be natural, be yourself.

Grammar and pronunciation: relative clauses
Exercise 8

- ■ Ask students to read the explanation and the sentences carefully. Then ask them to discuss the questions in pairs.

Answers
1 a, c, d, e, f 2 b, g, h; the clause goes between commas 3 defining 4 non-defining
5 non-defining

- ■ Refer students to the Grammar Reference on page 155.

Extra activity

Ask students to grade themselves 1 (not very good), 2 (OK), or 3 (very good) for each of the main areas in exercise 3. Tell them to share their grades with a partner. Ask students to advise each other on what sort of job they should get, and on how they should prepare for interviews.

Exercise 9   CD2/19

- Ask students to listen and mark the short pauses. Let students check their answers in pairs before discussing as a class.
- Play the recording again. Students listen and repeat.

> **Answers**
> **b** Personality tests, // which are very different kinds of tests, // measure how you do things.
> **g** Personality tests, // which have no right or wrong answers, // are more difficult to prepare for.
> **h** The best thing is to be natural, // which isn't easy I know.

Exercise 10

- Ask students to write the sentences. Do the first as an example to get them started. Let students check their answers in pairs before discussing as a class.

> **Answers**
> **1** My job, which I've been doing for two years, is very physically demanding. **2** The people I work with are all very ambitious. **3** The job I used to do was extremely stressful. **4** After much consideration, I turned the first job down, which actually turned out be a good decision. **5** I'd like a job where I can work from home.

Vocabulary

Exercise 11

Extra activity

- Ask students to work in pairs to match adjectives and opposites. In feedback, check the meaning of any unknown words.

Ask students to listen and repeat (after your model) words that are difficult to pronounce.

> **Answers**
> **1** pragmatic/idealistic **2** sociable/reserved **3** creative/unimaginative **4** organised/chaotic **5** trustworthy/unreliable **6** cheerful/bad-tempered **7** sensitive/thick-skinned **8** confident/hesitant **9** dynamic/apathetic **10** efficient/incompetent

> **Pronunciation note**
> Note the strong stress as marked on the answers above.

Exercise 12

- Ask students to choose three adjectives from exercise 11 or to describe themselves. Ask them to share their descriptions in pairs. Ask some confident students to describe themselves.

Exercise 13

- It is a good idea to model this activity first. Describe one or two different jobs, using the adjectives and phrases suggested in the activity. Ask the class to guess the job you describe.
- Divide students into pairs to describe the jobs. Tell them to find the relevant lists at the back of the Student's Book and prepare their descriptions.
- When they are ready, ask students to take it in turns to describe the jobs.

Animals at work

Write on the board *My pet*. Ask students, *Do you have or have you ever had a pet? What is/was it? How would you describe the animal's personality and personal traits? How would you describe your relationship?* Divide students into groups of three to talk about their pets.

Listening and speaking

Exercise 1

- Brainstorm working animals and write them on the board. Then ask students to work in pairs to talk about what they do.

> **Vocabulary and culture note**
>
> Dogs: **sledge dogs** (huskies) transport people and goods by pulling them on sledges over snow; **service dogs** such as guide dogs help people who have physical problems such as blindness or deafness; **sheepdogs** herd and protect sheep; **guard dogs** are used to protect property and people from thieves or violence; **hunting dogs** are used to hunt foxes, deer and other animals.
>
> Others: **horses** and **donkeys** are still used occasionally to pull carts or plough the land, but more often they are used recreationally or in sport; **ferrets** are used to catch rabbits; **cats** are used to catch mice and rats; **truffle pigs** are used to sniff out truffles underground
>
> Other countries: **pack animals** (e.g. **camels, llamas, horses, donkeys, mules**) transport people and things in places where there are no motor vehicles or where it is difficult to use them (for example in the desert or over mountains); **oxen** are used in farming; **logging elephants** are used to lift and transport heavy tree trunks; **dolphins** have been used to perform underwater tasks.

Exercise 2

- Ask students to work in pairs to predict. Elicit students' ideas but do not confirm or deny as the recording explains what animal-assisted therapy is.

> **Culture note (and answers)**
>
> The interview is with a doctor discussing using animals to assist people who have undergone a traumatic experience – stroking a dog/cat is calming. **Animal-assisted therapy** is when you use animals to help people who are depressed or autistic, or have behavioural problems.

Exercise 3   CD2/20

- Ask students to listen and answer the question. Let students check their answers in pairs before discussing answers as a class.

Audioscript

Interviewer   Dr Allen, we've been using animals to help us since time began. Anyone with pets knows how companionable a dog or a cat can be. And the beneficial aspects of stroking pets – stress reduction, lowering blood pressure – are also widely known. Is this what animal assisted therapy is all about?

Dr Allen   Partly. Animals are widely used in hospitals with sick people and in care homes with old people in this way – the more you stroke an animal and interact with it, the calmer and happier you become.

Interviewer   But that's not the whole story?

Dr Allen   No indeed. I think what we're really talking about when we talk about animal-assisted therapy is using animals in a goal-oriented way to aid traditional methods of therapy. Very seriously depressed people, people with behavioural problems and autistic children can all be helped by animal therapy. Therapy animals are also commonly used with rescue services or in disaster relief programmes for people who have undergone a traumatic experience.

Interviewer   But how?

Dr Allen   Well, people with these difficulties will often respond to animals in a way that they might not respond to fellow humans. So, for example, an autistic child who avoids social contact might form a bond with a dog and through that bond learn how to relate more to people. The more contact a person has with an animal, the more sociable they become with people.

Interviewer   So, the dog plays a more central role?

Dr Allen   Yes, that's right. The dog is not just a friend but plays a key role in the therapy programme. And by the way, we're not always talking about dogs, although dogs are very often used. Dolphin therapy – swimming with dolphins in a special pool – is a popular form of animal-assisted therapy. People say the more they swim with dolphins, the less depressed they feel. And equine therapy – that's therapy using horses – is often used with teenagers who have behavioural problems.

Interviewer So do all these therapies have some sort of scientific basis?

Dr Allen Well, to be honest, I have to say no. There are thousands of cases where improvements do seem to have been made, and the longer the therapy, the better the results. But at the moment, there is a lack of comprehensive scientific evidence that animal-assisted therapy has long-term effects which can be traced directly back to the therapy.

Interviewer Dr Allen, thank you.

Answers
Dogs, cats, dolphins and horses.

> **Vocabulary note**
> *goal-oriented* = trying to achieve a particular aim; *undergo a traumatic experience* = suffer a very bad and distressing experience; *bond* = strong connection

Exercise 4 CD2/20
- Give students time to read through the statements and answer any they can.
- Play the recording again. Ask students to listen and choose true or false. Let students check their answers in pairs before discussing as a class.

Answers
1 False 2 True 3 True 4 True 5 False

Exercise 5
- Ask students to discuss the questions in pairs or as a class.

Grammar and pronunciation: double *the* + comparative
Exercise 6 CD2/21
- Ask students to read the explanation carefully. Check the form and meaning.
- Play the recording for students to note the stress, rhythm and pauses.
- Play the recording again for students to listen and repeat.
- Refer students to the Grammar Reference on page 155.

Exercise 7
- Ask students to complete the sentences with their own ideas. Monitor and correct. Let students share their sentences with a partner.

Example answers
1 The more I work, the more I earn. 2 The older I get, the better I feel. 3 The more people worry, the worse things seem. 4 The more money people earn, the more they can buy.
5 The less you eat, the slimmer you get.

> **Grammar note**
> Point out the form: *the* + comparative; *the more* + noun, noun phrase or clause.
> The two clauses are separated by a comma.

Reading
Exercise 8
- Ask students to read the introduction and look at the photo. Ask them what they might expect to read about in the story.

Extra activity

Ask students if they know any stories of animals who have been involved in rescuing people.

Extra activity

Write the following phrases on the board and ask students in pairs to decide what they mean (answers in brackets):
1 *The more you learn, the more you earn.* (If you want a well-paid job, you should get good qualifications.)
2 *The more things change, the more they stay the same.* (Changes often bring more of the same thing.)
3 *The less said, the better.* (In a difficult situation, it is better to keep quiet.)
4 *The more you give, the more you get.* (If you are generous to other people, you will be rewarded with generosity in return.)
5 *The more, the merrier.* (Everybody is welcome.)

- Tell students to read the text quickly and say what they find out about the trip and the relationship between father and son.
- Give students a moment to read through the sentences then to match them to the gaps in the text. Let students check their answers with a partner before discussing as a class.

Answers
1 C 2 D 3 B

Vocabulary and culture note
The Horse Boy was written by Rupert Isaacson, a Texan horse trainer, who, after the trip to Mongolia in 2007, set up the **Horse Boy Foundation** and a horse trails centre to help autistic children. A movie of the story was made in 2009.

The author creates a very vivid atmosphere by using lots of descriptive verbs and adjectives such as *digs, scrambling, slips, heave, straining, dizzying, terrifying, fluttering, whip round.*

Grammar: participle clauses
Exercise 9
- Ask students to read the explanation carefully. Check the form and meaning.
- Ask students to underline examples. Let students compare answers with a partner before discussing as a class.

Answers
… the wide streak of white still clinging to the higher tops; … where a pair of ravens fly, cawing madly on the wind; … the great Siberian forest, stretching to infinity; Before us rises a great cairn set with animal skulls …; … prayers scribbled in Cyrillic script on loose sheets of paper, weighted down by heavy rocks, fluttering in the wind.

- Refer students to the Grammar Reference on page 155.

Exercise 10
- Ask students to choose the correct participles. Let them check their answers in pairs.

Answers
1 riding 2 filmed 3 making 4 Helped 5 limited

Grammar note
If students have problems, tell them to think about whether the verb is expressing an active or passive idea.

Exercise 11
- Ask students to rewrite the sentences. Do the first as a class as an example to get students started.

Answers
1 struggling with behaviour problems 2 Assigned to an individual horse 3 helping with the cattle 4 setting aside their negative attitudes.

Writing
Exercise 12
- Elicit two or three good or bad experiences from the class. Then put students in pairs to think of experiences they could write about.
- Give students a couple of minutes to write a short paragraph. Monitor and check. When they are ready, ask students to shorten sentences with participles.
- Ask students to show their paragraphs to a partner. Tell students to comment on each other's pieces of work, and point out errors if necessary.

A centuries-old occupation

Books closed lead-in activity

Ask students to say what they know about different kinds of fishing (e.g. rod-and-line, net, from the land, from a boat). If anyone has first-hand experience, get them to talk about it in detail.

Grammar: inversion

Exercise 1

- Ask the class to read and comment on the sentences, and answer the questions.
- Read through the information on inversion with them.

Example answers
1 The job was badly paid and I also had to work at weekends.
2 Members of the public are not allowed beyond this point under any circumstances.
3 As soon as he started his new job, the boss reduced his salary.
4 Few men continue in this job past the age of 30 because of the physical strain.
5 She had only just finished filing her reports when the afternoon's meetings began.

- Refer students to the Grammar Reference page on 155.

Exercise 2

- Ask students to complete the sentences individually, then check in pairs.
- Elicit the answers from the class as complete sentences.

Answers
1 had Sandy started
2 did the training last
3 has Jason regretted
4 did she want
5 will Ben get paid for his work

Vocabulary

Exercise 3

- Decide if you want this to be a dictionary exercise.
- Ask students to do this individually, then check with a partner.
- Elicit answers from the whole class.

Answers
1 A job is a general term for any work, whether short-term, long-term, manual or professional. A profession always involves training and qualifications and would be long-term.

2 A job as above; an occupation is a formal term for a person's work.

3 An education implies long-term general learning and teaching; training is related to a specific job or type of work.

4 An apprentice is someone learning a craft or trade by practising it; a student is usually learning in an academic situation.

5 Wages are the pay you get per hour, per day or per week, often for manual or lower-skilled jobs; a salary is monthly and refers to payment for a skilled full-time job.

Reading

Exercise 4

- Ask students to find the examples individually, then check in pairs.
- Elicit the sentences in a different order.

Answers

1 … such is the importance of the fishing industry that it employs 1.4 million people. / The fishing industry is so important that it employs 1.4 million people.

2 Not only does that mean no fish to eat, but it also means no money to buy other food. / That means both no fish to eat and no money to buy other food.

3 The floods, of course, do not bring only fish…. / As well as fish, the floods also bring …

Exercise 5

- Ask students to read the article and to discuss the highlighted words in pairs.
- Elicit ideas from the whole class.

Answers
concession: allowance
otters: a type of fish-eating mammal
retrieves: brings back
sheepdogs: dogs which are trained to move sheep around
net: a criss-cross material used to catch fish
catch: the fish that are caught
cubs: young otters
breed: to mate and produce babies
seasonal: only at some times of the year
monsoons: rainy seasons
eking out a living: living at a very low level, with great difficulty
subsidising his income: making extra, necessary money
apprentice carpenter: a young person learning to be a carpenter (working with wood)

Exercise 6

- Ask students to insert the sentences individually, then check in pairs.
- Elicit the answers from the class.

Answers
1 C 2 E 3 G 4 H 5 F 6 A 7 B

Making conversation

Write *Problems* on the
board. Ask students to think
of a problem they have
had this week. It could be
practical or emotional.
Then divide students into
groups of three and tell
them to discuss their
problems and offer solutions.

Vocabulary

Exercise 1

■   Ask students to work in pairs to match phrases to meanings.

■   In feedback, ask students to repeat the phrases after your model. Point out that
    the pronunciation of *Sorry* starts high, and falls then rises.

Answers
a 2, 3, 6 **b** 1, 4, 5

> **Vocabulary note**
> *I'm not with you* and *I didn't get that* are more informal and abrupt than the other
> phrases.

Listening: discussing problems

Exercise 2   CD2/22

■   Ask students to look at the picture. Ask, *Where are they? What sort of occasion
    is it? What do you think they are talking about?*

■   Play the recording. Ask students to listen and match speakers to topics.
    Let students check their answers in pairs before discussing as a class.

Audioscript

1

Liz	I don't think we've met. I'm Liz Martin from Sales.
Julia	Julia Biani. I'm an intern in the Research and Development department. So, you're in Sales?
Liz	Yes, we're up to our eyeballs at the moment.
Julia	Sorry, what was that again? Up to your eyeballs?
Liz	Oh, yes sorry. It's just an expression we use when we're busy.
Julia	Oh, I see. Why's that?
Liz	Oh, it's always the same at this time of year …

2

Boss	Have you settled in? How's the work going?
Employee	Fine, thanks … well so-so.
Boss	Oh dear, what do you mean by that? Aren't you enjoying the work?
Employee	Yes, but it's not quite what I expected. The team …
Boss	Mmm, so in other words, you're finding it difficult to get along with your colleagues.
Employee	Erm, well, yes.

3

Colleague 1	Can I ask you about something? I have a bit of a problem.
Colleague 2	Sure.
Colleague 1	My boss expects me to do filing and make coffee and things that are just not part of my job description. But I've only been here a couple of months, so …
Colleague 2	So, what are you trying to say? You're not sure whether you should talk to him about it?
Colleague 1	What I mean is that I'm worried I'll lose my job if I complain.
Colleague 2	OK, yes, I see your problem.

Answers
1 D 2 C 3 A

■ Play the recording. Ask students to listen and answer the question.

Answers
1 The speaker hasn't understood an expression which the other speaker has used.
2 The speaker has a problem which he doesn't want to talk about directly.
3 The speaker has a problem that she doesn't explain very clearly.

> **Vocabulary note**
> *intern* = a trainee employee fresh from college employed on a short-term contract for work experience; *up to your eyeballs with work* = very busy (so much work that a pile of it would go up to your eyeballs); *so-so* = it's OK (often said with a slightly negative meaning)

Exercise 4

■ Ask students to work in pairs to categorise the phrases. Monitor and prompt.

Exercise 5   CD2/23

■ Ask students to listen, check answers and repeat.

Answers
Asking for clarification: 2, 4, 7   **Checking what you think somebody has said:** 5, 6
Explaining what you mean: 1, 3, 6

Speaking: clarifying meaning
Exercise 6

■ Divide students into pairs and ask them to find and read their roles. Ask them to look at the dialogue prompts and think about what to say. Then ask students to role play the situation. Monitor and note errors and good language use.

■ When they have finished, ask students to go on to situation B.

Writing: a CV
Exercise 7

■ Ask students to read the advert quickly and say what job it is advertising. Then ask students to underline skills and qualities. Do the first quality as a class as an example.

■ Let students check answers in pairs before discussing as a class.

Answers
a <u>dynamic</u> and <u>efficient</u> PA with <u>German speaking ability</u>. The ideal candidate will have <u>some administration experience</u>, <u>exceptional organisational and time management skills</u>, and a <u>good working knowledge of Microsoft® Office</u>. You must be <u>self-motivated</u> and <u>have good</u> <u>teamwork skills</u> along with <u>strong communication skills</u>

> **Vocabulary note**
> *minutes* /'mɪnɪts/ = notes that record exactly what was said in a meeting

Exercise 8

■ Read through the tips as a class, and check any unknown words. Then ask students to read Lucy's CV and tick the points she has followed. In feedback, discuss whether it is a good CV.

Answers
All the points should be ticked. It is highly likely she will be invited for interview.

Extra activity

Ask students to think of two or three English expressions they have learned on the course and write them down. Then, in pairs, ask students to say their expressions. Their partner responds by showing they understand or by using an expression to show they don't. For example: *'I'm on cloud nine at the moment.' 'Sorry, I'm not with you.'* Or, *'I'm on cloud nine.' 'Oh, so you are really happy …'*

Extra activity

Ask students to write a list of problems they have. When they are ready, ask them to practise discussing them with a partner. Alternatively, do this as a mingle. Ask students to walk round and discuss one or two problems with three or four different students.

Vocabulary note
bullet points = dots that order different points to be made (as shown in the *How to …* box); *tailor* = write or change something so that it is specifically for the audience it is aimed at

Exercise 9

■ Ask students to write their own CV. Tell them to start by writing rough notes under each heading then write them up more neatly. Monitor and help with ideas and vocabulary.

Vocabulary note
references = names and contact details of people who will comment on your suitability for a job

Exercise 10

■ Ask students to exchange CVs and make comments and suggest improvements.
■ Ask students about their partner's CV. Ask, *What job might suit them? What impressions does the CV give?*

Alternative activity

You could do this as a co-operative pairwork activity. Ask students to turn the CV headings into questions (*How would you describe yourself? What academic qualifications do you have? Have you ever had a job? What was it? What achievements are you proud of? Do you have any skills?*). Then ask them to interview each other and take notes. Finally, tell them to work together to write each other's CVs, based on the answers they have.

Work culture

Speaking and vocabulary

Exercise 1

- Give students a moment to read the sayings. Then put them in pairs to discuss the questions.

Answers
1 **a** Work gets done more quickly when several people help. **b** It isn't healthy to work all the time and have no leisure time or leisure interests. **c** Women always have lots of work to do (in the household, with children). **d** Hard work is good for you. **e** You shouldn't start work early and work late as well. **f** If you get up early and get things done, you'll be more successful in life. **2, 3** and **4** Students' own answers

> **Culture note**
> These are all very old proverbs or sayings, many of them first recorded in the 17th century.

Exercise 2

- Ask students to work in pairs to complete the exercise. In feedback, check meaning by asking for examples of how to use the idioms.

Answers
1 nose 2 easy 3 socks 4 dog 5 feet
1, 3 and **4** mean to work hard.

> **Vocabulary and pronunciation note**
> A *grindstone* /ˈɡraɪndˌstəʊn/ was used to grind corn to make flour, and using one was very hard, physical work. Keeping your nose to the grindstone means concentrating and working hard.

Reading

Exercise 3

- Ask students to look at the title and predict what the text is about. Ask them to read the text quickly to check their predictions.
- Ask students to complete the article with the correct forms. Do the first as a class to get students started.

Answers
1 preferring 2 longest 3 compared 4 regularly 5 estimate 6 employees

> **Vocabulary note**
> *workstation* = place where you work (e.g. your desk); *workload* = amount of work you have to do; *fringe benefits* = extra ('on the side') benefits

Exercise 4

- Ask students to work in pairs to come up with sentences.

Example answers
British employees work their socks off. British employers keep their employees' noses to the grindstone. British employees work like dogs.

Books closed lead-in activity

Write one of the sayings in exercise 1 on the board (e.g. *The early bird catches the worm*). Ask students to guess and say what it means.

Exercise 5

■ Ask students to match words or phrases from the article to the definitions.
   Let them check their answers in pairs before discussing as a class.

> **Answers**
> 1 working day/working hours 2 part-time 3 bank holidays 4 annual leave 5 minimum
> wage 6 salary 7 fringe benefits

Exercise 6

Extra activity

Ask students to say what the other numbers in the text refer to.

■ Ask students to complete the table. Let them check their answers in pairs before
   discussing as a class.

> **Answers**
> Typical working day: 9 a.m. to 5 p.m.
> Average working hours: 43.6 per week
> Paid holiday per year: 28 days
> National minimum wage £4.98 (aged 18–20) or £6.08 (21 and over)

Exercise 7

■ If you didn't do it as a lead-in task to the reading (see extra activity), ask students
   to work in pairs to make notes under the headings. Monitor and help with ideas
   and information.

■ If your students have Internet access, ask them to research information about
   their country.

Exercise 8

■ Ask students to role play the conversation. Tell them to try to use expressions
   from the box.

Listening

Exercise 9 CD2/24

■ Ask students to read through the points carefully. Ask them if they know or can
   guess any answers.

■ Play the recording. Ask students to listen and make notes. Let them check their
   answers in pairs before discussing as a class.

■ Discuss any advice that was unusual or interesting.

Audioscript

PA	So, let me take you round and tell you a few things on the way. The first important thing I need to say is that you're expected to be punctual at all times. That means being on time in the morning and always making sure you arrive on time for meetings and appointments, especially if they're with people from outside the company. Being late is considered very unprofessional.
Employee	Right, of course.
PA	Dress … We do have an unwritten dress code. There are no formal rules about what you have to wear, but smart dress is the norm. You don't have to wear a suit, smart trousers and a shirt are fine. It's up to you if you want to wear a tie. But wearing jeans is frowned upon and it's not acceptable to wear shorts and flip-flops in summer.
Employee	Fine, I was expecting some sort of dress code.
PA	Mmm, good. I think, you'll probably find this is a reasonably relaxed environment to work in. As far as addressing people is concerned, we don't stand on ceremony – people usually call each other by their first names, apart from the big bosses. However, if you're ever unsure, use somebody's surname, that way you won't offend anybody. Oh, and we don't use professional or academic titles here at all.
Employee	That's good. At my last job people were much more formal.
PA	Well, management are very keen to promote a good working environment. It's quite usual to meet up with colleagues after work – well, actually, you're expected to socialise with your colleagues to a certain extent.
Employee	Right, well, I certainly have no objections to that. Could you tell me …

Answers

Punctuality: be on time for work and for meetings and appointments; don't be late it's unprofessional

Dress code: unwritten code, no formal rules; smart dress is the norm; no jeans, no shorts or flip-flops

Names and titles: first names, apart from big bosses; if unsure, use surname; don't use professional or academic titles

Socialising: meet up with colleagues after work; expected to socialise to a certain extent.

Vocabulary note

the norm = what people usually do; *frowned on* = something that people do not approve of

---

Exercise 10

- Ask students to work in pairs or small groups to make a list about local work culture, using the points given in exercise 9. Then ask them to think about how they can express these points using the useful expressions.
- Ask students to discuss the points. You could change partners or mix groups at this stage.

Writing

Exercise 11

- Ask students to work in small groups to make an information sheet. Tell them to use expressions from the *Useful expressions* box in exercise 10.
- Put the information sheets on the wall or pass them round the class. Find out which group has designed the most informative or most interesting sheet.

Extra activity

Have a class discussion about whether they think working conditions in the UK are fair or not. Ask students what they would change and why.

Celebrations and customs

Lead-in

Ask students to talk about a local, national or international celebration they know about and think is interesting and/or unusual. Have them explain what people do, what happens, when it takes place and why.

Exercise 1

- Ask students to work in groups of four and discuss the questions.
- Ask each group to appoint a secretary to keep notes on their answers.
- Have a class discussion where the secretaries present the results.

Exercise 2

- Ask students to read the sentences first to focus their reading.
- They should answer individually, then check in pairs.
- Elicit the answers as complete sentences.

> **Answers**
> 1 happiness has been invited in 2 she has been crowned 3 is said 4 being invited

Exercise 3

- Ask students to complete the sentences individually, then check in pairs.
- Ask for answers from the whole class as complete sentences.

> **Answers**
> 1 shows respect to the building and creates an environment where the house will look after its inhabitants
> 2 given money in an envelope.
> 3 which are written on lanterns in the street
> 4 do local people celebrate with singing, dancing and a torch-lit procession

Exercise 4

- Ask students to discuss the points in pairs or small groups.
- Ask one person to act as secretary and write down the ideas.
- As a class, have the secretaries feed back, and open up the discussion to the class.

Find out more!

Do some research about an aspect of this topic which interests you, for example:
- nocturnal festivals around the world
- Native American music
- wedding celebrations

Look on the Internet and in books in the library. In particular, have a look at the National Geographic website: www.nationalgeographic.com

Units 7 and 8

Unit 7 Review

Ask students to complete the exercises in class or set the review for homework. After they have completed the exercises, students should evaluate their own performance, using the self-assessment box.

Answers

Exercise 1

1 costumes; masks 2 balloons; streamers 3 making a speech; clapping
4 parade; acrobats

Exercise 2

1 It is thought to have started as a celebration of the beginning of summer. 2 In the past people are said to have decorated their houses with flowers for good luck. 3 The crowning of the May Queen is known to be a popular tradition still. 4 It is reported to be the busiest time of the year for English morris dancers

Exercise 3

1 been played 2 dancing 3 to find 4 to be occupied 5 to leave
6 being taken out

Exercise 4

1 for 2 cheaper 3 about 4 bring 5 receipt 6 wrap

Unit 8 Review

Answers

Exercise 1

1 C 2 B 3 B 4 C 5 C 6 A

Exercise 2

1 profession 2 a job 3 training 4 students 5 salary

Exercise 3

1 Every day lifeguards check their equipment, which has to be in perfect working order.
2 They put warning signs on areas of the beach which / that could be dangerous.
3 Lifeguards spend most of their time watching people who are playing or swimming in the sea. 4 Lifeguards rescue people whose behaviour indicates (that) they are having problems. 5 Lifeguards have to write reports on all the incidents (that) they have dealt with.

Exercise 4

1 featured 2 using 3 possessing 4 requiring 5 armed

Exercise 5

1 Rarely have I met such motivated people. 2 The more I got to know the people I worked with, the more I enjoyed the work. 3 Not only did I experience working life, I also got a job offer. 4 The more photocopies I did, the more I hated the job.

Exercise 6

1 catch 2 missed 3 with 4 follow 5 again 6 mean

9

The economy

Let's get started

Exercise 1

■ Ask students to look at the photo. Ask, *What can you see?* Put students in pairs to discuss the questions and the quotation.

> **Culture note**
> Paul Heyne was an economics lecturer for nearly a quarter of a century at the University of Washington in Seattle, USA. His best known work was the critically acclaimed textbook *The Economic Way of Thinking*.

Vocabulary and speaking

Exercise 2

■ Ask students to read through the words in the box in pairs and decide which ones mean rich and which mean poor. Let students check their answers in pairs before discussing as a class.

> **Answers**
> **Rich:** well off; wealthy; loaded; affluent
> **In the middle:** comfortable
> **Poor:** hard up; broke; destitute

Extra activity

Check students' understanding of the words by asking them to match the words to the following phrases (answers in brackets):

1 *I've got 300 euros in my pocket.* (loaded)

2 *I earn a bit more than I spend.* (comfortable)

3 *I have no money until I get paid.* (broke)

4 *I've lost my job and my house, and I need to claim money to live.* (destitute)

5 *We have a big house, large salaries and three cars.* (wealthy/well off)

Exercise 3

■ Ask students to work in pairs or small groups to read the facts and discuss the questions. Ask students which facts they found surprising or disturbing.

Answers
1 Since 1988 the rich have been getting richer. **2** 30%

Exercise 4

■ Ask students to work in pairs or small groups to discuss the questions.

> **Vocabulary note**
> *standard of living* = how many material possessions (e.g. car, house, holidays abroad) you have (as opposed to *cost of living* = how much things cost to buy)

9A Stone Age economics

Books closed lead-in activity

Write on the board, *In life, what matters to me the most is …* Ask students to complete the sentence in any way they wish. Elicit sentences from students and discuss any interesting sentences as a class.

Speaking and vocabulary

Exercise 1

- Ask students to look at the words in the box. Check meaning and pronunciation.
- Ask students to work individually to choose their six most important needs.

Exercise 2

- Ask students to compare their lists in pairs. You could start students off by describing your choices. Have a class discussion.

Exercise 3

- Ask students to read the quotation, look at the pyramid, and answer the question.

Answer
B

Exercise 4

- Ask students to work in pairs to place the needs on the pyramid and discuss the question.

Answers
Self-actualisation: creativity; Esteem: feeling valued by others; Love: family; Safety: job security; Physiological: sleep

Listening

Exercise 5

- Ask students to work in pairs to match ages to photos. Then ask them to discuss the questions. Have a whole-class discussion.

Answers
A Hunter gatherers B Information Age C Industrial Age D New Stone Age

> **Vocabulary and culture note (and answers)**
> **Hunter gatherers** are so-called because in their nomadic society they hunted animals and gathered fruit, nuts, etc. The **New Stone Age** involved the adoption of agriculture, larger settlements and the development of pottery and stone tools.
>
> The **Industrial Age** describes the period which began at the end of the 18th century with the introduction of factories and water- or steam-powered machines. It was at its height from the 1850s to 1980s. The **Information Age** began with the introduction of computers and mobile phones in the 1980s. We are living in this technological age now.

Exercise 6   CD2/25

- Play the recording. Ask students to listen and answer the questions. Let them check their answers in pairs before discussing as a class.

Audioscript

In his book *The Original Affluent Society*, the anthropologist Marshall Sahlins argued that the early hunter gatherers were in fact a rich society. There are two ways to be rich – either you produce a lot to fulfil all your wants, or you have very few needs and wants and these are easily fulfilled by producing only a little. The early hunter gatherers fall into this second category. If we measure their standard of living by modern standards, they look poor. We see a people who move from place to place constantly searching for food, with no leisure and few comforts. They must be unhappy by our economic rules, because they are failing in the accepted goal, which should be to keep obtaining more material comforts.

Traditionally, anthropologists and historians have described the life of hunter gatherers as not much better than that of animals. But what was the reality? In fact, they only worked a few hours per day, probably no more than four to five hours, much less than someone in agriculture or a modern-day factory. The goods they needed – stone, wood, bone and animal skin – were abundant, and access was free for anyone who wished to take it. But being nomads, they did not want to acquire many objects because they could only keep what was portable: a bow and arrow to hunt, whatever clothing was necessary to protect them from the elements, and some simple form of shelter was enough for hunters. Because they were not in the business of acquiring material comforts, their ultimate objective was purely their health. If they remained healthy, they could remain mobile and fit for hunting. In fact the hunter had really no sense of possession or of property and showed little interest in developing his technical equipment.

The advent of the New Stone Age, when man settled down in one place to grow crops and domesticate animals, and began to use more sophisticated tools, is generally seen by historians as an enormous leap forward. But this development, argues Sahlins, marks the beginning of the modern economics of scarcity which continues to this day. In this system the price of things depends on how scarce or abundant they are. And where has it brought us?

Thirty to forty per cent of the world's population are said to go to bed hungry each night. In the time of the greatest technological power, starvation is at its height. This paradox is Sahlins' whole point. The amount of hunger seems to increase with the evolution of culture. Hunter gatherers had a tiny number of possessions, but they were not poor.

Answers
He says hunter gatherers were a rich society because even though they didn't have much, they didn't need or want much either. In the modern world, 'the time of greatest technological power', thirty to forty per cent of the population go hungry.

Exercise 7 CD2/25
- Give students time to read through the options carefully and choose any that they already know the answer to.
- Play the recording again. Ask students to listen and choose the correct options. Let them check their answers in pairs before discussing as a class.

Answers
1 B 2 D 3 B 4 C 5 B 6 D 7 A

Grammar: *(a) few* and *(a) little*
Exercise 8
- Ask students to work in pairs to discuss the difference in meaning.
- Refer students to the Grammar Reference on page 156.

Exercise 9
- Ask students to complete the sentences. Let them check their answers in pairs before discussing as a class.

Answers
1 little 2 a few 3 a little 4 little 5 a few 6 few

Speaking
Exercise 10
- Ask students to work in pairs or small groups to discuss the questions.

Extra activity

Write the following words on the board and see if students can recall their opposites from the listening (answers shown in brackets): *abundant* (scarce); *many* (few); *much* (little); *settled down* (nomadic); *enormous* (tiny); *throw away* (acquire).

Extra activity

Ask students to write true sentences about their lives using these sentence starters:

1 *I have little interest in …, so …*

2 *A few of my friends have shown a little interest in …, so …*

3 *These days, few films or books …, so …*

Books closed lead-in activity

Ask students to make a list of products and services that they get for free. In feedback, ask whether they pay for anything which they think they should get for free.

Vocabulary

Exercise 1

■ Ask students to complete the sentences. Let them check their answers in pairs before discussing as a class.

> **Answers**
> 1 for 2 for 3 on 4 for 5 for 6 on

> **Vocabulary note**
> Note the forms: *spend/waste (money) on;* but *pay (money) for; get (something) for; hire (something) for; charge (somebody) for*

Speaking

Exercise 2

■ Ask students to work in pairs to discuss the quotations.

> **Culture note**
> **Milton Friedman** was an American economist, statistician and recipient of the Nobel Prize in Economics. He advised President Ronald Reagan. He wrote a book entitled *There's no such thing as a free lunch* in 1975.
>
> **Dr Madsen Pirie** is a British researcher and author.
> Both economists are on the right wing of politics.

Exercise 3

■ Ask students to work in pairs to discuss the questions.

Exercise 4

■ Discuss the advertisement and questions as a class.

> **Answers**
> A free trial of an encyclopaedia (they hope after this you'll buy it, either because you like it or because you can't be bothered to cancel it).

Listening

Exercise 5  CD2/26

■ Give students time to read the summaries carefully. Then play the recording. Ask students to listen and choose the best summary. Let them check their answers in pairs before discussing as a class.

Audioscript

Interviewer	So, Rowan, you're going to tell us about the economics of giving things away for free, so-called 'freeconomics'. I think the question everyone will want answered, certainly *I* do, is where's the catch? You don't really get anything free in this life, do you?
Rowan	Well, I'd beg to differ on that … The whole economics of the Internet is really very different to the traditional way of doing business. You really can get more for free now than you ever could before.
Interviewer	Can you give us some real, convincing examples of that?
Rowan	Sure. Let's look at some different web-based models. The one used by most newspapers, like the *Financial Times*, or by magazines is where they offer users of the site free access to the most recent material to encourage you to use the site. However, if you want access to older or more specific articles, they ask you to pay a small subscription fee.
Interviewer	It's a bit like a free sample, isn't it, trying to hook you to buy more.

Rowan	Yes, a bit, I suppose. Particularly in that only about one per cent of the free users ever buy the premium service. There are other sites that don't charge the user anything at all for using them. Instead, once they've got a large number of visitors, they then persuade advertisers to pay for advertising space on the site. Another approach would be still not to charge the user anything, but to convince them to register on the site and give their contact details. Then the company can sell these details on to marketing companies.
Interviewer	That's a bit cheeky of them.
Rowan	Maybe, but it's nothing new. But, um, anyway, what's really interesting about the economics of the Internet is that the marginal cost of getting a new customer is more or less zero.
Interviewer	Sorry, you've lost me there …
Rowan	What I mean is the cost of distributing the product is the same, whether you have 6,000 customers or six million. That's why there is pressure on companies, for example, music companies like Sony, to give music away for free over the Internet, because it's not really costing them anything to do so. Some have agreed to do this; others are resisting, threatening to sue any website that gives their music away for free. Their argument is that they make their money from CD sales, and free internet downloads decrease these sales. What's interesting is that more and more of the artists themselves are suggesting giving their music away. They lose out on sales to consumers, but they benefit from a bigger audience in other ways: they may sell more concert tickets or get more plays of their music on radio.

Answer
B

> **Vocabulary note**
> *a trick* = here, a clever tactic that makes people do or think something

Exercise 6 CD2/26

■ Ask students to listen again and answer the questions. Let them check their answers in pairs before discussing as a class.

Answers

Type of business	1 Examples	2 What's free	3 How they make money
Newspapers/ magazines	*Financial Times*	Access to recent articles	You pay a subscription for access to older articles
websites	None	Use of the site	Advertising or selling users' details to marketing companies
Music business	Sony	Some music is free to download, some not	From CD sales

Exercise 7

■ Ask students to work in pairs to discuss the phrases.

Answers
1 what is the disadvantage 2 get you very interested 3 a little naughty or wrong 4 I didn't understand you 5 fail to get

> **Vocabulary note**
> *I beg to differ* = I have a different opinion; *more or less zero* = almost but not exactly zero

Exercise 8

■ Ask students to work in pairs to discuss the question.

Example answer
The cost of distributing the product is the same, whether you have 6000 customers or 6 million.

Grammar: reporting verbs

Exercise 9 CD2/27

- Give students time to read through the sentences and recall or guess what the missing words are.
- Play the recording. Ask students to listen and complete the gaps. Let them check their answers in pairs before discussing as a class. Ask students to tell you the form after each reporting verb.

> **Answers**
> 1 to pay 2 them to register 3 to do; to sue 4 giving

> **Grammar note**
> Note the form: 1 persuade (somebody) to do; 2 convince (somebody) to do; 3 agree to do; threaten to do; 4 suggest doing

Exercise 10

- Ask students to read the explanation and put the verbs in the correct places. Let them check their answers in pairs before discussing as a class.

> **Answers**
> to + infinitive: 1 persuade 2 convince 3 offer 4 threaten
> the gerund: 5 admit 6 suggest
> a preposition + the gerund: 7 forgive 8 thank 9 accuse

- Refer students to the Grammar Reference on page 156.

Exercise 11

Extra activity ————→

Ask students to write five personal sentences using reporting verbs from exercise 10, e.g. *Last week, I criticised my sister for not doing her homework.*

- Ask students to write the sentences. Do the first as a class to get students started. Let them check their answers in pairs before discussing as a class.

> **Answers**
> 1 He congratulated me on passing my exam. 2 He asked me to open the window.
> 3 He advised me to accept the job. 4 He promised to let me know tomorrow. 5 He recommended taking the train. 6 He accused me of not caring. 7 He threatened to leave without me if I was late. 8 He criticised them for making the test so difficult.

Exercise 12

- Ask students to read the explanation and complete the rules. Let them check their answers in pairs before discussing as a class.

> **Answers**
> wouldn't; hadn't; couldn't; likes.

- Refer students to the Grammar Reference on page 156.

Extra activity ————

Ask students to write up their story as a blog entry, using useful expressions and reporting verbs.

Exercise 13

- Ask students to choose a situation and make a few brief notes about how to tell the story. Monitor and help with ideas and vocabulary.
- Ask students to prepare to speak by thinking about how to tell their story using the useful expressions.
- When they are ready, ask students to tell their stories in pairs or small groups.

Social entrepreneurs

Books closed lead-in activity

Write the names of some world-famous entrepreneurs on the board and ask students to tell you what they know about them, e.g. Thomas Edison (electric products), Henry Ford (cars), Bill Gates (Microsoft), Richard Branson (Virgin).

Speaking

Exercise 1

■ Ask students to work in pairs to define *entrepreneur* and discuss famous examples from their country.

> **Vocabulary and pronunciation note**
> An *entrepreneur* /ˌɒntrəprəˈnɜː(r)/ is somebody who starts new businesses and has a lot of success and makes money. They are often risk-takers.

Exercise 2

■ Ask students to work in pairs to discuss the questions on page 142 at the back of the Student's Book. Have a brief feedback and find out what answers different students gave.

■ Ask students to read the analysis on page 144. Tell them to discuss what they found out with a partner, using the expressions in the box. Find out how many potential entrepreneurs there are in the class.

Answers	
Safe option	Risk-taking option
1 Company	Working for yourself
2 Don't borrow	Happy to borrow
3 Team member	Leader
4 Hasn't tried such a scheme	Has tried a money-making scheme
5 Ballroom dancing	Mountain climbing
6 Wouldn't buy the shares	Would buy the shares

> **Vocabulary note**
> *it's your head on the block* = you will suffer if things go wrong; *put yourself forward* = be confident and volunteer to do things; *it never crossed your mind* = you didn't think of it; *keep your feet on the ground* = be sensible and don't take chances

Vocabulary

Exercise 3

■ Ask students to work individually to complete the collocations. They should then discuss the meanings with a partner. Ask students to put the new words in a sentence to show that they understand the meaning.

> **Answers**
> 1 tackle 2 raise 3 implement 4 recruit 5 foster

Extra activity

You could introduce a set of vocabulary around this topic: *take a risk/chance; have a go; gamble/take a gamble; make a tricky decision; put your head on the block; play safe*

> **Vocabulary note**
> *tackle a problem* = try to deal with a problem; *raise money* = collect money by working, asking for donations, etc. in order to buy, support or pay for something (e.g. *raise money for charity*); *implement* = put in place or start; *recruit volunteers* = encourage people to join (often by advertising); *promote/foster innovation* = encourage and support it

Reading

Exercise 4

- Ask students to look at the title and photos, then predict what they think a 'changemaker' might be.
- Ask students to read the text quickly and answer the questions. Let students discuss their answers in pairs before discussing as a class.

> **Answers**
> A changemaker is someone who finds a solution to a social or economic problem. No specific qualifications are required, just a lot of persistence.

> **Vocabulary and culture note**
> *innovative* = creative; *receptive* = open to ideas
>
> **Bill Drayton** founded **Ashoka** in 1981 to support leading social entrepreneurs. The organisation is currently in over 60 countries and supports the work of over 2,000 social entrepreneurs.

Exercise 5

- Give students a moment to look through the options. Then ask them to read the article and choose the correct words. Let students check their answers in pairs before discussing as a class.

> **Answers**
> 1 B 2 A 3 C 4 D 5 A 6 C

Exercise 6

Extra activity ────────────

- Ask students to research the text and find words to match the definitions.

> **Answers**
> 1 pressing 2 persistance 3 slum 4 rot 5 chunks

Extra activity

Write five key words or phrases about each project on the board (e.g. *attract rats, deplete the soil*).
Tell students to use the key words or phrases when recalling and retelling the texts.

> **Pronunciation note**
> Note the stress: per<u>si</u>stence

Exercise 7

- Ask students to take it in turns to explain the projects. In feedback, ask different students to tell you what they remember about the projects.

Speaking

Exercise 8

Extra activity ────────────

- Divide students into small groups to think of a problem and discuss the questions.

Exercise 9

- Ask students to complete the table with details of their project.

Exercise 10

- Ask each group to prepare their presentation using expressions from the box. When they are ready, ask groups to present their projects to the class.

Extra activity

Ask students to research another project on the Internet that is supported by Ashoka. Ask them to take notes about it then present it to the class.

Negotiating

Speaking
Exercise 1

- Lead in by asking students to look at the photo. Ask, *What are the people doing? Where are they? Have you ever had to negotiate? What was the situation?*
- Ask students to work in pairs to discuss the questions.

Listening: negotiating with a sales person
Exercise 2  CD2/28

- Ask students to read the situation and predict what the speakers might say.
- Play the recording. Ask students to listen and answer the questions. Let students check their answers in pairs before discussing as a class.

Audioscript

Student	Mmm, well the blue one is really nice, but it's a bit more than I was thinking of paying. £900 is a lot of money for a scooter that's four years old.
Salesman	How much did you have in mind?
Student	I wouldn't really want to spend more than £700.
Salesman	Sorry, I couldn't possibly let it go for that little. What about the red one we saw earlier?
Student	Yeah, well that one's *a lot* older. Would you be willing to drop the price a bit on the blue one? Perhaps meet me halfway?
Salesman	Look, to be honest, I'm in no great hurry to sell it. It only came in two days ago. If you were to come back in a month and it was still here, I might be prepared to come down a bit.
Student	No, I can't wait a month. Supposing I was to give you the full £900, what kind of warranty could you offer me?
Salesman	Standard warranty – three months.
Student	Oh. Look, can't you move on the price a bit or throw something else in, like a year's free service or …
Salesman	Sorry, I really can't. The fact of the matter is: I'm not making much on it as it is.
Student	OK. Well, I guess I'll have to leave it then. I may call you in a couple of weeks if I haven't found anything else.

> **Answers**
> 1 She doesn't buy one. 2 She feels that he isn't moving in her direction at all.

Exercise 3

- Ask students to work in pairs to discuss the questions. Have a whole-class discussion.

Exercise 4  CD2/28

- Play the recording again. Ask students to listen and complete the sentences. Let students check their answers in pairs before discussing as a class.

> **Answers**
> 1 have in mind 2 want to go higher 3 couldn't possibly 4 drop the price; halfway 5 might be prepared 6 Supposing; you offer me 7 fact of the matter 8 have to leave

> **Grammar note**
> Notice the use of the second conditional for hypothesis in the useful expressions, used when negotiating to present hypothetical arguments. In particular, notice the use of *Supposing* in place of *If* to make a supposition, and *If you were to (come back),* which is also used to make a supposition.

Books closed lead-in activity

Write the word *Swap* on the board, and explain its meaning. Tell students to think of three things they possess which they don't want anymore. Then put them into groups of three and ask them to tell their partners which possessions they no longer want and would like to swap. Tell students to negotiate so that they swap their possessions for things of similar value.

Extra activity

Check the vocabulary in the text by writing the following definitions on the board and asking students to find synonyms in exercise 4 (answers in brackets): *think of* (have in mind), *reduce* (drop, come down), *offer a price that is between yours and mine* (meet me halfway).

Pronunciation: sentence stress

Exercise 5   CD2/29

■ Ask students to look at the first three sentences and predict where they think the stress will fall. Then play the recording. Students listen and mark the stress. Let students check their answers in pairs before discussing as a class.

> **Answers**
> 2 I <u>wouldn't</u> really <u>want</u> to <u>spend</u> <u>more</u> than <u>£700</u>. 3 Sorry, I <u>couldn't</u> possibly <u>let</u> it <u>go</u> for that <u>little</u>.

> **Pronunciation note**
> The stress falls on words that carry most meaning.

Exercise 6

■ Ask students to practise saying the sentences in pairs. Monitor and listen for good sentence stress.

Speaking: getting a good deal

Exercise 7

Extra activity ────

■ Lead in by asking students what sorts of things housemates have to negotiate when living together. Elicit a list.
■ Divide students into groups of four. Ask each student to read the information carefully, and decide what their negotiating position should be. For example, ask them to decide whether they would prefer a large room or a lower rent, to do shopping or cooking.
■ When ready, ask the groups to role play the situation, using the useful expressions in the box. Monitor and note errors and good language use.

> **Grammar note**
> Notice the use of the second conditional for hypothesis in the useful expressions. Remind students of the form and use by referring them to exercise 4 again if necessary.

Exercise 8

■ Ask groups to compare answers. At the end, have a class discussion and find out which students got the best deal.

Writing: a report of a meeting

Exercise 9

■ Ask students to work in pairs to answer the questions. Brainstorm a list of details and write them on the board.

Exercise 10

■ Ask students to read the opening sentence and check their answers to exercise 9.

Exercise 11

■ Ask students to work in pairs to complete the information box.

> **Answers**
> **Subject:** to discuss new accommodation; **Participants:** student union representatives and the Dean of the University; **Action agreed:** to carry out an evaluation of existing accommodation

> **Vocabulary note**
> The *Dean* is a senior official at a university.

Extra activity

After students have prepared ideas, but before they do the role play, ask them to briefly work in pairs, writing a short simple dialogue using the expressions. Ask a few pairs to act out their dialogues. Point out errors of form and pronunciation. This prepares students to be more accurate when they do the actual role play.

Exercise 12

- Ask students to read through the words in the box. Check any unknown meanings or difficult pronunciations. Then ask students to work in pairs to discuss the form. In feedback, categorise the verbs according to what form they are followed by.

Answers
admitted that / doing; **argued** that; **commented** that; **complained** that; **considered** doing; **asked** if / someone to do; **offered** to do; **pointed out** that; **promised** that / to do; **say** that; **proposed** doing / that someone should do; **said** that; **suggested** doing / that; **urged** doing

> **Vocabulary and pronunciation note**
> *propose* = suggest (in a formal way); *urge* = encourage strongly
> Note the verbs with stress on the second syllable: ad<u>mit</u>, com<u>plain</u>, con<u>sid</u>er, pro<u>pose</u>, sug<u>gest</u>.

Exercise 13

Extra activity ──────────→

- Ask students to read the report and correct the verbs. Let them check their answers in pairs before discussing as a class.

Answers
1 Correct 2 Incorrect – had received 3 Correct 4 Incorrect – fallen 5 Incorrect – of putting 6 Correct 7 Incorrect – would consider 8 Correct 9 Incorrect – promised to carry out 10 Incorrect – meeting

> **Vocabulary note**
> *a full survey* = a thorough, official check of a building carried out by a surveyor

Exercise 14

- Lead in by eliciting negotiation situations that students could use as a resource from which to write the report.
- Ask students to summarise the report using bullet points as in exercise 11. Then ask them to note down briefly what different people said. Using their notes, students then write the report using reporting verbs.

Exercise 15

- Ask students to compare their work with a partner and to comment on errors and the use of reporting verbs.

Extra activity

Write the following sentence starters on the board: *Why don't you …;
I really think …; I'm afraid
I … ; In my opinion;
I think …; You really
should …; Shall I …;
Would you ….*

Ask students in pairs to complete the sentences. Then ask them to swap their sentences with another pair. The pairs must now report the sentences using the reporting verbs in exercise 12.

Books closed lead-in activity —→

Write on the board *private sector jobs* and *public sector jobs*. Brainstorm a list of jobs typical of each sector from the class. Ask, *Which sector would you like to work in and why?*

Vocabulary

Exercise 1

- Ask students to work in pairs to complete the phrases with the missing words. Do the first as a class as an example.

Answers
1 multinational 2 family 4 employed 5 NGO 6 company 7 civil 8 sector

Exercise 2

- Ask students to match the organisations to the descriptions. Let them check their answers in pairs before discussing as a class.

Answers
a 3 b 8 c 2 d 6 e 1 f 5 g 4 h 7

> **Vocabulary and pronunciation note**
>
> Note the stress: multinational corporation; co-operative; civil service; public sector
>
> The *third sector* refers to jobs in charitable organisations. **Civil servants** include parliamentary secretaries.

Exercise 3

- Ask students to work in pairs to think of examples. Have a whole-class discussion. Ask, *What is the third sector? Who works for the civil service? Which of these areas of working life appeal to you and why?*

Reading

Exercise 4

- Ask students to look at the headline and predict what the message of the article might be. Ask them to read the article quickly and answer the questions. Let students check their answers in pairs before discussing as a class.

Answers
Young people are becoming more interested in working in the public sector or for a charity.
The reputation of the private sector was damaged by the economic crisis of 2008 and they want to do a job that benefits others.

> **Vocabulary note**
> *shattered* = literally, broken into small pieces – here, it means destroyed or completely undermined; *tarnished* = literally, it means the gloss has been damaged – here, *a tarnished reputation* is one which has lost its credibility

Extra activity

Ask students to match *shake*, *tarnish* and *shatter* (verbs in the text) to the words below (answers in brackets): *silver* (tarnish), *dice* (shake), *a reputation* (tarnish/shatter), *confidence* (shake/shatter), *a windshield* (shatter), *metal* (tarnish), *a tambourine* (shake), *a belief* (shake/shatter), *a glass* (shatter).

Exercise 5

- Give students a moment to read through the questions. Check any unknown words and ask them to predict answers from their general knowledge.
- Ask students to read the article more carefully to find answers. Let them check their answers in pairs before discussing as a class.

Answers
1 boring, badly paid and with limited career opportunities 2 public sector and charity jobs 3 job security; high salary 4 It has been tarnished.

Listening

Exercise 6 CD2/30

■ Ask students to read the introduction and questions. Then play the recording. Let students check their answers in pairs before discussing as a class.

Audioscript

Interviewer	So, Kate, you finish university in June this year. Do you know what you're going to do next?
Kate	Mmm, actually I've already started applying for jobs.
Interviewer	Oh, I see. Can I just ask what you study?
Kate	Yes, I read English and politics.
Interviewer	OK, and what kind of jobs are you looking for?
Kate	Well, I've got two main ideas: one is to find a job in journalism. I did some writing for the university gazette, and I also managed to get some film and concert reviews published in the local paper in Warwick, where I study, so I have a bit of experience of that, and it's something I enjoy.
Interviewer	Do you have any idea how easy it is to get jobs in journalism?
Kate	It's really competitive. I'm not that hopeful. So my other idea is to work for a charity or an NGO, perhaps helping with writing newsletters or information leaflets, stuff like that.
Interviewer	I see, but the terms charity and NGO cover a lot of organisations. Can you tell me what kind of organisation appeals to you? Is there something specific?
Kate	Not really, as long as it helps people in some way. That's important to me. Either helping disadvantaged people or doing something to improve the environment. I'm quite open-minded about it. I mean it's not as if the job I choose now is going to be the one I have for the rest of my life. I'll probably work for a lot of different organisations. If I'm lucky, I might get more than one career … in charity work *and* in journalism.
Interviewer	Is the salary important to you?
Kate	Not *very* important. What's more important is that I like the people I work with and that I have enough freedom and flexibility to have a life outside work.
Interviewer	Can you just explain what you mean by that?
Kate	Yeah, that I can carry on doing the things I like doing in my free time – travelling, seeing my friends, doing yoga …
Interviewer	And lastly Kate, I have to ask you. You seem a very relaxed and confident person and these are not easy economic times … What do you think your future employer will be looking for? Why will they choose you ahead of other candidates?
Kate	I think qualifications are becoming less important, in the sense that everyone has them now, so you have to really care about the job you do. That's what I want to show an employer, that I'm keen, enthusiastic, passionate even …

> **Answers**
> 1 a journalist or working for an NGO/charity 2 She has experience of writing for the university magazine; she wants to help people. 3 enthusiasm and passion

Exercise 7 CD2/30

■ Give students time to read through the statements and answer any they can.
■ Play the recording. Students choose True or False. Let them check their answers in pairs before discussing as a class.

> **Answers**
> 1 True 2 True (competitive) 3 False 4 False (will work for a lot of organisations) 5 True
> 6 False (everyone has them now)

Grammar: indirect questions

Exercise 8

■ Ask students to work in pairs to complete the questions. In feedback, ask them to say which are indirect.

Exercise 9 ⊙ CD2/31

■ Play the recording. Ask students to listen and check their answers.
■ Discuss and note the form of indirect questions.

> **Answers**
> **1** you're going to do (indirect question) **2** you study/you are studying (indirect question) **3** are you looking **4** it is (indirect question) **5** appeals (indirect question) **6** Is the salary **7** you mean (indirect question) **8** your future employer will look for/be looking for (indirect question)

> **Grammar note**
> In an indirect question, the usual word order in questions changes to the word order typical of statements. So, *What time is it?* changes to *Do you know what time it is?* And *Where does he live?* changes to *Can you tell me where he lives*.

■ Refer students to the Grammar Reference on page 157.

Speaking

Exercise 10

■ Ask students to work in pairs to read through the categories and discuss the results. Check that students know what the categories are by asking them to tell you the types of job people might have in each sector.

> **Vocabulary note**
> *real estate* = buying and selling houses and other property

Exercise 11

■ Divide the class into groups of four to six. Tell students to prepare questions to ask, making sure some of their questions are indirect. Then tell them to take it in turns to interview people, making sure that everybody interviews at least two people.
■ Ask each group to collate their information, and then elicit what each group found out and note it on the board. Write up how many people in each group expressed a wish to work in which sector. Then ask groups to look at the information on the board and work out the percentage for each sector.

Extra activity

Ask students to work in pairs to think of and write down five questions that people typically ask at a job interview. Tell them to exchange their questions with another pair. They must now change the questions into indirect questions.

Extra activity

Ask students to imagine they are going to interview an expert or an employer in one of the sectors in the table in exercise 10. Tell them to work in pairs to choose a sector and prepare five indirect questions to ask. You could then pair students with someone from another pair to role play the interview: one student asks questions, the other improvises answers.

Starting your own business

Ask students, *If you could set up your own business, what sort of business would it be? Why would you set up such a business?* Ask students to think for a moment and then tell their partner.

Listening and speaking

Exercise 1

- Ask students to work in pairs or small groups to discuss the questions. Then ask students to tell you what answers they came up with to questions 3 and 4.

Exercise 2 CD2/32

- Give students a moment to read through the reasons. Check any unknown words.
- Play the recording. Ask students to listen and complete the reasons. Let them check their answers in pairs before discussing as a class.

Audioscript

Most people think that not having enough funds in the bank is the main reason for failure, but actually that's only the third most common mistake. The main reasons are first, that people start a business for the wrong reasons, thinking it's going to make them rich or that they're going to have a lot more free time, which is never the case; and secondly, that they have no previous experience of managing a business. They think a good idea will automatically translate into a profitable business. But it doesn't work like that.

Another factor that people often ignore is the importance of location. They have a good idea for a shop or a restaurant and then they take the first premises they find, not considering how easily their customers will find it or get to it.

Number five on the list is lack of planning, and the last is expanding too quickly. Some start-ups do very well in their first two years, expand, and then when business drops they are left with heavy bills that they can't pay.

> **Answers**
> 1 wrong reasons 2 management 3 funds 4 location 5 planning 6 Expanding

Exercise 3 CD2/32

- Ask students to listen and answer the question. Let them check their answers in pairs before discussing as a class.

> **Answers**
> They think it's going to make them rich or that they're going to have a lot more free time.

Exercise 4 CD2/33

- Give students time to read the situation and questions. Ask, *What advice would you give someone who wants to set up a business?*
- Play the recording. Ask students to listen then discuss the questions in pairs.

Audioscript

Adviser	So, I understand you'd like to set up your own business. How can we help?
Andrew	That's right, a friend and I would like to set up our own internet café and I wanted to find out how we go about getting a small business loan …
Adviser	OK, OK. Let's just start at the beginning. Can you tell me why you want to set up this café?
Andrew	Why? Um, because we've found some really nice premises and we think it's an excellent business opportunity.
Adviser	OK, fair enough. Where are these premises?
Andrew	It's a café in West Street that has a five-year lease.
Adviser	OK. That's a good location – convenient for university students. And have you managed a business before?
Andrew	Not really, no. But I've helped my father run his own restaurant for two years.
Adviser	Have you written a business plan?
Andrew	Well, we've worked out how much money we're going to need. And we've also calculated what our turnover needs to be to pay the rent and cover the other costs … But a formal plan, no.

Adviser	Well, that's the first thing to do. The bank will want to see a proper business plan. And it's also a very good exercise for you to do some careful planning before you begin. You say you need money … Do you have any funds of your own to invest?
Andrew	We've got some savings, about £7,000 between us.
Adviser	Good. And what do you need to borrow more for?
Andrew	We need a small loan to help us with set up costs, furnishing the café and putting in computers, but not more than £5,000, I don't think … Is there some kind of low-interest loan we can get, you know for small businesses?
Adviser	Yes, there is. It's also good that you have some money of your own to put in. So what I'm going to ask you to do is to take away this business plan document and fill it in. Then we can arrange another meeting to go through it in detail.
Andrew	OK, great. Well thanks for your time.

> **Answers**
> 1 an internet café 2 make a proper business plan

Exercise 5

■ Ask students to work in pairs to categorise the words. In feedback, ask students to tell you how they would explain each word.

> **Answers**
> Finance: lease, loan, low interest, savings, turnover
> Location: convenient, lease, premises

> **Vocabulary note**
> *lease* = the legal agreement allowing you to rent a property; *premises* = the building where the business is

Exercise 6 CD2/33

■ Ask students to listen again and take notes on Andrew's answers.

> **Answers**
> 1 We've found some really nice premises and we think it's an excellent business opportunity. 2 Not really, no. But I've helped my father run his own restaurant for two years. 3 We've got some savings, about £7,000 between us. 4 It's a café in West Street that has a five-year lease. 5 Well, we've worked out how much money we're going to need. And we've also calculated what our turnover needs to be to pay the rent and cover the other costs … But a formal plan, no.

Exercise 7

Extra activity ————→

■ Ask students to share their notes in pairs. Find out which pairs think the business will be a success and why.

Exercise 8

■ Divide students into pairs and ask them to choose a business and prepare details.

Exercise 9

■ Ask students to find a new partner and to prepare to speak by looking at the useful expressions and thinking about how to use them to ask for and give advice.

■ Ask students to act out their role plays. Monitor for errors and good language use.

■ When they have finished, ask students to change roles and repeat the role play.

Ask students in pairs to write a business plan. Give them the following headings: **1** name and type of company **2** premises and location **3** funding **4** business experience required **5** expenses **6** plans for development and expansion.

Ask them to write this plan as part of the preparation for the role play (exercise 8).

Doing the right thing

10

UNIT OVERVIEW

Topic	moral dilemmas, good practice at work, ethical travel, asking for advice, British and Canadian sense of humour
Reading	Don't stop snitching, The Stanford Marshmallow Experiment, Intelligent Travel (ethical travel), hoaxes
Listening	interview about unethical practices in the workplace, interview with a psychologist, people talking about giving advice
Grammar	past ability (*could/was able to*, etc.), future in the past, *better*, *should* and *ought to*
Function	giving advice
Vocabulary	types of behaviour, workplace crimes, personality, holidays
Pronunciation	homophone vowel sounds
Writing	a review of a TV documentary
Speaking	discussing course of action for a variety of workplace crimes, talking about changing your mind, presenting alternative plans to those of a developer, discussing English proverbs, discussing moral dilemmas
Culture	sense of humour

Books closed lead-in activity

Elicit some human character types from the class and write them on the board, e.g. serious, relaxed, studious, nervous, happy and so on. Ask students to think about how they would describe their own characters. Ask them to talk about themselves in groups of four, and see if their classmates agree with them.

Let's get started

Exercise 1

- Ask the class to read the quotations and comment upon them. Encourage them to discuss the ideas.

Exercise 2

- Ask students to discuss the questions and guess percentages. Write the guesses on the board.

Vocabulary and speaking

Exercise 3

- Give students a moment to read through the words. Check any difficult pronunciations.
- Put students in pairs to complete the table. Explain any words that students aren't sure of.

> **Answers**
> Being rational: Use . . . your head; common sense; reason; your judgement
> Being instinctive: Follow . . . your heart; your intuition; your feelings; your instincts
> Be just and honest: Play . . . fair; by the rules; straight; the game

Extra activity

Ask students in pairs to think of and describe situations where well-known people have been rational or instinctive. Ask some pairs to tell the class using phrases from exercise 3.

Exercise 4

■ Check that students know *former* (the one said or written first) and *latter* (the one said or written second). Then ask students to work in pairs or small groups to discuss the questions.

■ You could ask one person from each group to tell the class how rational each person in their group is.

Vocabulary and speaking

Exercise 1

- Give students time to read through the actions. Explain any unknown words or ask students to use a dictionary. Then ask students to work in pairs to discuss the actions.

> **Vocabulary note**
> *leak information* = to allow information that you have to get into the hands of the newspapers by, for example, secretly telling a journalist or putting it on the Internet anonymously; *testify against* = give evidence against; *spread a rumour* = pass on a rumour (something that might not be true)

> **Answers**
> 1 a 2 b 3 b 4 c 5 a 6 c 7 a

Reading

Exercise 2

- Ask students to work in pairs to discuss the words. Ask questions to check meaning, for example, *Which one sees a crime?* (witness) *Which one commits a crime?* (offender).

> **Vocabulary and pronunciation note (and answers)**
> A *witness* sees a crime; a *victim* suffers from a crime; an *offender* commits a crime; a *sentence* is a fine or period of time in jail that the judge gives an offender.
> Note the stress: *witness, victim, offender, sentence.*

Exercise 3

- Ask students to look at the heading. Ask if anyone knows what *snitching* might be. Then ask students to read the text and answer the questions. Let students check their answers in pairs before discussing as a class.

> **Answers**
> Snitching is telling on others – telling the police who has committed a crime. Everyone, including offenders, does it. Criminals want to stop it.

> **Vocabulary and culture note**
> *witness intimidation* = threatening witnesses so they don't report crimes or speak in court
> **Baltimore**, like New York, is a city on the east coast of the USA with a large, poor, urban underclass.

Exercise 4

- Ask students to read again and answer the questions. Let students check their answers in pairs before discussing as a class.

> **Answers**
> 1 You will receive severe punishment from the criminals you snitch on. 2 Criminals won't get caught. 3 To get a reduced sentence (punishment) from the courts. 4 It is part of a code of honour.

Books closed lead-in activity

Write on the board *Blowing the whistle*. Ask students in pairs to have a guess at what it means (without using a dictionary). Elicit a few ideas before revealing the answer (it means reporting or revealing that a person or institution is doing something wrong or illegal).

Extra activity

Ask students to discuss in what situations they would snitch on someone at school who has done something wrong, and in what situations they would not snitch.

Vocabulary

Exercise 5

■ Lead in by eliciting crimes or unethical practices in the workplace. Build up a list on the board.

■ Ask students to work in pairs to match the words to the definitions.

> **Answers**
> 1 corporate manslaughter 2 bribery 3 conflict of interest 4 theft 5 discrimination 6 fraud

> **Vocabulary and pronunciation note**
> *Manslaughter* is different from murder in that the wrongdoer had no actual intent to kill somebody.
> Note the stress and pronunciation: *bribery* /ˈbraɪb(ə)ri/; *manslaughter* /ˈmænˌslɔːtə(r)/; *discrimination*; *fraud* /frɔːd/.

Exercise 6

■ Ask students to discuss the question in pairs or small groups. Then have a whole-class discussion.

Listening

Exercise 7 CD2/34

■ Give students a moment to read the question. Then play the recording. Let students check answers in pairs before discussing as a class.

Audioscript

Interviewer	What I don't really understand is whether whistle-blowing on colleagues is an employee's duty or just a right, something they can do if they think it's appropriate.
Representative	Well, different companies have different policies on this. Some say it is just a right, others that it is a duty. But in most cases it depends on how serious the bad practice that's detected is. For example, let's imagine that you think one of your colleagues is offering bribes to a customer in order to win a big contract. Most companies would say in that case that you have a duty to inform the management.
Interviewer	But that's tricky, isn't it? Because the senior management may well have colluded in the bribe-giving. I mean, they may have given the OK for these illegal payments to be made.
Representative	Yes, it's very difficult for the employee who suspects unethical practice. For a start, he or she may not be sure of the information. And then, as you say, he may not know who actually gave the order or idea for the unethical practice. The truth is that often management doesn't openly sanction such behaviour, but it just turns a blind eye to it. In other words, it kind of chooses not to know.
Interviewer	OK, and what about a less serious case such as when you know one of your colleagues is helping themselves to office equipment – printer cartridges, let's say, which are a small item, but not cheap and can build up over time. Not many people would blow the whistle in that case, would they?
Representative	No, I don't think they would, unless they had a particular dislike for that colleague and wanted to see them fired or disciplined in some way, and that's another problem. But the right thing to do in that case would be to warn the colleague that what they were doing was pretty obvious. And that if it's obvious to you, then it might well be that a more senior manager had also noticed it, so they had better be careful and stop it before they get found out.
Interviewer	So, you're saying that rather than blow the whistle, in some cases we should intervene directly ourselves?
Representative	Yes, I am. I think that's the crucial point. It's up to all of us to make sure that business is conducted in an ethical way. Sometimes this will mean informing management if you suspect bad practice. In other cases it will mean taking direct action ourselves.

Extra activity

It is a good idea to research recent well-known cases of these crimes before the lesson. Write up a headline for each story you found and ask students if they can say what happened and what the crime was.

Answer

She talks about a colleague offering bribes to win a contract, and a colleague stealing stationery from the company.

> **Vocabulary note**
> *detect* = find out; *collude with* = be in agreement with (bad practice); *tricky* = difficult; *sanction* = agree with and permit to happen; *turn a blind eye* = pretend not to notice

Exercise 8 CD2/34

- Ask students to read the options carefully and choose any that they think they already know the answer to.
- Play the recording. Students listen and circle the correct options. Let students check their answers in pairs before discussing as a class.

> **Answers**
> 1 C 2 A 3 D 4 A

Exercise 9

- Ask students to work in pairs to discuss the questions. Have a whole-class discussion.

Pronunciation: vowel sounds

Exercise 10 CD2/35

- Ask students to work in pairs to decide on the sounds. Then play the recording. Students listen and check. Then play the recording again. Students listen and repeat.

> **Answers**
> /ɪ/: whistle, printer; /iː/: colleague, senior, illegal
> /ʊ/: would, look; /uː/: collude, truth, crucial
> /e/: many, ethical; /eɪ/: case, change, payment

> **Pronunciation note**
> Show students the different position of the lips involved in producing these sounds. The lips are wider when producing the long sound /iː/ than when producing the short sound /ɪ/. The lips are rounded when producing both /ʊ/ and the longer sound /uː/, but tighter and more pursed for /uː/. The lips are much wider when making the diphthong /eɪ/ than they are when making the short sound /e/.

Speaking

Exercise 11

- Give students a few minutes to read the cases, and then check for unknown words and general understanding.
- Ask students to work in small groups to discuss each case. Tell them to look at the *Useful expressions box* first, and think of one or two things to say before doing the first case. Monitor and prompt, and note errors and good language use.
- Ask students to compare ideas with another group, or ask a spokesperson from each group to summarise for the class what was said in their group.

> **Vocabulary note**
> Note the use of *need to*, *have to* and *should* to express strong and mild obligation in the useful expressions.

Extra activity

Ask students to work in small groups to prepare a short leaflet entitled 'Good practice at school'. Tell them to brainstorm advice for good practice (for example, *Don't copy other people's homework*), and then to express the advice in five or six bullet points.

Human nature

Books closed lead-in activity

Ask students to think of three things they could do at the age of eight which they can't do anymore (for example, *I could climb through the small hole in our garden wall*). Ask them to tell a partner. Elicit funny or interesting examples.

Extra activity

Ask students in pairs to design their own experiment to test whether students in their class are impulsive. In feedback, find out which pair has the best idea.

Vocabulary

Exercise 1

■ Ask students to work in pairs to match the adjectives. Ask students to say which ones are positive and which are negative.

> **Answers**
> 1 shy / outgoing 2 confident / insecure 3 impulsive / cautious 4 attentive / distracted
> 5 anxious / easygoing 6 naughty / well-behaved

> **Pronunciation note**
> Note the stress on the second syllable: *distracted, impulsive, attentive*

Exercise 2

■ Ask students to describe themselves as an eight-year-old child to their partner, using the words in exercise 1.

> **Example answer**
> I was an anxious child and I didn't like being on my own. However, I was attentive in class and very well-behaved.

Reading

Exercise 3

■ Ask students to look at the photo and headline. Check that they know what a *marshmallow* is. Ask, *What do you think the experiment might have been?*
■ Ask students to read the text and summarise the experiment. Let students try out their summaries on a partner before asking one or two students to summarise for the class.

> **Example answer**
> The experiment involved asking children to sit in a room with a marshmallow, and seeing if they could control the impulse to eat it. The immediate result was that while some children couldn't resist eating the marshmallow at all, others were able to. Fourteen years later, experimenters found that throughout their lives there had been big differences between the achievements of the impulsive children and the ones who could control impulses.

> **Vocabulary and culture note**
> *devoured* = ate quickly; *agonised* = worried a lot; *grabbed* = took quickly
>
> **Walter Mischel**, who was born in 1930, is an American psychologist. He specialises in personality theory and social psychology.
>
> The **SAT** is a standard test for admission to college in the USA.

Grammar: past ability

Exercise 4

■ Ask students to work in pairs to discuss the question about the excerpt. Then ask them to read the explanation and check.
■ Ask students to tell you about things they could do as small children, and to tell you about a situation when they had to show a specific ability. Elicit a few ideas.

Answer
Because it is describing an ability on one particular occasion.

> **Grammar note**
> There is a (very) subtle difference between *was able to* + infinitive, which stresses having the ability (*Tom was able to swim to shore because of his strong arms*), *managed to* + infinitive, which stresses reaching an aim (*He managed to open the lock after hours of trying*), and *succeeded in* + *-ing*, which stresses being successful (*I succeeded in passing all my exams*). To most intents and purposes, however, they are interchangeable.

■ Refer students to the Grammar Reference on page 158.

Exercise 5

■ Ask students to choose the correct options. Let students check their answers in pairs before discussing as a class.

Answers
1 could 2 was able to 3 managed to 4 couldn't/wasn't able to 5 could see
6 succeeded in avoiding 7 couldn't understand 8 could

Exercise 6

■ Ask students to write three sentences. Tell them to write them about their own experiences. Ask students to read out and check their sentences in pairs.

Listening

Exercise 7 CD2/36

■ Give students a moment to read the summarising sentences. Ask them to guess which one might be the correct answer.
■ Play the recording. Students listen and choose the best answer. Let them check their answers in pairs before discussing as a class.

Audioscript

Interviewer	So, what does the test really tell us about human nature? Because I imagine there are a lot of parents out there thinking, 'Oh My child is really impulsive. Are they going to end up failing in school, failing in their relationships and everything else?'
Psychologist	No, no, not at all. Because controlling your impulses is something that you can learn. Everybody wants the marshmallow as badly as the next person. The key is how you deal with the desire … how you control it.
Interviewer	So it's about will-power, then – mind over matter.
Psychologist	Sure. The kid who was about to eat it and then worked out a strategy to avoid doing that is the same kid who would later work out strategies for controlling other impulses that didn't serve his long-term interests. He is the one who stayed in to study for a couple of hours before going out to play basketball. Or the one who was going to hit his friend when he insulted him but thought better of it and just walked away. But there are strategies that can be learned. The experimenters at Stanford taught the kids some simple tricks – like pretending the marshmallow was just a picture or a cloud, and kids who previously hadn't been able to control themselves for 15 seconds were able to do so for 15 minutes. From simple strategies like that you get amazing results.

Answer
C

Alternative activity

Ask each student to write two true facts about themselves using expressions of ability, and one false 'fact' which is believable but not true. In pairs, students must ask questions about their partner's facts until they can guess which one is false.

Grammar: future in the past

Exercise 8

- Ask students to work in pairs to compare the sentences and underline the forms. Then ask students to explain the rule in their own words.

Answers
Tenses move one back, so *is* to *was*, *works* to *worked*, *will* to *would*, *don't* to *didn't*. In text A, the future form *will later work out* becomes, in text B, the future-in-the-past form, *would later work out*

- Refer students to the Grammar Reference on page 158.

Exercise 9

- Ask students to transform the sentences. Let them compare answers before having a whole-class discussion.

Example answers
2 She was going to apply to study in America, but her parents didn't want her to go abroad.

3 They were about to buy a big new apartment on the riverfront, but they decided to move to the country instead.

4 I promised I would help you to paint your room, but I'm afraid I was too busy.

5 The council was to build a huge new shopping mall in the city centre, but they built a library instead.

6 I hoped I was not going to be asked to make a speech, but then one of the speakers couldn't attend and I had to.

Speaking

Exercise 10

- Give students time to read the situations and prepare what to say. Monitor and help students who aren't sure what to talk about.
- Ask students to work in pairs to talk about their experiences.

Extra activity

Ask students to write three sentences about things they planned to do or promised to do last week but failed to. Ask them to tell their partner about what these things were and why they didn't happen.

Ethical travel 10C

Vocabulary

Exercise 1

- Ask students to complete the sentences with their own adjectives. Do the first as a class to get them started.

> **Vocabulary note**
> *tacky* = cheap, touristy and in poor taste

Exercise 2

- Ask students to work in pairs to compare their answers with the words in the box.

> **Answers**
> 1 remote 2 authentic 3 built-up 4 unspoilt 5 package 6 guided 7 eco-friendly

> **Pronunciation note**
> Note the stress on the second syllable: *authentic, remote, unspoilt*.

Speaking

Exercise 3

- Ask students to work in pairs to discuss the questions before discussing as a class.

Reading

Exercise 4

- Ask students to look at the headline. Ask, *What is 'intelligent travel'?* Elicit several suggestions.
- Ask students to read the text quickly, and in feedback ask them what they found out about intelligent travel from the text.
- Give students time to read through the sentences in the exercise. Then ask them to read the text carefully and match the sentences. Let students check their answers in pairs before discussing as a class.

> **Answers**
> 1 D 2 B 3 A 4 E

> **Vocabulary and culture note**
> *paved* = covered with cement; *enhances* = improves; *incentives* = reasons to do something positive
> **Baja** (lower) **California** is the southern part of the Californian peninsula. It is part of Mexico.

Exercise 5

- Discuss the question as a class.

> **Answer**
> The key is to be aware of how you and your money fit into the place you are visiting – to sustain the geographical character of a place and to be proactive.

Books closed lead-in activity

Ask students to tell a partner about when they go on holiday: where to, what they do, and who they go with. In feedback, find out about students' holidays.

Extra activity

Ask students to give you examples of remote places, authentic culture, unspoilt areas and built-up areas in their country.

Extra activity

Ask half the class (in pairs) to make a list of the advantages of tourism, and half the class to list disadvantages. In feedback, find out which is the longer list.

Pronunciation: homophone vowel sounds

Exercise 6　CD2/37

- Ask students to match the words. Do the first as a class to get them started.
- Play the recording. Students listen and check. Then put students in pairs to practise saying the words.

> **Answers**
> 1 wild　2 cruise　3 worse　4 role　5 neighbour　6 build　7 wise　8 plants　9 stuff

Speaking

Exercise 7

Extra activity

Divide students into groups of four. Students choose one of the following roles: a local politician, a villager, an environmentalist, a resort developer. Tell students they are going to debate the building of the resort. Tell students to prepare their arguments according to their role, then to discuss the plans in exercise 7, and compromise on how they should be adapted.

- Ask students to read the information and plans. In feedback, ask, *In what ways are the plans insensitive to the inhabitants? How do they affect the environment?* Elicit several ideas.
- Divide students into groups of three or four to draw up new plans. Monitor and help with ideas.
- When they are ready, ask students to prepare to speak about their new plans, and to decide who is going to make the presentation.
- Ask a spokesperson from each group to come to the front of the class and present their group's ideas. At the end, vote on which set of plans should be implemented.
- Refer students to the DVD about saving the Amazon together. Video worksheet on page 140.

The right thing to do

10D

Speaking

Exercise 1

- Ask students to work in pairs to discuss the quotation.

Exercise 2

- Ask students to read the proverbs carefully, and check any words they don't know. Then put them in pairs to discuss the questions.

Answers

1 *Before criticising …* This means that you shouldn't criticise someone until you know what his life is like and what his thoughts are.

2 *If you're …* This means that if you've already done and said the wrong thing, stop, because doing or saying anything else will only make it worse.

3 *Don't burn …* Remember to be civil when leaving a situation (e.g. job).

4 *A problem …* It is good to talk about a problem with somebody because you feel better afterwards.

5 *Fortune favours …* Being brave and taking chances often results in success.

6 *If it …* If something works, even if it is old and scruffy, don't try to change or improve it.

7 *An eye …* You shouldn't seek revenge if something wrong is done to you, because it only results in more people getting hurt.

8 *Sometimes you …* This means you have to do or say things to people which may hurt them but will be for their own good in the end.

Listening: the usefulness of advice

Exercise 3

- Ask students to discuss the questions in pairs.

Exercise 4 CD2/38

- Give students time to read through the attitudes, and check any unknown words.
- Play the recording. Ask students to match speakers to attitudes. Let students check their answers in pairs before discussing as a class.

Audioscript

Speaker 1 In my experience, people don't really listen to advice. Usually they've already made up their mind what they're going to do and are just sounding it out. What they really want is affirmation that they've made the right decision. If you say to them, 'No, I don't think you should do that. It would be better to do such and such,' they'll pretend to listen, but actually they won't follow your advice.

Speaker 2 Too much is made of moral dilemmas, if you ask me. I think most of us know instinctively what the right thing to do is in a particular situation. Usually, if people are in a dilemma, it's because they are looking for someone to help them justify doing the wrong thing. For example, if they find £50 lying in the street, they will look for some justification to keep it. You know, they might say 'Oh, I lost £20 myself in the same way two months ago. This must be fate … returning it to me.'

Speaker 3 It's true that people rarely take advice from others. But does that mean we would be better off not giving advice at all? I don't think so. Even if it's wasted on another person, working through these kinds of problems is a very useful exercise – it helps you to formulate your own judgements about what's right and wrong.

Speaker 4 I think it's very important to get your worries or problems out into the open. Asking others for advice is a way of doing that. But actually what I do, and what I'd recommend everyone does, is whenever I'm facing a dilemma, I apply this simple test. If I took this course of action and my mum found out, what would she say? Or if my actions were reported on the front page of the newspaper,

Books closed lead-in activity

Tell students a 'problem' you have. You could turn it into a little story, e.g. *I left home in a hurry this morning, and I think I've lost the key to the front door of my apartment.* Ask students to give you some advice.

how would I feel about that? I find thinking about how others might react to what you do really helps to focus the mind.

Answers
1 E 2 D 3 C 4 B

Exercise 5 CD2/38

■ Ask students to listen again and complete the sentences. Let them check their answers in pairs before discussing as a class.

Answers
1 made up 2 follow 3 justify 4 take 5 working 6 formulate 7 facing; apply

> **Vocabulary note**
> *make up your mind* = decide; *follow advice* = do what they have been advised to do; *justify* = give a good reason why; *face a dilemma* = have a difficult problem

Exercise 6

■ Ask students to work in pairs to discuss the question.

Grammar: *better, should* and *ought to*
Exercise 7

■ Ask students to look at the forms in pairs and discuss them. Check that students understand form and use.
■ Ask students to complete the sentences. Let students check their answers in pairs.

Answers
1 hurry 2 walking 3 bite 4 to lose; (to) risk 5 to get 6 to tell 7 get

> **Grammar note**
> Note the different forms: *had better* + infinitive without *to*; *be better* + infinitive with *to*; *be better off* + *-ing*.
>
> *had better* is stronger than *should* and *ought to* when used to give advice. It means you really should. The other forms are not as strong.
>
> Compare *You had better tell him* (there is an obligation on you to do so) to *You'd be better off telling him* (this would be good for you).

■ Refer students to the Grammar Reference on page 158.

Exercise 8

■ Ask students to discuss the question in pairs.

Answers
1 had 2 would 5 would 7 would

> **Vocabulary note**
> Note the use of *far* and *much* to strengthen the advice in *It's (far/much) better to …*

Speaking: giving advice
Exercise 9

■ Give students time to read through the situations and check any unknown words.
■ Divide students into groups of three to five. Discuss what they should say. Elicit pieces of advice using *better*, *should* and *ought to*, and correct any errors.

Extra activity

Ask students to discuss the following questions:

1 *When did you last give or take advice?*

2 *Do you usually follow your friends' advice?*

Writing: review of a TV documentary

Exercise 10

- Ask students to look at the photo and title. Ask, *What type of text is it? What type of TV programme is it about?*
- Ask students to read the review and answer the question. Let them check their answers in pairs before discussing as a class.

> **Answer**
> The filmmakers did not get the permission of the subjects of the documentary and this made the reviewer feel uncomfortable watching it.

> **Vocabulary note**
> *Untouched* and *unspoilt* both describe a natural place that has not been developed by modern civilisation.

Exercise 11

- Check that students understand *voyeuristic* (taking pleasure in watching other people, even when they are suffering or being exploited). Then ask students to discuss the questions in pairs.

Exercise 12

- Ask students to find and underline the sections. Let them check their answers in pairs before discussing as a class.

> **Answers**
> 1 the latest episode in the popular series *Disappearing Planet* made by Birdsview Productions, which aims to record parts of our natural world before they disappear
> 2 tells the story of one of the few remaining tribes still untouched by western civilisation
> 3 The documentary is beautifully filmed and well researched.
> 4 I still felt uncomfortable watching: it seemed voyeuristic.
> 5 I cannot give it my approval.

Exercise 13

- Lead in by brainstorming recent documentaries writing ideas on the board, and asking whether students think they are exploitative or voyeuristic.
- Ask students to work in pairs to follow the instructions and write a review.

Extra activity

Once students have written reviews, use them as the basis for a 'TV interview'. Tell students to prepare questions based on the headings in exercise 13 (for example, *What exactly were the aims of the documentary?*). Then mix pairs. Students take turns to interview each other about the programmes they have reviewed.

10E You've got to laugh

Books closed lead-in activity

Ask students who can tell a joke in English. You could start by telling them one yourself. Encourage students to tell a joke they know to the class.

Vocabulary and speaking

Exercise 1

■ Ask students to work in pairs to discuss the questions.

Exercise 2

■ Ask students to complete the phrases with the verbs. Do the first as a class to get students started. Let students check their answers in pairs before discussing as a class.

> **Answers**
> 1 play 2 see 3 take 4 laugh 5 make 6 tell 7 be

Exercise 3

■ Ask students to work in pairs to discuss the questions. In feedback, ask students to give examples to show they understand the meanings of the phrases.

> **Answers**
> **a** to play a trick on someone; to make fun of someone or something **b** to see the funny side of something; to take nothing too seriously; to laugh at yourself **c** to be witty

Extra activity

Ask students to think of other phrases they know under each heading.

Unkind: *laugh at someone, poke fun at someone, play a practical joke on someone*

Relaxed: *make a joke about life/yourself*

Intelligent: *be clever or quick-witted*

Listening

Exercise 4  CD2/39

■ Lead in by asking students what they know about British or Canadian humour. Ask, *What adjectives would you use to describe their humour?*

■ Ask students to listen and answer the question. Let students compare answers in pairs before discussing as a class.

Audioscript

Recently a Lapland Theme Park in the New Forest was forced to close. Visitors had been promised snow, cabins, happy elves and animals, but in fact there was more mud than snow, the cabins were like the kind of huts you get on a building site, some of the elves weren't that happy, and at least one of the animals was made of plastic. The reaction? Rather than anger, a great laugh went up. This laugh told you two things. The first is that the British enjoy a blunder. It's part of our national identity: the Millennium Dome with nothing inside, Terminal 5 at Heathrow where bags were regularly lost, a shoddy Lapland theme park. These were almost made to help us British laugh at ourselves.

But we're not the only ones to do this. Take Canada. Canada borders the US, and speaks the same language. The problem for Canadians is that no one can really tell a Canadian from an American unless the Canadian is speaking French. They are constantly made aware that they have a more dominant and more famous neighbour.

They are irritated by this, but they try to laugh. A recent Canadian book called *Coping with Back Pain* did so well that the Americans printed their own edition. But the Americans called it *Conquering Back Pain* because America is a can-do nation. It doesn't cope, it conquers and overcomes. In response to this Canadians were quick to work out their own jokes. The Canadian version of Julius Caesar's memoirs? *I came, I saw, I coped*. In that sense they are like the British – they know they have faults but they've learned to see the funny side and enjoy it.

Answers
British – an ability to laugh at themselves
Canadian – they've learned to see the funny side of having a dominant neighbour

Vocabulary and culture note
shoddy = untidy and of poor quality; *cope with* = deal with or manage
Lapland is the area to the north of Sweden, Norway and Finland. **The Millennium Dome** is a huge exhibition space built south of the Thames in London to celebrate the year 2000. It has lost a lot of money and it has been hard to find things to use it for.
Terminal 5 is the new terminal at London's largest airport, Heathrow. When it opened, there were many problems with computer systems which resulted in huge delays.
Julius Caesar's memoirs were titled *Veni, Vidi, Vici* (I came, I saw, I conquered).

Exercise 5 CD2/39

- Give students time to read through the statements and answer any they can.
- Play the recording. Students listen and choose True or False. Let students compare answers in pairs before discussing as a class.

Answers
1 True 2 True 3 True 4 False (conquering) 5 False (joke about themselves)

Reading
Exercise 6

- Ask students to read through the multiple choice questions to focus their reading.
- Ask them to read the article and answer the questions individually.
- They can then check their answers in pairs.
- Elicit the answers from the whole class.

Answers
1 B 2 C 3 B 4 C 5 A

Exercise 7

- Ask students to get into groups of four to discuss the four questions.
- Ask each group to appoint a secretary to keep short notes of their ideas on each question.
- Elicit responses from the secretaries, and encourage further discussion by the class.

Exercise 8

■ Ask students to read about the other hoaxes on page 131 and decide individually what they think.

■ They can then work in groups of four to share their ideas.

■ Elicit answers from the class and encourage further discussion.

The rise of China

Lead-in

Ask the class to give you any information they can about China.

Exercise 1

- Ask students to note down the main point of each paragraph individually, then check in pairs.
- Elicit suggestions from the whole class.

> **Answers**
> **Paragraph 1:** China was advanced in the past and will be again in the future.
> **Paragraph 2:** Industry and the economy have been improving for 30 years.
> **Paragraph 3:** Transport systems have been improved.
> **Paragraph 4:** China has invested heavily in technology.
> **Paragraph 5:** This trend looks set to continue in the future.

Exercise 2

- Ask students to answer the questions individually, then check in pairs.
- Elicit answers from the class, having one student ask a question and another answer it.

> **Example answers**
> 1 The Chinese economy may be twice as big as the USA's by 2050.
> 2 They have invested $750 billion in improving the rail network, and more cities will have metros.
> 3 They have invested in a space programme and computer technology.
> 4 They are young and educated, and 50 per cent of graduates and managers are women.

Exercise 3

- Ask students to work in groups of three: Student A says a statement and Student B reports it to Student C. Then Student B says a statement and Student C reports it to Student A, and so on.

Find out more!

Do some research about an aspect of this topic which interests you, for example:
- China's instant cities
- the rise of Shanghai
- can China go green?
- rare natural resources in China

Look on the Internet and in books in the library. In particular, have a look at the National Geographic website: www.nationalgeographic.com

Units 9 and 10

Unit 9 Review

Ask students to complete the exercises in class or set the review for homework. After they have completed the exercises, students should evaluate their own performance, using the self-assessment box.

Answers
Exercise 1
1 tackle 2 civil 3 implement 4 foster 5 recruit 6 self 7 raise

Exercise 2
1 me to write 2 to lend 3 on having 4 that I should approach 5 borrowing
6 of providing 7 would 8 for not having; to come

Exercise 3
1 a little 2 little 3 a few 4 little 5 few 6 a few

Exercise 4
1 Do you know how much this car is/costs? 2 Would you be willing/able/prepared to negotiate on the price? 3 Supposing I brought/were to bring my old car in exchange?
4 That sounds good/fine/OK. 5 Can you tell me what time you are open/you open?

Unit 10 Review

Answers
Exercise 1
1 anxious 2 unspoilt 3 authentic 4 judgement

Exercise 2
1 e 2 d 3 f 4 a 5 c 6 b

Exercise 3
1 was 2 was 3 were 4 were 5 aren't 6 are 7 would have 8 was 9 would

Exercise 4
1 managed to 2 could not/didn't manage to 3 succeeded in resisting 4 could also/were also able to 5 were also able to

Exercise 5
1 should 2 ought 3 would 4 had

Video Worksheets Answer Key

1 A Chinese Artist in Harlem

1 The statistics show that New York City is a huge city with a population of over 8 million people, and it is also quite a crowded place compared to other places in the USA (thousands more people per square kilometre). There is a greater mix of races and origins than in the USA as a whole: there are fewer white persons and more Asian and black persons, as well as more people of Hispanic origin. The number of foreign born people is four times higher than in the USA as a whole.

2 Harlem is a neighbourhood in the Manhattan borough of New York City. It is populated in large part by African Americans.

4 1 Shanghai **2** his father **3** 1990 **4** tourists **5** Cultural **6** children

5 1 True.

2 False. (She doesn't think children can only learn using books, paper and pencils.)

3 False. (According to the video, he sees beyond ethnicity. He says that all children are the same.)

4 True.

5 True.

6 False. (He believes his work is important because it introduces children to a wider world.)

6 1 cosmopolitan **2** melting pot **3** merge **4** calligraphy **5** make a living **6** easel **7** cultural ambassador **8** benefit **9** learn first hand **10** ethnicity **11** broaden their horizons

4 Crop Circles

1 Bigfoot / the Yeti: Bigfoot is described in reports as a large, hairy, ape-like creature, ranging between 2 and 3 m tall, weighing in excess of 230 kg, and covered in dark brown hair. It inhabits forests, mainly in the Pacific northwest region of North America.

Stonehenge: Stonehenge is a prehistoric monument made up of a circular setting of large standing stones located in the English county of Wiltshire. It is at the centre of the most dense complex of Neolithic and Bronze Age monuments in England, including several hundred burial mounds.

The Bermuda Triangle: The Bermuda Triangle is a region in the western part of the North Atlantic Ocean where a number of aircraft and surface vessels allegedly disappeared mysteriously. Popular culture has attributed these disappearances to the paranormal or activity by extraterrestrial beings.

UFOs: Unidentified Flying Object is the term for any apparent aerial phenomenon whose cause cannot be easily or immediately identified by the observer. The term UFO is popularly used as a synonym for alien spacecraft.

The Loch Ness Monster: The Loch Ness Monster is a cryptid that is reputed to inhabit Loch Ness in the Scottish Highlands. The most frequent speculation is that the creature represents a line of long-surviving plesiosaurs.

4 1 False **2** True **3** True **4** True **5** False **6** True

5 1 animals (carved) **2** the gods **3** so enormous **4** broken (suddenly) **5** (creative) art **6** military operation

6 1 phenomenon **2** carved **3** puzzles **4** formations **5** bent **6** canvas **7** markers **8** flatten **9** combing **10** apocalyptic

7 The Great Kite Fight

3 1 Crazy **2** five **3** 250 **4** almost everyone (in the town) **5** at peace **6** 1,500 **7** large **8** easier **9** pull

4 1 captured **2** breaks **3** points

5 1 True **2** False (northerly) **3** True **4** False (they relax and have fun) **5** False (they have both) **6** True

6 1 eating three meals a day / food **2** equal **3** teamwork **4** maniac; enthusiast

7 1 passionate **2** planting **3** legend **4** huge **5** fighter jets **6** bombers **7** distinct **8** twisted **9** tug of war **10** clings

8 Gauchos of Argentina

3 1 b **2** a **3** a **4** a

4 1 strict **2** run **3** adjust **4** utilise

5 A 1 to **2** to **3** up **4** by
  B 1 into **2** for **3** to **4** to **5** after
  C 1 In **2** of **3** to **4** to **5** to
  D 1 for **2** to **3** of

6 1 adapt **2** terrain **3** remote **4** self-reliant **5** cruel **6** respect **7** code of ethics **8** hospitable **9** heritage

10 Saving the Amazon Together

1 (suggested answers)

1 Conservation of the Amazonian tropical rain forest is important because it is home to millions of rare and exotic species of insects, plants, animals and birds.

2 The Amazon tropical rainforest is under threat from deforestation due to human settlement, land development and industry such as mining.

4 1 The team is going to mark the borders of the new national park.

2 They want to search for criminals such as illegal gold miners who might be harming the landscape.

3 They want to seek cooperation with the tribes who live next to the park's land, and convince them to help protect the park's borders.

5 1 C **2** A **3** B **4** B **5** B

6 1 national park **2** hectares **3** species
4 park warden **5** indigenous people
6 tribes **7** patrol **8** hydraulic gold mining
9 erodes **10** silt **11** mercury **12** operating

A Chinese Artist in Harlem

Narrator: With a population of approximately eight million, the huge cosmopolitan city of New York is a melting pot of immigrant communities. Sometimes, this diversity results in clashes between cultures. Other times, positive outcomes result from the merging of backgrounds and traditions. Artists in particular often use their cultural differences to learn from each other. One such artist, Mingliang Lu, has taken his skills to Harlem to enable others to learn about and understand Chinese art.

Born in Shanghai, Ming has studied Chinese art for the majority of his life. At a very young age, he learned about calligraphy and painting from his father and has continued to paint through the more difficult times in his life. Ming moved to the U.S. in 1990, and today lives in New York where he continues to create beautiful landscapes, flowers, animals, and even the symbol of the United States: the eagle.

Mingliang Lu, Artist: When I first came to America, my only skills were art. I didn't have other skills. I used my art to make a living.

Narrator: When he first arrived in the U.S., Ming set up his easel and drew and painted portraits of tourists in order to survive. But even for professional artists, drawing on the street is not the easiest way to make a living. So, Ming eventually stopped painting on the street, and began to work for the New York Chinese Cultural Centre. Through them, he brought his skills to Harlem and the children of Public School 36.

Ming: What is this?

Pupils: Circle.

Ming: It is a circle, right? OK. So I just draw. I change the colour. What colour this?

Pupils: Yellow.

Ming: OK. I just put this – you see this? For the ear.

Amy Chin, Executive Director, New York Chinese Cultural Centre: As we all know, a lot of artists are not employed being artists. So I'm hoping that what we do is to provide them this opportunity, to really practise in the field that they've been trained for.

Ming: OK, this time I take it this way … Little circle one … Yeah, you very good job. Good.

Narrator: Teaching at the public school, though, is more than just an opportunity for Ming; the programme benefits the children as well. Head teacher Cynthia Mullen Simons says the programme is important to her Year Four pupils.

Cynthia Mullen Simons, Head Teacher: You cannot teach solely by the book, paper and pencil. They have to become involved. We need our students to hear, first hand, people from various cultures talk about their ethnicity.

Ming: Too much water … I show you this, not too much water, you see …

Narrator: From time to time Ming stops to help each child get his or her painting just right. The kids view Ming as their teacher from China, but Ming sees beyond ethnicity. He just sees pupils who want to learn how to paint a tiger.

Ming: Chinese children, American children, Hispanic children and black children, they are all the same. No difference.

Narrator: Even though New York is already established as a diverse international city, programmes like the Chinese Cultural Centre's still make a considerable difference.

Chin: When we bring these programmes in, the kids get to see real people from another culture and to relate to them on many different levels.

Simons: What we don't want to do to our students is to make them ignorant to others and what others can bring. Our students need to understand that we are all human beings, that we all have different backgrounds … different experiences … and that's what makes us so interesting.

Narrator: These days, in addition to being an artist, Ming is also serving as a kind of cultural ambassador for his country. In the long run, Ming's art may open the door to a whole different world for these children.

Ming: I feel like I am doing very important work, and it makes me really happy to teach calligraphy and painting to the children. I'm introducing them to a wider world of Chinese culture, giving them a greater understanding of Chinese people in the world and broadening their horizons.

Narrator: Ming is not only good in his role as a teacher, he is also excellent in his role of cultural ambassador. In Harlem, this Chinese artist has found a job that makes more than just a living; it makes a difference.

Mysterious Crop Circles

Narrator: The beautiful rolling countryside of England has a long history. But in recent years, there's been a strange phenomenon here; one which people all over the world have been studying with great interest: crop circles. These strange and mysterious circles have many people – even some scientists – asking who or what could have made them.

Since the beginning of time, human beings have created signs such as unusual constructions or animals carved into the hillsides. Some people suggest that different cultures may have constructed them as ways of communicating with aliens. Others say that ancient peoples must have created them to please the gods. Did people create these crop circles, or are they messages made by aliens from outer space? The question has been the cause of much debate.

Reg Presley, Crop Circle Researcher: I walked into the first crop circle in 1990, and I thought, "Hmm … I love puzzles." And what I did was said, "Right, I'm going to try and find out what this puzzle's all about." I think probably 95 per cent of them are man-made. But there's one particularly here, just over on the hill – Milk Hill – it's so enormous, that you can't even see the other side of the crop formation.

Narrator: Presley then explains that the formation is over a kilometre wide. He feels that people couldn't have made such an enormous circle without other people knowing about it. He also points out that these formations appear all over the world. He tells of a circle in a forest near Vancouver, Canada. In it, only the top two metres of the trees were bent and shaped in a circle. Remarkably, the trees were not broken suddenly and quickly, but bent over – without breaking – when they were arranged.

Presley has also heard of ice circles, in which a circle of ice is missing from a body of water while the area around it remains frozen. For Presley, a connection between these mysterious circles almost certainly exists, but to a young Englishman named Matthew, they're not all that mysterious.

Matthew, Crop Circle Maker: Yeah, a lot of circles have been appearing in this area. It's lovely landscape, and the fields are just very clean and open like a canvas.

Narrator: In the area near Matthew's home, many crop circles have recently appeared. While he will not admit to making any of these, Matthew has offered to demonstrate exactly how crop circles are made.

Matthew: Well, if there are aliens out there doing it, they're using stomper boards and these little markers. Because, I mean, there's things there, like combing effects, which are people going around and around and around the same area, flattening it down. That wouldn't be there with aliens, I'm sure.

Narrator: In fact, Matthew thinks aliens would more likely use a faster, instantaneous technique; something obviously real to everyone – even him. Matthew's never seen this kind of evidence. The only crop circles he's seen are undoubtedly made by humans.

As Matthew and his team begin the long evening task of making a crop circle, he talks about some of the beliefs regarding them. He explains how people imagine seeing extraterrestrials, strange balls of light, or UFOs when they see a crop circle. Matthew, however, claims that crop circle design is actually a creative art done by human beings. He also explains that teams sometimes challenge each other to amaze the public by showing what they can do in an evening.

Matthew: It is a bit like a military operation. You've got to get in, do the job, get out, not get caught, you know. It's SAS I suppose. Who dares wins. I'm a little bit worried about some of the beliefs I hear going around. Some of the stuff is a bit apocalyptic.

Narrator: At times, Matthew is disturbed by some of the beliefs about crop circles. He thinks that some people are using the circles to push their own unusual theories. In his years of making crop circles, Matthew's never seen any evidence that aliens made them. In his opinion, crop circles are definitely not signs of intelligent life in outer space. But perhaps opinions like Matthew's are a sign of one kind of intelligent life – intelligent life on Earth!

The Great Kite Fight

Narrator: Once a year, the people of Shirone, Japan, leave their quiet lives behind them and take part in an activity about which they are absolutely passionate. They become so enthusiastic about a competition that local residents have given it a name. They call it *Tako Kichi*: Kite Crazy.

Kazuo Tamura, Kite Enthusiast: 'Kite Crazy' refers to people who really love kites. People who think more about kites than getting their three meals a day. Even when they go to bed, they can't fall asleep because they see kites flying over their beds.

Narrator: Normally Shirone is a quiet and peaceful place, like many other towns that are found in northern Japan. Farmers work hard through the spring to plant their rice, but when the work is done, they're ready to have some fun at a five-day festival that celebrates the open sky – the Great Shirone Kite Fight.

The Great Kite Fight began 250 years ago. According to legend, a giant kite was given to a village leader by the local lord. The kite was so huge that it damaged houses and crops when it came crashing down. Soon after, villagers who were angry or upset started using kites to fight one another. Eventually, these battles evolved into a festival where people rid themselves of some stress every spring.

Kite madness comes to Shirone every June, and affects people of all ages. Residents both old and young join the fun, and just about anybody who can cling to a piece of kite rope gets involved. The town is transformed into a giant kite factory as rival teams prepare for battle. Playgrounds, car parks, driveways and even schools become work areas. Kazuo Tamura is an internationally known kite-flying team leader.

Tamura: This event is very important to me. It's not just a question of having a good time. Somehow, underneath a sky that's full of kites, everyone seems equal. And no one flies a kite in times of war. So the festival is like a sign that we're at peace.

Narrator: Shirone festival kites are made by hand and put together carefully and precisely. Teams spend hours designing, constructing and painting their creations. Each kite has a distinct colourful design to capture the special look that symbolises a particular team.

Finally, opening day arrives. Fifteen hundred kites are designed, decorated and ready to be flown. The biggest kites are called *odako*. They're difficult to get into the air, but 13 different teams have come to try their best.

Other teams prefer the smaller kites called *rokako*, which are much easier to fly – more like fighter jets while the *odako* are like heavy bombers.

For centuries, the battle of the kites has taken place along Shirone's central river, the Nakanokuchi. The competing teams stand on opposite sides of the river. The goal is for one team to capture another team's kite and pull it from the sky. Once one team has captured another team's kite, it's time for the real competition to begin. Team members desperately cling to their kite ropes, doing everything they can to keep their grip. Unfortunately, in the tug of war, both of the kites are twisted, pulled, and basically destroyed. Finally, when one team's rope breaks, a winner is declared. Extra points are given to the winning side for every inch of rope it captures from the losing team.

All along the river, teams get involved in clashes that quickly lead to open war. The battles often spread to the town, and almost everyone gets involved.

By the end of day one, thousands of the smaller kites have been destroyed, but not everyone has been able to enjoy the competition. The large *odako* kites are still not flying. The teams can't even get the huge *odakos* into the air. Without a stable northern wind, the larger kites are helpless. The *odako* teams must wait for a change in the weather, and hope that they're ready when the north wind finally arrives. While they wait, the teams step back from the excitement of the riverside to ensure that their ropes are strung correctly. These ropes are made by hand, which makes them extremely strong so they can serve two purposes: controlling the kite, and standing up to the tugs of war. Teamwork constitutes another important part of the kite competition.

Tamura: The most important thing is teamwork. Everyone runs around clinging to the same rope, so they have to work together. This is very important. Without teamwork, these kites won't fly; they'll fall right to the ground.

Narrator: On the third day of this five-day festival, there's still no northern wind, and everyone's very disappointed. But when evening falls the kite fighters still manage to have a good time. Everyone welcomes the chance to relax, have some fun and go a little crazy. On the fifth and final day of the competition, the wind continues to deliver disappointment, but at the last minute something wonderful happens. With just one hour remaining, a northern wind comes down along the river. At last, the oversized kites are released from their earthly imprisonment.

Now, finally, Tamura's team will have its only chance to compete before the festival ends. The young men on Tamura's team have managed to capture the competing team's kite. Now the tug of war begins. It's a situation that requires both skill and passion; luckily Tamura's team has plenty of both.

Tamura: People call me a kite maniac. I am a kite enthusiast. That's just me. They call me a kite maniac, but I don't think I'm all that crazy.

Narrator: The two teams are nearly exhausted, but the battle continues. Neither will stop until the war is won, but the ropes remain firmly tied together across the river. One set of kite ropes finally breaks and it belongs to the rival team. It looks like Tamura's team is the winner!

So are the people of Shirone really Kite Crazy? Most of the residents become very excited at this time of year. But if it's some type of craziness, it's not a dangerous one. In a good year, every kite is destroyed, but the people of Shirone never seem to feel sorry. They know that next spring, the kites will live again. For now, there are no signs that the 'Kite Craziness' will disappear any time soon. In fact, among everyone who appears affected by it, no one seems to want to find a cure.

The Gauchos of Argentina script

Narrator: In the country of Argentina, cowboy life has scarcely changed over the past three centuries. The gaucho is a hero here; for most people, he is a legendary figure that is larger than life. But in the far reaches of the country, there are still men for whom the gaucho is more than a legend. For them, it is their life; they are the gauchos of Argentina. The cowboy life of the gaucho came to Argentina from Spanish culture. It created a unique type of men who were as hardy and self-reliant as the animals for which they cared. The word 'gaucho' means 'outcast', or one who doesn't belong to a specific society or group. There are as many kinds of gauchos as there are varied terrains in Argentina. There are gauchos on the soft flat pampas of Corrientes, on the windswept plains of Patagonia, and in the wooded hills of Salta.

Don José Ansola, a 76-year-old horseman, seems to be the 'classic gaucho', and one who treasures his residence in a remote region of Corrientes. He believes solitude helps to keep gaucho life in its purest form.

Don José Ansola, Corrientes Gaucho: If I couldn't live in the campo, the countryside – an unthinkable thought – I don't know what I'd do.

Narrator: According to Don José, he would rather live in a poor little house in the country than in a palace in the city. Don José's 400-square-kilometer ranch in Corrientes is far from everything, so Don José depends entirely on his horses to travel. As a result, he and his three sons spend much of their time finding and catching the wild horses that run free in the countryside. The horses must then be 'broken' so that they'll allow people to ride them.

Ansola: Breaking a horse is a slow process, taking more than a year. This is something the horse learns to put up with.

Narrator: The gaucho explains that the horse must adjust to using a saddle and reins so the riders aren't thrown off later. The treatment seems cruel, but according to Don José it's actually not. The training, he says, often seems harsher than it is.

Ansola: We love our horses, and in the end, they love us in return. This is the traditional way of training a horse in Argentina – the gaucho way.

Narrator: Being a gaucho, though, is more than a life of solitude and caring for horses and cattle. The gaucho way of life has its own strict code of ethics. Hospitality and respect for others are as much a part of this lifestyle as the art of breaking horses. Argentina is nearly the last place where this code of ethics and the demanding lifestyle of the gaucho still exist. The country is home to nearly 150,000 gauchos, who are very much a part of the national identity. There are gauchos in all parts of the country, even 2,000 kilometres south of Buenos Aires, on the edge of Antarctica in Patagonia.

The harsh terrain of this region has its own type of gaucho as well. Here, the gauchos raise sheep, not cattle, and even more surprisingly, many speak English. Many of the ancestors of Patagonian gauchos were immigrants from Scotland. Several of these settlers came to the area during the 19th century, including the ancestors of Eduardo Halliday and his father, Jimmy. These two gauchos run a ranch in Patagonia, and for them, this strange terrain seems like the perfect place to live. The Hallidays enjoy living in the region for a number of reasons. For Jimmy, the most refreshing aspect about living in Patagonia is that there's space everywhere so he can see far in all directions. The land is also rich, he says, and produces everything that he and his family need. Life on the plains of Patagonia is difficult, even harsh, but the gauchos here have learned how to adjust and succeed. Eduardo has lived his entire life on the family ranch and has learned the traditional ways from his father. The goal of every gaucho is self-reliance, and these gauchos of Patagonia are no different. Because the ranch is so remote, father and son have to utilize everything they have available. This also means they don't abandon anything quickly and often use and reuse everything they have, including their bags and their boots. After all, it's a long way to go to buy new ones.

Gauchos are experts at adjusting to their surroundings. Here, they've learned to use a local weapon called a 'boleadora'. Made of leather and small stones, boleadoras are still used to hunt rhea. Pursuing the small flightless birds is no problem, but hitting them can be tough. As the gauchos fly like the wind along the plains on their strong horses, the rheas run swiftly ahead of them. It's an exciting chase, but the rheas get away – this time. Twenty-nine hundred kilometers north of Patagonia is the region of Salta. Here the stony hills and rough terrain have produced yet another different kind of gaucho. The gauchos here were once fierce soldiers for Argentina, and they won recognition and respect in the Argentine war of independence from Spain. They're famous for their huge leather chaps and red ponchos, and often celebrate their proud traditions in an annual parade. One of the best horsemen in the area is Rudecindo Campos. Rudecindo loves being a gaucho and says that it's the life he's always wanted.

Rudecindo Campos, Salta Gaucho: In life there are all kinds of people: engineers, doctors, and gauchos. I knew I had to choose one or the other. I have always had a gaucho soul and I like being a gaucho.

Narrator: However, choosing the life of a gaucho means more than just working with horses. Just as it is in Corrientes, a strict code of ethics and principles is essential to the gaucho lifestyle in Salta as well.

Don Coco Campos, Rudecindo's Father: It's not only knowing how to catch an animal with a rope, use a saddle or ride a horse. It's also about being good and kind. When you ask a gaucho a favour, he must not refuse. He does it.

Narrator: At times, it's difficult to make enough money working as a gaucho. In order to survive, Rudecindo must work at a part-time job so he can continue training horses. He specialises in training a strong little horse from the area called a 'criollo'. It's one of the few animals that can round up cattle in this rough terrain covered with thorns. To protect themselves from the environment, horse and rider rely on their special leather chaps. The thick leather protects the pair from injuries as they round up the last of the cattle. In Salta, each time the gauchos successfully return the cattle safely back to the ranch, there's a lively fiesta, a celebration in which women have always had an important role. Rudecindo's wife, who comes from the city, talks about life on the ranch.

Rudecindo's wife: It's very difficult to adapt to the slower pace of the campo. In the city, you live faster and you are less attentive to nature. We've lost that in the city. We've lost some of our humanity, which my husband hasn't lost. He's not caught up in the trivia of everyday life. You can really get consumed by small things, and you forget what's important.

Rudecindo: If I go into town for two weeks, I can't wait to get home to the horses, to the smell of the countryside, and the wet earth after a rain. I love this life.

Narrator: In the end, the story of today's gaucho may be one of adaptation; to climate, to landscape, and to traditional ways of life that sustain them.

Ansola: For Argentina, it's very important for people to treasure this proud and honourable legacy. We must be sure that whatever else happens to us, we never lose our heritage, our gaucho way of life.

Narrator: Don José is not alone in his dream. The proud and self-reliant gauchos of Corrientes, Patagonia and Salta are all helping to retain the traditional lifestyle of the gauchos of Argentina.

Saving the Amazon Together

Narrator: Brazil's Amazon rainforest has millions of different types of insects, plants, animals and birds, many of which are exotic and rare. Scientists have yet to record all of the varied species of life here. However, the Amazon is far from a paradise. There are a number of threats that have put it in crisis. It's quickly being destroyed by widespread deforestation from human settlement and land development.

Therefore, a concerned group has been brought together in an effort to help save it. The expedition has come to define the borders and the rules of a newly created national park, Tumucumaque. The park is enormous – about 3.8 million hectares – but it only employs five people, not nearly enough staff to care for it.

The Brazilian government established the national park and allocated funds for its administration. However, legislation is one thing; it's quite another to make a park a reality. The first step is to mark the borders of the park. Another major issue is one of monitoring. The area is so vast that it's extremely difficult to regulate effectively.

The team is part of the Amazon Region Protected Areas programme. The experts come from different organisations. Christoph Jaster is a Brazilian government park warden. He's joined by Claudio Maretti from the World Wildlife Fund and Jawapuku Wayapi, a member of the indigenous people on neighbouring lands.

Claudio Maretti, World Wildlife Fund: Somebody needs to come here and do the job, and that's what we are doing.

Narrator: Their mission is twofold. First, they have come to search for criminals, such as illegal gold miners who may be harming this precious, newly protected landscape. They've also come on a diplomatic mission, seeking cooperation with neighbouring tribes that live alongside park lands. Jawapuku Wayapi says that by working with each other, the authorities and his people can protect the new park from being invaded by illegal commercial activity.

From here, the journey will become even more challenging as they move into the more remote and untravelled areas of the forest. There are no roads in this remote area surrounding the park, and few airstrips, so water is the most efficient and practical way to travel, but it's not an easy journey. Dangerous currents and majestic waterfalls have stopped all but a few explorers and fortune seekers from ever coming here.

Maretti: This is the largest obstacle, the most important that we have to cross.

Narrator: They construct a pulley system using ropes and wheels to get the boats to the top of the waterfall.

After their heavy lifting, the team is exhausted, but they still need to continue moving. Park manager Christoph Jaster wants to track down a gold mine seen from the air. According to his GPS, it should be nearby.

Maretti: We're going back, trying to find an entrance here – a small river or a track in the forest.

Narrator: Once they've found the track, the team will simply need to follow it to its source: the illegal mine. Hydraulic gold mining in the Amazon erodes the soil and creates silt in rivers, negatively affecting the habitats of countless species of plants and animals. However, the most dangerous aspect of the process is the mercury used to extract the gold, which can poison wildlife and create health risks for neighbouring indigenous communities.

Authorities hope to create a partnership with the local Wayapi tribe, supplying them with boats and fuel so that they can help patrol the new park's borders. According to Claudio Maretti, this is an unusual collaboration, but obviously one that could benefit both sides.

Far up the river, the team finds a path that appears to have been made by miners. Together with an armed police unit, they follow it deep into the forest. Eventually, as they get closer to the suspected mining site, the team comes across a frightened miner named Francisco. He agrees to lead them several miles to the gold mine.

Once at the mining site, the team realises the degree of damage from just one mining operation. It turns out that the mine has been operating illegally for nearly two decades. But it appears that the mine isn't really very profitable.

Christoph Jaster, Park Manager: They just obtain 70, 80, or at maximum 100 grams of gold per month. And that's too poor. They are looking for other places to mine. That will be a positive moment for us to convince them to leave this place.

Narrator: Francisco says that the mine's owner will be angry but that he was thinking of closing the operation down anyway and moving to another location. In time, the forest will repair the damage caused by the mine, but the mercury pollution will last much longer.

The team has found the mine, but their mission is not over yet. Jaster leads the others to a remote airstrip built years ago by a mining company. Upon their arrival, the team finds two unexpected residents. Jose and his wife Madeleina have lived here for 18 years, mining gold with a small dredge, and surviving by farming, hunting and fishing. The team posts a signboard to make it clear that this land is a national park now. Unfortunately for the couple, non-employees are prohibited from living in it. The wardens don't want to leave the couple homeless, but there's no way around the rules. Or is there…?

Jaster may be able to pay the couple a salary to monitor and maintain the airstrip. It's another way to get the local residents to support the new reserve instead of discriminating against them or ignoring their needs.

The team has finished its work and, for now, the expedition can return down the Amazon. The gold miners have been sent on their way, the Wayapi have agreed to help patrol the new park's borders, and the park's western border has been marked.

Little by little, the beautiful, lawless wilderness of the Tumucumaque rainforest is becoming a well-defined and protected national park. The rainforest and the amazing animal and plant diversity in this region now stand a better chance of surviving because conservationists and indigenous peoples are working to save the Amazon together.

Workbook Answer Key

Unit 1

Page 4 Vocabulary

1 **1** a painter **2** a musician **3** a film director **4** a playwright **5** a photographer **6** a poet **7** an actor **8** a novelist

2 **1** lyrics **2** stage **3** cast **4** portrait **5** encore **6** auditions **7** sketch **8** gigs

3 **1** creativity **2** play **3** appearance **4** sold **5** collectors **6** disappointing **7** performance **8** illegally

4 **1** B **2** C **3** D **4** A **5** E

5 **1** sets **2** opening **3** sketches **4** model **5** piece

Page 5 Listening

1 one hour

2 **1** F **2** E **3** C **4** A **5** B

3 **1** moving **2** not … the point **3** witty, very long **4** obvious, Still **5** Quite imaginative

4 **A** 5 **B** 3 **C** 1 **D** 2 **E** 4

Pronunciation

1 2, 3, 5, 6, 7 and 10 contain the /ʌ/ sound.

Page 6 Grammar

1 **1** are always saying **2** not possible **3** will arrive **4** will rehearse **5** will have **6** not possible **7** will generally do **8** not possible **9** will always go **10** will get **11** will go **12** are always trying **13** will often have **14** not possible

2 **1** have you been doing **2** have been recording **3** haven't finished **4** have you got **5** have written **6** have been trying **7** have been touring **8** have been working **9** have admired **10** have actually played

3 **1** the **2** a **3** the **4** Ø **5** the **6** Ø **7** a **8** the

4 **1** Ø **2** the **3** a **4** Ø **5** the **6** Ø **7** a

Page 7 Grammar Plus

1 **1** have opened, R **2** have been browsing, D **3** has gained, R **4** has been **5** have bought, R **6** has been going, D **7** have seen **8** has reached, R

2 **2** don't use **3** tell **4** play **5** share **6** have **7** involves **8** enters **9** appears **10** fights **11** defeats **12** is undergoing **13** are losing **14** seems **15** are now developing

3 circled verbs: **2** will not use **3** will tell **5** will sometimes share **6** will have **7** will usually involve **8** will enter **9** will appear **10** will fight **11** will defeat

4 **1** am always stuffing them into my bag **2** is always forgetting his wallet **3** is always telling ridiculous jokes **4** are forever treading on my feet

5 **1** an **2** an **3** – **4** – **5** – **6** the **7** – **8** – **9** the **10** – **11** a **12** a **13** – **14** a **15** –

Pages 8–9 Reading

1 **1** B **2** C **3** A

2 Yes, they probably do.

3 **1** C **2** A **3** D **4** C **5** B

4 **1** claim **2** overtake **3** damaging **4** suffering **5** willing **6** decent **7** return **8** principally

5 **1** damage **2** suffer **3** decent **4** overtook **5** claim **6** willing **7** principally **8** return

6 **1** to **2** for **3** from **4** on **5** in **6** on

Page 10 Everyday English

1 **1** find **2** appeal **3** like **4** mood **5** keen **6** mind **7** fan **8** stand **9** on **10** thing **11** of **12** of

2 **1** majority of **2** quarter of **3** One in **4** most popular **5** as many … as **6** Over

3 (suggested answers) **1** Are there any in the stalls? **2** And how much are they? **3** Would there be a discount for 15 people? **4** OK. Could I book 15 tickets, then? **5** Sorry, I'm not with you. **6** OK. I'll take those, I guess. **7** What time does the show start? **8** And how can I collect the tickets?

Page 11 Writing

1 **1** early years; for the last ten years **2** venue; it took place **3** amazing; disappointing; for the most part, it was **4** piece; they opened with; for the most part, it was **5** applause; fans; impatient **6** it is well worth seeing

2 Missing elements are: **1** (Introduction), the where of **2** (The occasion of the concert) **4** (The details) and **5** (The audience's reaction).

3 (suggested answers) **[B] In the last five years, Kings of Leon have gone from being a cult group with a small dedicated following to one of the world's biggest rock bands.** Last week I took a friend to see one of their concerts, which the newspaper had asked me to review. **[D] It took place at the Wembley Arena in London, which is an enormous venue.** It was the opening concert in their world tour which will take in six countries and over 30 venues. I am not a huge fan of their music and so my expectations were not very high.

In fact, it was an excellent show and I came away still humming some of their tunes. [C] **They opened with** *Use Somebody,* **their catchy new single, but in fact then continued to play mostly older material.** Kings of Leon do not really put on a show as such. There are no big video screens at the back, no impressive laser lights. All there is to watch are four musicians playing their instruments. But the lack of visual stimulation doesn't actually matter, because the music is so good and they play with such passion. For two hours I was spellbound.

[A] **The audience, a mixture of die-hard fans and people who had been attracted more recently by their more commercial songs, loved it.** At £70 per ticket it's not a cheap concert, but if you appreciate good musicianship and great song-writing, I would thoroughly recommend seeing them.

4 **1** cult **2** humming **3** catchy
4 spellbound **5** thoroughly

Unit 2

Page 12 Vocabulary

1 **1** border **2** abroad **3** volunteer
4 touch **5** emigrate

2 **1** poor **2** human **3** medical **4** global
5 environmental **6** economic

3 **1** charitable **2** practical **3** established
4 extensive **5** religious **6** profitable

4 **1** a three-hour journey **2** a 120-metre high
building **3** a world-famous park **4** a high-profile
photographer **5** a long-running dispute **6** some
last-minute changes **7** reddish-brown hair

5 **1** to **2** to **3** in **4** – **5** from … to
6 over / – **7** in … with **8** –

6 **1** timetable, time zone **2** healthcare, health check
3 market place, market research **4** newsletter, news
story **5** sunburn, sunlight **6** road sign, road works

Page 13 Listening

1 **A** good deal, Greek island, mates **B** police,
speeding, 60% **C** career, Royal Festival Hall, series
of concerts

3 **1** T **2** F **3** F **4** F **5** T **6** T

4 **1** heading **2** come by **3** queuing up
4 growing **5** getting back **6** attaches
7 associate **8** rubbed off

5 **1** rubbed off **2** come by **3** associate
4 getting back **5** heading (for)

Pronunciation

1 **1** striking /aɪ/ **2** highly /aɪ/ **3** picking /ɪ/
4 driving /aɪ/ **5** difficult /ɪ/ **6** incentive /ɪ/
7 Britain /ɪ/ **8** skilled /ɪ/

2 1, 2, 3, 5 and 6 follow the rule for /ɪ/. 7, 8, 10, 11
and 12 follow the rule for /aɪ/.

Page 14 Grammar

1 **1** We both like tennis. **2** Neither of us eats fish.
3 None of the participants was under 16 years old.
4 Each country has different immigration rules.
5 Either you can go or I can. **6** Some want to
study abroad and others don't. / Some don't want
to study abroad but others do. **7** No volunteer had
previous experience of this kind of work. **8** Every
contract lasts three months.

2 **1** arrived **2** was raining **3** had decided
4 took **5** had made / made **6** climbed **7** ran
8 unrolled **9** sat down **10** had gone **11** was
coming up / came up **12** realised **13** was
blocking

3 **1** had ever won **2** had met **3** had been crying
4 had been looking forward to **5** had
prepared **6** hadn't been waiting **7** had
sold **8** had lost **9** had been working **10** had
been getting

4 **1** set up / ~~used to set up~~ / ~~would set up~~ **2** took
/ ~~used to take~~ / ~~would take~~ **3** belonged / used
to belong / ~~would belong~~ **4** recruited / used to
recruit / would recruit **5** had / used to have /
~~would have~~ **6** worked / used to work / would
work **7** was / ~~used to be~~ / ~~would be~~
8 telephoned / used to telephone / would
telephone **9** gave / ~~used to give~~ / would give
10 thought / ~~used to think~~ / ~~would think~~

Page 15 Grammar Plus

1 **1** Neither … nor **2** both **3** None
4 either … or **5** Each **6** both … and
7 all **8** Some **9** Every

2 **1** B **2** C **3** A **4** C **5** A

3 **2** (often would go) In the past people
would often go/often went for walks in the
countryside. **3** (would use to travel) In the
Middle Ages people would travel / used to travel /
travelled on horseback or on foot. **4** (used to like)
I didn't use to like / didn't like salty food, but now
I do. **5** (would be) My dad says he used to be /
was really good at maths when he was at school.

Pages 16–17 Reading

1 Because the judge ruled that the child was already
well cared for in her native country.

2 **1** B **2** A **3** B **4** C

3 **1** B **2** D **3** C **4** D **5** C **6** A **7** B

4 **1** In the 1850s **2** War orphans from Europe
and Asia **3** 20,000 **4** The Joint Council on
International Children's Services **5** UNICEF

5 **1** T **2** F **3** F **4** T **5** F

Page 18 Everyday English

1 1 absolutely 2 a bit 3 pretty 4 totally
5 a bit 6 absolutely

2 1 Unfortunately 2 Actually 3 Luckily 4 Well
5 anyway

3 1 visited 2 rose 3 fell / dropped 4 went

Page 19 Writing

1 1 world-famous destination 2 three-hour
3 lived 4 used to inhabit 5 Most 6 45-minute
7 either 8 awe-inspiring façade 9 will avoid
10 have ever visited

2 1 I would like to give travellers some practical
advice about the best way to visit it. 2 Petra
is situated in the south of Jordan, a three-hour
journey by car from the capital, Amman. 3 It is
a unique place, a city carved out of the rock … /
Walk down the Siq, a long narrow passage
with high rocks on either side and at the end
you will catch a glimpse of the Treasury with
its awe-inspiring façade. This massive building
is the tomb of a Nabataean king and is carved
out of the pink rock that surrounds it. 4 The
Bedouins in the area used to inhabit the same
caves until quite recently, but they were moved
out by the government in the 1980s. Now the
site is purely for visitors. 5 Petra is without
doubt one of the most beautiful places I have
ever visited …

Unit 3

Page 20 Vocabulary

1 1 different 2 worse 3 spoiled 4 have
transformed 5 in decline

2 1 population 2 birth 3 older 4 expectancy
5 group

3 1 hyper 2 semi 3 micro 4 semi
5 semi 6 hyper 7 ultra 8 hyper

4 1 chewed 2 snack 3 takeaway 4 out
5 course 6 go, sit

5 1 pre 2 under 3 multi 4 trans 5 over
6 mis 7 re 8 inter

Page 21 Listening

1 She mentions 2, 4 and 5.

2 1 C 2 D 3 B 4 C 5 A 6 D

Pronunciation

1 1 magical S 2 change S 3 gum H 4 longer H
5 technology S 6 guess H

2 1 guarantee H 2 generous S 3 finger H
4 danger S 5 gunpowder H 6 biology S
7 logical S 8 generate S

Page 22 Grammar

1 1 are you doing 2 am not going to spend
3 is staying 4 'll ask 5 'll mind 6 's only taking
7 finishes 8 'll give 9 Are you doing
10 're having / are going to have 11 's coming
12 's going to introduce 13 'll bring 14 are you
doing / are you going to do 15 am going
16 're vaccinating / are going to vaccinate 17 are
you going to get 18 're taking / going to take
19 'll walk / are going to walk 20 're getting up /
going to get up / will get up 21 leaves

2 1 The population will have reached nine
billion. 2 The temperature will have increased
by 2–3 degrees. 3 People will be living to over
100 years. 4 Medical scientists will have eliminated
inherited diseases. 5 Computers will be thinking
like humans. 6 Everyone will be eating genetically-
modified food. 7 People will be using multi-
language translators. 8 Scientists will have
discovered new ways to store electricity.

3 1 will have built 2 will have stopped 3 will
have been using, will have forgotten 4 will have
been thinking 5 will have eliminated

Page 23 Grammar Plus

1 2 E 3 F 4 A 5 D 6 C

2 1 A 2 C 3 A 4 B 5 B

3 1 a will have planted b will have been planting
2 a will have negotiated b will have been negotiating
3 a will have left b will have been staying

4 1 will have finished, will love 2 will have
changed 3 will be flying 4 will have been,
will be celebrating / will celebrate 5 will have
graduated, will have to 6 will be sitting

5 1 will be lying 2 will have made 3 will have
finished 4 will be preparing 5 will have been
working

Pages 24–25 Reading

1 1 How people, young and old, use technology.
2 that the iPad is very useful for old people.

2 1 A 2 B 3 A 4 B

3 1 C 2 A 3 F 4 D

4 1 B 2 C 3 A 4 A

5 1 incompetent 2 technophobic 3 inadequate
4 infirm 5 varying 6 isolated

Page 26 Everyday English

1 1 convinced / certain 2 might / may 3 see
4 unlikely 5 well 6 chance 7 definitely
8 way

2 1 Personally, I find it amazing that 2 considering
how much food 3 The way I see it 4 as far as

I am concerned   **5** Statistics show us that if
6 due to the fact that

3 (suggested answers)   **1** I'm afraid I'm not free
tonight.   **2** Yes, that would suit me better.
3 Great. See you then.

4 (suggested answers)   **1** Hello, I would like to make
an appointment with the bank manager.   **2** Would
some time this week be possible?   **3** I'm afraid I'm
not available on Thursday.   **4** Yes, that would be
fine. Thank you.

5 **1** attend   **2** invite   **3** convenient   **4** sincerely

Page 27 Writing

1 A

2 He is in favour of it. (*In my opinion, there is no doubt
that the benefits of genetic engineering outweigh its
disadvantages;* and the contents of paragraphs 2
and 3.)

3 **1** however   **2** therefore   **3** in contrast to
4 in addition   **5** despite   **6** all things considered

4 **1** outweigh   **2** provoke   **3** examine   **4** treat
5 diagnose   **6** suffer   **7** spend   **8** question

Unit 4
Page 28 Vocabulary

1 **1** remarkable   **2** peaceful   **3** overpopulation
4 sceptical   **5** unsettling   **6** scarce   **7** puzzling
8 villains   **9** heroes

2 **1** achieved   **2** gained   **3** reach   **4** survive
5 attempt   **6** fulfil   **7** accomplish   **8** took on
9 discover

3 **1** C   **2** E   **3** D   **4** A   **5** B

4 **1** raised / dashed   **2** confirmed / dispelled
3 seized / wasted   **4** carried through / abandoned
5 hit / missed   **6** met / didn't live up to
7 fulfilled / failed to achieve   **8** kept / broke

Page 29 Listening

1 **1** He believed in a perfect society where people
shared equally.   **2** No, it wasn't successful.

2 **1** Voyage   **2** poverty   **3** craftsmen   **4** 70
5 poor   **6** the Civil War   **7** president   **8** four
9 industry   **10** (less than) 50

3 **1** Because it's difficult to think about sharing
when you don't have enough even for yourself.
2 The Icarians were never well-organised or
prepared.

Pronunciation

2 **1** certain /ɜː/   **2** learn /ɜː/   **3** wear /eə/
4 careful /eə/   **5** unfair /eə/   **6** world /ɜː/
7 hurt /ɜː/   **8** parent /eə/   **9** birthday /ɜː/
10 merchant /ɜː/

3 **1** bird /ɜː/   **2** rare /eə/   **3** repair /eə/
4 work /ɜː/   **5** nowhere /eə/   **6** turn /ɜː/

Page 30 Grammar

1 **1** is   **2** was announced   **3** was standing   **4** are /
have been counted   **5** changed   **6** feel   **7** reach /
have reached   **8** is / has been elected

2 **1** after   **2** As soon as/When   **3** before
4 Following/After   **5** Prior to   **6** Until

3 **1** When   **2** Prior to / Before   **3** Until
4 On   **5** As soon as / When / After

4 **1** must have been   **2** could have predicted
3 can't have had   **4** might have been
5 must have voted

Page 31 Grammar Plus

1 **1** B   **2** A   **3** C   **4** A   **5** C   **6** A   **7** C   **8** B

2 A – a fact, B – certainty   **1** There could have
been a huge explosion which destroyed life on
the planet.   **2** The climate may have changed
suddenly.   **3** Robots couldn't have rebelled against
their masters.   **4** Animals might have adapted to
the changing climate.

3 **1** must be   **2** can't have driven   **3** must have
reached   **4** can't feel

4 **1** They may (still) join us on Saturday.   **2** Jenny
could be preparing for her driving test.   **3** Susie
might not have been invited to the party.   **4** John
can't have been at home yesterday.   **5** The driver
must have been talking on the phone when the
accident happened.

Pages 32–33 Reading

2 **1** seek   **2** opt for   **3** row   **4** halt   **5** riddle
6 urges   **7** curb   **8** boost   **9** drive   **10** calls for
11 acts

3 **1** The government is acting to halt the immigration
row.   **2** Young people are choosing a life of
leisure.   **3** Nasa is asking for an increase to the
space programme budget.

5 **1** f   **2** d   **3** a   **4** g   **5** b   **6** e   **7** c

6 **1** F   **2** F   **3** T   **4** T   **5** T   **6** F   **7** T

7 **1** exoplanets   **2** planets like Earth   **3** dwarf stars
4 extraterrestrial life   **5** planets of other stars that
have life

8 **1** We have not had the necessary technology.
2 lines 25–29: 'a rocky planet roughly the size of
Earth orbiting in the habitable zone – not so close
to the star that the planet's water has evaporated
away, nor so far out that it has frozen into ice'

Page 34 Everyday English

1 **1** He must have known the weather was going
to be bad.   **2** He might have lost radio contact

with base camp.   **3** He may have fallen and hurt himself.   **4** He can't have been able to climb very far in those conditions.   **5** He may / might well have taken shelter in a cave somewhere.   **6** He is likely to have taken enough emergency supplies with him.

2 1 must   **2** likely   **3** probably   **4** would **5** definitely   **6** may

3 (suggested answers) **1** He might have been delayed. / Perhaps he left his mobile at home. **2** I must have made some serious mistakes. / Perhaps I didn't answer the question properly. **3** He can't have sold his car. / He probably decided to enjoy the sunny weather.   **4** He / She must have won some money. / Perhaps it was a present from a rich relative.   **5** A fire might have started in the town. / There was probably an accident somewhere.

Page 35 Writing

1 1 common   **2** puzzling   **3** distressed   **4** weird **5** astonishing   **6** sceptical   **7** intense

2 1 whenever   **2** suddenly   **3** gradually **4** still   **5** just then

3 4, 2, 3, 1, 5 (or 4, 1, 3, 2, 5)

Unit 5

Page 36 Vocabulary

1 1 application   **2** course   **3** prospects **4** academic   **5** degree   **6** requirements **7** gain   **8** activities   **9** vocational   **10** get

2 1 historian   **2** psychologist   **3** biologist **4** designer   **5** physicist   **6** politician **7** lawyer   **8** economist

3 1 out, out   **2** up, along   **3** by   **4** in, out of **5** down to   **6** for, down

Page 37 Listening

1 1 It's a prize ceremony for the students who are going to leave the school this year.   **2** The speaker used to be a pupil there.   **3** university and what happens after it

2 A

3 1 D   **2** A   **3** C   **4** B   **5** A   **6** A

Pronunciation

1 Berlin, Milan, Madrid

2 degree, career

Page 38 Grammar

1 1 is it, F   **2** have you, R   **3** wasn't it, F **4** shall we, R   **5** did you, R   **6** shouldn't I, F **7** do you, R   **8** would you, R

2 1 would certainly accept   **2** would not have applied   **3** will have to   **4** would not have

5 had gone   **6** pass   **7** have (general truth) / will have   **8** would not be facing   **9** had (now) / had had (then)   **10** do not think   **11** were

3 1 Jonah is currently studying a practical subject at university.   **2** Millie didn't go to medical school: she studied / is studying drama.   **3** Olivia is doing media studies.

4 1 had, would   **2** would   **3** had, would   **4** would

Page 39 Grammar Plus

1 1 aren't I   **2** shall we   **3** should you   **4** doesn't she   **5** am I   **6** shall we   **7** could you   **8** will it **9** am I   **10** shall we

2 1 hadn't been   **2** would have studied   **3** would be **4** had passed   **5** had gone   **6** could have become   **7** had spent   **8** would have learnt/learned   **9** would be   **10** hadn't worried   **11** would have done   **12** had known

3 2 had passed, would be studying / would study 3/2 **3** would be, had followed 2/3   **4** had, wouldn't have applied 2/3   **5** had got down, wouldn't have to 3/2   **6** had taken, would have 3/2

4 1 have applied for the university course (I wanted to do) if it hadn't been so expensive   **2** hadn't married the boss's daughter, he wouldn't be the manager now   **3** advise you what course to take if I knew what your interests are   **4** study systematically, (I'm sure) you'll do well in your final exams   **5** be a successful business consultant (now) if she hadn't taken Business Studies at university **6** has a first-class degree, they / it's normal for them to get a better job

Pages 40–41 Reading

1 1 1 verb   **2** adjective   **3** noun   **4** adverb **2 1** + someone + to infinitive   **2** + on + gerund form of verb   **3** –   **4** + adjective

2 1 A   **2** D   **3** D   **4** B

3 1 vocational   **2** business studies, product design

4 1 B   **2** C   **3** D   **4** A   **5** C   **6** D

5 1 Because they simply reflect the fast-changing needs of the work place.   **2** Falmouth college **3** Because there was a shortage of detectives. **4** They were horrified.   **5** He means it is a mysterious subject that is difficult to understand and surrounded by secrecy, almost like magic.

Page 42 Everyday English

1 What the right thing to do is: 2, 4, 6; What you can choose to do or not do: 3, 7; What others want you to do: 1, 5, 8

2 1 're supposed   **2** 're required   **3** 're expected **4** is it up to us   **5** should   **6** are we required **7** don't have   **8** ought

3 **1** to take out **2** expenses **3** afford to
4 repaying it / repayments / paying it back
5 lend **6** charge **7** owe **8** earn **9** spend

Page 43 Writing

1 She doesn't have A levels or a Baccalaureate.

2 **1** I developed a keen interest in **2** rewarding
3 Part of my job was to **4** I am convinced that
5 allow me to **6** I am optimistic that

Unit 6

Page 44 Vocabulary

1 **1** split **2** molten **3** covered **4** continents
5 collision **6** bombarded

2 **1** impossible **2** illegal **3** uninteresting
4 insufficient / inadequate **5** illegible
6 impolite **7** irrelevant **8** immature
9 unpredictable

3 **1** unsuccessful **2** unnecessary **3** imperfect
4 unimaginable **5** unwelcome **6** unmeasurable
7 illiterate **8** impatient **9** inefficient
10 unmovable

4 **1** c **2** b **3** f **4** a **5** e **6** d

Page 45 Listening

1 **1** Many things, including medicine, writing and
shipbuilding. They built impressive monuments,
revealing their skills in geometry and stonemasonry.
2 It contained items unseen for 3,000 years which
taught us a lot about their lives and beliefs.

2 **1** C **2** D **3** A **4** F **5** B

3 **1** Tomb raiders or grave robbers. **2** Because things
get lost in translation. **3** Damaging fragile artefacts
(and losing them to foreign museums). **4** Whether
we are happier today than the ancient Egyptians
were. **5** Placing poison or radioactive materials
there (and/or putting a curse on the tomb).

Pronunciation

1 **1** spe<u>c</u>ific **2** <u>a</u>rtefacts **3** <u>ch</u>aracters
4 trans<u>la</u>tion **5** <u>la</u>nguages **6** <u>g</u>overnment
7 con<u>di</u>tion **8** <u>fa</u>scinates **9** <u>pri</u>mitive **10** <u>ea</u>rlier

2 **1** <u>in</u>terview **2** <u>po</u>verty **3** e<u>mo</u>tion **4** <u>a</u>rgument
5 <u>tee</u>nager **6** lin<u>gui</u>stic **7** intro<u>duce</u>
8 <u>pra</u>ctical **9** <u>cu</u>ltural **10** <u>news</u>paper
11 <u>fle</u>xible **12** ad<u>van</u>tage

Page 46 Grammar

1 **1** they **2** their **3** she **4** her **5** them **6** their

2 **1** travelling **2** to believe **3** to see **4** talking
5 finding out **6** building **7** to go **8** to visit
9 come back **10** being **11** thinking **12** doubt
13 to see

3 **1** to write, looking **2** to talk / talking **3** to tell /
telling **4** to put, to sign **5** to say (although

'saying' is possible, providing students recognise
the situation it implies, i.e. that he didn't stop
talking about volunteering)

4 **1** my teeth checked **2** my eyes tested **3** it fixed /
repaired / checked **4** it cut / done **5** them
painted / redecorated **6** it cleaned / washed

Page 47 Grammar Plus

1 **1** takes, their **2** they, expect, them **3** deserves,
their **4** introduces, themselves, their **5** knows,
their **6** is, themselves, they, are, they,
are **7** dreams, has to, their **8** decides, they,
want, theirs **9** talks, themselves, feels **10** knows,
them, they, make, their, their

2 **1** to call **2** to leave **3** to buy **4** analysing
5 opening / to open **6** to feed **7** to
remember **8** watching **9** to have **10** to persuade

3 **1** living **2** feeling **3** talking **4** to keep
5 practising **6** to make **7** feel **8** to make
9 to go out **10** go **11** to change
12 to stay out **13** going **14** studying
15 to choose **16** to do

4 **2** had / got my shoes repaired by a local cobbler
3 am having / am getting my roof repaired
4 will have / will get the interior designed by a
professional designer **5** had / got my car serviced
two weeks ago **6** will have / will get the flights
booked for us

Pages 48–49 Reading

1 (suggested answer) In the <u>USA</u>, the law varies from
state to state, with <u>some states following British
law</u> and <u>others having their own laws.</u> <u>Courts</u> in
<u>most states will rule that the treasure belongs to
the finder</u>, but in <u>some states the court will rule in
favour of the landowner</u> so as not to encourage
people to go treasure hunting on other people's
land. The found items will only <u>become the
property of the finder/landowner after a certain
period has been spent trying to trace the owner.</u>
However, <u>any item over 100 years old</u>, which might
be considered to be of archaeological interest, <u>can
become the property of the government.</u>

2 B

3 A

4 **1** C **2** A **3** C **4** B **5** D **6** C

5 **1** ransacked **2** earth-shattering **3** hull
4 looters **5** timber **6** replicas **7** soil
8 deemed

Page 50 Everyday English

1 **1** than **2** a little **3** as **4** harder **5** as

2 **1** is easier than **2** (just) as important as
the Romans **3** are better (now) than (they
were) **4** is more exciting than learning from a
book **5** more expensive to make

3 **1** designed **2** purpose **3** aimed **4** presented
5 recommend **6** aims

Page 51 Writing

1 **1** Because he has always been interested in 20th
Century history. **2** He describes it as 'easy to
read'. **3** Ordinary people, as well as those with a
particular interest in military history. **4** (suggested
answer) There were mistakes made in the war and
these could have led to a very different conclusion. If
that had happened, the world could be very different
today. **6** Yes. Anyone who is interested in finding
out what shaped the world we live in today.

2 1, 2, 4, 6

3 **1** b **2** d **3** a **4** c

Unit 7

Page 52 Vocabulary

1 **1** farewell **2** speech **3** fireworks **4** fancy
5 mask **6** garland **7** street **8** parade
9 acrobats **10** clapping **11** banner

2 **1** e **2** c **3** b **4** f **5** a **6** d

3 **1** infancy **2** childhood **3** elderly
4 adolescence **5** teenagers

4 **1** We all got together at my house. **2** We were
celebrating the end of term. **3** We really enjoyed
ourselves. **4** Everyone let their hair down. **5** Some
people dressed up in funny costumes. **6** Afterwards
we let off some fireworks. **7** We stayed up very
late. **8** It was a great way to mark the end of school.

Page 53 Listening

1 To celebrate the birthday of a great civil rights
activist.

2 C

3 **1** B **2** C **3** A **4** D **5** C

Pronunciation

1 **1** h<u>o</u>nour **2** <u>wh</u>ole **3** <u>k</u>new **4** <u>foreig</u>ner
5 dou<u>b</u>t **6** lis<u>t</u>en **7** han<u>d</u>some **8** colum<u>n</u>
9 hal<u>f</u>

2 **1** hopeless **2** kinetic **3** wasted **4** film
5 herb **6** amnesty

Page 54 Grammar

1 **1** being divided **2** being thrown **3** to be
carried **4** to be killed **5** being drowned
6 to be banned **7** to be played

2 **1** being slightly injured **2** to be replaced **3** to
be given a present **4** being treated / to be
treated like a child **5** to be tidied before I come
home **6** being kept waiting **7** to be done /
doing **8** to be invited to the party

3 **1** She is understood to have left the
country. **2** This is considered to be a major

achievement. **3** The wedding is estimated to have
cost €20,000. **4** He is thought to be hiding from
the police. **5** It is claimed that he acted alone.

4 **1** is believed to be about to make an
announcement **2** is known that the criminal is
dangerous **3** are understood to have taken part
in the ceremony **4** are not expected to change in
the next 24 hours **5** is hoped that we can keep
this tradition going **6** is said to have begun in
Europe thousands of years ago

Page 55 Grammar Plus

1 **1** not being appreciated **2** being sent **3** to
be done **4** not to have been paid **5** being
interrupted **6** being cheated **7** being told / to
be told **8** not have been informed

2 **1** is thought **2** is said **3** was believed
4 was known

3 **1** not to have been **2** to have made **3** to have
been **4** to be **5** not to have committed

4 **1** a that the two Hollywood stars got married in
secret last weekend **b** are rumoured to have got
married in secret last weekend **2** **a** reported that
the celebrity couple have adopted a child **b** are
reported to have adopted a child **3** **a** believed
that love is the most important factor in a marriage
b is believed to be the most important factor in a
marriage **4** **a** assumed that someone who marries
a rich person is interested only in their money
b is often assumed to be interested only in their
money **5** **a** said that many marriages fail because
of money problems **b** are said to fail because of
money problems

Pages 56–57 Reading

1 **1** Glastonbury **2** Hop Farm **3** Camp Bestival
4 Paradise Gardens **5** Latitude **6** Download

2 **1** B **2** A **3** D **4** D **5** B **6** C

3 **1** the middle ages **2** Latitude **3** a Sunday
newspaper **4** gourmet meals / local produce
5 to escape from urban life (and relax) **6** in the
countryside

4 **1** B **2** C **3** B **4** C **5** A **6** C

Page 58 Everyday English

1 **1** origin **2** do **3** day when **4** benefits
5 significance **6** celebrate **7** place
8 commemorates **9** mark

2 **1** for **2** at **3** of **4** back **5** for **6** up

3 Customer: 2, 3, 5   Sales assistant: 1, 4, 6

4 **1** I'm looking for a **2** you show me some
3 How much is it? **4** Have you got anything
cheaper? **5** What's it made of? **6** Can I
bring it back? **7** Can you wrap it up **8** you
take off

Page 59 Writing

1 1 Fortunately   2 In fact   3 Naturally   4 Funnily enough   5 To be honest

2 1 D   2 A   3 F   4 E   5 C   6 B

3 1 Naturally   2 In fact   3 To be honest
4 Fortunately

Unit 8

Page 60 Vocabulary

1 Across 2 monotonous   4 secure   5 prestigious
6 badly(-paid)   8 rewarding

Down 1 low   3 stimulating   4 stressful
7 (badly-)paid

2 1 rewarding   2 monotonous   3 prestigious
4 secure   5 badly-paid

3 1 efficient   2 organised   3 dynamic   4 creative
5 trustworthy   6 cheerful   7 confident
8 sociable

4 1 trustworthiness, trustworthy   2 efficiency,
inefficient   3 confidence, unconfident
4 organisation, disorganised   5 logical,
illogical   6 reliability, unreliable   7 dynamism,
undynamic   8 motivated / motivating,
unmotivated / demotivated / demotivating
9 sociability, unsociable   10 sensitivity, insensitive
11 competence, competent   12 literacy, illiterate

Page 61 Listening

1 1 E   2 F   3 A   4 D   5 C

2 1 follow a career   2 asked for anything better
3 afford to make any mistakes   4 runs the
business   5 feel quite a lot of responsibility
6 term; monotonous; career prospects
7 pull together; support   8 electricians; make
more money   9 lasted

Pronunciation

1 1 She_/j/_ is quite_ambitious_actually.   2 A
lot_of people_ask you_/w/_if you can_advise
them.   3 The_/j/_ interview didn't go_/w/_
at_all_as_I_/j/_expected_it to.   4 I_/j/_applied
for_a job as_a porter_in_a hotel.   5 I_/j/_ordered_a
tomato_/w/_and cheese sandwich.   6 I go_/w/_out_
of the_/j/_office_every two_/w/_hours to get some
fresh_air.

Page 62 Grammar

1 1 which / –   2 who / that   3 whose   4 which / –
5 which / that   6 which / that / –   7 which / that /
– 8 which   9 who

2 1 going   2 over-prepared   3 interviewing
4 trained   5 asking   6 advertised

3 1 you learn (about something)   2 better paid
it is / better the pay (is)   3 the competition for

skilled jobs (is)   4 older you get   5 more slowly
the time goes   6 the better

4 1 does she raise a family   2 was the number of
applications   3 had he heard the news   4 does he
realise   5 should you attempt   6 have I come across

Page 63 Grammar Plus

1 1 who   2 which / that / –   3 which   4 that /
which   5 which   6 which   7 which   8 who / that

2 2 Mrs Judie Onslow, who is my physics teacher,
holds a PhD in astrophysics.   4 Poles, who became
EU citizens in 2004, are famous for their mobility in
the job market.   5 Renting a flat in the city centre,
which you can afford easily with your salary, will save
you two hours of commuting to work every day.

3 1, 3

4 1 The greater, the more effective   2 The more
monotonous, the more apathetic   3 The closer,
the healthier

5 1 given responsibility for the project   2 attending
the seminar   3 Arriving early at the lecture
hall   4 Puzzled by what the lecturer had said

6 1 did they realise   2 did I find out   3 can our
employees   4 do I come across   5 had the
plane taken off   6 was the job rewarding   7 did
he feel   8 did the company follow   9 had he
sent   10 will I stop

Pages 64–65 Reading

1 danger, loneliness, culture clashes

2 1 B   2 B   3 A   4 B   5 D   6 A

3 Phil Moneypenny has developed qualities he
lacked before. Claire Skinner likes knowing she's
helping people and the challenge of living in basic
conditions.

5 4 **a)** hypothermia, stamina   **b)** intense, blank,
rugged   **c)** fazed by

Page 66 Everyday English

1 1 was   2 catch   3 missed   4 with
5 follow   6 by   7 other   8 saying

2 1 What do you mean by   2 In other words
3 So are you saying   4 I'm not with

3 1 I didn't quite catch that   2 you mean   3 don't
know what you mean   4 other   5 was that
6 I mean is

4 1 missed   2 with   3 mean   4 by   5 wanted
6 words

Page 67 Writing

1 1 A   2 B   3 B   4 C   5 A   6 C   7 A

2 a 6   **b** 5   **c** 1   **d** 4   **e** 6   **f** 2

Unit 9

Page 68 Vocabulary

1 **1** rich **2** wealthy **3** well **4** comfortable
5 affluent **6** poor **7** destitute **8** hard

2 **1** on **2** for **3** for **4** for **5** on

3 **1** family business **2** NGO **3** e-company
4 civil service **5** multinational corporation
6 self-employed

4 **1** tackle, solve **2** advertise for, train **3** search
for, apply for **4** join **5** owe, repay
6 implement **7** assess, take **8** run, retire from

Page 69 Listening

1 **1** supermarket food (buy one, get one free);
(online) film rental; a network of homes you can
stay in free **2** another of the same item; a free
two-week subscription; a place to stay when
travelling

2 **1** supermarket **2** one week **3** waste
4 lucky one **5** online film **6** one film
7 your computer **8** extra charges
9 more film **10** stay overnight **11** own home
12 hotel bills **13** local people

3 **1** get one free **2** local rental store, mail rental
company **3** hotel

Pronunciation

1 **1** F **2** F **3** R **4** F **5** F **6** R **7** R **8** F
(Question 5 you would expect to have rising
intonation, but it's not really an open question:
it expects the answer 'no'.)

Page 70 Grammar

1 **1** a few **2** a little **3** little **4** a few **5** few

2 **1** to buy **2** to dress **3** to let **4** for not taking
5 of taking **6** for putting **7** to put **8** to
take **9** getting on

3 **1** was / is **2** had started / started **3** had not
tried / did not try **4** went / had gone **5** is /was
6 couldn't **7** were **8** had started / started
9 had just used **10** hadn't had / didn't have

Page 71 Grammar Plus

1 **1** a little **2** very little **3** a few **4** little **5** very few

2 **1** organising **2** cheating **3** for being **4** to
file **5** eating out

3 **1** advised me not to buy / against buying
2 denied having seen **3** insisted on buying /
that we buy **4** promised to help / that he would
help **5** recommended going and seeing
6 told me to move out

4 **1** to deal / that he would deal with the problem
the next / following day **2** that they had been
waiting there for over an hour **3** her students that
they would be writing a test the next / following

week **4** (that) (perhaps) the advertisement could
seem slightly misleading **5** if / whether I had ever
been disappointed with one of those products
6 I met her there that evening **7** (that) he had
not finished **8** where we were going to stay

5 **1** the current inflation rate is **2** much money you
are ready to invest in this house **3** the cheapest
youth hostels are **4** the best bank to obtain a
student loan is **5** you were yesterday between
6 and 8 p.m. **6** you are coming back

Pages 72–73 Reading

2 A

3 C

4 **1** A **2** B

5 **1** C **2** D **3** E **4** A

6 **1** Eugene Ciewinski: a landscape painted on his
living room wall / Gerry Simons: 30 steaks / Kelly
Holmes: nothing / Greg Parsons: a huge variety of
things (restaurant meals, plasma TV screen, security
gates) **2** You don't have to do direct trades with
just one other person and there are 75,000 members
in the network. **3** That they will lose tax revenue
because people do not declare goods that are traded.

7 **1** A **2** B **3** C **4** C

Page 74 Everyday English

1 **1** to lend **2** about appearing **3** would
4 went **5** in mind **6** share **7** good **8** 'll take

2 **1** What kind of deposit did you have in mind?
2 Would you be prepared to accept just two
months'? **3** That sounds fair. **4** How would you
feel about two people sharing a room? **5** And
if we were to redecorate the bathroom, would
you share the cost? **6** No, I'm sorry. I couldn't
possibly do that. **7** Supposing we wanted to leave
early, would we get a refund?

3 **1** go **2** recommend **3** possibility **4** try
5 thing **6** advising **7** going **8** would

Page 75 Writing

1 (suggested answers) **1** was 32, down 15 on
last year **2** was only two-thirds of what they
had before **3** people to give their ideas for
recruiting more members **4** putting up
some posters **5** performing a demonstration
dance **6** agreed and suggested that the best place
and time would be **7** that there was a problem with
having club night on a Monday when most people felt
too tired **8** she thought that was not a problem and
that it was the only time the gym was available **9** the
organising committee for screening only one film last
year **10** the film club for this **11** that we should
look for another space **12** to research this and report
back at the next meeting **13** meeting again in a
week to decide who was going **14** to put up some
posters **15** everyone for their ideas

Unit 10

Page 76 Vocabulary

1 **1** Use: common sense, reason, your head, your judgement **2** Follow: your feelings, your heart, your intuition **3** Play: by the rules, fair, straight, the game

2 **A** theft **B** bribery **C** corporate manslaughter **D** discrimination

3 **1** naughty **2** tricks **3** spread **4** gossiping **5** told **6** insecure **7** fun **8** side

4 **1** d **2** a **3** f **4** c **5** b **6** e

5 **1** eco-friendly / green; rip off **2** unspoilt; off the beaten track **3** authentic / genuine; built-up / developed

Page 77 Listening

1 a daytime TV talk show

2 **1** To see what members of the public would do when faced with a moral dilemma. **2** Actors and passers-by **3** Yes, probably

3 **1** F **2** T **3** T **4** F **5** F **6** F **7** F **8** T

Pronunciation

2 **1** second syllable **2** second syllable **3** second syllable **4** opportunity

Page 78 Grammar

1 **1** I could swim 40 lengths. **2** I was able to swim 40 lengths. **3** I succeeded in swimming 40 lengths. **4** I managed to swim 40 lengths.

2 **1** could see **2** could hardly speak / was hardly able to speak **3** managed to get / was able to get / succeeded in getting **4** couldn't get / wasn't able to get **5** managed to arrive / succeeded in arriving **6** couldn't believe **7** managed to control / succeeded in controlling **8** could see **9** managed to get / succeeded in getting **10** never managed to do / never succeeded in doing **11** could not wait **12** could not bring / wasn't able to bring

3 **1** is due to **2** was intending **3** would have kept **4** sold **5** was always going to **6** will drop **7** is about to **8** is going to **9** was going to **10** was expected **11** was about to **12** was due to **13** would have been

Page 79 Grammar Plus

1 **1** couldn't **2** managed to **3** could **4** managed to **5** could

2 **1** PO, was able to **2** PO, were able to **3** GA, was able to / could **4** GA, could **5** PO, wasn't able to / couldn't

3 **2** was sure they were going to announce the name of the winner the next / following day **3** have called Jeff (yesterday) to let him know I wouldn't be there until later **4** knew that she could always ask us to help her **5** would have finished revising for the exam by the end of that week **6** had to leave early that afternoon because I was meeting my landlord **7** was going to start learning Chinese **8** was worried that something terrible was about to happen **9** was due to arrive at ten o'clock **10** could have borrowed by bike any time you liked

4 **1** 'd better **2** ought not to **3** be better off taking **4** 'd better not **5** you should ask

Pages 80–81 Reading

1 (possible answers) **Know:** It's the tallest mountain in the world. Lots of people try to climb it, but not many succeed. **Want to know:** Why are they thinking of closing it? What will happen to the climbers?

2 (possible answers) Everest is very polluted. The government of Nepal gets a lot of money from visitors and climbers. 20,000 people visit Everest each year.

4 **1** street children (living around the main station) **2** Indian visitors **3** uncomfortable **4** tired **5** learning much but are happy to be there **6** with finding food and safe places to sleep **7** more direct experience of the children's working lives

5 C

6 **1** rehabilitate **2** gape **3** (profound) misery **4** limbs **5** battle **6** spot **7** takings **8** lucrative **9** packs **10** peer

Page 82 Everyday English

1 **1** ought to / should / had better **2** be better **3** were you **4** ask **5** better **6** think of / about **7** off buying / getting **8** should / ought to

2 **1** case **2** question **3** establish **4** duty **5** advise **6** interests

3 **1** our duty to make sure this doesn't happen again **2** a case of bribery **3** to establish (a/the reason) why he did it **4** advise against acting now **5** the company's interests (for us) to make a statement

Page 83 Writing

1 **1** D **2** A **3** C **4** B **5** E

Workbook Audioscripts

Unit 1, Listening, Exercises 2 and 3  CD1/02

1 I saw a young girl who stood on the plinth and threw paper roses into the crowd. I didn't catch one but someone near me did. There was a message on it. It said that the girl's friend had died of a disease called Cystic Fibrosis and it gave the name of a website where you could go and donate money to find a cure for it. It was quite moving.

2 The guy I saw was displaying his own paintings. He had four portraits, but you couldn't really make out who they were of. I think one was of the Dalai Lama. I think he was hoping that someone in the art world would see them and buy one. It seemed a bit commercial to me and not really the point.

3 When I was there, a mime artist – the kind you see quite often in public places in big cities – stood without moving on the plinth for one hour. He was dressed to look like the stone figure of Lord Nelson that stands on the top of the column in the middle of Trafalgar Square. Quite intelligent and witty really, but not something you could watch for very long – at least not for an hour.

4 This woman – she must have been about 45 or so – was lifted up and she got out a mop and a bucket and spent the next 55 minutes cleaning the top of the plinth. I don't know what point she was trying to make really: that she'd spent a lot of her life doing boring cleaning work? That we need to look after our public buildings? It wasn't really obvious. Still, she got a big cheer from the crowd at the end.

5 We went on the last day hoping to see something special, and I think it probably was a bit more original than some of the other things that had come before it. A woman was making a model of a man out of bread rolls. She began with the legs, putting bread rolls over two upright sticks. He looked a bit like the Michelin man. Somebody told me that it was supposed to be in the style of the artist who set up the whole project, Antony Gormley. Quite imaginative, I thought.

Unit 1, Pronunciation, Exercise 1 CD1/03

/æ/ cat, stack, hat, bag, sang
/ɒ/ top, stock, hot, blog, song
/ʌ/ but, stuck, hut, cut, sung

Unit 1, Pronunciation, Exercise 1 CD1/04

1 young **2** column **3** public **4** project
5 something **6** one **7** other **8** commercial
9 model **10** bucket

Unit 1, Everyday English, Exercise 4 CD1/05

N = Nick, T = Ticket agent

N Have you got any tickets left for this Saturday?

T Yes, we've still got a few.

N Are there any in the stalls?

T Sorry, no, we've none left in the stalls, but there are a few in the circle.

N And how much are they?

T £32.

N Would there be a discount for 15 people?

T Yes, there's a 20% discount on groups of 12 or more.

N OK. Could I book 15 tickets then?

T OK, but I'm afraid they're not all in the same place.

N Sorry, I'm not with you.

T Well, six are in row D and the other nine are in row E.

N OK. I'll take those, I guess.

T OK. I'll book those for you now.

N What time does the show start?

T The doors open at 7 pm and the show starts at 8 pm.

N And how can I collect the tickets?

T We can post them to you or, if you prefer, you can collect them at the door.

Unit 2, Listening, Exercises 3 and 4  CD1/06

I = Interviewer, C = Commentator

I In the studio today is Philip Turner, an expert in migration at the Institute of Economic Studies, who I hope is going to shed some light on recent trends in UK migration. Welcome, Philip.

C Thanks. Good to be here.

I So, Philip, it's pretty apparent that the majority of the Polish migrant workers who came here in the last four or five years are heading home now. Why is that? Is there no longer any work for them?

C Well, some Polish workers held highly-qualified jobs – doctors and nurses and so on–but most of them didn't. They did rather unglamorous work such as potato picking or cleaning, driving buses, working on building sites, that kind of thing. And yes, that work is more difficult to come by. We'll actually miss them, particularly in agriculture, because even though a few people here complained about immigrants taking British jobs, these weren't actually the jobs that British people were queuing up to take.

I But that isn't the whole story, is it? That doesn't explain why we are also losing skilled workers …

C Probably the main reason why they're leaving is that the exchange rate, which was once seven zloty to the pound, now gives only around four. At the same time the Polish economy is growing at a faster rate than ours, and key workers like nurses and plumbers are more and more in demand back home. On top of that, there's the incentive of getting back to the relatives or families they left behind.

I And you say we'll miss them …

C Well, yes I think Britain will be a poorer place for not having them. Not just because it's a reminder that our own economy isn't doing so well, which of course it isn't, but because Polish culture was good for us.

I Can you expand on that?

C Yes, for a start it's a much less cynical culture than ours – it attaches great importance to traditional values like hard work and community and looking after your family. These are values that we associate more with our parents' generation. In fact, in a way it has been a bit like going back to another era.

I I know what you mean. A striking example of that is the way that Polish people working in bars or restaurants treat you as a customer – I find them incredibly polite and friendly compared to your average English waiter.

C Exactly. It's pretty simple and obvious, you'd think, but I'm afraid we British are in danger of losing that kind of basic social manners. But perhaps some of this culture has rubbed off on us and even though the Poles are returning, perhaps a little bit of Polish attitude will remain. I think that's one of the important things about migration … When cultures mix, often they influence each other in a positive way.

Unit 2, Pronunciation, Exercise 1   💿 CD1/07

1 striking   **2** highly   **3** picking   **4** driving
5 difficult   **6** incentive   **7** Britain   **8** skilled

Unit 2, Pronunciation, Exercise 2   💿 CD1/08

1 immigrant   **2** simple   **3** quickly   **4** migrant
5 little   **6** relative   **7** behind   **8** excited
9 promise   **10** reminder   **11** hostile   **12** like

Unit 3, Listening, Exercises 1 and 2   💿 CD1/04

Perhaps you remember a scene from the film, or book, *Willy Wonka and the Chocolate Factory*, where he produces a magical piece of chewing gum that is a three-course meal all in one: tomato soup followed by roast beef and finishing with blueberries and ice cream. Fantasy, you think? Maybe not.

The idea of nano-foods is not to miniaturise food. Instead, nano-researchers in universities and food companies are talking about methods that will be able to design foods at a molecular level and bring any flavour, texture or taste to our mouths in whatever form we wish – through chewing gum, drinks, or anything else for that matter.

Realistically, such technology may be for the more distant future, but nano-science is already changing methods of food production today. It is clear that nano-packaging will be the first commercial application. Boxes and wrappers will contain anti-bacterial agents that will make our food safer and last longer. The next step is that we will then see nano-particles introduced into the foods themselves, so that you will not have to boil milk or water to remove the bacteria. Nano-science will also transform the lives of people with food allergies. If you are lactose intolerant, for example – in other words, allergic to milk – no problem. The lactose can be removed from the milk by nano-filtering and replaced with some other sugar.

All this sounds scary, but perhaps it is less frightening than the amount of chemicals and preservatives we add to our food now to make it last longer. Defenders of the technology say these are natural solutions which mean we can do away with these harmful chemicals. Opponents, on the other hand, say we're playing with fire. They argue that we don't yet know enough about the effects of these nano-particles to test them out on large numbers of people. They are worried that changing the molecular structure of food could have much deeper consequences. 'When I drink a glass of milk,' says one critic, 'I want to know that it's going to my stomach, not that tiny particles could arrive at some part of my brain that could be changed for the worse.'

Unit 3, Pronunciation, Exercise 1   💿 CD1/10

1 magical   **2** change   **3** gum   **4** longer
5 technology   **6** guess

Unit 3, Pronunciation, Exercise 2   💿 CD1/11

1 guarantee   **2** generous   **3** finger   **4** danger
5 gunpowder   **6** biology   **7** logical   **8** generate

Unit 4, Listening, Exercises 1 and 2   💿 CD1/12

J = Journalist, C = Curator

J So, you run a museum here dedicated to the Icarian movement. Can you tell us a little more about it?

C Sure. The movement was founded by a Frenchman, Etienne Cabet, in the 1840s. He had written a book some years earlier called *The Voyage to Icaria*, which was a kind of blueprint for a perfect society.

J And what was his idea for a perfect society? How would it work?

C Essentially, it was based on socialist principles. In fact, Karl Marx was an early fan of his. The idea was that if everyone shared the work that needed to be done and shared their property with each other, they could eliminate poverty.

J I see. So, how did this Frenchman come to live in the USA?

C He felt France was an undemocratic country where poor people were exploited. So, he went across Paris and other French cities looking for people who were willing to join him in establishing a new society. He gathered together a range of people with different skills – farmers, craftsmen, tailors, and so on – and in 1848 less than 100 – about 70 of them in total – set sail for America and landed in Texas.

J But we're in Iowa now.

C That's right. The conditions for farming were poor in Texas and they ran out of supplies, so they moved north and set up their community at Nauvoo, and then at Corning just near here in Iowa.

J And were they able to live according to Cabet's socialist principles?

C No, they always struggled for money, except during the American Civil War when they were able to get a good price for the food they produced. I'm pretty sure that some also found it difficult to share all they had. It's not easy to share or to get along with others when you are constantly worrying about not having enough yourself.

J Who was in charge though? Or did they decide things together?

C There was a president who was elected each year (women didn't have the vote though), and four officers: one for finance, one for farming, one for industry and one for education. But they were never well organised or prepared and the whole movement ended after less than 50 years.

Unit 4, Pronunciation, Exercise 1  CD1/13

1 The Voyage to Icaria, which was a kind of blueprint for a perfect society.

2 The idea was that if everyone shared the work …

3 But they were never well organised or prepared …

Unit 4, Pronunciation, Exercise 2  CD1/14

1 certain **2** learn **3** wear **4** careful **5** unfair **6** world **7** hurt **8** parent **9** birthday **10** merchant

Unit 4, Pronunciation, Exercise 3  CD1/15

1 bird **2** rare **3** repair **4** work **5** nowhere **6** turn

Unit 4, Everyday English, Exercise 2  CD1/16

One thing's certain: he must have changed his plans and given up on reaching the summit. The bad weather is likely to have closed in quite fast, and so he probably wouldn't have had time to radio back. He would definitely have been more preoccupied with how to protect himself from the storm. My guess is that he may have decided to sit tight until the storm blows over. I think we should do the same and then send out a search party.

Unit 4, Everyday English, Exercise 5  CD1/17

1 Remember that the main aim here is to make the mark less visible.

2 Whatever you do, don't use bleach.

3 So, first of all, use a wet sponge to remove as much ink as possible.

Then, dry it with a towel and spray the ink mark with hairspray.

Finally, dry it again and put it in the washing machine.

4 If that doesn't work, wash it again two or three times.

5 Is that clear?

Unit 5, Listening, Exercises 2 and 3  CD1/18

There are few people who are lucky enough to know from a young age what they want to do in life, and I'm guessing that there are not that many of you in the audience today. Certainly when I went off to university at 18 I had no idea what I was going to do afterwards ... and that's not an issue necessarily. The problem comes when you get to your third year and you still have no real idea.

It's a common scenario – we all go through it. You've had a great couple of years, enjoyed yourself, made lots of friends – probably not done quite as much work as you should have – and now you're trying to focus on your final exams. But at the back of your mind there's a niggling thought that won't go away: 'What on earth am I going to do when this is over?'

I'm not trying to scare you or anything. I just want to give you one piece of advice. When you get to college, you'll find an enormous number of possibilities for extra-curricular activities: sports clubs, theatre clubs, charity work, the Student Union for those interested in events-organising or politics. You should take advantage of these, because one of them may just lead to something – you never know.

Just for fun, I joined a group in my first year that was making up comedy sketches. My subject was history and politics so it really had nothing to do with my studies. Anyway, we wrote and practised a show and then took it to the Edinburgh theatre festival at the end of the year. It went down quite well with audiences and a couple of critics, and so I carried on writing comedy sketches, some of which we performed in Edinburgh the following year.

In my third year, I submitted a couple of my favourite sketches to a TV production company called Talkback, and much to my surprise I got a letter back asking if I'd like to test out as a junior writer on their light entertainment writing team.

I realise not everyone will be as lucky as I was, but I hope you see my point. If you get out there and get involved, things will happen. You'll make useful contacts, new avenues will open up and you'll find that when you leave university, the prospect of getting a job doesn't seem frightening at all – in fact, it might seem rather exciting.

Unit 5, Pronunciation, Exercise 1  CD1/19

1 Denver **2** London **3** Kansas **4** Bristol **5** Berlin **6** Auckland **7** Milan **8** Madrid

Unit 5, Pronunciation, Exercise 2 CD1/20

1 student **2** prospects **3** degree **4** subject **5** career **6** pupil **7** future **8** college **9** tutor

Unit 5, Grammar, Exercise 1 CD1/21

1 It's not rocket science, is it?

2 You haven't seen my pen anywhere, have you?

3 It was great to hear that Jane had passed her exams, wasn't it?

4 Let's take a break, shall we?

5 You didn't study history at university, did you?

6 I should have known better, shouldn't I?

7 I don't suppose you know what date the summer term ends, do you?

8 You wouldn't like to see a movie tonight, would you?

Unit 5, Everyday English, Exercise 3 CD1/22

B = Bank employee, K = Kim

B   Hello, how can I help you?

K   I'd like to take out a student loan.

B   OK. Is it for your tuition fees?

K   No, it's really to cover my living expenses. I already get help with tuition fees.

B   I see. And how much do you need to borrow?

K   Well. It depends. I can't afford to pay a lot of interest. What is the interest rate?

B   It's fixed at 0.5% over the base lending rate.

K   And when do I have to start repaying it?

B   Not until your salary is over £15,000 per year.

K   I see. So, is there a limit on how much you can lend me?

B   Yes, up to £4,000 per year.

K   And is there a charge for setting up the loan?

B   No, our service is free. Can I just ask, do you have any other debts at the moment?

K   Well, I owe £700 to my credit card company, but I also earn about £100 per week from my part-time job.

B   I see, and how much is your accommodation?

K   I spend £60 per week on rent.

B   OK. Well, I don't see any problems … If you'd like to fill out these forms then …

Unit 6, Listening, Exercises 2 and 3 CD1/23

1 Now? In the UK? I … no, I don't think there is discrimination in companies against women anymore. In fact, to be honest, I can't remember a time when women have had it so good. Any woman who is prepared to work hard and dedicate themselves to their work … there's no position that they shouldn't be able to reach. I can't think of any profession … well, almost none – restaurant chefs are pretty male-dominated still – where they can't reach the top. Talk about a glass ceiling is just nonsense; in fact I think it's often just an excuse people make for not achieving as much as they hoped to.

2 The problem is that, unlike men, women have always had several different roles … different lives if you like. There's their working life, their family life and also their personal life. They have to balance these. Fewer women go for the top jobs because they are not prepared to compromise their family and personal lives to get there. I don't think that's

unreasonable and I don't think it means they are being discriminated against. On the contrary, I think it shows that they are more rounded individuals than a lot of men.

3 I run my own company so I suppose you could say I've reached the top. I'm also a mother of two. I've managed to do both things because I've introduced a lot of family-friendly policies into the company. People in the company work flexibly, not sticking to 9–5 hours. Sometimes they work from home. We also have a crèche and childcare facilities so that people can bring their children into work if they need to. That's modern life, and bosses who can't accept that and accommodate employees with families shouldn't be running businesses, frankly.

4 We have a problem – you only have to look at the statistics to see that: less than one fifth of politicians are women; about 12% of company directors are women. And as far as I'm concerned, there's only one way to tackle the problem. There's no point just having good intentions and saying 'we must try to get more women into top jobs'. We need to bite the bullet and introduce quotas: a quota of 40% women in these two professions would be a good start.

5 The barrier you're talking about is not necessarily just imposed by men. I think it's partly in the nature of men and women. Women aren't as aggressive as men, they generally don't attach the same importance to job status, and they don't fight as hard to get to those senior positions. There are a few women who do, and by and large they get what they want. But like men who do the same thing, it means pretty much devoting your whole life to your career.

Unit 6, Pronunciation, Exercise 1 CD1/24

1 dedicate **2** dominate **3** compromise **4** family
5 profession **6** policy **7** company **8** personal
9 position **10** statistic

Unit 6, Pronunciation, Exercise 2 CD1/25

1 interview **2** poverty **3** emotion **4** argument
5 teenager **6** linguistic **7** introduce **8** practical
9 cultural **10** newspaper **11** flexible **12** advantage

Unit 6, Everyday English, Exercises 2 and 3 CD1/26

C = Chairperson, F = Freddie, K= Karen

C   So, today's topic is 'Women in sport should receive the same prize money as men.' Let's begin with the arguments against this proposition. I'd like to introduce Freddie Fletcher, who will speak for five minutes, and then we'll hear from Karen, who will speak in favour of equal prize money. Freddie …

F   Thank you. Firstly I would like to emphasise that I am not a male chauvinist and that in principle I don't have a problem with women getting the same prize money. If, that is – and it's a big 'if' – they are being asked to do the same as men. But often that isn't the case. In tennis, for example, men play the best of five sets and women the best of three. Logically, women should then get three fifths the amount of prize money. But they don't. In addition, there's the question of economics and how much revenue …

K … I'd like to draw attention to something Freddie said about the economics of sport. He said that the market should decide. But I disagree completely. It's essential that we don't allow the market to decide, because the market is run by men for men. I would also like to point out that in the top 100 richest sports people last year, there wasn't a single woman.

Unit 7, Listening, Exercises 2 and 3 CD1/27

I = Interviewer, P = Peter

I OK. So now it's time to welcome Peter Ginsberg, who has come in to give us some ideas on how we can celebrate Martin Luther King Day. Peter, I think a lot of people out there appreciate having the day off and they generally know who Martin Luther King was, but what if they'd like to commemorate it in some way that seems more … appropriate, if you like … to do something that would really honour his memory.

P Well, first of all, Doug, thanks for inviting me onto your show. What you've just said exactly sums up how we see it. We have a national Martin Luther King Day in this country for a reason: and that's that we continue to honour him by carrying on the great work that he did and keeping his dream alive.

I And what is that dream, according to you?

P His dream was that all the peoples of the world could live together in harmony regardless of their ethnicity, their religion, their colour and their social background.

I So can you give us some examples of the kind of activity we can do this Martin Luther King Day?

P Well, a very simple thing you can do is to celebrate diversity by eating varied food: Puerto Rican rice-and-beans, a Chinese stir-fry, or a peach pie from Atlanta, Dr King's home town. Get your kids to make multi-coloured paper chains to decorate the house. Explain to them that the different colours represent different kinds of people all linked together. You can also make it a day when you lend a helping hand to each other. So kids can help Mom with the housework or cooking. You could visit an elderly neighbour who lives alone and take him or her something nice to eat. In everything you do, try to think how Dr King tried to promote harmony. So, avoid arguments over what TV programme to watch; be generous and share what you have with others; don't put others down or make them feel small.

I That's interesting. I actually thought you were going to come and tell us to perhaps read a bit more about the man and his work, to listen to his speeches and so on. But what you're saying is: just be conscious of how he wanted people to behave towards each other and try to act on that in all the little things you do that day.

P Precisely. Of course you can do those things you mentioned: listening to his speeches is a very inspiring experience. But I think little, conscious actions are an even better way to honour his memory. If you can take these further, beyond just his anniversary itself, and perhaps carry on doing a bit of voluntary community work or something, all the better.

Unit 7, Pronunciation, Exercise 1 CD1/28

1 honour **2** whole **3** knew **4** foreigner **5** doubt
6 listen **7** handsome **8** column **9** half

Unit 7, Pronunciation, Exercise 2 CD1/29

1 silent *h* honest honour hopeless whenever
2 silent *k* know kinetic knock knife
3 silent *t* often fasten wasted ballet
4 silent *l* film talk calm folk
5 silent *b* debt lamb combing herb
6 silent *n* amnesty solemn autumn column

Unit 7, Everyday English, Exercise 4 CD1/30

SA = Shop assistant, C = Customer

SA Hi. Can I help you?

C Yes, I'm looking for a belt for my brother.

SA We've got lots of belts. Do you know what kind? Leather, cotton, plastic?

C Not really. Can you show me some examples?

SA Sure. They're over here.

C I like this one. How much is it?

SA That's £40.

C Er … Have you got anything cheaper?

SA There are some reduced in the sale over there.

C OK. I'll look at those.

C This is nice. What's it made of?

SA It's part leather, part fabric.

C I like it, but what happens if he doesn't. Can I bring it back?

SA Yes, but we can't refund your money. We can only exchange it for another item.

C OK. I'll take it. Can you wrap it up for me?

SA I'm sorry, we can only do that on Saturdays, when there are more of us working in the shop.

C OK, never mind. Can you take off the price tag, though?

SA Of course.

Unit 8, Listening, Exercises 1 and 2 CD1/31

1 In itself it's not that stimulating a job, and I was never going to follow a career in it. But I met some really interesting people. Usually I was just ferrying equipment from one place to another and fetching things from the nearest town, because the film location was out in the country, miles from anywhere. But I also got to take some of the actors to and from the set where they were shooting back to the hotel. The best was Dustin Hoffman. He was a really nice guy – very funny and not at all self-important. As a summer job, I couldn't have asked for anything better.

2 It's my sister-in-law's business and I knew from her how stressful it can get. It's someone else's big day and you can't afford to make any mistakes: everything has to be just right. Sometimes people can get a little too involved. I remember on one occasion the bride coming to the reception hall about two hours before the ceremony to check that all the tables were laid out as she wanted. But she didn't like the way that the flowers at the centre of each table had been done and she stood over us for an hour while we re-arranged them.

3 It was a perfect job for me because I love animals anyway – I'm going to study veterinary science at college next year. I've known the lady who runs the business for years because we sold her some rabbits when I was about 12. (We kept rabbits at home and they were always reproducing.) What's interesting about it is that it's more than just selling pet food – a lot of times people come in to ask you for advice about animal care and I really enjoy that aspect of it. Also, when customers come in to buy a pet, you feel quite a lot of responsibility to make sure *they* know what they're letting themselves in for and that the pet is going to be properly looked after.

4 I think the right term for this kind of work is a 'Mcjob' – monotonous, badly-paid, with few career prospects, but do you know what? I really enjoyed it. The food we were serving was pretty awful, but because it was cheap, standardised fast food, the customers kept coming. So we were really busy on our feet most of the time … and I think what happens in that situation is that as a team you kind of pull together and support each other through what's a fairly unpleasant experience. The rest of the staff were fantastic and I made some really good friends – we often used to go out together after the evening shift.

5 All my friends from university thought I was mad when I took this job, but I'd read an article that said that people in trades like this – electricians, plasterers, roofers and so on – actually make more money than people following so-called professional careers like accountancy or law. And since I've always liked physically demanding work … and I'm quite good with my hands, I thought I'd give it a go. In fact I didn't learn as much as I'd hoped to: it was all fairly mechanical stuff – cutting lengths of pipe, installing water tanks – and often working in really cramped and hot conditions in people's attics. I only lasted two months and then I quit.

Unit 8, Pronunciation, Exercise 2  CD1/32

1 She is quite ambitious actually.
2 A lot of people ask you if you can advise them.
3 The interview didn't go at all as I expected it to.
4 I applied for a job as a porter in a hotel.

5 I ordered a tomato and cheese sandwich.
6 I go out of the office every two hours to get some fresh air.

Unit 8, Reading, Exercise 5  CD1/33

a pay rise, hypothermia, intense, fatalities, black spots, remote areas, culture clashes, blank, fazed by, stamina, resolve, harvests, rugged, a glimpse

Unit 8, Everyday English, Exercise 2  CD1/34

H = Headmistress, NT = New teacher

H So, Stephen. How are things going?
NT Not bad. It was a bit of a shock at first, teaching the top class.
H What do you mean by a shock?
NT Well, at training college we focused on teaching Grade 1 literacy and numeracy.
H In other words, basic reading and arithmetic.
NT Yes, and the top class here is quite advanced.
H I see. So, are you saying that it's too difficult?
NT Sorry, I'm not with you.
H I mean, perhaps you should stick to lower levels.
NT Oh no, it's OK. It was just a bit of a surprise at first.

Unit 9, Listening, Exercises 1 and 2 CD1/35

1 Two loaves of bread for the price of one. Wow! That's a good deal ... Or is it? The trouble with most regular supermarkets' *buy one, get one free* food offers is that often that second item goes bad before you have a chance to use it. How many times have you had to throw away a loaf of bread or a carton of milk because it's past its use-by date? So, here at Lucky Shopper Supermarkets, on selected items, you can buy one item of food and get a voucher to claim the second item of food free any time within one week. This way you will save money and at the same time prevent unnecessary waste. So get down to your local Lucky Shopper and take advantage of our unique *buy one, get one free* offers! Lucky Shopper – aren't you the lucky one?

2 Filmfifty is the new way to enjoy your favourite films at home. We are now the biggest online film rental service in the country. At the moment you have two options: your local rental store or mail rental companies. Let's face it, the local rental store isn't great. They probably don't have the film you want because others got there first. If they do, they will rent it to you for 24 hours and charge you another day if you fail to return it on time. The mail rental company is a little more flexible, but who wants to wait two days to get their film in the post? You want to watch it now. That's where Filmfifty comes in. Subscribe for a year and then choose one film a week to watch. We'll send it direct to your computer to download, where it will remain active for one week. No waiting, no disappointment and no extra charges. This month we're offering customers a free two-week trial. Just go on to our website at filmfifty.com and sign up. Filmfifty – less hassle, more film.

3 Would you love to travel more but feel you can't afford to stay in expensive hotels? Couch surfing with Sleepsurf is the answer. We bring together a network of people from all over the world just like you, offering them the chance to stay overnight in someone's house free. Yes, that's right, free. All you have to do is make your own home available for other members as and when you can. Just consider the benefits. No hotel bills, a friendly welcome, the chance to meet local people in a place that's foreign to you, receiving exotic visitors in your own home. Interested? Then visit Sleepsurf.com. There are no strings attached, no hidden charges. Just sign up and join the couch surfing community.

Unit 9, Pronunciation, Exercise 2  CD1/36

1 What is it going to cost you?

2 How much do you normally pay?

3 Can I help you?

4 Why should you pay so much?

5 That's a good deal ... Or is it?

6 Are you looking for a new washing machine?

7 Is the Excelsior hotel too expensive for you?

8 Where can I find a supermarket?

Unit 9, Everyday English, Exercise 3 CD1/37

BA = Business adviser, E = Entrepreneur

BA Good morning. So, how can I help?

E Well, I've got an idea for a mobile coffee shop and I want to know how I go about getting a street trading licence.

BA Well, I'd recommend going to the City Council. Is it just one site you want to operate at?

E Not really. I want to move around. The station in the morning, the main shopping street at lunchtime, and so on. Is there a possibility of getting a multi-site licence?

BA Mmm. That's tricky. I think you ought to try applying for a single licence to begin with. But actually the first thing you should do is go and talk to the Council about your plans.

E So, are you advising me to be completely open with them from the start?

BA Yes, they're very friendly. But before going there, make sure you have all the details. My advice would be to write a clear business plan and take it to them.

E Thank you. That's very helpful.

Unit 10, Listening, Exercises 2 and 3 CD1/38

I = Interviewer, R = Reviewer

I So, you watched a re-run of *The Oprah Show*. Any surprises or was it pretty much what you expected?

R It wasn't the regular show, actually. It was her 'What would *you* do?' series that I saw. It's a series of staged situations, where actors play out a scene in front of passers-by to see how people react.

Basically the passers-by are faced with a kind of moral dilemma – should they intervene in some way or not?

I What kind of situations?

R Well, the first was a classic teenage bullying situation. It was in a public park and there were four girls and three of them are teasing the other one and being mean to her, saying things like, 'You're such a loser' and 'It's no wonder nobody likes you'. Meanwhile, the girl who's being bullied is getting more and more visibly upset.

I And what do the passers-by do? Does anyone step in?

R Practically all of the men just keep on walking, but most of the women do stop and give the three mean girls a piece of their mind. When they were interviewed afterwards about it, the women who intervened mostly said it was either because they empathised (they remember being in the same situation themselves when they were young) or that they felt worried for the girl's physical safety. Quite a few thought that it was going to come to blows pretty soon.

I And what did it make you think about how you would have reacted?

R Yeah, well, that's where it becomes interesting ... from a psychological point of view ... and I guess that's the value of a programme like this. You could just say it was voyeuristic, but of course it makes you think about the right thing to do. I hope I would have told the mean girls to back off ...

I And what was the other situation?

R Yeah ... I don't know about this one. It was more sensational somehow, like it was trying to get a reaction from the audience. What happens is you see a well-dressed woman walking near the station during a busy commuter time and suddenly she collapses – you imagine from a stroke or something. Within seconds people are around her, covering her with a coat to keep her warm, calling for an ambulance. Then they do the same thing with an older man, badly dressed, a bit dirty – could be a homeless guy. About 70 people go past before anyone stops to do anything. Some even just step over him ...

I Mmm, but perhaps people are afraid ... He could be mentally ill or a drunk ...

R Yes, I know. That's why it seemed a slightly unfair experiment. But then, when you think about it, that's not really an excuse for doing nothing ...

I So, overall would you watch the show again?

R I might. I think it has a serious point to it. And if it helps people to be more aware of their moral duty to help others in difficulty, then I think that's a very positive thing ...

Unit 10, Pronunciation, Exercise 1  CD1/39

1 dilemma **2** intervene **3** psychological **4** teasing

Unit 10, Pronunciation, Exercise 2  CD1/40

1 aware **2** bully, put, but **3** commuter, opportunity, full **4** empathise **5** voyeuristic, boy

Unit 10, Everyday English, Exercise 2 CD1/41

TA = Travel agent, C = Customer

TA Hi. Can I help you?

C Yes. We're looking for a beach holiday this summer … for two weeks in July.

TA OK. Did you have anywhere particular in mind?

C Well, definitely somewhere hot. We were thinking of Spain, but we don't want to go anywhere too crowded. We'd prefer to give the big resorts a miss.

TA And have you got a budget? I mean, is money an issue for you?

C Well, we just wanted to get an idea of the price of things first.

TA I see. Well, there are some fantastic deals on Spanish resorts at the moment.

C Are they package holidays – with everything included?

TA That's right. I'll show you some examples.

C Could we look at some villas instead?

TA Yes, of course. How many of you are there?

C We're a family of four. Two adults and two children, 12 and 14.

Placement Test

1 My name _____ Asia.

  a am **b** is **c** are **d** have

2 They _____ from Italy.

  a am **b** is **c** are **d** have

3 My uncle _____ two cars.

  a is **b** are **c** have got **d** has got

4 We live in _____ house.

  a a **b** an **c** two **d** old

5 There _____ twenty students in my class.

  a has got **b** have got **c** are **d** is

6 _____ he _____ in Amman?

  a Do / live **b** Do / lives **c** Does / live
  d Does / lives

7 **A:** Do you like tennis?

  B: No, I _____.

  a do **b** does **c** don't **d** doesn't

8 My brother can _____ the piano very well.

  a play **b** plays **c** to play **d** to plays

9 I'd like _____ bread, please.

  a a **b** an **c** some **d** any

10 Bill and Mary _____ for a bus at the moment.

  a wait **b** waits **c** is waiting **d** are waiting

11 Why _____ our teacher _____ us a test today?

  a does / give **b** is / give **c** are / giving
  d is / giving

12 My grandfather _____ a professional football player in 1950!

  a is **b** was **c** were **d** could

13 A famous king _____ in this city.

  a live **b** don't live **c** lived **d** living

14 Last year, we _____ to London for three days.

  a go **b** is going **c** goes **d** went

15 You _____ talk when your teacher is talking.

  a mustn't **b** has to **c** have **d** must to

16 Yesterday the class _____ take an exam.

  a must **b** had to **c** have to **d** did must

17 My parents _____ have mobile phones when they were young.

  a use to **b** didn't use to **c** doesn't used to
  d don't use to

18 Alexandria is a _____ city than Cairo.

  a small **b** smaller **c** smallest **d** not small

19 My toothache is _____ than yesterday. I need a dentist.

  a bad **b** good **c** best **d** worse

20 Everest is the _____ mountain in the world.

  a highest **b** higher **c** high **d** most high

21 Rachel _____ at university when she leaves school.

  a is going to studies **b** is going
  c is going to study **d** is going study

22 That's a _____ song. Play it again.

  a beauty **b** beautiful **c** beautifully
  d most beautifully

23 It's raining and I _____ my umbrella.

  a haven't brought **b** hasn't brought
  c haven't bring **d** didn't brought

24 In 1969, a human _____ on the Moon.

  a land **b** landed **c** is landing **d** has landed

25 Daphne plays the guitar really _____.

  a good **b** goodly **c** best **d** well

26 Ali lives in Dubai, but at the moment he _____ English in London.

  a studies **b** has studied **c** is studying
  d will study

27 I think people _____ their cars in the future.

  a fly **b** will **c** will fly **d** flying

28 Why _____ late for school?

  a always is he **b** is always he **c** he is always
  d is he always

29 Who _____ my cake? It was here a minute ago.

  a did take **b** has taken **c** was taking **d** takes

30 He _____ football last year.

  a used to **b** has played **c** used to play
  d played

31 What _____ when you told her the truth?

  a happened **b** did happened
  c has happened **d** was happening

32 How _____ have you had your new car?

  a long **b** long time **c** much time **d** many time

33 They met each other _____ their studies.

  a during **b** while **c** for **d** when

34 What _____ when I phoned you last night?

  a have you done **b** were you doing
  c had you done **d** did you

35 Oh no, we haven't got _____ cereal left, so we must buy another packet.

  a many **b** some **c** none **d** any

36 We don't have _____ before the train leaves.

  a long **b** much **c** little **d** few

©2013 National Geographic Learning, a part of Cengage Learning PHOTOCOPIABLE

37 Look at those dark clouds. It _____ very soon.

a will rain   b rains   c would rain
d is going to rain

38 Don't cry, Sally. I _____ you another ice-cream.

a 'll buy   b am buying   c buy   d 'd buy

39 I am writing _____ about the treatment I received in your restaurant.

a for complain   b a complain
c for to complain   d to complain

40 We _____ as soon as she gets here.

a begin   b will have begun   c will begin
d are beginning

41 They left after they _____ their meal.

a finishing   b had finished   c were finishing
d have finished

42 Have you ever been to _____ United States of America?

a a   b an   c the   d [no article]

43 I'd like _____ ticket to _____ Giza, please.

a a / the   b a / [no article]   c the / the
d [no article] / a

44 I hate school terms because I have to get up _____.

a more early   b earlier   c earliest   d earlily

45 How _____ people volunteered to help us?

a much   b many   c some   d lots

46 If you eat _____ fruit, you'll become sick.

a a few   b too few   c a little   d too little

47 You _____ for hours. Take a break and start again later!

a painted   b were painting   c have painted
d have been painting

48 Generations of my family have been living in this house _____ 1901.

a in   b from   c for   d since

49 Mike _____ by the time I arrived, so I didn't see him.

a went   b has gone   c had gone   d was going.

50 English school children wear a uniform, but in the USA, children _____ wear a school uniform.

a mustn't   b don't have to   c shouldn't
d don't must

51 Let's _____ a new website for our school.

a start   b to start   c starting   d started

52 How about _____ T-shirts to raise money?

a sell   b to sell   c selling   d to selling

53 Is this the _____ you have?

a big   b biggest   c bigger   d most big

54 It was the best pizza I _____.

a have ever eaten   b ever eat   c was eating
d ever eaten

55 As _____ as I am concerned, it's a bad idea.

a soon   b long   c far   d if

56 I wouldn't buy that laptop if I _____ you.

a am   b will be   c were   d have been

57 What _____ you give me if I cleaned your bedroom?

a will   b do   c can   d would

58 That's the man _____ brother owns the English bookshop.

a who   b that   c whose   d which

59 I can't give you this book. It _____ to someone else.

a owns   b lends   c borrows   d belongs

60 James _____ me if I knew Maritin's phone number.

a told   b said   c asked   d demanded

61 A cheetah runs _____ faster than a cow!

a slightly   b a bit   c many   d a lot

62 A cricket team and a football team _____ have eleven players.

a either   b every   c neither   d both

63 I don't like junk food _____.

a either   b too   c neither   d both

64 Sheila is someone _____ achieves 100% on everything.

a who   b when   c whose   d which

65 Chess _____ on a board.

a plays   b is played   c has played   d had played

66 Currently, many types of animals _____ by humans.

a kill   b are being killed   c are killing   d is killed

67 Have you any idea when _____?

a starts the film   b does the film start
c the film starts   d the film start

68 The policeman asked me if I _____ the burglar the night before.

a would see   b had seen   c saw
d was seeing

69 They _____ you 10% off at that shop if you spend over 100 euros.

a have given   b 'll give   c 'd give   d gave

70 We'd love to come if we _____ any spare time.

a have   b will have   c would have   d had

71 I _____ if I'd known he was coming too!

a wouldn't have come   b won't have come
c wouldn't come   d hadn't come

72 My uncle is a very _____ business

© 2013 National Geographic Learning, a part of Cengage Learning PHOTOCOPIABLE

man. He's made millions!

a success b succeed c successful
d unsuccessful

73 At the weekends, my mum makes us all
_____ some housework before we can
go out.

a do b make c clean d have

74 You _____ wear a coat because it's cold
outside.

a would better b had better to C had better
d would be better to

75 Judith comes from Boston, _____ she?

a isn't b hasn't c wasn't d doesn't

76 She _____ borrowing my clothes without
asking – it's annoying.

a keeping on b always c is always d is keeping

77 This _____ delicious. Can you give me
the recipe?

a tasty b is tasting c tastes d tasteful

78 I'm really looking _____ my holidays.

a forward to going b forward to go c forward
d forward to

79 Harry joined the army _____ he was
under eighteen.

a however b although c despite d if

80 Her parents _____ her to practise the
violin every day before lunch.

a let b made c forced d insisted

81 William has very _____ close friends.

a little b few c a little d a few

82 Your hair looks nice. _____?

a Did you do them b Have you had it done
c When have you done it d Was it done

83 I would rather we _____ at home this
evening.

a stay b will stay c would stay d stayed

84 Three ships were _____ in the storm.

a disappeared b vanished c gone d lost

85 The engineer pushed a button and the bridge
_____.

a was raising b lifted c raised d rose

86 Can you tell me what time _____?

a the train leaves b does the train leave
c leaves the train d will leave the train

87 Helen _____ Lawrence to make a
doctor's appointment.

a reminded b remembered c suggested
d said

88 The victim was attacked _____ a large
stone.

a from b by c with d for

89 Tennis is a great sport. You should _____.

a take it up b take up it c take up
d up take it

90 By this time tomorrow we will _____ in
Sydney.

a arrive b have arrived c have been arriving
d be arriving

91 Hi Miranda, I _____ you for ages.

a didn't see b haven't seen c hadn't seen
d don't see

92 He doesn't play football any more but he
_____.

a used to playing b used to c got used to
d was used to

93 I wish you _____ making that horrible
noise.

a will stop b stopped c would stop
d would have stopped

94 The roads are icy. Drive carefully, _____
you?

a aren't b don't c won't d wouldn't

95 I think we should drive. _____ we'll
have to take the train.

a Unless b Otherwise c Provided d If

96 You _____ blonde hair when you were
a baby.

a would have b was having c used to have
d had had

97 He should _____ a long prison sentence
for what he did.

a give b be give c have given
d have been given

98 No sooner _____ the door than she
realised her keys were still inside.

a had she closed b she had closed
c did she close d she closed

99 It was _____ hot an afternoon that
everyone fell asleep.

a so b such c very d too

100 Don't worry. I'm not really crying.
I _____ onions, that's all!

a chop b was chopping c had chop
d have been chopping

(1 mark for each correct answer. Total _____ /100)

1–25 Elementary
26–50 Pre-Intermediate
51–80 Intermediate
81–100 Upper-Intermediate

© 2013 National Geographic Learning, a part of Cengage Learning PHOTOCOPIABLE

Progress Test Unit 1

Part 1: Listening CD3/02

1 You will hear five speakers talking about cultural activities they did in London. The first time you listen, put the number of the speaker next to the correct activity (A–G).

(1 mark for each correct answer: Total __/5)

A A play at the theatre _____

B An art exhibition _____

C A pop concert _____

D A classical concert _____

E A photographic exhibition _____

F A stage musical _____

G A comedy show _____

2 Listen again and mark these sentences True or False.

(1 mark for each correct answer: Total __/5)

1 Speaker 1 feels this kind of art can help you to get to know someone better.   True / False

2 Speaker 2 felt that this performance was fresh and original.   True / False

3 Speaker 3 had very good seats for the show.   True / False

4 Speaker 4 saw a performance in an art gallery.   True / False

5 Speaker 5 found the show she saw funny.   True / False

Part 2: Grammar

3 Put the verbs into the correct tense to complete this interview with an artist (present simple, present continuous, present perfect simple or present perfect continuous).

(1 mark for each correct answer: Total __/6)

Interviewer:	So you were last in the UK in 2008 for an exhibition at the Tate gallery. What _____ (do) here now?
Artist:	Well, I _____ (just / return) from Italy where I _____ (live) for the last two years.
Interviewer:	Are there plans for a new show in London?
Artist:	People _____ (always / ask) me that. No, I _____ (decide) not to do any more shows until next year. I _____ (work) too hard lately and I need time to stop and think.

4 Complete these sentences using *a, the* or nothing.

(1 mark for each correct answer: Total __/4)

1 Can you tell me where _____ main Post Office is, please?

2 That's _____ lovely jacket. Where did you get it?

3 _____ gold is always a safe investment.

4 Let's go and see _____ film tonight, shall we?

Part 3: Vocabulary

5 Put in the right word to complete each definition about the arts and artists.

(1 mark for each correct answer: Total __/10)

1 The part of the theatre where the actors stand is called the _____.

2 All the actors together in a film or play are called the _____.

3 To get a part in a film or play, actors have to do an _____.

4 A pop or rock concert is also called a _____.

5 The place where a concert or show takes place is known as the _____.

6 A painting or photograph of a person is called a _____.

7 A _____ is a quick or rough drawing done by an artist.

8 A painting of the countryside is known as a _____.

9 A _____ is a person who tells jokes as a profession.

10 A _____ is a person who plays a musical instrument.

Part 4: Communication

6 Transform these sentences using the words given.

(2 marks for each correct answer: Total __/10)

1 Well, I like some of it.
Well, _____.
(appeals)

2 No, I don't really like it.
No, _____. (thing)

3 Yes, I love Kings of Leon.
Yes, I _____. (fan)

4 Yes, when I feel like it.
Yes, when _____.
(mood)

5 No, I don't. It has bad associations with my last summer holiday.
No, _____. (reminds)

© 2013 National Geographic Learning, a part of Cengage Learning PHOTOCOPIABLE

Part 5: Reading

7 Read the text and choose the right word (A–D) to complete the passage.

(1 mark for each correct answer: Total __/5)

1 A other **B** again **C** not **D** any

2 A eye **B** vision **C** sight **D** visual

3 A person **B** participant **C** member
D constituent

4 A to watch **B** looking **C** watching
D to be seen

5 A who **B** when **C** it **D** which

A new play starting in London this week is inviting its audience to fall asleep during the performance. I think we all have at some time or (1) _____ fallen asleep during a film or play, perhaps after a hard day's work or a big meal. In the theatre, it is particularly easy to nod off because there is usually less (2) _____ stimulation than at the cinema. The lights are dim and there is little movement to keep your attention. All the same, when it happens, you feel embarrassed – as if you have failed to participate correctly as a (3) _____ of the audience.

But should you feel this way? Surely it is the job of the actors, the director and the production team to present something that is worth (4) _____, and if they don't, you cannot be blamed. Nick Woodruff, the American critic, argues the opposite. Theatre, according to him, is no different from a football match or a concert: it needs the participation of both a performer and a spectator or audience to be successful.

The new play, *Lullaby*, (5) _____ opens at The Barbican this week, promises to send its audience to sleep for 90 minutes of the performance, using lighting and special sound effects. An interesting idea, but according to Woodruff's definition, it won't be successful theatre.

8 Now answer these questions.

(1 mark for each correct answer: Total __/5)

1 What two conditions make it easier to fall asleep in the theatre? _____

_____

2 How do people react if they fall asleep in the theatre? _____

3 Is this the right reaction according to Nick Woodruff? _____

4 How long is the play *Lullaby*? 90 minutes, less than 90 minutes or more than 90 minutes?

_____

© 2013 National Geographic Learning, a part of Cengage Learning PHOTOCOPIABLE

Progress Test Unit 2

Part 1: Listening  CD3/03

1 You will hear an interview about an international youth camp run by UNESCO – the United Nations Educational, Scientific and Cultural Organization. Listen and choose the correct answer: A, B, C or D.

(2 marks for each correct answer: Total __/10)

1 The camp is for:
   A anybody who is interested.
   B 20–30 students.
   C high school students.
   D university students.

2 The camp takes place:
   A in different places each year.
   B at UNESCO's headquarters in Paris.
   C on the UK's east coast.
   D in the USA.

3 The organisers hope that students:
   A will become experts on global issues.
   B will use their experience to further cultural integration.
   C will continue to work for UNESCO.
   D will organise similar camps in their own countries.

4 The camp is aimed at:
   A future political and social leaders.
   B future Nobel Peace Prize winners.
   C future construction workers.
   D future diplomats.

5 Conflict resolution workshops teach students:
   A about the main causes of conflict.
   B how to find a solution to conflict without aggression.
   C how to resolve international conflict situations.
   D case studies of high profile conflict situations.

Part 2: Grammar

2 Choose the correct form of the verb.

(1 mark for each correct answer: Total __/4)

1 Each of those organisations *does / do* excellent work.

2 We have two alternatives: both of them *sounds / sound* fine.

3 None of those holiday resorts really *appeals / appeal* to me.

4 I have two brothers: neither of them *has / have* ever been abroad.

3 Complete the text using the past simple, past continuous or past perfect. Use *would* and *used to* instead of the past simple where possible.

(1 mark for each correct answer: Total __/6)

In the 1980s, the French Atomic Energy Commission (1) _____ (regularly / test) nuclear weapons in the Pacific. The testing site for these weapons (2) _____ (be) a small French island. Each test (3) _____ (cause) world-wide protests. After Greenpeace (4) _____ (protest) peacefully but unsuccessfully against the tests, the organisation (5) _____ (decide) to illegally enter the island testing zone with their ship *The Rainbow Warrior*. While the ship (6) _____ (wait) in the port of Auckland, New Zealand in July 1985, two French agents sank the ship and one man was drowned.

Part 3: Vocabulary

4 Complete the second part of each phrase.

(2 marks for each correct answer: Total __/20)

1 The Sydney Opera House is a **world-**_____ tourist attraction in Australia.

2 **Humanitarian** _____ is funded by individuals, organisations and governments.

3 Most **asylum** _____ are granted asylum because it is unsafe to return to their own countries.

4 Coordinating **relief** _____ is an increasingly international task.

5 The sheer amount of help provided by volunteers around the world is **awe-**_____.

6 Young people in Somalia have grown up in a country divided by **civil** _____.

7 Floods have claimed more lives that any other **natural** _____.

8 **Labour** _____ trends show that in Britain one fifth of the population is economically inactive.

9 The area of Kashmir in south Asia has been the subject of a **long-**_____ territorial dispute.

10 **Race** _____ in the USA were positively influenced by the election of the country's first black President.

 © 2013 National Geographic Learning, a part of Cengage Learning PHOTOCOPIABLE

Part 4: Reading

5 **Read the text. Match sentences A–F to gaps 1–4. There are two extra sentences.**

(2 marks for each correct answer: Total ___/10)

A She lifted it out. It was very heavy.

B She was sure that there was a lot of buried treasure in the area.

C Metal detectors cost a lot of money.

D Her interest continued as she grew up.

E She wanted to write a book about archaeology.

F When she heard the noise, she dug down to see what it was.

A treasure seeker's story

In 2001, Janet Lyons became a household name when her story was printed on the front page of all the national newspapers, and she was interviewed on many TV stations. Janet was a treasure seeker. As a child, the idea of finding treasure buried in the ground had fascinated her. She wanted to dig up a box full of gold, silver and jewels herself.
(1) _____. At university she studied archaeology, and took part in many interesting digs around the world.

After university she worked in a museum in the northeast of England, in a place near the Roman wall and areas where the Vikings had landed and lived.

(2) _____. But there was no money to do a lot of digging for the museum, and most of her work time was spent in an office studying and recording the objects in the museum.

In 1999, however, Janet bought herself a metal detector, and, using her knowledge of the places where the Romans and Vikings had lived, she started her own explorations. The metal detector told her when there was anything metal underground by making a noise.
(3) _____ Often it was not very interesting. She found an old bicycle one day, a spoon from somebody's picnic another day, and various other things. But sometimes she found good things like a Roman coin or part of an old knife.

Then in 2002 she got lucky. She was using her metal detector in a field where she knew there had been a large Viking village. Suddenly the machine made a very loud, continuous noise. Janet got her spade and dug down into the earth. About half a metre down she hit something hard. She dug carefully all around, and then using her archaeological skills, removed the last bits of earth to see what she had always dreamed of – a wooden box.
(4) _____. When she opened it, the box was full of beautiful Viking objects – jewellery, cups and money – all in gold and silver. It was worth millions of pounds, and was an extremely important find. It soon became national news and was later put into Janet's museum as the main exhibition.

© 2013 National Geographic Learning, a part of Cengage Learning PHOTOCOPIABLE

Part 1: Listening 🔊 CD3/04

1 **You will hear five people over 100 years old talking about what keeps them healthy. Match each speaker (1–5) with the reason that they talk about (A–F). There is one extra heading.**

(1 mark for each correct answer: Total __/5)

A sharing experiences _____

B having a purpose in life _____

C social interaction _____

D regular fitness training _____

E eating an apple a day _____

F healthy nutrition _____

2 **Listen again. Are these sentences true or false?**

(1 mark for each correct answer: Total __/5)

1 Speaker 1 is often alone.   True / False

2 Speaker 2's habit started as a child.   True / False

3 Speaker 3's habits have changed over the years.   True / False

4 There was a tragic event in speaker 4's life.   True / False

5 Education still interests speaker 5.   True / False

Part 2: Grammar

3 **Choose the correct future form.**

(1 mark for each correct answer: Total __/5)

A: What (1) _____ / *will you* do tomorrow?

B: I'm not sure yet. I (2) *'m going to give / 'll give* you a call later.

A: What time (3) *are you leaving / will you leave* on Sunday?

B: Well, the plane (4) *goes / is going* at 14.10. But the motorway to the airport is always busy so I think I (5) *'ll set off / am setting off* quite early.

4 **Complete the text with the correct form of the future perfect, future continuous or future perfect continuous.**

(1 mark for each correct answer: Total __/5)

What environmental goals (1) _____ (we / achieve) by the end of 2020? At the end of the decade, most of the world's countries (2) _____ (work) towards common environmental goals for 11 years. According to the Copenhagen Accord from 2009, by 2020 110 countries (3) _____ (cut) their carbon emissions by a large amount. However, countries (4) _____ (set) their own targets each year, so cuts will vary. All countries (5) _____ (fight) to limit global warming to an increase of under 2°C. Richer countries will help poorer countries to achieve their environmental targets.

Part 3: Vocabulary

5 **Complete the words with the correct prefix.**

(1 mark for each correct answer: Total __/6)

1 You need a _____scope to see nanoparticles.

2 _____ sound scans are used to examine organs inside the body.

3 We only drink _____-skimmed milk.

4 He never stops moving. He's completely _____ active.

5 Even good restaurants have a _____wave.

6 Too much _____ violet light can damage your skin.

6 **Rewrite the words and phases in bold using the words in the box in the correct form.**

(1 mark for each correct answer: Total __/4)

| improve   reform   spoil   transform |

In Nottingham, a city in the centre of the UK, a new public transport policy has (1) **completely changed** the city. In a bid to reduce traffic in the city centre, the city decided to (2) **update** its transport system with the introduction of trams in 2004. Some feared a tram system would (3) **negatively affect** the look of the town, but the trams have become very popular with passengers. In addition, the city has (4) **made** its bus service **better** with new bus lanes and new buses.

1 _____

2 _____

3 _____

4 _____

Part 4: Communication

7 **Underline five sentences in these formal emails which are not appropriate in style.**

(2 marks for each correct answer: Total __/10)

> Hi Mr Stevens
>
> Thank you for your letter. We would be very interested to meet you. Do you want to come round this week? Would Tuesday at 9 am be convenient? Or what about Wednesday?
> I would be grateful if you could let us know as soon as possible.
>
> See you then
> Alexandra Robinson

© 2013 National Geographic Learning, a part of Cengage Learning PHOTOCOPIABLE

Dear Mrs. Robinson

Thank you for your mail. I'm afraid I am not available on Tuesday or Wednesday. What are you doing next week? How about meeting on Thursday?

Yours sincerely
Zack Stevens

Part 5: Reading

8 **Read the text about Ireland and choose the right word to complete the text.**

(1 mark for each correct answer: Total __/5)

From poor relation to wealthy country

At the end of the 1980s, the Republic of Ireland was one of Europe's poorest countries with a (1) _____ economy: high unemployment (18%) and a huge national debt. Many people were forced to leave the country to find work. Ten years later, Ireland had a booming economy known as 'the Celtic Tiger.' In 1999 unemployment was 6% and the national debt (2) _____. In a short space of time, Ireland had become one of Europe's wealthiest countries.

Both globalisation and Europeanisation played key roles in the transformation of the Irish economy. With lightning speed, Ireland went from being a country with little industry and an economy based mainly on agriculture, to a country which (3) _____ a centre of global high-tech industries and services such as computers, computer software, chemicals and pharmaceuticals. Multinational companies were attracted by Ireland's very low tax rates for companies, and the fact that it was an English-speaking country with a young labour force. It was also – (4) _____

its euro-sceptic neighbour the UK – committed to the European Union and the common European currency. Ireland attracted not only huge amounts of international investment, but also EU aid to improve education and transport.

Ireland's economy (5) _____ to grow in the first years of the new millennium. But in 2008 Ireland was hit hard by the global economic crisis and its economy began to shrink as rapidly as it had grown.

1 **A** changing **B** growing **C** struggling
 D expanding

2 **A** will be halved **B** is halved **C** was halved
 D had been halved

3 **A** was going to become **B** became
 C had become **D** is becoming

4 **A** with respect to **B** unlike **C** in addition
 to **D** except for

5 **A** continued **B** stopped **C** began
 D finished

9 **Complete the information.**

(1 mark for each correct sentence: Total __/5

1 Unemployment was _____ at the end of the eighties and _____ at the end of the nineties.

2 People called the growing economy the _____.

3 Traditionally, Ireland's main economic sector was _____.

4 The two main causes of the economic boom were _____ and _____.

5 Ireland's low _____ was one reason for multinational companies to choose Ireland.

Part 1: Listening  CD3/05

1 **You will hear an interview about the future of space travel. Listen and choose the best answer (A, B, C or D) to each question according to what you hear.**

(2 marks for each correct answer: Total __/10)

1 The new era of space travel will focus on:

  A sending robots close to the Sun.

  B sending people to other planets.

  C medical research.

  D sending spaceships into deep space.

2 The problem at the moment with sending craft into deep space is:

  A the high cost.

  B spacecraft have to be unmanned.

  C it takes a long time to reach it.

  D it is too dangerous.

3 Solar sails:

  A are a recent invention.

  B were invented nearly 100 years ago.

  C have been used widely for a long time.

  D have never been tested.

4 The main advantage of solar sails is that:

  A the spacecraft doesn't need heavy fuel tanks.

  B they can use light and solar wind energy.

  C they help the spacecraft to change direction quickly.

  D the solar panels are quite small.

5 The main disadvantage of light as a power source is that:

  A the spacecraft cannot go very fast.

  B the spacecraft stops when there is no light.

  C there needs to be another power source as well.

  D the spacecraft takes a long time to pick up speed.

2 **Listen again and complete these sentences. Use ONE word (or number) per space.**

(1 mark for each correct answer: Total __/4)

1 Deep space means _____ our own solar system.

2 Voyager 1 was launched in _____ and took 40 years to reach the edge of the solar system.

3 Solar sails were originally proposed by _____ and a Russian scientist called Zander.

4 At the moment solar-powered spacecraft can only carry a small payload, like a _____.

Part 2: Grammar

3 **Look at the sentences below and cross out the verb which is NOT possible.**

(1 mark for each correct answer: Total __/5)

1 The crew was very relieved when the shuttle *landed / was landing / had landed* safely.

2 The rocket launch was delayed until ground control *made / was making / had made* all the necessary checks.

3 There was a great tension in the air while the astronauts *waited / were waiting / had waited* for countdown to begin.

4 About three minutes after the rocket *will take / takes / has taken* off, the solid rocket boosters (SRBs) separate from the spacecraft.

5 Once the SRBs have separated, they *will fall / fall / have fallen* back into the ocean.

4 **Look at the sentences below and cross out the time conjunction which is NOT possible.**

(1 mark for each correct answer: Total __/5)

1 People are only allowed to be astronauts *after / following / when* strict medical tests.

2 What happens *once / when / while* the rockets and spacecraft have separated?

3 Do the astronauts lose consciousness *while / during / after* the launch?

4 How many astronauts survived *after / following / when* the Challenger shuttle exploded?

5 It seems that some were still alive *until / before / prior to* the shuttle crashed in the sea.

Part 3: Vocabulary

5 **Circle the correct words to complete the text.**

(1 mark for each correct answer: Total __/6)

Our (1) *solar / galaxy / universe* system is made up of the sun in the middle and a group of planets which are in (2) *particles / eclipse / orbit* around it. The force that keeps these bodies circling the sun is known as (3) *mass / gravity / light*. There are also smaller objects. Occasionally they enter the earth's atmosphere in the form of (4) *meteors / moons / satellites*, or what we call 'shooting stars'. Many people are dedicated to 'listening' to distant stars and planets, and hope that we will one day (5) *receive / pick / broadcast* a message from advanced life forms. We have also (6) *transmitted / analysed / collected* signals into space in the hope that someone might be listening, but we might have to wait thousands of years for a reply – if one comes at all.

© 2013 National Geographic Learning, a part of Cengage Learning PHOTOCOPIABLE

Part 4: Communication

6 Yesterday Tom gave instructions to Sophie on how to tune her TV. Complete this conversation between them.

(2 marks for each correct answer: Total __/8)

Tom: So, how did it go? Did you manage to tune the TV?

Sophie: Well, I managed to get three channels working but not the others.

Tom: That's strange. I think the aerial cable (1) _____ _____ been damaged.

Sophie: It may (2) _____ _____ been. Part of it was under a heavy wardrobe.

Tom: Well you should check that first (3) _____ _____. But if it is, (4) _____ _____ replacing it yourself, whatever you do. Call me.

Part 5: Reading

7 Read the text about the colonisation of space and chose the correct words (A,B,C or D) to complete it.

(1 mark for each correct answer: Total __/5)

There is no doubt that the space race of the late 20th Century is over. The sad truth is that times of peace are not good for investment in science. That is why following the end of the Cold War governments scaled back their investment in space programmes.

However, as more and more countries become industrialised, competition for the world's (1) _____ resources will intensify. One obvious consequence of this could be more wars between nations. But another possible result could be that, before any such conflicts begin, the search for raw materials (2) _____ into space and we see a whole new generation of space colonies appearing.

There is no shortage of theories about how these colonies would exploit the resources of other planets. One theory has it that colonists on the Moon would use the Moon's minerals to generate energy (3) _____ could then be beamed back to Earth, replacing polluting power plants. Other theories suggest that the discovery of new minerals on other planets in our solar system could enable us to find more efficient and environmentally friendly solutions to our food, transport and communications needs.

All this (4) _____ like a distant dream, but there are those who argue that we have the capability to start this research now. "We already have the International Space Station and the ability to land men on the Moon," says one NASA scientist. "We need to start making use of these capabilities now before our own resources run (5) _____ and it's too late. The Moon would be an obvious place to start because from a colony there we can launch missions much more easily to other planets."

1 A unlimited **B** limited **C** limit **D** limiting

2 A is extending **B** has extended **C** extend **D** extends

3 A in which **B** which **C** whose **D** from which

4 A sounds **B** appears **C** sees **D** portrays

5 A off **B** away **C** downwards **D** out

8 Are these statements true or false?

(1 mark for each correct answer: Total __/5)

1 The original space race is now finished.   True / False

2 The author regrets that science advances quicker in times of war.   True / False

3 It will take another war to prompt people to look for resources on other planets.   True / False

4 Many ways in which people could use the resources of other planets have been suggested.   True / False

5 The NASA scientist thinks we have the technology to start building space colonies now.   True / False

Progress Test Unit 5

Part 1: Listening CD3/06

1 You will hear five students talking about their gap year – a year out between school and university doing something different. Match the speakers (1–5) to the correct topics (A–F). There is one extra heading.

(1 mark for each correct answer: Total __/5)

A Gaining experience _____

B Helping people _____

C Travelling the world _____

D Taking a break _____

E Getting better results _____

F Making a decision _____

2 Complete the sentences with the correct word.

(1 mark for each correct answer: Total _____/5)

1 Speaker 1 got a _____ job in Sydney, Australia.

2 Speaker 2 found a marine _____ programme in Spain.

3 Speaker 3 got _____ work in different companies.

4 Speaker 4 was a volunteer in Uganda on a project organised by the _____ in her home town.

5 Speaker 5 worked as a _____ porter in a hotel.

Part 2: Grammar

3 Rewrite the sentences using the words given.

(1 mark for each correct answer: Total __/5)

1 Ahmed wants to study medicine but his grades weren't high enough.

If Ahmed had got _____

_____.

2 Lucy doesn't have a place at university because she didn't pass her exams.

If Lucy had passed _____

_____.

3 Damon didn't save any money before university, so he had to take out a huge loan.

If Damon had _____.

4 Pierre wants to study in the USA but he doesn't have the money.

Pierre would _____.

5 Maria hopes to get a place at university and leave home.

If Maria gets _____.

4 Complete the dialogues with the correct question tags.

(1 mark for each correct answer: Total __/5)

1 You saw that new film, _____
Yes, I saw it at the weekend.

2 I like your phone. It's new, _____?
Yes, I got it yesterday.

3 You speak Spanish, _____?
No, just Portuguese.

4 You've brought my book back, _____?
Yes, I have it right here.

5 He didn't go home, _____?
I don't know.

Part 3: Vocabulary

5 Write the word for the definitions.

(1 mark for each correct answer: Total __/5)

1 Lessons and lectures in a particular subject at university are called a _____.

2 Somebody who studies or teaches history is a _____.

3 The place where university buildings are located is the _____.

4 The money that you pay for tuition is called _____.

5 Somebody who studies or teaches biology is a _____.

6 Complete the phrases in bold with the correct words.

(1 mark for each correct answer: Total __/5)

An exchange year is a great way to **experience new** (1) **c**_____. You can **make useful** (2) **c**_____ and **put ideas** from your lectures **into** (3) **p**_____. To **get the** (4) **b**_____ out of your year, you need to be open to new ideas and ready to **take** (5) **r**_____.

Part 4: Communication

7 Match the questions with the correct answers.

(2 marks for each correct answer: Total __/10)

1 Can you afford to go to university? _____

2 Do you have any savings? _____

3 Do you owe any money? _____

4 How much do you earn? _____

5 What living expenses do you have? _____

A I've saved a little but not much.

B I don't have a regular income.

C I don't have enough money without borrowing.

D I don't have any debts at all.

E Well, I spend most of my money on rent.

© 2013 National Geographic Learning, a part of Cengage Learning PHOTOCOPIABLE

Part 5: Reading

8 Read the text. Match sentences A–G to gaps 1–5. There are two extra sentences.

(2 marks for each correct answer: Total __/10)

A Shuffle through my papers, arrange my books, make a cup of tea and discipline myself for a few hours of serious work until dinner.

B I never go to lectures as I don't find them very useful.

C Make another cup of tea.

D Go to a two-hour tutorial and realise I didn't do the preparation.

E Lectures aren't compulsory but we don't have that many, so I usually attend them all.

F If I'm feeling especially diligent, I might work.

G Most of that is often spent trying to find the set texts that I need for my classes.

Diary of a student

9.20: Switch off alarm clock.

9.40: Get up, throw on clothes and run to lecture hall, just in time for the 10 o'clock lecture. (1) _____.

11.00: Go to the coffee shop for breakfast, then get down to work. I usually do a couple of hours in the library before lunch. (2) _____. The library has a complicated system involving searching for hours on the computer and then looking on shelves only to find that the books have disappeared without trace.

13.00: Lunch. Chat with friends, eat sandwich, perhaps play a game of pool. Then I check my email and Facebook™ page and prepare for a few hours of hard slog in my room.

14.00: (3) _____ I usually have an essay or two to write or texts to read, and I find I work best when I have a concrete task and a deadline. Otherwise it's amazing how attractive going food shopping or doing your washing can seem when endless hours of reading stretch before you.

16.45: (4) _____ Then force myself to go to the library for an hour and try and hunt down a few more books.

18.30: Dinner. Cook pasta or something easy, sit around chatting with flatmates, then watch a bit of TV.

Evening: (5) _____. Otherwise, I'm involved in student plays so I might go to a rehearsal or to watch another production. Later I might meet friends or go to a party in somebody's room. Always end up going to bed much too late.

© 2013 National Geographic Learning, a part of Cengage Learning PHOTOCOPIABLE

Progress Test Unit 6

Part 1: Listening  CD3/07

1 **You will hear an interview with an archaeologist. Decide if the sentences are true or false.**

(1 mark for each correct answer: Total ___/10)

1	Paula Smith is a TV presenter.	True / False
2	Paula Smith works full time as a TV presenter.	True / False
3	She has always worked in TV.	True / False
4	She started out in TV by chance.	True / False
5	They knew the show was going to be successful.	True / False
6	There is a book and DVD of the TV series.	True / False
7	She travels to many different places for the TV.	True / False
8	Her husband is a TV presenter, too.	True / False
9	Paula has no time for anything but filming and family.	True / False
10	More people are interested in archaeology because of the programme.	True / False

Part 2: Grammar

2 **Complete the sentences with somebody, nobody or everybody.**

(1 mark for each correct answer: Total ___/6)

1 As I walked home that night, I thought that _____ was following me down the dark street, but when I turned round to look, there was _____ there.

2 I wrote an email inviting _____ I know to my birthday party, but on my birthday, _____ came! I realised later that I had forgotten to send the email!

3 I asked _____ in the class if they had seen my gold pen, but they hadn't. Eventually, _____ from another class found it.

3 **Complete the sentences with the correct form (infinitive + to, infinitive without to or gerund) of the verb in brackets.**

(1 mark for each correct answer: Total ___/4)

1 Mike said he didn't mind _____ me to the station. (drive)

2 The children were allowed _____ in the park. (play)

3 The teacher made the students _____ five extra exercises. (write)

4 Do you enjoy _____ English? (study)

Part 3: Vocabulary

4 **Complete the sentences with the correct form of the words in the box.**

(1 mark for each correct answer: Total ___/6)

engage	series	design	aim	style	present

There have been many different (1) _____ of programmes on TV about history. Their (2) _____ are sometimes quite different. Some of them are (3) _____ to give the viewers general information about a particular period in history. Others (4) _____ quite detailed facts about one particular person or event. Whatever type of programme it is, it must (5) _____ the viewers, or nobody will watch it. That is why the (6) _____ of the presenter is very important.

5 **Add the correct negative prefix to these words.**

(½ mark for each correct answer: Total ___/4)

1 _____logical

2 _____capable

3 _____moral

4 _____sufficient

5 _____regular

6 _____predictable

7 _____polite

8 _____adequate

Part 4: Communication

6 **Complete the dialogue.**

(1 mark for each correct answer: Total: ___/10)

A: So what did you do in you free time when you were young, Granddad?

B: Life was much quieter (1) _____ it is today, John. There weren't (2) _____ many kinds of entertainment as you have. No TV, no CDs, no mp3s, no DVDs, no computers.

A: It sounds as if life was much (3) _____ than it is now!

B: No, it wasn't bad at all. It was (4) _____ interesting than it is now. We made our own entertainment. We played games, sang songs, and talked (5) _____ more than people do now. It (6) _____ to be great fun to play with my friends in the street.

A: But the games you played weren't as good (7) _____ the ones I play on my computer, were they?

B: I think they were (8) _____ . They were old traditional games. And we played with other people, not just with a machine.

A: Well, I think my computer games are (9) _____ exciting.

B: Yes, but you don't meet (10) _____ many people as I did.

© 2013 National Geographic Learning, a part of Cengage Learning **PHOTOCOPIABLE**

Part 5: Reading

7 Read the text and choose the best answer.

(2 marks for each correct answer. Total ___/10)

1 The Ancient Egyptians settled in northern Africa because:

   A the river Nile was there.

   B they were tired of their nomadic existence.

2 The Ancient Egyptians established their culture:

   A because they were good at mathematics.

   B and then became good at mathematics.

3 They are famous for:

   A their science, building and music.

   B their medicine, building and art.

4 A society needs to be secure in order to:

   A produce art.

   B have a good army.

5 We know they were a highly developed civilisation:

   A because we can still see the things they produced.

   B because we still find the things they produced amazing.

Ancient Egypt

The river Nile in northern Africa was probably the main reason for the initial settlements in Egypt. There was a constant supply of water, and they developed clever ways to divert it to irrigate the fields. This led to people staying in one place after generations of nomadic existence.

The basis of Egyptian existence was probably firmly established around 4500 years ago. The surviving monuments created by this civilisation, such as the world famous pyramids, provide us with evidence of just how sophisticated the people were in the areas of mathematics and construction with stone.

Besides developing good trading relations, and a good system of writing, the Ancient Egyptians were also a powerful military presence in the area, which protected its citizens and also dominated other peoples in the area.

Beyond this, they were also significantly advanced in medicine and made what was probably the world's first attempts at shipbuilding. An important part of what they left to us today is their art; art is usually a sign that society has become secure enough to develop a cultural life and to enjoy the luxury of aesthetic pastimes.

The fact that we still wonder at what they produced shows just how advanced they were.

© 2013 National Geographic Learning, a part of Cengage Learning PHOTOCOPIABLE

Progress Test Unit 7

Part 1: Listening CD3/08

1 **You will hear an interview with an actor. Listen and complete the statements. Use one or two words per space. You will hear the extract twice.**

(1 mark for each correct answer: Total __/10)

1 He decided to become an actor when he was _____.

2 The first play he performed in was *Death of* _____.

3 When he first performed in a play, he didn't feel _____.

4 He says actors in films get better _____ than actors in stage plays.

5 He was attracted to American films by their _____.

6 The film that most influenced him was *American* _____.

7 The setting of the film is a _____ in America

8 The theme of the film is becoming _____.

9 It made a strong impression on him because it captured a particular _____.

10 He was a _____ when he saw the film.

Part 2: Grammar

2 **Transform these sentences using the words given.**

(1 mark for each correct answer: Total __/5)

1 People say that Australians have always enjoyed parties. Australians _____ (said)

2 Festivals should be a time of happiness. Festivals _____ (supposed)

3 The general opinion is that big weddings are too expensive. Big weddings _____ (thought)

4 Historians believe that Dragon Boat racing started in China. Dragon Boat racing _____ (believed)

5 People used to say that the bride arrived on horseback. The bride _____ (said)

3 **Put the verbs into the correct form (passive infinitive or gerund) to complete the sentences.**

(1 mark for each correct answer: Total __/5)

1 She insists on _____ if there are any changes in the schedule. (inform)

2 If you are under 18 you have _____ by an adult. (accompany)

3 I'd like _____ if there is any news. (tell)

4 Not many people enjoy _____ for a new job. (interview)

5 If you tell them you are a student, you will avoid _____ the full adult fare. (charge)

Part 3: Vocabulary

4 **Choose the correct word to complete each sentence.**

(1 mark for each correct answer: Total __/10)

1 Armistice Day on 11th November *commemorates / remembers / reminds* the end of the First World War.

2 We're going to give her a *departure / going / farewell* party when she leaves.

3 I went to the fancy *dress / clothes / costume* party in a penguin suit.

4 He *did / told / made* a great speech at the conference.

5 They had decorated the room with balloons and paper *bands / streamers / strips*.

6 The carnival began with a big *parade /march / demonstration* of dancers and musicians through the streets.

7 People argue about when *mid / medium / middle* age starts: some say 40, others 50.

8 *Adulthood / Adolescence / Infancy* occurs during your teens, generally speaking.

9 They celebrated the *birth / born / baby* of their first child.

10 My great grandparents are in their *mid age / late age / old age*.

Part 4: Communication

5 **Complete the responses by using the words given.**

(2 marks for each correct answer: Total __/10)

1 The festival began in the 16th century.
The festival _____.
(dates)

2 I will never forget my 16th birthday.
Me neither. _____ occasion. (memorable)

3 Why are we going to the Post Office? It's my 17th birthday today.
Exactly! You're 17 today, so _____ to drive. We are going to get your licence. (allow)

4 I'm going to take my driving test tomorrow.
What age _____ first drive in your country? (can)

 © 2013 National Geographic Learning, a part of Cengage Learning PHOTOCOPIABLE

5 Do you like firework displays?

No, I _____. (boring)

Part 5: Reading

6 Read the text and choose the right sentences (A–G) to complete the passage. There are two extra sentences.

(2 marks for each correct answer: Total __/10)

Did you miss World Mole Day on 23 October? (1) _____. It's not a day dedicated to the adorable little creatures that dig up our gardens, if that's what you were thinking. A mole, in this case, refers to a unit of measurement used in chemistry which was discovered by Amedeo Avogadro in 1800. (2) _____. It has grown into a celebration of science and learning in general and is now quite popular among science teachers.

You could be forgiven for missing it, because it came so soon after 21 October which was Apple Day, and just before National Sleep-in Day on 30 October. (3) _____. If you look at the calendar, you will find that there is at least one on every day of the year. Some are clearly just marketing opportunities, like National Potato Day, to get people to consume more of that particular item. (4) _____. For example, Plant a Tree Day or No Smoking Day.

But there is an argument that having special days for everything diminishes their importance. In most cases, we are told to do something on these days that we should probably be doing every day, like eating more fruit, or not smoking. (5) _____. It would be far better if we confined ourselves to commemorating important historical events, like the end of a war or the birth of a great person.

A Why are there so many 'special days'?

B I did.

C It's rather like having a 'Brush your teeth' day.

D The day is not only dedicated to this single discovery, though.

E More and more people are commemorating them anyway.

F Others are there to raise awareness of an important social or environmental problem.

G I haven't got the time to celebrate them all.

Progress Test Unit 8

Part 1: Listening 🄲 CD3/09

1 **You will hear a report about the dos and don'ts of job applications. Listen and choose the correct answer, A, B, C or D.**

(2 marks for each correct answer: Total __/10)

1 Job applicants can sometimes be tempted to:
   A give up when there are too many applicants.
   B make up experience.
   C do something different.
   D enter competitions.

2 Charlotte Cole had a female applicant who:
   A put up posters of her favourite politician.
   B ran a political campaign.
   C asked for an interview in the car park.
   D advertised herself on posters.

3 Charlotte Cole had a male applicant who:
   A cancelled his interview by telegram.
   B sang about himself.
   C sent somebody to sing about him.
   D sang at his interview.

4 Charlotte Cole thinks stunts are a waste of time unless:
   A the stunt is really original.
   B the candidate is extremely well qualified.
   C the candidate has an excellent personality.
   D the stunt is well-thought out.

5 Amir Khan warns applicants not to send:
   A recommendations.
   B gifts.
   C applications by post.
   D CVs.

Part 2: Grammar

2 **Rewrite the parts of the sentence in bold using either a relative clause or a participle clause.**

(1 mark for each correct answer: Total __/5)

Famous film stars inspire many to dream of an acting career. For many people (1) **who want** _____ to become a film actor, reality is a long way from the dream. Film actors are often on location (2) **and live** _____ away from their family and friends for months on end. The hours (3) **worked** _____ every day range from 14 to 20. (4) **As they are mentally exhausted** _____ after filming, actors (5) **with** _____ successful careers often sacrifice their personal life for success.

3 **Rewrite the sentences so that they have similar meanings.**

(1 mark for each correct answer: Total __/5)

1 You need the right qualifications and you also need the right personality.
   Not only _____.

2 You shouldn't lie about your qualifications under any circumstances.
   Under no circumstances _____.

3 Job applicants with more work experience are more attractive to employers.
   The more work experience _____.

4 It's only when you start your first real job that you realise your students days are over.
   Only when you _____.

5 If you work hard, you can play hard.
   The harder _____.

Part 3: Vocabulary

4 **Complete the words using the letters given.**

(1 mark for each correct answer: Total __/10)

1 To succeed in many jobs you need to be d_____ and get things done.

2 Students who are more interested in practical training can consider becoming an a_____.

3 N_____ is the ability to deal with numbers.

4 In many jobs it is important to be t_____ rather than sensitive.

5 Cooperating on a project is an example of t_____.

6 A s_____ is the money that you earn every month.

7 Jobs where people help others are usually extremely r_____.

8 P_____ is finding a solution to a difficult situation.

9 Jobs such as university professors, scientists or doctors are generally seen as p_____.

10 Doctors and teachers often describe their jobs as interesting and s_____.

Part 4: Communication

5 **Complete the phrases using one word.**

(1 mark for each correct answer: Total __/8)

You didn't understand the meaning of something.

1 Sorry, I'm not _____ you.

2 Sorry, I don't know what you _____.

© 2013 National Geographic Learning, a part of Cengage Learning PHOTOCOPIABLE

You didn't hear something properly.

3 Sorry, I didn't quite _____ that.

4 Sorry, I _____ that.

You need to ask for clarification.

5 What do you _____ by that?

6 What are you trying to _____?

You want to explain what you mean.

7 What I wanted to _____ is ...

8 What I _____ is ...

Part 5: Reading

6 **Read the text and choose the right word to complete the text.**

(1 mark for each correct answer: Total ___/5)

1 A plucking **B** pluck **C** to pluck **D** plucked

2 A have to **B** had to **C** have had to
D would have to

3 A off **B** in **C** out **D** up

4 A With **B** As **C** For **D** By

5 A sticking **B** to stick **C** stuck **D** stick

6 A wanted **B** had **C** tried
D managed

Student jobs

I used (1) _____ chickens, geese and turkeys. I hated the work but it was well-paid and, living in a rural area, there wasn't much part-time work. It was monotonous work, but I think the worst thing was the smell and the fact that I always had sore, red fingers.

I used to work in an ice-cream van in the summer holidays. If it was good weather, then we were always rushed off our feet and customers could be really unpleasant if they (2) _____ stand in the queue for too long. My worst moment was when I dropped an ice-cream on a small child's head when I was bending down to give it to him. He screamed his head off and his parents were not too pleased.

I once had a summer job tasting new cake recipes for a large food company. I had to try out several variations and mark down on a sheet which ones I liked best and why. All my friends were green with envy, but after a few weeks of constantly eating cake I was more than happy to give it (3) _____.

(4) _____ a student I had a weekend job with a local fruit producer. My job was (5) _____ the little sticky labels onto apples. I did that eight hours a day with a 30-minute lunch break. Boring is not the word.

I had a two-week student job where I (6) _____ to dress up in a bear costume and hand out sweets to children in a shopping centre as part of a promotion. The costume was hot and heavy but it didn't bother me because it was a very rewarding job. The look on the small kids' faces was just magical sometimes.

7 **Decide if the statements are true or false.**

(1 mark for each correct answer: Total ___/5)

1 The first student thought the worse thing about the work was that it was boring.   True / False

2 The second student had a busy time when it was sunny.   True / False

3 The third student's friends were jealous.   True / False

4 The fourth student didn't think the work was boring.   True / False

5 The fifth student couldn't stand wearing a costume.   True / False

© 2013 National Geographic Learning, a part of Cengage Learning PHOTOCOPIABLE

Progress Test Unit 9

Part 1: Listening 🔊 CD3/10

1 You will hear three students talking about the kind of organisation they would like to work for when they graduate. The first time you listen, put the number of the speaker next to the correct organisation (A–F).

(½ mark for each correct answer: Total __/3)

A The civil service _____

B A multinational _____

C An e-company _____

D The family business _____

E The public sector _____

F An NGO _____

2 Listen again and complete the statements. Use ONE word per space.

(1 mark for each correct answer: Total __/7)

Speaker 1

1 His father has his own _____ firm.

2 His father advises companies on _____ law, which doesn't interest him.

3 He would like to work in the _____ Ministry.

Speaker 2

4 His brother's job is to make _____ films for Red Bull.

5 His brother says the atmosphere at work is very friendly and _____.

Speaker 3

6 She has been working non-stop for _____ years.

7 She says her work in Africa will not exactly be a _____.

Part 2: Grammar

3 Underline the correct form to complete this conversation between a business adviser (BA) and a young entrepreneur (E)

(1 mark for each correct answer: Total __/10)

E: I apologise (1) *to be / for being / by being* late. Thank you (2) *agreeing / for agreeing / of agreeing* to see me.

BA: So, how can I help you today?

E: Well, I've got (3) *a few / few / little* ideas for starting up a new business and I'd like your advice.

BA: OK. Well I should say first of all that I'm not going to persuade (4) *you doing / you to do / to do* one thing or another. I have (5) *a few / a little / little* experience of business – I ran my own company for 12 years – so I can give you advice, but you are completely free to refuse (6) *for taking / taking / to take* it. OK?

E: Yes, I understand. The thing is I need to borrow about £60,000. Do you recommend that I (7) *shall go / will go / should go* to the bank, or

would you encourage (8) *to find / me finding / me to find* a business partner?

BA: Funnily enough, someone asked me a very similar question only yesterday. I told him that he (9) *has / had / had had* to decide first whether he wanted to share the risk or not. And I'll give you the same advice. If you think there are (10) *little / a few / few* risks, then go to the bank. If you don't feel so confident, then find a partner to share the risk.

Part 3: Vocabulary

4 Complete the sentences by putting the opposite of the bold words in each space. Use one word per space.

(1 mark for each correct answer: Total __/10)

1 He didn't **deny** that he was only interested in money: he openly _____ it.

2 They both earn decent salaries, so they're not **badly off**: they're _____-_____.

3 The **rich** represent about 10% of the population, while the _____ represent about 20%.

4 You see a lot of **poverty** in some parts of London, but also great _____ in others.

5 In our area, about 40% work is in the **public** sector and about 60% in the _____ sector.

6 We can't just **ignore** the problem of poverty in our cities; we have to _____ it.

7 I don't want to **discourage** volunteering. I think it's great. It's something we should _____.

8 The business got unemployed people working, but it **lost** money. These projects have to _____ money to be successful.

9 She is always developing new projects. As soon as she **closes** one down, she _____ _____ another.

10 I'm not **an employee of a company**; I'm _____-_____.

Part 4: Communication

5 Complete these phrases from a negotiation using the words given.

(2 marks for each correct answer: Total __/10)

1 If I offered you £300 for your bike, would you accept?

If _____ £300 for your bike, would you accept? (were)

2 Can you lower the price?

Would _____ the price? (willing)

3 What price were you thinking of?

How much _____? (mind)

4 £300 is too little for me to accept.

I _____ as little as £300. (possibly)

5 In that case I won't buy it.

I think I _____. (leave)

© 2013 National Geographic Learning, a part of Cengage Learning PHOTOCOPIABLE

Part 5: Reading

6 Read this blog from a community website and choose the best word (A, B, C or D) to complete it.

(1 mark for each correct answer: Total __/6)

1 A and   **B** but   **C** until   **D** only

2 A require   **B** demand   **C** request   **D** pledge

3 A laying   **B** lying   **C** spreading
   D landing

4 A at   **B** on   **C** in   **D** after

5 A out   **B** off   **C** inside   **D** around

6 A should   **B** must   **C** ought   **D** have

I just heard about this wonderful idea and thought I would share it with all you people who hate waste and unnecessary consumption. It's a new community called Freeconomy and the basic idea is about local exchange of goods and services.

One example is 'Toolshare'. I don't know about you, but I am always buying tools just to do one job, like repairing a leaking gutter, (1) _____ to find that I never use them again. The idea of Toolshare is that you post a (2) _____ on the website for the tool you need and someone else in the community offers to lend it to you.

Another example is 'Skillshare'. This doesn't just mean helping someone out who is having trouble fixing their car or (3) _____ a carpet. The idea is that the local person who possesses the skill you need comes round and actually teaches you how to do a particular job, so that the next time you are able to do it yourself without assistance. I like this idea particularly because (4) _____ the end it helps to make people more independent and reduces the need to buy in extra services.

Other ideas are 'Spaceshare' and 'Landshare' where you give up extra space you have in or (5) _____ your home so that people can store things temporarily – in your garage for example – or use the land to grow some vegetables.

This is not bartering; in other words, not just a way of replacing money with payment in kind. With Freeconomy you don't *have* to give something in return for what you receive. It's just about helping each other out as people in every community (6) _____ to do, and at the same time reducing our impact on the environment. It's based on the principle of 'what goes around, comes around' and I really like it.

7 Complete these statements according to the information given in the blog.

(1 mark for each correct answer: Total __/4)

1 The idea of Freeconomy is to reduce

    _____.

2 With 'Skillshare', you don't just help people; you _____.

3 One reason people might want extra space is

    _____.

4 Bartering is when people _____.

© 2013 National Geographic Learning, a part of Cengage Learning PHOTOCOPIABLE

Progress Test Unit 10

Part 1: Listening CD3/11

1 You will hear an interview with the manager of a travel company. Listen and complete the statements below using one or two words per space. You will hear the extract twice.

(1 mark for each correct answer: Total __/10)

1 The company is called 'Go_____ Travel'.
2 Jessica describes herself as a _____ at heart.
3 Her holidays are not typical _____ holidays.
4 Her company always tries to use the tourist industry that _____.
5 In Tanzania, clients can do safaris and _____.
6 On their expedition to Mount Meru, you walk up the mountain and _____.
7 The interviewer describes their pricing policy as very _____.
8 Clients put together their own holiday from a menu of _____.
9 There is no _____ on the price of each activity.
10 The company adds _____ to the final price.

Part 2: Grammar

2 Use a 'future in the past' form of the words in brackets to complete these sentences.

(1 mark for each correct answer: Total __/5)

1 We would _____ (have / wait) for you, but we were worried we'd miss the show.
2 I _____ (be / go) to tell her that her hair looked awful, but it seemed cruel.
3 The band _____ (be / due) to come onstage at 9pm but they didn't start playing until 10.30.
4 She _____ (be / expect) to get A grades in her exams, but she got two Bs and a C.
5 Sorry I _____ (be / go) to pay you the money back yesterday, but I forgot to go to the bank.

3 Choose the correct form to complete these sentences.

(1 mark for each correct answer: Total __/5)

1 At the age of four, she *could speak / succeeded in speaking* four languages.
2 When we got to the top of the mountain, we *could / managed to* see for miles.
3 *Could you post / Were you able to post* the letters in time?
4 I *couldn't / didn't manage to* swim until I was 18 years old.
5 After about ten unsuccessful attempts, he finally *could / managed to* get the car started.

Part 3: Vocabulary

4 Put the correct verb into each space to complete these statements.

(1 mark for each correct answer: Total __/10)

People say that in business it's dangerous to (1) _____ your heart; instead you should (2) _____ your common sense. If you do this and (3) _____ by the rules, you will be successful.

If you (4) _____ rumours about people and (5) _____ about them behind their backs, then it will come back to bite you.

Someone in the company (6) _____ the information to the press that the company had turned off the heating in their offices to save money. It was supposed to be a joke, but unfortunately, the management did not (7) _____ the funny side of it.

The jokes that people most commonly (8) _____ are those which (9) _____ fun of other people and those where people (10) _____ at themselves: their weight or lack of education, or something like that.

Part 4: Communication

5 Complete this conversation between a travel agent (TA) and a customer (C). Use one word per space.

(1 mark for each correct answer: Total __/10)

TA: So, how can I help you today?
C: We'd like to have a holiday near the sea this summer. A friend told me that we (1) _____ to book soon in case all the good deals get taken. But the important thing for us is that it (2) _____ be somewhere quiet.
TA: I see. Well in that case I think you'd be better (3) _____ renting a villa rather than staying in a hotel. Did you have any particular country in (4) _____?
C: Yes, we were thinking of Portugal. But we've got quite a small (5) _____. Don't you think a villa will be very expensive?
TA: Not necessarily. How many of you are (6) _____?
C: We are a family of four.
TA: OK. I'll give you a brochure to take away and look at so that you can (7) _____ an idea of prices and locations. But it (8) _____ be better not to wait too long, because these villas get booked (9) _____ quite quickly.
C: OK. We (10) _____ better get a move on. We'll have a look and call you in a couple of days.

Part 5: Reading

6 Read this account of a psychological experiment and choose the best answer (A, B, C or D) to each question.

(2 marks for each correct answer: Total __/10)

Everyone deceives themselves at one time or another. It is part of our nature. A good example is when we

© 2013 National Geographic Learning, a part of Cengage Learning PHOTOCOPIABLE

apply for a job and are rejected. Generally people will try to cover their feelings of disappointment and rejection by saying things to themselves like, "It wasn't really the right job for me anyway" or "They weren't a very nice company".

In their famous experiment of 1984, Quattrone and Tversky, two eminent psychologists, explored this phenomenon: to what extent do people deceive themselves, persuading themselves that something is true, when in fact it isn't. Thirty-eight students were told that they were going to take part in an experiment that would help them understand their current health status.

First, the students were instructed to submerge their arms in cold water for as long as they could bear it. Next, they were asked to do some exercises, like cycling exercises. Then half of them they were given a short lecture in which they were told that people who were more tolerant to cold water after exercise had better health, would live longer and be less likely to have heart disease. The other half were told the opposite – that intolerance to cold water showed a healthy body. Finally, they were all asked to put their arms into cold water again for as long as they could.

The results were as you have probably guessed. Each half of the group of students deceived themselves into believing they were healthy by either holding their arms in water for longer or taking them out more quickly than usual. But most tellingly, on being questioned no-one admitted that they had tried to alter the outcome of the experiment.

1 The author thinks that self-deception is:

   A dangerous because we hide our real feelings.

   B a good way to protect ourselves against being hurt.

   C a natural phenomenon among human beings.

   D very useful in the right circumstances.

2 The aim of the experiment was to find out:

   A why people deceive themselves.

   B whether people deceived themselves particularly about their health.

   C what the health status of the students really was.

   D how much people deceive themselves.

3 In the first stage of the experiment, the students had to:

   A keep their arms in cold water for as long as they could.

   B do some exercises.

   C listen to a lecture.

   D put their arms in cold water to test how cold it was.

4 The students were divided into two groups in order to:

   A see which was the healthier group.

   B be told different things about the significance of the test.

   C separate those who deceived themselves from those who didn't.

   D manage the experiment more easily.

5 The real confirmation that people deceive themselves was that:

   A the first group held their arms in for longer.

   B the second group held their arms in for less time.

   C both groups did exactly what they thought indicated a healthy heart.

   D everyone denied trying to influence the results.

End of Term Test 1 (first version)

Part A

Listening CD3/12

1 You will hear five artists talking about their work. Match the speakers (1–5) to the aspects of their life that they talk about (A–F). There is one extra heading.

(1 mark for each correct answer: Total __/5)

A Self-discovery through art

B Expressing emotion

C Street art as protest

D Artistic freedom

E Financial security

F Character development

2 Listen and choose the correct answer (A, B, C or D).

(2 marks for each correct answer: Total __/10)

1 Speaker 1 became a full-time artist:
  A straight after college.
  B after a couple of years of work.
  C when she was middle-aged.
  D after she had retired from work.

2 Speaker 2:
  A always has a clear idea what to make.
  B lets the materials inspire him.
  C produces sculptures on demand.
  D uses his imagination.

3 The murals that speaker 3 helps create:
  A have a story behind them.
  B are inspired by him.
  C use complicated techniques.
  D are illegal.

4 According to speaker 4, costumes:
  A can make people look good.
  B are works of art.
  C determine how you view somebody.
  D are very difficult to sew.

5 Speaker 5 wants to produce music that:
  A reflects the times we live in.
  B makes people feel happy.
  C is good background music.
  D changes people.

Grammar

3 Complete the dialogues with the correct form of the verb.

(1 mark for each correct answer: Total __/14)

1 When (you / go) _____ on holiday?

– The week after next. I (wait) _____ for my new passport for weeks. I hope it arrives soon.

2 What (they / do) _____ when they were arrested?

– Well just before the police arrived, they (write) _____ graffiti on the factory wall.

3 What do you think you (do) _____ in five years' time?

– Well, I hope I (graduate) _____ from university by then, but otherwise I don't have a clue.

4 She (always / complain) _____ about her job, but she never looks for a new one.

Well, I'm pretty sure that she (not find) _____ such a good job anywhere else.

5 (you / go) _____ to university if you had known how much it would cost?

– Yes, definitely. I (not be) _____ the person I am today if I hadn't done the course.

6 So (you / enjoy) _____ the film?

Well, I went to see it because I (read) _____ the book, but the book was much better.

7 It's 8 o'clock! We (sit) _____ here for over an hour soon!

– OK, if he (not come) _____ in ten minutes, we'll go.

4 Rewrite the sentences so that the second sentence has a similar meaning.

(2 marks for each correct answer: Total __/16)

1 Both of them are hard-working.

Neither _____ lazy.

2 Can I just check if you are over 16?

You are over 16, _____?

3 Unless they invest in technology, their economy will suffer.

If they _____, their economy will suffer.

4 I fell asleep during the film.

I fell asleep while we _____ the film.

5 Take this aspirin and you'll feel much better.

Once you _____, you'll feel much better.

6 I'm sure there was a logical explanation.

There must _____ a logical explanation.

© 2013 National Geographic Learning, a part of Cengage Learning PHOTOCOPIABLE

7 We stayed with my grandmother every summer when I was a child.

We used _____ every summer when I was a child.

8 The government plans to spend more money on wind turbines.

The government is _____ more money on wind turbines.

Vocabulary

5 **Complete the text by putting the word in brackets into the correct form.**

(1 mark for each correct answer: Total __/10)

Trade in valuable wild animals is big business. International (1) (cooperate) _____ means that wildlife trade – even for (2) (plenty) _____ species – must follow strict regulations. But it is each country's (3) (responsible) _____ to ensure that documentation matches official (4) (require) _____. The trade is extremely (5) (profit) _____ as the traffickers, (6) (expense) _____ are low, most species are caught in countries where many people live in (7) (poor) _____ and hunters receive little (8) (pay) _____ for catching the animals and birds. One third of global sales are illegal and (9) (fortunate) _____ three out of four animals smuggled illegally die during transport. Without stricter penalties for trafficking, it is (10) (doubt) _____ whether the situation will change.

6 **Choose the correct word (A, B, C or D) to complete the sentences.**

(1 mark for each correct answer: Total __/10)

1 To get a part in the play, actors need to attend the _____ on Friday.

A cast **B** set **C** run **D** audition

2 The date for the group's concert in London has been announced, but the exact _____ is as yet unknown.

A encore **B** gig **C** venue **D** performance

3 A large proportion of environmental work is done by volunteers with _____ organisations.

A public **B** extensive **C** practical
D charitable

4 The Geneva Convention regulates the protection of _____ who are forced to leave their country for racial, religious or political reasons.

A economic migrants **B** foreigners
C refugees **D** asylum seekers

5 A significant drop in the birth _____ is giving rise to problems in many European countries.

A number **B** rate **C** expectancy
D population

6 Supporters of 'slow food' argue that we should be producing and _____ good regional food.

A savouring **B** chewing **C** grabbing
D snacking

7 A common utopia is a world in which all pain and suffering have been _____.

A exploited **B** destroyed **C** fought
D eliminated

8 I have a dream which I am striving to _____.

A complete **B** accomplish **C** fulfil
D succeed

9 After completing my degree, I hope to do _____ research in the same subject.

A undergraduate **B** postgraduate
C vocational **D** higher

10 We are all determined to _____ the best out of our time at university.

A take **B** gain **C** make **D** get

Part B

Communication

7 **Write the dialogues using the words in brackets.**

(1 mark for each correct answer: Total __/10)

Booking theatre tickets

1 Ask what time the evening performance is. (start)

_____?

2 Say there are no more tickets for the evening performance. (sold out)

I'm afraid _____.

Phoning Greenpeace

3 Ask for information about how to volunteer. (mind)

_____?

4 Ask how old the person phoning is. (could)

_____?

Making arrangements with a friend

5 Ask your friend if they want to come to your house. (round)

_____?

6 Ask your friend if they can come to your house instead. (about)

_____?

Giving instructions

7 Tell your listener that if they are not sure, they shouldn't touch anything. (doubt)

_____?

© 2013 National Geographic Learning, a part of Cengage Learning PHOTOCOPIABLE

8 Ask the speaker if they can repeat the instructions. (through)

_____?

Applying for a student loan

9 Tell the manager you would like to borrow some money. (take out)

_____

10 Ask the student how much they spend on day-to-day living. (high)

_____?

Reading

8 **Read the text about growing food on the moon and choose the right words to complete the text.**

(2 marks for each correct answer: Total __/10)

When Neil Armstrong landed on the Moon in 1969, people assumed it wouldn't be long (1) _____ Moon colonies were part of the lunar landscape. People began to dream of living, working and holidaying on the Moon. Over 40 years later, we are no nearer to creating colonies on the Moon than we were when Apollo 11 landed. However, it has been reported that the American space agency NASA hopes that they (2) _____ a temporary Moon colony by 2025 – both as a base for further research on the Moon and for exploration missions to Mars.

Two of the problems facing scientists until now were how to (3) _____ food and water without importing them from Earth. Relatively large quantities of water ice have recently been discovered in the south polar region of the Moon. However, growing food poses more of a problem (4) _____ the chemicals and minerals needed to grow food are not available on the Moon.

A team of scientists in Arizona has now come up with a light-weight, portable, lunar greenhouse which grows vegetables without soil. The greenhouse can be constructed (5) _____ ten minutes and will provide vegetables in about a month. Nutrients and water to grow the vegetables will come from the astronauts' own waste, providing a sustainable cycle.

Shelter from the Moon's extreme temperatures and ultraviolet radiation is also an important factor for future colonists. In early 2010, an international team discovered a giant 'lava tube' – a huge hole which is protected by lava and which could be the site of the Moon's first colony.

1 **A** when **B** before **C** prior to **D** once

2 **A** will establish **B** will be establishing **C** will have established **D** will have been establishing

3 **A** utilise **B** grow **C** transport **D** provide

4 **A** although **B** while **C** unless **D** since

5 **A** under **B** within **C** below **D** before

9 **Decide if the sentences are true (T) or false (F).**

(1 mark for each correct sentence: Total __/5)

1 There has been little progress towards establishing a base on the Moon. True / False

2 Some of the problems associated with Moon colonies have been solved. True / False

3 Scientists have discovered lunar lakes containing fresh water. True / False

4 Eventually, vegetables could be grown without outside supplies. True / False

5 Future colonists might live in greenhouse-like structures. True / False

Writing

10 **Look at the paragraph structure for a short story. Then read the first three paragraphs of a short story that starts** _I couldn't believe my eyes . . ._ **Complete the story by writing paragraphs 4 and 5. Write about 100 words.**

Paragraph 1: Introduce the characters
Paragraph 2: Describe the characters and set the background to the story
Paragraph 3: Describe the events leading up to the main event
Paragraph 4: Describe the main event
Paragraph 5: Write the ending: keep it open and mysterious

Sample answer

I couldn't believe my eyes. There was Jack, leaning over me and smiling. There wasn't a bruise or a mark on him. But how was it possible?

Jack was a confident, funny guy. I'd met him at a party and we'd got on really well. We started going to football matches together and generally hanging out.

The night that it happened, we were taking a walk down to the river. I'd taken off my shoes and we were walking on the soft grass by the side of the road. The sun had gone down but it wasn't quite dark.

Suddenly _____

© 2013 National Geographic Learning, a part of Cengage Learning PHOTOCOPIABLE

End of Term Test 1 (second version)

Part A

Listening CD3/12

1 Listen and choose the correct answer (A, B, C or D).

(2 marks for each correct answer: Total __/10)

1 Speaker 1 became a full-time artist:

  A straight after college.

  B after a couple of years of work.

  C when she was middle-aged.

  D after she had retired from work.

2 Speaker 2:

  A always has a clear idea what to make.

  B lets the materials inspire him.

  C produces sculptures on demand.

  D uses his imagination.

3 The murals that speaker 3 helps create:

  A have a story behind them.

  B are inspired by him.

  C use complicated techniques.

  D are illegal.

4 According to speaker 4, costumes:

  A can make people look good.

  B are works of art.

  C determine how you view somebody.

  D are very difficult to sew.

5 Speaker 5 wants to produce music that:

  A reflects the times we live in.

  B makes people feel happy.

  C is good background music.

  D changes people.

2 You will hear five artists talking about their work. Match the speakers (1–5) to the aspects of their life that they talk about (A–F). There is one extra heading.

(1 mark for each correct answer: Total __/5)

  A Self-discovery through art

  B Expressing emotion

  C Street art as protest

  D Artistic freedom

  E Financial security

  F Character development

Grammar

3 Rewrite the sentences so that the second sentence has a similar meaning to the first.

(2 marks for each correct answer: Total __/16)

1 Both of them are hard-working.

  Neither _____ lazy.

2 Can I just check if you are over 16?

  You are over 16, _____?

3 Unless they invest in technology, their economy will suffer.

  If they _____, their economy will suffer.

4 I fell asleep during the film.

  I fell asleep while we _____ the film.

5 Take this aspirin and you'll feel much better.

  Once you _____, you'll feel much better.

6 I'm sure there was a logical explanation.

  There must _____ a logical explanation.

7 We stayed with my grandmother every summer when I was a child.

  We used _____ every summer when I was a child.

8 The government plans to spend more money on wind turbines.

  The government is _____ more money on wind turbines.

4 Complete the dialogues with the correct form of the verb.

(1 mark for each correct answer: Total __/14)

1 When (you / go) _____ on holiday?

  – The week after next. I (wait) _____ for my new passport for weeks. I hope it arrives soon.

2 What (they / do) _____ when they were arrested?

  – Well just before the police arrived, they (write) _____ graffiti on the factory wall.

3 What do you think you (do) _____ in five years' time?

  – Well, I hope I (graduate) _____ from university by then, but otherwise I don't have a clue.

4 She (always / complain) _____ about her job, but she never looks for a new one.

  Well, I'm pretty sure that she (not find) _____ such a good job anywhere else.

5 (you / go) _____ to university if you had known how much it would cost?

  – Yes, definitely. I (not be) _____ the person I am today if I hadn't done the course.

6 So (you / enjoy) _____ the film? Well, I went to see it because I (read) _____ the book, but the book was much better.

7 It's 8 o'clock! We (sit) _____ here for over an hour soon!

– OK, if he (not come) _____ in ten minutes, we'll go.

Vocabulary

5 Choose the correct word (A, B, C or D) to complete the sentences.

(1 mark for each correct answer: Total __/10)

1 To get a part in the play, actors need to attend the _____ on Friday.

A cast **B** set **C** run **D** audition

2 The date for the group's concert in London has been announced, but the exact _____ is as yet unknown.

A encore **B** gig **C** venue **D** performance

3 A large proportion of environmental work is done by volunteers with _____ organisations.

A public **B** extensive **C** practical **D** charitable

4 The Geneva Convention regulates the protection of _____ who are forced to leave their country for racial, religious or political reasons.

A economic migrants **B** foreigners **C** refugees **D** asylum seekers

5 A significant drop in the birth _____ is giving rise to problems in many European countries.

A number **B** rate **C** expectancy **D** population

6 Supporters of 'slow food' argue that we should be producing and _____ good regional food.

A savouring **B** chewing **C** grabbing **D** snacking

7 A common utopia is a world in which all pain and suffering have been _____.

A exploited **B** destroyed **C** fought **D** eliminated

8 I have a dream which I am striving to _____.

A complete **B** accomplish **C** fulfil **D** succeed

9 After completing my degree, I hope to do _____ research in the same subject.

A undergraduate **B** postgraduate **C** vocational **D** higher

10 We are all determined to _____ the best out of our time at university.

A take **B** gain **C** make **D** get

6 Complete the text by putting the word in brackets into the correct form.

(1 mark for each correct answer: Total __/10)

Trade in valuable wild animals is big business. International (1) (cooperate) _____ means that wildlife trade – even for (2) (plenty) _____ species – must follow strict regulations. But it is each country's (3) (responsible) _____ to ensure that documentation matches official (4) (require) _____. The trade is extremely (5) (profit) _____ as the traffickers, (6) (expense) _____ are low, most species are caught in countries where many people live in (7) (poor) _____ and hunters receive little (8) (pay) _____ for catching the animals and birds. One third of global sales are illegal, and (9) (fortunate) _____ three out of four animals smuggled illegally die during transport. Without stricter penalties for trafficking, it is (10) (doubt) _____ whether the situation will change.

Part B

Communication

7 Write the dialogues using the words in brackets.

(1 mark for each correct answer: Total __/10)

Booking theatre tickets

1 Ask what time the evening performance is. (start)

_____?

2 Say there are no more tickets for the evening performance. (sold out)

I'm afraid _____.

Phoning Greenpeace

3 Ask for information about how to volunteer. (mind)

_____?

4 Ask how old the person phoning is. (could)

_____?

Making arrangements with a friend

5 Ask your friend if they want to come to your house. (round)

_____?

6 Ask your friend if they can come to your house instead. (about)

_____?

Giving instructions

7 Tell your listener that if they are not sure, they shouldn't touch anything. (doubt)

_____?

© 2013 National Geographic Learning, a part of Cengage Learning **PHOTOCOPIABLE**

8 Ask the speaker if they can repeat the instructions. (through)

_____?

Applying for a student loan

9 Tell the manager you would like to borrow some money. (take out)

_____

10 Ask the student how much they spend on day-to-day living. (high)

_____?

Reading

8 Decide if the sentences are true (T) or false (F).

(1 mark for each correct sentence: Total __/5)

1	There has been little progress towards establishing a base on the Moon.	True / False
2	Some of the problems associated with Moon colonies have been solved.	True / False
3	Scientists have discovered lunar lakes containing fresh water.	True / False
4	Eventually, vegetables could be grown without outside supplies.	True / False
5	Future colonists might live in greenhouse-like structures.	True / False

9 Read the text about growing food on the moon and choose the right word to complete the text.

(2 marks for each correct answer: Total __/10)

When Neil Armstrong landed on the Moon in 1969, people assumed it wouldn't be long (1) _____ Moon colonies were part of the lunar landscape. People began to dream of living, working and holidaying on the Moon. Over 40 years later, we are no nearer to creating colonies on the Moon than we were when Apollo 11 landed. However, it has been reported that the American space agency NASA hopes that they (2) _____ a temporary Moon colony by 2025 – both as a base for further research on the Moon and for exploration missions to Mars.

Two of the problems facing scientists until now were how to (3) _____ food and water without importing them from Earth. Relatively large quantities of water ice have recently been discovered in the south polar region of the Moon. However, growing food poses more of a problem (4) _____ the chemicals and minerals needed to grow food are not available on the Moon.

A team of scientists in Arizona has now come up with a light-weight, portable, lunar greenhouse which grows vegetables without soil. The greenhouse can be constructed (5) _____ ten minutes and will provide vegetables in about a month. Nutrients and water to grow the vegetables will come from the astronauts' own waste, providing a sustainable cycle.

Shelter from the Moon's extreme temperatures and ultraviolet radiation is also an important factor for future colonists. In early 2010, an international team discovered a giant 'lava tube' – a huge hole which is protected by lava and which could be the site of the Moon's first colony.

1 A when **B** before **C** prior to **D** once

2 A will establish **B** will be establishing **C** will have established **D** will have been establishing

3 A utilise **B** grow **C** transport **D** provide

4 A although **B** while **C** unless **D** since

5 A under **B** within **C** below **D** before

Writing

10 Look at the paragraph structure for a short story. Then read the first three paragraphs of a short story that starts *I couldn't believe my eyes …* Complete the story by writing paragraphs 4 and 5. Write about 100 words.

Paragraph 1: Introduce the characters
Paragraph 2: Describe the characters and set the background to the story
Paragraph 3: Describe the events leading up to the main event
Paragraph 4: Describe the main event
Paragraph 5: Write the ending: keep it open and mysterious

Sample answer

I couldn't believe my eyes. There was Jack, leaning over me and smiling. There wasn't a bruise or a mark on him. But how was it possible?

Jack was a confident, funny guy. I'd met him at a party and we'd got on really well. We started going to football matches together and generally hanging out.

The night that it happened, we were taking a walk down to the river. I'd taken off my shoes and we were walking on the soft grass by the side of the road. The sun had gone down but it wasn't quite dark.

Suddenly _____

Part A

Listening CD3/13

1 You will hear five speakers talking about their work. The first time you listen, put the number of the speaker next to people that they work with (A–F).

(1 mark for each correct answer: Total __/5)

A with a group of talented women _____

B with a mix of people from different backgrounds _____

C with men trying to get out of the profession _____

D with a group of very ambitious men _____

E with a group of untidy men _____

F mainly with women who are mothers _____

2 Listen again and mark the statements about each speaker True or False.

(1 mark for each correct answer: Total __/10)

Speaker 1

1 Speaker 1 thinks women are generally less concerned about promotion at work.　　　True / False

2 He thinks it's wrong that the majority of head teachers are men.　　　True / False

Speaker 2

3 He says most investment bankers don't worry about the morality of their job.　　　True / False

4 The reason a lot of people do it is to earn a lot of money quickly.　　　True / False

Speaker 3

5 Preparing for weddings can bring a lot of pressure with it.　　　True / False

6 She thinks that being a trainee can be as good an education as going to university.　　　True / False

Speaker 4

7 His work involves directing short films.　　　True / False

8 He gets a salary to do something he enjoys.　　　True / False

Speaker 5

9 Her colleagues are all people who have had difficulties of their own.　　　True / False

10 She works as a volunteer (i.e. with no salary).　　　True / False

Grammar

3 Transform these sentences. Use up to four words per space.

(2 marks for each correct answer: Total __/30)

1 The garage is going to repair my car.

I'm going to _____ at the garage.

2 The optician is going to test my eyes to see if I need glasses.

I'm going to _____ at the opticians to see if I need glasses.

3 We were never forced to do any housework.

My parents never made _____.

4 After college she got a job with a law firm.

After college she went _____ a lawyer.

5 The police catch very few drivers who break the speed limit.

Most drivers who break the speed limit avoid _____.

6 I wish my boss would recognise the work I do.

I'd really like _____ by my boss for the work I do.

7 People think that wind turbines are a bad idea.

Wind turbines _____ a bad idea.

8 People believe that the custom of giving birthday presents originated in China.

The custom of giving birthday presents is _____ in China.

9 I went to look at a flat yesterday and the owner turned out to be an old friend.

The person _____ to look at yesterday turned out to be an old friend.

10 Attenborough wrote and narrated the documentary which tells the story of life on Earth.

_____ Attenborough, the documentary tells the story of life on Earth.

11 You don't get many chances in life to find a really enjoyable job.

You get _____ chances in life to find a really enjoyable job.

12 "If they put my music on their website without permission, I'll sue them."

He _____ if they put the music on their website.

13 "Let's go out for dinner tonight, shall we?"

She _____ out for dinner.

14 My original intention was to study in America, but the costs were too high.

I _____ in America, but the costs were too high.

© 2013 National Geographic Learning, a part of Cengage Learning PHOTOCOPIABLE

15 The plane left at 10.30 a.m., two hours later than scheduled.

The plane _____ at 8.30 a.m., but it was delayed two hours.

Vocabulary

4 Put the word in brackets into its correct form to complete these sentences.

(1 mark for each correct answer: Total __/10)

1 Pierre de Coubertin was against women's sports in the Olympics because "they were _____". (practice)

2 If you are a _____ person, it means you like to win. (compete)

3 After the presentation, my sister made a short _____. (speak)

4 Too many children in Africa still die during _____. (infant)

5 Medicine is not just a job; it's a _____. (call)

6 We need someone we can depend on; Tom is just too _____. (rely)

7 It can be through music, art, writing, but children need a way to express their _____. (create)

8 Most people think that taking home some pens and paper from work isn't _____. (thief)

9 I wasn't very _____ during my maths lessons, so I never learned much. (attend)

10 Crete is still a relatively _____ island. (spoil)

5 Underline the word on the left that collocates with the word(s) on the right.

(1 mark for each correct answer: Total __/10)

1 *raise / lift / rise* awareness

2 *alike / equal / equivalent* rights

3 *make / do / perform* your fair share

4 *study / learning / tuition* fees

5 *place / rest / put* your feet up

6 *foster / grow / build* innovation

7 *apply / employ / implement* a project

8 *play / follow / use* your heart

9 *a led / conducted / guided* tour

10 *use / try / make* your head

Part B

Communication

6 What should you say in these situations? Use the word in brackets to make natural sentences.

(2 marks for each correct answer: Total __/10)

1 You want your audience to take particular notice of some statistics.

I'd like _____ these statistics. (attention)

2 You want the shop assistant to put the item you have bought in special gift paper.

Can _____? (wrap)

3 You did not hear what someone said to you.

I'm sorry. I _____. (catch)

4 You are trying to negotiate a lower price.

Would _____? (prepared)

5 You want to advise your friend to wait a bit before buying a new computer.

You would _____ before buying one. (better off)

Reading

7 Read the text about the benefits of hosting big sporting events and choose the correct missing sentences (A–F) to complete it.

(2 marks for each correct answer: Total __/10)

A But it is very rare that these systems actually meet the community's long-term needs.

B There are many other problems, such as finding accommodation for all the athletes.

C Those cities who just bid to host them benefit in the same way.

D So instead you have to look for the indirect benefits.

E But is it worth it?

F Or even a bronze for that matter.

If making money were an Olympic event, no city hosting the games would win a gold medal. (1) _____ In fact when you balance all the costs against all the income, there has never been an Olympic Games that has made a profit. That is because the costs of security and improving the infrastructure are not included in the Olympic budgets, but are usually provided by government.

(2) _____ Studies have shown that here, too, predictions about how much the event will boost tourism or create new industries are often over-optimistic. What big sporting events like the Olympics or World Cup do seem to do, however, is to increase the international reputation of the city in question. By hosting the event they are saying, "We welcome everyone from all over the world to a celebration of sporting achievement." But strangely, that international recognition seems to come not only to those cities that actually host the events. (3) _____

Many Olympic cities justify the spending because they gain new roads, transit systems, affordable housing, sports facilities and other infrastructure improvements. (4) _____

So are there any benefits? Well, there is one which is undeniable, and that is the civic pride that local people feel from putting on a successful event. All the eyes of the world are your city, and naturally that makes people proud. (5) _____ That is another question.

© 2013 National Geographic Learning, a part of Cengage Learning PHOTOCOPIABLE

8 Mark these statements True or False.

(1 mark for each correct answer: Total __/5)

1 Governments generally end up   True / False
paying the whole cost
of the event.

2 It is proven that big sporting   True / False
events don't increase tourism.

3 A city can increase its international   True / False
standing just by offering to hold
a big sporting event.

4 The improvements made to the   True / False
city for the event generally don't
benefit the citizens after it.

5 The citizens themselves dislike all   True / False
the attention.

Writing

9 Match the phrases below to the right type of writing. There are two phrases per type.

Writing types

A A review of a TV documentary

B A CV

C A report of a meeting

D A description of a memorable event

E A book review

Phrases

1 Ran the University Film Society for one year and produced the film *A Student's Life*. _____

2 To be honest, I was not really looking forward to it. _____

3 It is definitely worth seeing, if you have the chance. _____

4 It has a very good index of useful websites at the back. _____

5 Riham pointed out that there was little accommodation available for rent. _____

6 Self-motivated and independent worker with a keen interest in ecology. _____

7 Naturally I felt anxious, but my sister, who is very down-to-earth, calmed my nerves. _____

8 It's written for young adults who are about to leave home for the first time. _____

9 It is part of a series that aims to explore the psychology of volunteering. _____

10 It was agreed that we should refer this question to the Principal. _____

© 2013 National Geographic Learning, a part of Cengage Learning **PHOTOCOPIABLE**

End of Term Test 2 (second version)

Part A

Listening CD3/13

1 Listen again and mark the statements about each speaker True or False.

(1 mark for each correct answer: Total __/10)

Speaker 1

1 He thinks women are generally less concerned about promotion at work.   True / False

2 He thinks it's wrong that the majority of head teachers are men.   True / False

Speaker 2

3 He says most investment bankers don't worry about the morality of their job.   True / False

4 The reason a lot of people do it is to earn a lot of money quickly.   True / False

Speaker 3

5 Preparing for weddings can bring a lot of pressure with it.   True / False

6 She thinks that being a trainee can be as good an education as going to university.   True / False

Speaker 4

7 His work involves directing short films.   True / False

8 He gets a salary to do something he enjoys.   True / False

Speaker 5

9 Her colleagues are all people who have had difficulties of their own.   True / False

10 She works as a volunteer (i.e. with no salary).   True / False

2 You will hear five speakers talking about their work. The first time you listen, put the number of the speaker next to people that they work with (A–F).

(1 mark for each correct answer: Total __/5)

A with a group of talented women _____

B with a mix of people from different backgrounds _____

C with men trying to get out of the profession _____

D with a group of very ambitious men _____

E with a group of untidy men _____

F mainly with women who are mothers _____

Grammar

3 Transform these sentences. Use up to four words per space.

(2 marks for each correct answer: Total __/30)

1 The garage is going to repair my car.
I'm going to _____ at the garage.

2 The optician is going to test my eyes to see if I need glasses.
I'm going to _____ at the opticians to see if I need glasses.

3 We were never forced to do any housework.
My parents never made _____.

4 After college she got a job with a law firm.
After college she went _____ a lawyer.

5 The police catch very few drivers who break the speed limit.
Most drivers who break the speed limit avoid _____.

6 I wish my boss would recognise the work I do.
I'd really like _____ by my boss for the work I do.

7 People think that wind turbines are a bad idea.
Wind turbines _____ a bad idea.

8 People believe that the custom of giving birthday presents originated in China.
The custom of giving birthday presents is _____ in China.

9 I went to look at a flat yesterday and the owner turned out to be an old friend.
The person _____ to look at yesterday turned out to be an old friend.

10 Attenborough wrote and narrated the documentary which tells the story of life on Earth.
_____ Attenborough, the documentary tells the story of life on Earth.

11 You don't get many chances in life to find a really enjoyable job.
You get _____ chances in life to find a really enjoyable job.

12 "If they put my music on their website without permission, I'll sue them."
He _____ if they put the music on their website.

13 "Let's go out for dinner tonight, shall we?"
She _____ out for dinner.

14 My original intention was to study in America, but the costs were too high.
I _____ in America, but the costs were too high.

© 2013 National Geographic Learning, a part of Cengage Learning PHOTOCOPIABLE

15 The plane left at 10.30 a.m., two hours later than scheduled.

The plane _____ at 8.30 a.m., but it was delayed two hours.

Vocabulary

4 Underline the word on the left that collocates with the word(s) on the right.

(1 mark for each correct answer: Total __/10)

1 *raise / lift / rise* awareness

2 *alike / equal /equivalent* rights

3 *make / do / perform* your fair share

4 *study / learning / tuition* fees

5 *place / rest / put* your feet up

6 *foster / grow / build* innovation

7 *apply /employ / implement* a project

8 *play / follow / use* your heart

9 *a led / conducted / guided* tour

10 *use / try / make* your head

5 Put the word in brackets into its correct form to complete these sentences.

(1 mark for each correct answer: Total __/10)

1 Pierre de Coubertin was against women's sports in the Olympics because "they were _____". (practice)

2 If you are a _____ person, it means you like to win. (compete)

3 After the presentation, my sister made a short _____. (speak)

4 Too many children in Africa still die during _____. (infant)

5 Medicine is not just a job; it's a _____. (call)

6 We need someone we can depend on; Tom is just too _____. (rely)

7 It can be through music, art, writing, but children need a way to express their _____. (create)

8 Most people think that taking home some pens and paper from work isn't _____. (thief)

9 I wasn't very _____ during my maths lessons, so I never learned much. (attend)

10 Crete is still a relatively _____ island. (spoil)

Part B

Communication

6 What should you say in these situations? Use the word in brackets to make natural sentences.

(2 marks for each correct answer: Total __/10)

1 You want your audience to take particular notice of some statistics.

I'd like _____ these statistics. (attention)

2 You want the shop assistant to put the item you have bought in special gift paper.

Can _____? (wrap)

3 You did not hear what someone said to you.

I'm sorry. I

_____. (catch)

4 You are trying to negotiate a lower price.

Would _____? (prepared)

5 You want to advise your friend to wait a bit before buying a new computer.

You would _____ before buying one. (better off)

Reading

7 Mark these statements True or False.

(1 mark for each correct answer: Total __/5)

1 Governments generally end up paying the whole cost of the event. — True / False

2 It is proven that big sporting events don't increase tourism. — True / False

3 A city can increase its international standing just by offering to hold a big sporting event. — True / False

4 The improvements made to the city for the event generally don't benefit the citizens after it. — True / False

5 The citizens themselves dislike all the attention. — True / False

8 Read the text about the benefits of hosting big sporting events and choose the correct missing sentences (A–F) to complete it.

(2 marks for each correct answer: Total __/10)

A But it is very rare that these systems actually meet the community's long-term needs.

B There are many other problems, such as finding accommodation for all the athletes.

C Those cities who just bid to host them benefit in the same way.

D So instead you have to look for the indirect benefits.

E But is it worth it?

F Or even a bronze for that matter.

If making money were an Olympic event, no city hosting the games would win a gold medal. (1) _____ In fact when you balance all the costs against all the income, there has never been an Olympic Games that has made a profit. That is because the costs of security and improving the infrastructure are not included in the Olympic budgets, but are usually provided by government.

(2) _____ Studies have shown that here, too, predictions about how much the event will boost tourism or create new industries are often over-optimistic. What

© 2013 National Geographic Learning, a part of Cengage Learning PHOTOCOPIABLE

big sporting events like the Olympics or World Cup do seem to do, however, is to increase the international reputation of the city in question. By hosting the event they are saying, "We welcome everyone from all over the world to a celebration of sporting achievement." But strangely, that international recognition seems to come not only to those cities that actually host the events. (3) _____

Many Olympic cities justify the spending because they gain new roads, transit systems, affordable housing, sports facilities and other infrastructure improvements. (4) _____

So are there any benefits? Well, there is one which is undeniable, and that is the civic pride that local people feel from putting on a successful event. All the eyes of the world are your city, and naturally that makes people proud. (5) _____ That is another question.

Writing

9 **Match the phrases below to the right type of writing. There are two phrases per type.**

Writing types

A A review of a TV documentary

B A CV

C A report of a meeting

D A description of a memorable event

E A book review

Phrases

1 Ran the University Film Society for one year and produced the film *A Student's Life.* _____

2 To be honest, I was not really looking forward to it. _____

3 It is definitely worth seeing, if you have the chance. _____

4 It has a very good index of useful websites. _____

5 Riham pointed out that there was little accommodation available for rent. _____

6 Self-motivated and independent worker with a keen interest in ecology. _____

7 Naturally I felt anxious, but my sister, who is very down-to-earth, calmed my nerves. _____

8 It's written for young adults who are about to leave home for the first time. _____

9 It is part of a series that aims to explore the psychology of volunteering. _____

10 It was agreed that we should refer this question to the Principal. _____

Part A

Listening CD3/14

1 You will hear a critic giving a review of TV documentary *Jamie's American Food Revolution*. The first time you listen, mark the statements below True or False.

(1 mark for each correct answer: Total __/5)

1 Jamie Oliver's British healthy eating campaign focused on children. True / False

2 In the new programme, he persuades a local DJ to join his US campaign. True / False

3 Jamie Oliver is aware that people may laugh at poor Americans. True / False

4 The children are free to choose between his dish or another. True / False

5 Overall, the reviewer recommends us to watch this programme. True / False

2 Listen again and complete these statements. Use ONE word per space.

(1 mark for each correct answer: Total __/10)

1 Jamie Oliver's British healthy eating campaign had _____ success.

2 Americans do not take _____ to people telling them what to do.

3 The DJ asks him who made him '_____' to decide what they eat.

4 Huntingdon is _____ the unhealthiest city in America.

5 People who eat well in America are generally _____.

6 The danger with the programme is that people will laugh or get _____.

7 When he first visits the school, he is _____ by the food they are eating.

8 According to the US Department of Agriculture, French fries are a _____.

9 Jamie Oliver cooks them a meal of _____ chicken and foccacia bread.

10 It is to the _____ of the programme makers that they will stay in Huntingdon.

Grammar

3 Put each verb in brackets into the correct tense.

(1 mark for each correct answer: Total __/12)

1 I _____ (have) guitar lessons for the last two months but I _____ (not / make) much progress.

2 Most actors that I _____ (know) are very superstitious and _____ (always /perform) some ritual before the opening night.

3 He _____ (arrive) home yesterday morning completely exhausted because he _____ (work) since 9 a.m. the day before.

4 _____ (you / do) anything tonight? There's a play at the theatre I want to see. It _____ (start) at 7.30 p.m.

5 I'm reading this Jane Austen novel for my English exam. By the time I _____ (finish) reading it, I _____ (read) it five times in all.

6 I'm sorry – I feel terrible. If I _____ (listen) to your advice, we _____ (not / be) in this situation now.

4 Choose the correct word to complete each sentence.

(1 mark for each correct answer: Total __/8)

1 _____ of them knows that the other is applying for the same job.
A None B Neither C Every D Both

2 _____ of the volunteers gets paid a little pocket money.
A Every B All C Both D Each

3 Can you wait a few days _____ I give you an answer?
A before B while C prior to D during

4 The award ceremony took place shortly _____ the race was over.
A when B as soon as C following D after

5 It is _____ to be a long time before people colonise space.
A probable B probably C likely
D possible

6 It _____ have been an aeroplane: there's no other explanation.
A must B might C may D can't

7 I'd like a job _____ I can be free to make my own decisions.
A which B whose C where D when

8 She accused me _____ her ideas.
A to steal B of stealing C for stealing
D that I stole

5 Choose the correct complete auxiliary verb to complete the sentences.

(1 mark for each correct answer: Total __/10)

1 It's very complicated to organise your own holiday. You _____ be better off getting a package holiday.

2 You _____ better hurry up or you'll miss your train.

© 2013 National Geographic Learning, a part of Cengage Learning PHOTOCOPIABLE

3 Can you give me a hand, when you _____ finished what you're doing?

4 If I hadn't been wearing a helmet, I _____ have injured myself very badly.

5 Even experienced actors _____ tell you that they get nervous before going on stage.

6 You _____ to see another doctor and get a second opinion, if you are worried.

7 I imagine reading takes up a lot of your time, _____ n't it?

8 This time next week, I will _____ lying on a beach in Antigua.

9 The weather _____ been getting progressively worse for three days before the storm hit us.

10 Occasionally one of the lights _____ not work, but we have few other technical problems.

Vocabulary

6 Choose a word (A, B, C or D) to complete each of these collocations.

(1 mark for each correct answer: Total __/10)

1 The venue was a big concert _____ near the river.

   A room **B** chamber **C** hall
   D compartment

2 There has been a _____ war going on between the two parties for years.

   A interior **B** national **C** domestic **D** civil

3 They came to the UK as _____ seekers because they were not safe in their own country.

   A refuge **B** asylum **C** protection **D** shelter

4 The government's ambition is to _____ child poverty.

   A abolish **B** eliminate **C** remove **D** rid

5 The country has _____ resources, being rich in oil and minerals.

   A plenty **B** scarce **C** full **D** abundant

6 The socialists were voted out and we now have a _____ government.

   A right-sided **B** right-handed **C** right
   D right-wing

7 What are the entry _____ to study as an undergraduate at Oxford?

   A requirements **B** needs **C** obligations
   D credentials

8 My living _____ in London are really high.

   A spending **B** fees **C** expenses **D** bills

9 The most important thing for people is these uncertain times is job _____.

   A security B safety C certainty
   D confidence

10 It may look difficult, but if you just use your common _____, you'll learn quickly.

   A intelligence **B** mind **C** wits **D** sense

7 Find the word which doesn't fit in the group and explain why it doesn't fit.

(1 mark for each correct answer: Total __/10)

1 a landscape a sketch a drawing a sculpture
_____

2 a stage a cast a set props
_____

3 a musician an orchestra a group a band
_____

4 shuttle budget surcharge all-inclusive
_____

5 foreigner stranger migrant refugee
_____

6 versatile tiny small-scale extensive
_____

7 borrow owe afford pay back
_____

8 childhood adolescence teenager middle age
_____

9 job apprentice vocation profession
_____

10 bribery murder fraud discrimination
_____

Part B

Communication

8 What should you say in these situations? Use the word in brackets to make natural sentences.

(2 marks for each correct answer: Total __/10)

1 Someone invites you to a jazz concert, but jazz is not your taste. Thank them and explain why you are refusing.

Thanks, but _____.
(thing)

2 You are interested in volunteering for the Red Cross. Call them and ask politely for them to send you some information.

_____? (wondered)

3 You want to arrange to meet someone for coffee one day this week. Ask them which day is convenient.

_____. (suit)

4 You are instructing someone how to fit a new light switch. Warn them not to do this with the electricity still switched on.

_____. (whatever)

5 Someone is explaining how to use a computer program but you are confused by the explanation.

_____ (follow)

© 2013 National Geographic Learning, a part of Cengage Learning **PHOTOCOPIABLE**

Reading

9 Read the text about illegal immigrants crossing from Mexico into the United States at a town called Arriaga. Choose the correct missing sentences (A–F) to complete it. There is one extra sentence.

(2 marks for each correct answer: Total ___/10)

A Soon nearly a hundred people had surrounded the truck.

B In Nicaragua, he had a single mother and seven siblings.

C Migrants have been risking their lives for years making this crossing.

D Its agents are directed not to check for documentation nor to turn people over to the police.

E A half mile or so down the length of track, two railcars sat motionless amid the high weeds.

F It's better to wait for the next train than to lose a leg.

The morning I arrived in Arriaga, a dry, hot wind was wrapping plastic garbage bags against barbed-wire fencing at the edge of town. The main street ran straight across the railroad tracks, which appeared deserted. (1) _____.

Then Francisco Aceves put a whistle between his lips. Aceves is an engineer who runs a branch of the federal migrant protection agency called Grupo Beta. (2) _____. "Grupo Beta! Agua!" Aceves shouted, blowing his whistle. There was movement in the weeds. A young man with a bandanna around his forehead stepped out, straightening his back as he emerged. Another came out behind him, and then another, and a woman, and six more men, the weeds parting and people climbing out. (3) _____. "Make a line!" Aceves cried. "Here's water for you! Who wants a can of tuna? Anybody have a headache?"

Aceves handed out booklets instructing migrants that even if they have no documentation, no one is supposed to rob or abuse them. It contained other pieces of advice: in some parts of where you're going, the days can go above 50 degrees; there are thieves on the roads; don't get on trains while they're moving. (4) _____.

I asked how they would respond if they got to the USA, somehow avoiding all the illegal immigration enforcement, and then Americans said to them, Boys, I'm sorry you came all this way, but without papers there isn't any work for you here. One Nicaraguan man, Ramos said, "I'll keep looking. I'll find my own work."

Another Honduran man leaned in, his voice urgent. "Look," he said, "they're going to offer you seven dollars an hour. That seems like a lot of money. But do you know what rent costs? You're going to want to visit the cantina. How are you going to eat?"

A look of uncertainty flickered across Ramos's face. (5) _____. He was 21 years old. "If a door is closed on me, I'll open another one," he said, and he radiated the big smile. "I have to go live in the land of marvels."

10 Answer these questions.

(1 mark for each correct answer: Total ___/5)

1 How does the text suggest illegal immigrants make the crossing into the US from Arriaga?

2 Where were the migrants when Aceves blew his whistle?

3 What rights do migrants have, even without papers?

4 What point is the Honduran man making about the pay they will get in the USA?

5 What does Ramos mean by 'the land of marvels'?

Writing

11 Do you think studying abroad is a good idea or a bad idea? Explain the arguments on both sides and give your conclusion. Follow the structure below and include arguments for and against. Write around 250 words.

Structure

A Introduction: presentation of opinion

B Main arguments

C Additional arguments

D Opinions against

E Conclusion: repetition of opinion

Arguments for

- the chance to learn about a different culture
- the chance to experience a different style of learning
- working in a foreign language

Arguments against

- the cost
- being away from friends and family
- re-establishing yourself and finding a job after you return

© 2013 National Geographic Learning, a part of Cengage Learning PHOTOCOPIABLE

End of Year Test (second version)

Part A

Listening 🔘 CD3/14

1 Listen again and complete these statements. Use ONE word per space.

(1 mark for each correct answer: Total __/10)

1 Jamie Oliver's British healthy eating campaign had _____ success.

2 Americans do not take _____ to people telling them what to do.

3 The DJ asks him who made him '_____' to decide what they eat.

4 Huntingdon is _____ the unhealthiest city in America.

5 People who eat well in America are generally _____.

6 The danger with the programme is that people will laugh or get _____.

7 When he first visits the school he is _____ by the food they are eating

8 According to the US Department of Agriculture, French fries are a _____.

9 Jamie Oliver cooks them a meal of _____ chicken and foccacia bread.

10 It is to the _____ of the programme makers that they will stay in Huntingdon.

2 You will hear a critic giving a review of TV documentary, *Jamie's American Food Revolution*. The first time you listen, mark the statements below true or false

(1 mark for each correct answer: Total __/5)

1 Jamie Oliver's British healthy eating campaign focused on children.   True / False

2 In the new programme, he persuades a local DJ to join his US campaign.   True / False

3 Jamie Oliver is aware that people may laugh at poor Americans.   True / False

4 The children are free to choose between his dish or another.   True / False

5 Overall the reviewer recommends us to watch this programme.   True / False

Grammar

3 Choose the correct word to complete these sentences.

(1 mark for each correct answer: Total __/8)

1 _____ of them knows that the other is applying for the same job.

    A None   **B** Neither   **C** Every   **D** Both

2 _____ of the volunteers gets paid a little pocket money.

    A Every   **B** All   **C** Both   **D** Each

3 Can you wait a few days _____ I give you an answer?

    A before   **B** while   **C** prior to   **D** during

4 The award ceremony took place shortly _____ the race was over.

    A when   **B** as soon as   **C** following   **D** after

5 It is _____ to be a long time before people colonise space

    A probable   **B** probably   **C** likely   **D** possible

6 It _____ have been an aeroplane: there's no other explanation.

    A must   **B** might   **C** may   **D** can't

7 I'd like a job _____ I can be free to make my own decisions

    A which   **B** whose   **C** where   **D** when

8 She accused me _____ her ideas.

    A to steal   **B** of stealing   **C** for stealing   **D** that I stole

4 Choose the correct complete auxiliary verb to complete these sentences.

(1 mark for each correct answer: Total __/10)

1 It's very complicated to organise your own holiday. You _____ be better off getting a package holiday.

2 You _____ better hurry up or you'll miss your train.

3 Can you give me a hand, when you _____ finished what you're doing?

4 If I hadn't been wearing a helmet, I _____ have injured myself very badly.

5 Even experienced actors _____ tell you that they get nervous before going on stage.

6 You _____ to see another doctor and get a second opinion, if you are worried.

7 I imagine reading takes up a lot of your time, _____n't it?

8 This time next week, I will _____ lying on a beach in Antigua.

9 The weather _____ been getting progressively worse for three days before the storm hit us.

10 Occasionally one of the lights _____ not work, but we have few other technical problems.

5 Put each verb in brackets into the correct tense.

(1 mark for each correct answer: Total __/12)

1 I _____ (have) guitar lessons for the last two months but I _____ (not / make) much progress.

2 Most actors that I _____ (know) are very superstitious and _____ (always /perform) some ritual before the opening night.

3 He _____ (arrive) home yesterday morning completely exhausted because he _____ (work) since 9 am the day before.

4 _____ (you / do) anything tonight? There's a play at the theatre I want to see: it _____ (start) at 7.30 pm.

5 I'm reading this Jane Austen novel for my English exam. By the time I _____ (finish) reading it, I _____ (read) it five times in all.

6 I'm sorry – I feel terrible. If I _____ (listen) to your advice, we _____ (not / be) in this situation now.

Vocabulary

6 Find the word which doesn't fit in the group and explain why it doesn't fit.

(1 mark for each correct answer: Total __/10)

1 a landscape   a sketch   a drawing   a sculpture
_____

2 a stage   a cast   a set   props
_____

3 a musician   an orchestra   a group   a band
_____

4 shuttle   budget   surcharge   all-inclusive
_____

5 foreigner   stranger   migrant   refugee
_____

6 versatile   tiny   small-scale   extensive
_____

7 borrow   owe   afford   pay back
_____

8 childhood   adolescence   teenager middle age
_____

9 job   apprentice   vocation   profession
_____

10 bribery   murder   fraud   discrimination
_____

7 Choose the word (A, B, C or D) that completes these collocations

(1 mark for each correct answer: Total __/10)

1 The venue was a big concert _____ near the river.

   A room   **B** chamber   **C** hall   **D** compartment

2 There has been a _____ war going on between the two parties for years.

   A interior   **B** national   **C** domestic   **D** civil

3 They came to the UK as _____ seekers because they were not safe in their own country.

   A refuge   **B** asylum   **C** protection   **D** shelter

4 The government's ambition is to _____ child poverty.

   A abolish   **B** eliminate   **C** remove   **D** rid

5 The country has _____ resources, being rich in oil and minerals.

   A plenty   **B** scarce   **C** full   **D** abundant

6 The socialists were voted out and we now have a _____ government.

   A right-sided   **B** right-handed   **C** right
   D right-wing

7 What are the entry _____ to study as an undergraduate at Oxford?

   A requirements   **B** needs   **C** obligations
   D credentials

8 My living _____ in London are really high.

   A spending   **B** fees   **C** expenses   **D** bills

9 The most important thing for people is these uncertain times is job _____.

   A security   **B** safety   **C** certainty
   D confidence

10 It may look difficult but if you just use your common _____, you'll learn quickly.

   A intelligence   **B** mind   **C** wits   **D** sense

Part B

Communication

8 What should you say in these situations? Use the word in brackets to make natural sentences.

(2 marks for each correct answer: Total __/10)

1 Someone invites you to a jazz concert, but jazz is not your taste. Thank them and explain why you are refusing.

   Thanks, but _____.
   (thing)

2 You are interested in volunteering for the Red Cross. Call them and ask politely to be sent some information.

   _____? (wondered)

3 You want to arrange to meet someone for coffee one day this week. Ask them which day is convenient.

   _____? (suit)

4 You are instructing someone how to fit a new light switch. Warn them not to do this with the electricity still switched on.

   _____. (whatever)

5 Someone is explaining how to use a computer programme but you are confused by the explanation.

   _____ (follow)

© 2013 National Geographic Learning, a part of Cengage Learning **PHOTOCOPIABLE**

Reading

9 Read the text about illegal immigrants crossing from Mexico into the United States at a town called Arriaga. Choose the correct missing sentences (A–F) to complete it. There is one extra sentence.

(2 marks for each correct answer: Total __/10)

A Soon nearly a hundred people had surrounded the truck.

B In Nicaragua he had a single mother and seven siblings.

C Migrants have been risking their lives for years making this crossing.

D Its agents are directed not to check for documentation nor to turn people over to the police.

E A half mile or so down the length of track, two railcars sat motionless amid the high weeds.

F It's better to wait for the next train than to lose a leg.

The morning I arrived in Arriaga, a dry, hot wind was wrapping plastic garbage bags against barbed-wire fencing at the edge of town. The main street ran straight across the railroad tracks, which appeared deserted. (1) _____.

Then Francisco Aceves put a whistle between his lips. Aceves is an engineer who runs a branch of the federal migrant protection agency called Grupo Beta. (2) _____. "Grupo Beta! Agua!" Aceves shouted, blowing his whistle. There was movement in the weeds. A young man with a bandanna around his forehead stepped out, straightening his back as he emerged. Another came out behind him, and then another, and a woman, and six more men, the weeds parting and people climbing out. (3) _____. "Make a line!" Aceves cried. "Here's water for you! Who wants a can of tuna? Anybody have a headache?"

Aceves handed out booklets instructing migrants that even if they have no documentation, no one is supposed to rob or abuse them. It contained other pieces of advice: in some parts of where you're going, the days can go above 50 degrees; there are thieves on the roads; don't get on trains while they're moving. (4) _____.

I asked how they would respond if they got to the USA, somehow avoiding all the illegal immigration enforcement, and then Americans said to them, Boys, I'm sorry you came all this way, but without papers there isn't any work for you here. One Nicaraguan man, Ramos said, "I'll keep looking. I'll find my own work."

Another Honduran man leaned in, his voice urgent. "Look," he said, "they're going to offer you seven dollars an hour. That seems like a lot of money. But do you know what rent costs? You're going to want to visit the cantina. How are you going to eat?"

A look of uncertainty flickered across Ramos's face. (5) _____. He was 21 years old. "If a door is closed on me, I'll open another one," he said, and he radiated the big smile. "I have to go live in the land of marvels."

10 Answer these questions.

(1 mark for each correct answer: Total __/5)

1 How does the text suggest illegal immigrants make the crossing into the US from Arriaga?

2 Where were the migrants when Aceves blew his whistle?

3 What rights do migrants have, even without papers?

4 What point is the Honduran man making about the pay they will get in the U.S.?

5 What does Ramos mean by 'the land of marvels'?

Writing

11 Do you think studying abroad is a good idea or a bad idea? Explain the arguments on both sides and give your conclusion. Follow the structure below and include the arguments for and against. Write around 250 words.

Structure

A Introduction: presentation of opinion

B Main arguments

C Additional arguments

D Opinions against

E Conclusion: repetition of opinion

Arguments for

- the chance to learn about a different culture
- the chance to experience a different style of learning
- working in a foreign language

Arguments against

- the cost
- being away from friends and family
- re-establishing yourself and finding a job after you return

Tests Answers and Audioscripts

Placement test

1 b	**26** c	**51** a	**76** c
2 c	**27** c	**52** c	**77** c
3 d	**28** d	**53** b	**78** d
4 a	**29** b	**54** a	**79** b
5 c	**30** d	**55** c	**80** c
6 c	**31** a	**56** c	**81** b
7 c	**32** a	**57** d	**82** b
8 a	**33** a	**58** c	**83** d
9 c	**34** b	**59** d	**84** d
10 d	**35** d	**60** c	**85** b
11 d	**36** a	**61** d	**86** a
12 b	**37** d	**62** d	**87** a
13 c	**38** a	**63** a	**88** c
14 d	**39** d	**64** a	**89** a
15 a	**40** c	**65** b	**90** b
16 b	**41** b	**66** b	**91** b
17 b	**42** c	**67** c	**92** b
18 b	**43** b	**68** b	**93** c
19 d	**44** b	**69** b	**94** c
20 a	**45** b	**70** d	**95** b
21 c	**46** d	**71** a	**96** c
22 b	**47** d	**72** c	**97** d
23 a	**48** d	**73** a	**98** a
24 b	**49** c	**74** c	**99** a
25 d	**50** b	**75** d	**100** d

The scores on this Placement Test correspond to the books at these levels:

1–25 Elementary

26–50 Pre-intermediate

51–80 Intermediate

81–100 Upper intermediate

Progress Tests

Unit 1

Part 1: Listening

1 **1** E **2** C **3** F **4** D **5** B

2 **1** True **2** False **3** False **4** False **5** True

Part 2: Grammar

3 **1** are you doing **2** have just returned **3** have been living **4** are always asking/always ask **5** have decided **6** have been working

4 **1** the **2** a **3** – **4** a

Part 3: Vocabulary

5 **1** stage **2** cast **3** audition **4** gig **5** venue **6** portrait **7** sketch **8** landscape **9** comedian **10** musician

Part 4: Communication

6 **1** Some of it appeals to me **2** it's not (really) my (kind of) thing **3** I'm a (big) fan of Kings of

Leon **4** when I'm in the (right) mood **5** it reminds me of my last summer holiday

Part 5: Reading

7 **1** A **2** D **3** C **4** C **5** D

8 **1** a hard day's work/a big meal (2 marks) **2** they feel embarrassed **3** Yes **4** more than 90 minutes

Listening audioscript 💿 CD3/02

It was very interesting. The shots were all portraits of famous people, but they had been taken in uncharacteristic situations. So for example, there was one of the actor Ian McKellen, not on stage or from a film, but just reading a book quietly at home. It gave you an insight into the real person, behind their artist's persona ... and you felt you knew them better. I think, if they are well taken, photos have the power to do that.

We went to a gig at the Shepherd's Bush Empire. It used to be a traditional theatre, but now it's used for concerts ... and some stand-up comedy too, I think. It's a really nice venue – not too big and quite comfortable. I didn't like the band much, though, I have to say. This was their first major tour and they had been described as one of the most original new groups around, but I couldn't see that. The tickets were £30 each as well, which wasn't funny.

We were very lucky to get tickets, actually. The show's sold out for the next three months, but when we were at the box office, there was someone returning two seats for the following night. So we bought them immediately. They weren't the best position – high up in the gallery – and the stage looked pretty small from there, but you could hear all the songs perfectly ... It was a little more difficult when the actors were speaking, but I knew the story very well, anyway, so it didn't matter.

It was an outdoor event ... in a very beautiful setting. It was a sculpture garden next to an old house and the weather was beautiful – a calm, warm, summer evening. The music suited the atmosphere perfectly: pieces by Handel and some other composer I hadn't heard of. During the interval we had strawberries and cream – it was all very English!

This was a show that I saw in Hamburg too, but I liked it so much that I thought I would go again. There are a lot of very amusing pieces – mostly from the 1960s, but a few more recent ones like a painting by Damien Hirst and a film by the Japanese artist Murakami, which has Kirsten Dunst singing 'Turning Japanese' in the streets of Tokyo, which is also good fun. If you get a chance to see it, it's called 'The Pop Years' ... I'd really recommend going.

Unit 2

Part 1: Listening

1 **1** C **2** D **3** B **4** A **5** B

Part 2: Grammar

2 **1** does **2** sound **3** appeal **4** has

3 1 would regularly test **2** used to be **3** had caused **4** decided **5** was waiting **6** sank

Part 3: Vocabulary

4 1 famous **2** humanitarian aid **3** asylum seekers **4** relief operations **5** awe-inspiring **6** civil war **7** natural disaster **8** labour market **9** long-running **10** race relations

Part 4: Reading

5 1 D **2** B **3** F **4** A

Listening audioscript  CD3/03

Interviewer So tell us about the international youth camp.

Camp organiser Well, each year UNESCO organises a student summer camp. This gives about 60 high school students from around the world the chance to work together for three weeks.

Interviewer And this takes place in the USA?

Camp organiser That's right, in Maryland, on the east coast of the US.

Interviewer What are the goals of this international camp?

Camp organiser Well, we hope that students will use the knowledge and experience they gain at the camp to promote peace and cultural integration when they return home to their own countries. The programme gives students a framework to interact about peace and global issues, and on completion of their stay students are given the title of 'Builders of the Universe'.

Interviewer Sorry, did you say 'Builders of the Universe'?

Camp organiser Yes, builders in the sense that we hope that these students will go on to become leaders in their country who can contribute to building a future peaceful world order.

Interviewer I see … Can you give us some concrete examples of the types of events students participate in?

Camp organiser Well, there are political classes of course. For example the Model United Nations Conference in which students discuss global issues, or the 'ABC of a Builder of the Universe class', which focuses on case studies of Peace Nobel laureates. There are also field trips to the White House and the Capitol in Washington DC, and the United Nations Headquarters in New York. Erm, then there are the Conflict Resolution workshops: these provide an opportunity for students to acquire a set of tools to resolve conflicts peacefully.

Interviewer Right. But in addition to political classes, there are also cultural events?

Camp organiser Yes, the Creative Arts classes allow students to make exhibitions of their work using various techniques, for example collage and sculpture. And the Ethnic Festival is a great opportunity for students to share their cultural heritage. Students put on cultural performances which include music, poetry, dances and ethnic songs, as well as the tasting of traditional food from Africa, Asia, India and Europe.

Unit 3

Part 1: Listening

1 1 C **2** E **3** F **4** A **5** B

2 1 False **2** True **3** False **4** True **5** True

Part 2: Grammar

3 1 are you doing **2** 'll give **3** are you leaving **4** goes **5** 'll set off

4 1 will we have achieved **2** will have been working **3** will have cut **4** will be setting **5** will be fighting

Part 3: Vocabulary

5 1 micro **2** ultra **3** semi **4** hyper **5** micro **6** ultra

6 1 transformed **2** reform **3** spoil **4** improved

Part 4: Communication

7

Hi Mr Stevens

Thank you for your letter. We would be very interested to meet you. Do you want to come round this week? Would Tuesday at 9 am be convenient? Or what about Wednesday? I would be grateful if you could let us know as soon as possible.

See you then

Alexandra Robinson

Dear Ms Robinson

Thank you for your mail. I'm afraid I am not available on Tuesday or Wednesday. What are you doing next week? How about meeting on Thursday?

Yours sincerely

Zack Stevens

Part 5: Reading

8 1 C **2** D **3** C **4** B **5** A

9 1 18% / 6% **2** the Celtic tiger **3** agriculture **4** globalisation and europeanisation **5** tax rates

Listening audioscript  CD3/04

Speaker 1 I have a big family – I had four children and now I have grandchildren and great-grandchildren. I even have a great-great-granddaughter now, so that's five generations! It's my family and friends that keep me young. A lot of my relatives live locally, so there's always somebody popping in most days. Nearly all the people I grew up with have died now, of course, but some of their children come to visit me, too.

Speaker 2 My father lived to a ripe old age – he was 97 when he died and he always said it was local apples. I have an apple every day too. Always have done since I was young. My parents used to give us an apple cut up before dinner each day. So I've carried on the family tradition (chuckles) …. I only ever have one a day, though. After all they say: An apple a day keeps the doctor away, don't they?

Speaker 3 I've lived in the mountains all my life. I love the area, the mountain air. This was my parents' farm … We've always had goats and sheep. When we were kids, my mother made cheese from the goat's milk and we ate that for breakfast and lunch – sometimes dinner too. We didn't eat much meat … My mother made bread and we used to trade some of the cheese for olive oil. We buy more produce today from outside, but my diet hasn't really changed much over the years.

Speaker 4   I was devastated when my wife died … I still can't believe she isn't here. We were married for 68 years … Like two pieces of a jigsaw puzzle we were. We got through everything together – including the death of our first child, which was a terrible time … We always supported each other and told each other everything. I think that's what kept us going. We always had each other.

Speaker 5   I used to be a teacher. I taught until I was 75. I still follow all the educational debates, and until a couple of years ago I used to write articles myself. A lot has changed in the way we treat young people today … I've always believed in the power of education, thought that every child has the right to an equal chance. A lot of children today take it for granted. They waste their time at school. I tried to make kids realise that you often don't get another chance.

Unit 4

Part 1: Listening

1 1 D **2** C **3** B **4** A **5** D

2 1 beyond **2** 1977 **3** Einstein **4** robot

Part 2: Grammar

3 1 was landing **2** was making **3** had waited
4 will take **5** have fallen

4 1 when **2** while **3** while **4** following
5 prior to

Part 3: Vocabulary

5 1 solar **2** orbit **3** gravity **4** meteors **5** receive
6 transmitted

Part 4: Communication

6 1 must have **2** well have **3** of all
4 don't try

Part 5: Reading

7 1 B **2** D **3** B **4** A **5** D

8 1 True **2** True **3** False **4** True **5** True

Listening audioscript   CD3/05

Presenter   The next era of space travel is going to be concerned with sending spacecraft into deep space, in other words beyond our own solar system. The main problem at the moment is the time that it takes to get there. Voyager 1, which was a robotic unmanned spacecraft, was launched in 1977 and took 40 years to reach the edge of the solar system. So what sort of technologies could be used in future space missions to accelerate this process? In the studio I have Harvey Smith, an ex-NASA technician to answer this and other questions. Harvey, is there any technology already available to us that could make deep space missions a reality?

Harvey   Well, there's one technology which has been around for a long time but is only now just coming into its own … and that's solar sails. These were originally

proposed by Einstein and a Russian scientist Friedrich Zander as early as the 1920s.

Presenter   And how do they work?

Harvey   Well one of the major difficulties in getting a spacecraft to the edge of the solar system is the amount, and weight, of the fuel needed to travel such a long distance. Solar sails are large panels that propel the spacecraft using light energy – the energy of the sun – instead of wind energy, like ordinary sails. This does away with the need to carry any other fuel on board.

Presenter   It sounds fantastic. Are there any disadvantages in using them?

Harvey   Well, up to now they haven't been used much because the initial acceleration is so low. They only have the power to carry a small payload, such as a robot. It would be almost impossible to power a manned spacecraft with them. But … and this is a big but … because the light is a continuous source of power, the solar sails help the craft to continue accelerating up to speeds of 90 kilometres per second.

Presenter   Could you just give some comparison to explain to our listeners how fast that is?

Harvey   Yes, that's the equivalent of travelling from London to New York in just over a minute. Or to compare to the Voyager probe that you mentioned earlier, it would take about eight years, rather than 40, to reach the edge of the solar system.

Unit 5

Part 1: Listening

1 1 D **2** A **3** F **4** B **5** E

2 1 bar **2** research **3** temporary **4** church
5 night

Part 2: Grammar

3 1 If Ahmed had got higher grades, he would have studied medicine.   **2** If Lucy had passed her exams, she would have had a place at university.   **3** If Damon had saved some money before university, he wouldn't have had to take out a huge loan.   **4** Pierre would study in the USA if he had the money.   **5** If Maria gets a place at university, she'll leave home.

4 1 didn't you?   **2** isn't it?   **3** don't you?
4 haven't you?   **5** did he?

Part 3: Vocabulary

5 1 course **2** historian **3** campus **4** fees
5 biologist

6 1 challenges **2** contacts **3** practice **4** best
5 responsibility

Part 4: Communication

7 1 D **2** A **3** E **4** B **5** F

Part 5: Reading

8 1 E **2** G **3** A **4** C **5** F

Listening audioscript   CD3/06

Speaker 1   I felt really burnt out in the last year at school. I studied really hard and then did a lot of revision for the exams. So I knew I didn't want to go straight to university. I decided to wait a year, but I couldn't afford to hang round and do nothing. But I couldn't afford to go anywhere either. Then my parents said they would pay for a ticket to Australia if I supported myself. So I went over there and got a bar job in Sydney. It was hard work, but it was just so different from studying. I loved it and I learned a lot about working with different kinds of people.

Speaker 2   I applied to university to study marine biology, but I didn't get a place at the university I really liked. So I decided to wait a year and try and get some experience. I was already a good scuba diver, and when I found a marine research programme in Spain where I could help with conservation surveys, I knew that was right for me. I had a fantastic time, and with this on my CV, I got the university place that I wanted. It was definitely worth taking the year out.

Speaker 3   I didn't really know which subject to study at university – business or art. I'd enjoyed the business classes I did at school but didn't know if I wanted an office job. So my careers adviser at school suggested I take a year out and get some work experience in different kinds of business environments. I went to various agencies with my CV and got temporary work with different companies. After a few months, I knew that I wanted to work in business and applied for a place at university. Now all that experience I gained is coming in handy – I can relate what I'm learning to the practical work I did.

Speaker 4   I took a year out before teacher training college to work with a volunteer project in Uganda in East Africa. It was a project organised by the church in my home town. I'm not actually a member of the church but they needed volunteers and they knew I was interested in teaching. I helped teach children English in two different schools. My job was to take small groups of students and just practise what the teacher had taught. There were no books or paper or pens. Just a board and chalk. And the classes were so big – 50 or 60 in a class – it was really difficult for the teacher to give the students any sort of individual attention. The teachers did a fantastic job, though. It made me appreciate that you don't need equipment to be a good teacher.

Speaker 5   I didn't actually do a gap year. I, err, well I failed my exams. I just didn't put the work in … It was my own fault, but it was still a big shock when I got my results. Anyway, I decided to retake the two subjects I failed and work at the same time so I could save up for university. I got a job as a night porter at a hotel. It meant I could spend some of the time studying when things were quiet and still go to classes. It worked fine and I was able to pass my exams second time round.

Unit 6

Part 1: Listening

1 **1** True   **2** False   **3** False   **4** True   **5** False
   6 True   **7** True   **8** False   **9** True   **10** True

Part 2: Grammar

2 **1** somebody; nobody   **2** everybody; nobody   **3** everybody; somebody.

3 **1** driving   **2** to play   **3** write   **4** studying

Part 3: Vocabulary

4 **1** series   **2** aims   **3** designed   **4** present
   5 engage   **6** style

5 **1** illogical   **2** incapable   **3** immoral
   4 insufficient   **5** irregular   **6** unpredictable
   7 impolite   **8** inadequate

Part 4: Communication

6 **1** than   **2** as   **3** worse   **4** more
   5 much   **6** used   **7** as   **8** better
   9 more   **10** as

Part 5: Reading

7 **1** a   **2** b   **3** b   **4** a   **5** b

Listening audioscript   CD3/07

Interviewer   Paula Smith, you're one of the most successful archaeologists around right now. For those listeners who for some strange reason haven't heard of you yet, tell us something about yourself.

Paula Smith   Well, I'm 38 years old. I'm married with two young children, and recently I have been presenting The Archaeology Show on TV.

Interviewer   But you used to work at a university, didn't you?

Paula Smith   I still do, but the TV work has been more important in the last six months.

Interviewer   So how did you get into TV work?

Paula Smith   Well, by accident really. I was working on a dig at a Roman villa in the west of England when the TV people came to film us because I had found some very beautiful and complete mosaics, which are unique in Britain. After I had finished the interview, the producer asked me if I would be interested in presenting a series on archaeology.

Interviewer   And that show became very successful.

Paula Smith   Yes, it did. To everyone's surprise. When started we thought it would be a late-night programme that only a few people watched, but suddenly everyone got interested in archaeology.

Interviewer   And you did the book of the series.

Paula Smith   Yes, and it became a bestseller, and so did the DVD of the series. So it has all been quite a change.

Interviewer   I was just wondering how you manage it, you know with your children and work.

Paula Smith   Well, I go to the university most days when I am at home, so I can live a normal life, but when I am away filming it gets quite difficult. I have to change all my lectures because I am travelling a lot to talk about different archaeological sites all over Britain. I can only do it because my husband supports me 100 per cent. He knows what it means to me, and we both know it won't be forever. So right now, he looks after our children when I am away, and we split all the household jobs. At weekends I spend all my time with my family or away filming. I don't have time for anything else.

Interviewer   Is it hard being a woman in archaeology?

Paula Smith   Not really. Archaeology is hard work when you are on a dig, but I have always enjoyed being out in the field. I prefer it to the university work really. And the TV work is new and interesting, and I am really pleased to be able to make so many people interested in our past history. I still get nervous before we start filming, but once I'm talking about things that I love, I can handle it.

Unit 7

Part 1: Listening

1 **1** at school   **2** a salesman   **3** nervous
   4 pay/money/paid   **5** atmosphere   **6** Graffiti
   7 small(ish) town   **8** an adult   **9** mood
   10 teenager

Part 2: Grammar

2 **1** are said to have always enjoyed parties **2** are supposed to be a time of happiness **3** are thought to be too expensive **4** is believed to have started in China **5** was said to arrive on horseback

3 **1** being informed **2** to be accompanied **3** to be told **4** being interviewed **5** being charged

Part 3: Vocabulary

4 **1** commemorates **2** farewell **3** dress **4** made **5** streamers **6** parade **7** middle **8** adolescence **9** birth **10** old age

Part 4: Communication

5 **1** dates back to the 16th century **2** It was a (really) memorable occasion. **3** you are allowed **4** can you **5** I find them (a bit) boring

Part 5: Reading

6 **1** B **2** D **3** A **4** F **5** C

Listing audioscript  CD3/08

Interviewer When did you first decide to become an actor?

Actor I guess when I was at school. I performed in a school play – it was *Death of a Salesman* by Arthur Miller – and I really enjoyed it ... I didn't feel nervous at all.

Interviewer And how did you end up doing films rather than stage plays? Was it because the money was so much better?

Actor Well, of course it is better, but I don't really think that was the deciding factor. I was, anyway, in my teens, a big fan of American films and there was something about them, the atmosphere of them, that really drew me towards them.

Interviewer Did any one film in particular influence you?

Actor Yes, absolutely. *American Graffiti*, which is a George Lucas film – the guy who directed the *Star Wars* films. I don't know if you've seen it. Well for the benefit of those who haven't, it's about a group of high school kids living in a smallish town in America and it's their last night before going off to college. It's all about growing up and becoming an adult and leaving your past behind. They all realise that this change is about to happen, but none of them feels very comfortable about it.

Interviewer And why did it make such an impression on you?

Actor Because it captured a particular mood so perfectly. I was a teenager at the time myself. And that feeling of not wanting to grow up and face responsibilities is very strong. It's stayed in my mind ever since. It's my dream to be involved in a film as poignant as that, but they don't make many.

Unit 8

Part 1: Listening

1 **1** C **2** D **3** C **4** B **5** B

Part 2: Grammar

2 **1** wanting **2** living **3** (which/that) they work **4** Exhausted **5** who have

3 **1** Not only do you need the right qualifications, you need the right personality. **2** Under no circumstances should you lie about your qualifications. **3** The more work experience job applicants have, the more attractive they are to employers. **4** Only when you start your first real job do you realise that your student days are over. **5** The harder you work, the harder you can play.

Part 3: Vocabulary

4 **1** dynamic **2** apprentice **3** numeracy **4** thick-skinned **5** teamwork **6** salary **7** rewarding **8** problem-solving **9** prestigious **10** stimulating

Part 4: Communication

5 **1** with **2** mean **3** catch **4** missed **5** mean **6** say **7** say **8** mean

Part 5: Reading

6 **1** C **2** B **3** D **4** B **5** B **6** B

7 **1** False **2** True **3** True **4** False **5** False

Listing audioscript CD3/09

Presenter In today's competitive job market, particularly for graduates, it's tempting to think of an unusual way to stand out of the crowd when making a job application. And some of those stunts and tricks can really be quite creative. Charlotte Cole, head of human resources at a large marketing company, says two in her experience particularly stand out.

Charlotte I once had an applicant who put posters of herself in our car park. They were professionally printed posters, the sort you get in political campaigns. And they were literally everywhere, even on the windscreens of cars. It was pretty weird and I'm afraid we didn't even give her an interview. Another applicant sent a singing telegram – a messenger arrived with the applicant's CV and then sang a song about why this person should get the job. We did give him an interview but erm ... he didn't get the job in the end. ... In general, I'd say that unless the applicant has excellent qualifications and skills, we would be more likely not to consider them if they tried stunts like these.

Presenter Marketing executive Amir Khan agrees.

Amir I would recommend that job applicants be very careful about using any sorts of tricks to try and get noticed. In particular if people might see those tricks as an attempt to bribe them to get a job. We've had applicants who have sent tickets to football or tennis matches, lottery tickets, cakes, flowers, cuddly toys ... And I'm afraid each time, we've returned whatever has been sent – along with the candidate's CV and application.

Presenter So how can you get that all-important interview when there are so many others out there applying for the same job? The answer, it seems, is to simply make sure your CV and covering letter fit the job that is being advertised. According to Charlotte, relevance is the key.

Charlotte I always look at the covering letter which accompanies the CV. If it's a standard letter which the applicant has obviously sent out with several applications, then I don't take the application any further. And if it's very long and basically repeats the information in the CV, then I feel that's a sign that the applicant is not focused on the job. So my advice is, make sure your CV and in particular your covering letter are relevant to the position you are applying for.

Unit 9

Part 1: Listening
1 1 A **2** B **3** F

2 1 legal **2** trade **3** Foreign **4** promotional
5 intimate **6** six **7** holiday

Part 2: Grammar
3 1 for being **2** for agreeing **3** a few
4 you to do **5** a little **6** to take **7** should go
8 me to find **9** had **10** little

Part 3: Vocabulary
4 1 admitted **2** well-off **3** poor **4** wealth
5 private **6** tackle **7** promote/foster/encourage
8 make **9** sets up **10** self-employed

Part 4: Communication
5 1 I were to offer you **2** you be willing to
3 did you have in mind? **4** I couldn't possibly
accept **5** I'll leave it (then)

Part 5: Reading
6 1 D **2** C **3** A **4** C **5** D **6** C

7 1 waste and unnecessary consumption **2** teach them how to do something **3** to store things; to grow some vegetables **4** offer goods or services *in return for* other goods or services

Listening audioscript CD3/10
My father wanted me to join his legal practice when I finish law school. He's had his own business for the last 30 years. He advises local companies on trade law mainly, but it's not really the type of law that interests me. If I wanted to do that I could go and work in the legal department of a big multinational and probably earn loads of money. I'm actually more interested in politics, so when I finish I'm going to go and take the civil service exams and try to get a job in a government department – the Foreign Ministry, I hope.

My brother landed this amazing job with Red Bull™ when he left college, filming promotional films for them at sports events like the winter Olympics and Formula 1 races. Absolutely fantastic! He travels all over the world. I'm not a photographer, but I have studied marketing and I'd love to get a job with them. I know they're actually a big multinational, but he says it's more like working for a family business – you know, very friendly and intimate.

My first ambition is to travel and see the world a bit before I settle into a full-time hospital job. I'll qualify as a doctor at the end of this year. It's been six years of non-stop hard work, and if I go straight into a public sector job, who knows when I'll next get a chance to do something different. So I'm going to volunteer to do some work with the Red Cross in Africa. It's not exactly a holiday, I know, but it should be very interesting and it's also a very worthwhile cause.

Unit 10

Part 1: Listening
1 1 Lightly **2** traveller **3** package **4** exists already **5** treks **6** cycle down **7** transparent
8 options **9** extra charge **10** 20%

Part 2: Grammar
2 1 have waited **2** was going **3** were due
4 was expecting/was expected **5** was going

3 1 could speak **2** could **3** Were you able to post **4** couldn't **5** managed to

Part 3: Vocabulary
4 1 follow **2** use **3** play **4** spread **5** gossip/talk/speak **6** leaked **7** see **8** tell **9** make
10 laugh

Part 4: Communication
5 1 ought **2** should/must **3** off **4** mind
5 budget **6** there **7** get **8** would **9** up
10 had

Part 5: Reading
6 1 C **2** D **3** A **4** B **5** D

Listening audioscript CD3/11
Presenter I'm pleased to welcome Jessica Farrow to the studio to talk about her company, Go Lightly Travel. Jessica, I believe yours is a travel company with a slightly different approach. Can you just explain to our listeners what it is you do exactly?

Jessica Hello, Jim …. Yes, of course. I'm a traveller myself. I've spent a lot of time over the years travelling to different parts of the world, putting together my own itineraries, doing my own research about where are the best places to stay, what are the best ways to get to a country and then to travel about once you're there … and I wanted – essentially – to share this … the benefit of my experience with other people.

Presenter So you put together packages for people … But these are not your typical package holidays, are they?

Jessica No, not at all. The main principle for us is always how we can use the local tourist industry that already exists, and if the right tourist service doesn't exist then we work with local people … to provide that service.

Presenter Can you give us an example of that?

Jessica Sure. One of the trips we organise is to Tanzania and we can do walks and safaris and so on, but we also wanted to organise cycling trips near Mount Meru. So we looked for a local partner and found this fantastic operator who rents out bicycles that you can ride down one side of the mountain, so you can walk up and cycle down.

Presenter And I understand also that your pricing is very transparent too.

Jessica Well, I hope so. How it works is that customers, once they've decided where they want to go, choose from a menu of options – like the walks and cycle expeditions I just described – and the price of these is all given on the website without any extra charge from us. Then at the end they add up all the elements and we add 20 per cent for our own research and work.

Aspire End of Term Test 1 (first version)

Part A

Listening

Exercise 1

1 E **2** D **3** A **4** F **5** B

Exercise 2

1 C **2** B **3** A **4** C **5** D

Grammar

Exercise 3

1 are you going/have been waiting **2** were they doing/had been writing **3** will be doing/will have graduated **4** is always complaining/won't find **5** Would you have gone/wouldn't be **6** did you enjoy/had read **7** will have been sitting/doesn't come

Exercise 4

1 Neither of them is lazy. **2** You are over 16, aren't you? **3** If they don't invest in technology, their economy will suffer. **4** I fell asleep while we were watching the film. **5** Once you have taken this aspirin, you'll feel much better. **6** There must have been a logical explanation. **7** We used to stay with my grandmother every summer when I was a child. **8** The government is going to spend more money on wind turbines.

Vocabulary

Exercise 5

1 cooperation **2** plentiful **3** responsibility **4** requirements **5** profitable **6** expenses **7** poverty **8** payment **9** unfortunately **10** doubtful

Exercise 6

1 D **2** C **3** D **4** C **5** B **6** A **7** D **8** C **9** B **10** D

Part B

Communication

Exercise 7

1 What time does the evening performance start? **2** I'm afraid the evening performance is sold out/all the tickets for the evening performance are sold out. **3** Would you mind giving me some information about how to volunteer? **4** Could I ask how old you are?/Could you tell me how old you are? **5** Do you want to come round to my house? **6** How about coming round to my house instead? **7** If in doubt, you shouldn't touch anything. **8** Can you go through that/the instructions again? **9** I'd like to take out a loan. **10** How high are your living expenses?

Reading

Exercise 8

1 B **2** C **3** B **4** D **5** B

Exercise 9

1 True **2** True **3** False **4** True **5** False

Writing

Exercise 10

Sample answers

I couldn't believe my eyes. There was Jack, leaning over me and smiling. There wasn't a bruise or a mark on him. But how was it possible?

Jack was a confident, funny guy. I'd met him at a party and we'd got on really well. We started going to football matches together and generally hanging out.

The night that it happened, we were taking a walk down to the river. I'd taken off my shoes and we were walking on the soft grass by the side of the road. The sun had gone down but it wasn't quite dark.

Suddenly we heard the noise of tyres and a silver car appeared around the corner. It was driving fast and its lights were full on. As it drove straight at us, I heard Jack shout something. It sounded like, 'Not now, it wasn't supposed to be now.' The car crashed into him and I was thrown to the side of the road.

I closed my eyes for a few minutes and tried to work out if I was hurt. When I opened them, there was Jack. Smiling. I smiled back. And that's when I realised it wasn't Jack at all.

Listening audioscript – Exercise 1  CD3/12

Speaker 1 Anybody who's an artist will tell you that you don't do art for the money. I didn't give up my day job until I was in my mid-40s … There came a time when I just wasn't satisfied with being a part-time artist and I decided to take the plunge. I suppose I was lucky. I'd already built up a customer base as a book illustrator and I've never had to worry about money. Some people say you have to be hungry to be a true artist, but I don't buy the starving-artist scenario. I can produce better art when I don't have to worry where the next month's rent is coming from.

Speaker 2 I make sculptures from things that other people would throw away. Old metal pipes, rusty nails, plastic cartons, old tyres … I never have a preconceived idea of what I'm going to make. I find the materials and let them dictate the piece of work that I create. I love that feeling that there are no boundaries. I'm not limited by what my own imagination can produce, only what I can find. Of course, there are people who think what I do isn't art … But I would say it's very hard to say what isn't art. To me art is any way people express their creativity.

Speaker 3 I work with disadvantaged kids, creating murals on walls and tunnels in the city. We work in connection with the city council trying to brighten up unattractive areas, so we're not talking illegal street art here. What is important is not so much the murals themselves but what the kids discover about themselves while making the murals. I teach the kids certain techniques, but the inspiration for what we paint comes from them. The pictures are like an ongoing dialogue between each kid and their inner self. Each mural tells a story about who has painted it and what has been going on in their lives.

Speaker 4 I got into my present job rather by accident. I've always loved handicrafts and particularly sewing. I've made my own clothes for years. Anyway, one year I helped out at the local amateur dramatics productions when they needed somebody to make costumes and I was just fascinated by how powerful clothes are – how you can use clothes to manipulate somebody's perception of a character and their personality. It's an amazing skill. When people ask me what I do, I say I build characters. I take a conceptual idea of what a character is about and give it a physical form through a costume. It's an incredibly fulfilling experience.

Speaker 5 I think what I'm trying to do through music is articulate feelings. I never write songs that tell a story … If I'd wanted to do that, I'd have become a novelist or a poet. I want to make people feel pain, compassion, joy … Music is incredibly powerful: it can change your mood, how you feel about yourself and your view of life. I get a lot of my inspiration from observing people and watching how they interact in situations with other people. Music to me is never about producing songs that reflect the current trend or that you can eat dinner to in a restaurant. It has to have a deeper meaning.

Aspire End of Term Test 1 (second version)

Part A

Listening

Exercise 1

1 C **2** B **3** A **4** C **5** D

Exercise 2

1 E **2** D **3** A **4** F **5** B

Grammar

Exercise 3

1 Neither of them is lazy. **2** You are over 16, aren't you? **3** If they don't invest in technology, their economy will suffer. **4** I fell asleep while we were watching the film. **5** Once you have taken this aspirin, you'll feel much better. **6** There must have been a logical explanation. **7** We used to stay with my grandmother every summer when I was a child. **8** The government is going to spend more money on wind turbines.

Exercise 4

1 are you going/have been waiting **2** were they doing/had been writing **3** will be doing/will have graduated **4** is always complaining/won't find **5** Would you have gone/wouldn't be **6** did you enjoy/had read **7** will have been sitting/doesn't come

Vocabulary

Exercise 5

1 D **2** C **3** D **4** C **5** B **6** A **7** D **8** C **9** B **10** D

Exercise 6

1 cooperation **2** plentiful **3** responsibility **4** requirements **5** profitable **6** expenses **7** poverty **8** payment **9** unfortunately **10** doubtful

Part B

Communication

Exercise 7

1 What time does the evening performance start? **2** I'm afraid the evening performance is sold out/ all the tickets for the evening performance are sold out. **3** Would you mind giving me some information about how to volunteer? **4** Could I ask how old you are?/Could you tell me how old you are? **5** Do you want to come round to my house? **6** How about coming round to my house instead? **7** If in doubt, you shouldn't touch anything. **8** Can you go through that/the instructions again? **9** I'd like to take out a loan. **10** How high are your living expenses?

Reading

Exercise 8

1 True **2** True **3** False **4** True **5** False

Exercise 9

1 B **2** C **3** B **4** D **5** B

Writing

Exercise 10

Sample answers

I couldn't believe my eyes. There was Jack, leaning over me and smiling. There wasn't a bruise or a mark on him. But how was it possible?

Jack was a confident, funny guy. I'd met him at a party and we'd got on really well. We started going to football matches together and generally hanging out.

The night that it happened, we were taking a walk down to the river. I'd taken off my shoes and we were walking on the soft grass by the side of the road. The sun had gone down but it wasn't quite dark.

Suddenly we heard the noise of tyres and a silver car appeared around the corner. It was driving fast and its lights were full on. As it drove straight at us, I heard Jack shout something. It sounded like, 'Not now, it wasn't supposed to be now.' The car crashed into him and I was thrown to the side of the road.

I closed my eyes for a few minutes and tried to work out if I was hurt. When I opened them, there was Jack. Smiling. I smiled back. And that's when I realised it wasn't Jack at all.

Listening audioscript – Exercise 1  CD3/12

Speaker 1   Anybody who's an artist will tell you that you don't do art for the money. I didn't give up my day job until I was in my mid-40s … There came a time when I just wasn't satisfied with being a part-time artist and I decided to take the plunge. I suppose I was lucky. I'd already built up a customer base as a book illustrator and I've never had to worry about money. Some people say you have to be hungry to be a true artist, but I don't buy the starving-artist scenario. I can produce better art when I don't have to worry where the next month's rent is coming from.

Speaker 2   I make sculptures from things that other people would throw away. Old metal pipes, rusty nails, plastic cartons, old tyres … I never have a preconceived idea of what I'm going to make. I find the materials and let them dictate the piece of work that I create. I love that feeling that there are no boundaries. I'm not limited by what my own imagination can produce, only what I can find. Of course, there are people who think what I do isn't art … But I would say it's very hard to say what isn't art. To me art is any way people express their creativity.

Speaker 3   I work with disadvantaged kids, creating murals on walls and tunnels in the city. We work in connection with the city council trying to brighten up unattractive areas, so we're not talking illegal street art here. What is important is not so much the murals themselves but what the kids discover about themselves while making the murals. I teach the kids certain techniques, but the inspiration for what we paint comes from them. The pictures are like an ongoing dialogue between each kid and their inner self. Each mural tells a story about who has painted it and what has been going on in their lives.

Speaker 4   I got into my present job rather by accident. I've always loved handicrafts and particularly sewing. I've made my own clothes for years. Anyway, one year I helped out at the local amateur dramatics productions when they needed somebody to make costumes and I was just fascinated by how powerful clothes are – how you can use clothes to manipulate somebody's perception of a character and their personality. It's an amazing skill. When people ask me what I do, I say I build characters. I take a conceptual idea of what a character is about and give it a physical form through a costume. It's an incredibly fulfilling experience.

Speaker 5   I think what I'm trying to do through music is articulate feelings. I never write songs that tell a story … If I'd wanted to do that, I'd have become a novelist or a poet. I want to make people feel pain, compassion, joy … Music is incredibly powerful: it can change your mood, how you feel about yourself and your view of life. I get a lot of my inspiration from observing people and watching how they interact in situations with other people. Music to me is never about producing songs that reflect the current trend or that you can eat dinner to in a restaurant. It has to have a deeper meaning.

Aspire End of Term Test 2 (first version)

Listening

Exercise 1

1 F **2** C **3** A **4** E **5** B

Exercise 2

1 True **2** True **3** False **4** True **5** True
6 True **7** False **8** True **9** False **10** False

Grammar

Exercise 3

1 get/have my car repaired **2** get/have my eyes tested **3** us do any housework **4** on to become/be **5** being/getting caught **6** to be recognised **7** are thought to be **8** believed to have originated **9** whose flat I went **10** Written and narrated by **11** few **12** threatened to sue them **13** She suggested going/asked if we should go **14** was going/intending to study **15** was due/scheduled to leave

Vocabulary

Exercise 4

1 impractical **2** competitive **3** speech **4** infancy **5** calling **6** unreliable **7** creativity **8** theft **9** attentive **10** unspoilt

Exercise 5

1 raise **2** equal **3** do **4** tuition **5** put **6** foster **7** implement **8** follow **9** guided **10** use

Communication

Exercise 6

1 to draw your attention to **2** you wrap it (up) for me, please **3** didn't (quite) catch that **4** you be prepared to lower/reduce/decrease/drop the price **5** be better off waiting (a bit)

Reading

Exercise 7

1 F **2** D **3** C **4** A **5** E

Exercise 8

1 False **2** False **3** True **4** True **5** False

Writing

Exercise 9

1 B **2** D **3** A **4** E **5** C **6** B **7** D
8 E **9** A **10** C

Listening audioscript – Exercise 1 CD3/13

Primary school teaching in the UK is definitely a female-dominated profession. The reasons for that are fairly obvious. First of all, we get school holidays off, of course, which for those who have school-age children – and there a lot of those – is very convenient: it means they don't have to organise extra childcare. Secondly, it's a very people-oriented job and thirdly it doesn't have a strong career structure. You're either a teacher or a head teacher, so it suits the majority of women, who tend to be less career-minded than men. Actually what you find is that most primary head teachers are men, which is a little unfair, I think.

Investment banking definitely has got a bad name in the last few years. People associate it with greedy men who just want to get rich quickly and don't care about who gets hurt along the way. In fact you'd be surprised to learn that the majority of people working in it don't really agree with the ethics of it either. Quite a lot of the ones I work with – me included – plan to spend no more than ten years earning as much as they can and building up some kind of financial security for themselves (and their families, if they have them) and then to go off and do something more worthwhile, like teaching or working for an NGO.

I've been training as a florist for the last two years. It's a local shop where I've helped out on Saturdays and busy days since I was 14. It's a great atmosphere, but it does get pretty stressful too, particularly if we have a big wedding to prepare for. The thing is that the other women I work with are real artists: incredibly gifted at flower arranging. I could have gone to college but they offered me an apprenticeship and I thought, why not? I'll probably learn more here than I would there. Anyway, I can always go back to studying later if I get bored of this and I'll have acquired a useful skill along the way.

We do what's called post-production work on short films – advertisements and that kind of thing. What that means is we touch up the films and add special effects using computer technology. I taught myself, just playing around on my computer at home when I was a teenager. It's really good fun – I often feel like I'm being paid to play. But we work long hours, because we have to work to tight deadlines. I can do shifts of up to 16 hours, from nine in the morning to one am the next day. We're a group of six guys and the office is a bit like a male student flat, I'm afraid: lots of dirty coffee cups and smelly feet.

One of the things I like about my job is that there is so much variety in the people you work with. In my branch, there is an ex-army officer, a girl who used to work as a dietician, a former drugs counsellor, a man who ran his own removals company for ten years, a former bank manager. But we all share one thing in common, which is a wish to help people in difficulty. The CAB is an advice service for people who are facing some kind of crisis; they're in financial trouble or they have problems with noisy neighbours … that kind of thing. The advice we give is free, because we're government-funded. It's very satisfying work.

Aspire End of Term Test 2 (second version)

Listening

Exercise 1

1 True **2** True **3** False **4** True **5** True
6 True **7** False **8** True **9** False **10** False

Exercise 2

1 F **2** C **3** A **4** E **5** B

Grammar

Exercise 3

1 get/have my car repaired **2** get/have my eyes tested **3** us do any housework **4** on to become/be **5** being/getting caught **6** to be recognised **7** are thought to be **8** believed to have originated **9** whose flat I went **10** Written and narrated by **11** few **12** threatened to sue them **13** She suggested going/asked if we should go **14** was going/intending to study **15** was due/scheduled to leave

Vocabulary

Exercise 4

1 raise **2** equal **3** do **4** tuition **5** put **6** foster **7** implement **8** follow **9** guided **10** use

Exercise 5

1 impractical **2** competitive **3** speech **4** infancy **5** calling **6** unreliable **7** creativity **8** theft **9** attentive **10** unspoilt

Communication

Exercise 6

1 to draw your attention to **2** you wrap it (up) for me, please **3** didn't (quite) catch that **4** you be prepared to lower/reduce/decrease/drop the price **5** be better off waiting (a bit)

Reading

Exercise 7

1 False **2** False **3** True **4** True **5** False

Exercise 8

1 F **2** D **3** C **4** A **5** E

Writing

Exercise 9

1 B **2** D **3** A **4** E **5** C **6** B **7** D **8** E **9** A **10** C

Listening audioscript – Exercise 1 CD3/13

Primary school teaching in the UK is definitely a female-dominated profession. The reasons for that are fairly obvious. First of all, we get school holidays off, of course, which for those who have school-age children – and there a lot of those – is very convenient: it means they don't have to organise extra childcare. Secondly, it's a very people-oriented job and thirdly it doesn't have a strong career structure. You're either a teacher or a head teacher, so it suits the majority of women, who tend to be less career-minded than men. Actually what you find is that most primary head teachers are men, which is a little unfair, I think.

Investment banking definitely has got a bad name in the last few years. People associate it with greedy men who just want to get rich quickly and don't care about who gets hurt along the way. In fact you'd be surprised to learn that the majority of people working in it don't really agree with the ethics of it either. Quite a lot of the ones I work with – me included – plan to spend no more than ten years earning as much as they can and building up some kind of financial security for themselves (and their families, if they have them) and then to go off and do something more worthwhile, like teaching or working for an NGO.

I've been training as a florist for the last two years. It's a local shop where I've helped out on Saturdays and busy days since I was 14. It's a great atmosphere, but it does get pretty stressful too, particularly if we have a big wedding to prepare for. The thing is that the other women I work with are real artists: incredibly gifted at flower arranging. I could have gone to college but they offered me an apprenticeship and I thought, why not? I'll probably learn more here than I would there. Anyway, I can always go back to studying later if I get bored of this and I'll have acquired a useful skill along the way.

We do what's called post-production work on short films – advertisements and that kind of thing. What that means is we touch up the films and add special effects using computer technology. I taught myself, just playing around on my computer at home when I was a teenager. It's really good fun – I often feel like I'm being paid to play. But we work long hours, because we have to work to tight deadlines. I can do shifts of up to 16 hours, from nine in the morning to one am the next day. We're a group of six guys and the office is a bit like a male student flat, I'm afraid: lots of dirty coffee cups and smelly feet.

One of the things I like about my job is that there is so much variety in the people you work with. In my branch, there is an ex-army officer, a girl who used to work as a dietician, a former drugs counsellor, a man who ran his own removals company for ten years, a former bank manager. But we all share one thing in common, which is a wish to help people in difficulty. The CAB is an advice service for people who are facing some kind of crisis; they're in financial trouble or they have problems with noisy neighbours … that kind of thing. The advice we give is free, because we're government-funded. It's very satisfying work.

Aspire End of Year Test (first version)

Listening

Exercise 1

1 True **2** False **3** False **4** True **5** True

Exercise 2

1 limited **2** kindly **3** king **4** officially **5** rich
6 angry **7** disgusted **8** vegetable **9** roast
10 credit

Grammar

Exercise 3

1 have been having; have not made/am not
making **2** know/have known; will always perform/
always perform **3** arrived; had been working **4** are
you doing; starts **5** have finished/finish; will have
read **6** had listened; would not be

Exercise 4

1 B **2** D **3** A **4** D **5** C **6** A **7** C **8** B

Exercise 5

1 would **2** had **3** have **4** would **5** will
6 ought **7** does **8** be **9** had **10** does/will

Vocabulary

Exercise 6

1 C **2** D **3** B **4** B **5** D **6** D **7** A
8 C **9** A **10** D

Exercise 7

1 sculpture – all the others are types of drawing
or painting **2** cast – all the others are objects in a
theatre **3** a musician – all the others are more than
one person **4** shuttle – all the others are to do with
the cost of a holiday **5** stranger – all the others are
people from abroad **6** versatile – all the others relate
to size **7** afford – all the others relate to lending and
borrowing **8** teenager – all the others are stages
of life **9** apprentice – it's the only one which is a
person **10** murder – it's not a workplace crime

Communication

Exercise 8

Suggested answers

1 jazz isn't really my thing **2** I wonder if you could
send me some information, please **3** Which day suits
you best **4** Whatever you do don't fit the new switch
without turning the electricity off **5** I'm sorry. I don't
follow.

Reading

Exercise 9

1 E **2** D **3** A **4** F **5** B

Exercise 10

1 By jumping on a train **2** Hiding in the tall weeds
3 The right not to be abused or robbed **4** That even

though it seems a lot, the cost of living is high
5 The land of dreams and amazing opportunities

Listening audioscript – Exercise 1  CD3/14

Jamie Oliver is on a mission to get people eating
healthily. Having already tried, with limited success, to
improve the food served in British school canteens, he
has now taken his healthy food campaign to America.
Has he bitten off more than he can chew? His new TV
series, Jamie's American Food Revolution, will give you
the answer.

But I suspect you already know. Americans are great
believers in individual freedom and do not take kindly
to the government, or anyone else for that matter,
telling them what to do. As one local radio DJ on the
programme tells him, 'We don't want to sit around
and eat lettuce all day. Who made you king?'

The first programme in the series sees Oliver travelling
to Huntingdon, West Virginia, officially the unhealthiest
city in America, to persuade families to think more
carefully about the way they eat. Jamie Oliver is an
enthusiastic food missionary, but he seems rather naive
about American society. There is a real political divide
in the US between people who eat correctly, who are
generally rich, and people who eat badly, who are
generally poor. I am sure it is not his intention to make
fun of poor ignorant Americans, but there is a danger
people may watch this programme, and either point
their fingers and laugh or get very angry.

He visits an elementary school, where they are
serving up 'breakfast pizza' (eggs, sausage and
cheese) to 450 children. Disgusted by this and by
the chicken nuggets and French fries (classed as a
vegetable by the US Department of Agriculture) that
follow for lunch, he cooks a meal of roast chicken
and foccacia bread the next day. The alternative on
the menu is pepperoni pizza. No prizes for guessing
which the kids go for.

This may be a doomed experiment, but it is good
television and to the programme makers' credit they
are going to stay in Huntingdon for the whole of the
series, rather than moving on to laugh at some other
provincial townsfolk.

Aspire End of Year Test (second version)

Listening

Exercise 1

1 limited **2** kindly **3** king **4** officially
5 rich **6** angry **7** disgusted **8** vegetable
9 roast **10** credit

Exercise 2

1 True **2** False **3** False **4** True **5** True

Grammar

Exercise 3

1 would **2** had **3** have **4** would **5** will
6 ought **7** does **8** be **9** had **10** does/will

Exercise 4

1 have been having; have not made/am not making
2 know/have known; will always perform/always

perform   **3** arrived; had been working   **4** are you doing; starts   **5** have finished/finish; will have read   **6** had listened; would not be

Exercise 5

1 B   **2** D   **3** A   **4** D   **5** C   **6** A   **7** C   **8** B

Vocabulary

Exercise 6

1 sculpture – all the others are types of drawing or painting   **2** cast – all the others are objects in a theatre   **3** a musician – all the others are more than one person   **4** shuttle – all the others are to do with the cost of a holiday   **5** stranger – all the others are people from abroad   **6** versatile – all the others relate to size   **7** afford – all the others relate to lending and borrowing   **8** teenager – all the others are stages of life   **9** apprentice – it's the only one which is a person   **10** murder – it's not a workplace crime

Exercise 7

1 C   **2** D   **3** B   **4** B   **5** D   **6** D   **7** A   **8** C   **9** A   **10** D

Communication

Exercise 8

Suggested answers

1 jazz isn't really my thing   **2** I wonder if you could send me some information, please   **3** Which day suits you best   **4** Whatever you do don't fit the new switch without turning the electricity off   **5** I'm sorry, I don't follow.

Reading

Exercise 9

1 E   **2** D   **3** A   **4** F   **5** B

Exercise 10

1 By jumping on a train   **2** Hiding in the tall weeds   **3** The right not to be abused or robbed   **4** That even

though it seems a lot, the cost of living is high   **5** The land of dreams and amazing opportunities

Listening audioscript – Exercise 1    CD3/14

Jamie Oliver is on a mission to get people eating healthily. Having already tried, with limited success, to improve the food served in British school canteens, he has now taken his healthy food campaign to America. Has he bitten off more than he can chew? His new TV series, Jamie's American Food Revolution, will give you the answer.

But I suspect you already know. Americans are great believers in individual freedom and do not take kindly to the government, or anyone else for that matter, telling them what to do. As one local radio DJ on the programme tells him, 'We don't want to sit around and eat lettuce all day. Who made you king?'

The first programme in the series sees Oliver travelling to Huntingdon, West Virginia, officially the unhealthiest city in America, to persuade families to think more carefully about the way they eat. Jamie Oliver is an enthusiastic food missionary, but he seems rather naive about American society. There is a real political divide in the US between people who eat correctly, who are generally rich, and people who eat badly, who are generally poor. I am sure it is not his intention to make fun of poor ignorant Americans, but there is a danger people may watch this programme, and either point their fingers and laugh or get very angry.

He visits an elementary school, where they are serving up 'breakfast pizza' (eggs, sausage and cheese) to 450 children. Disgusted by this and by the chicken nuggets and French fries (classed as a vegetable by the US Department of Agriculture) that follow for lunch, he cooks a meal of roast chicken and foccacia bread the next day. The alternative on the menu is pepperoni pizza. No prizes for guessing which the kids go for.

This may be a doomed experiment, but it is good television and to the programme makers' credit they are going to stay in Huntingdon for the whole of the series, rather than moving on to laugh at some other provincial townsfolk.

Notes

Notes

Notes

Notes